Souvenirs of Cicero

SOUVENIRS OF CICERO

Shaping Memory in the Epistulae ad Familiares

FRANCESCA K. A. MARTELLI

OXFORD
UNIVERSITY PRESS

OXFORD
UNIVERSITY PRESS

Oxford University Press is a department of the University of Oxford. It furthers
the University's objective of excellence in research, scholarship, and education
by publishing worldwide. Oxford is a registered trade mark of Oxford University
Press in the UK and certain other countries.

Published in the United States of America by Oxford University Press
198 Madison Avenue, New York, NY 10016, United States of America.

© Oxford University Press 2024

All rights reserved. No part of this publication may be reproduced, stored in
a retrieval system, or transmitted, in any form or by any means, without the
prior permission in writing of Oxford University Press, or as expressly permitted
by law, by license, or under terms agreed with the appropriate reproduction
rights organization. Inquiries concerning reproduction outside the scope of the
above should be sent to the Rights Department, Oxford University Press, at the
address above.

You must not circulate this work in any other form
and you must impose this same condition on any acquirer.

CIP data is on file at the Library of Congress

ISBN 978–0–19–776196–0

DOI: 10.1093/oso/9780197761960.001.0001

Printed by Integrated Books International, United States of America

For dfjm

Contents

Preface	ix
Note on the Text	xi
Introduction: Receiving Cicero's Letters—A Brief History	1
1. Letters to the Editor: Constructing the Editor in *Fam.* 16	33
2. Enclosing the Collection: Frames of Meaning in *Fam.* 1 and *Fam.* 15	58
3. Reorienting the Collection: Cicero as Addressee and the Arena of Letters in *Fam.* 8	85
4. Ordering the Collection: History and Counter-History in *Fam.* 10–12	113
5. Structures of Feeling: The Household of *Familiaritas* in *Fam.* 13	162
Conclusion	195
Appendix: The Chronological Order of Letters in Fam. *10–12*	209
Bibliography	221
Index Locorum	235
Index	243

Preface

THIS BOOK HAS taken ten years or so to come together and owes much to the friends and colleagues who have inspired, taught, and kept me company along the way. It began and ended in conversation with John Henderson and has been sustained by countless exchanges with him in the interim, as well as by the example of his own inimitable understanding of Cicero, letters (and emails), and most other things besides. Above all, by his humanity. Many classicists have benefited from John's transformational mentorship, and I feel blessed to be able to count myself among them.

I have been very fortunate in my colleagues at UCLA, who have borne with me and this project for the duration of its planning and have all left their imprint on it somehow. Two colleagues in particular, David Blank and Amy Richlin, have taught me so much about Cicero and other material related to this study. Knowing that they might one day have to read this book has (I hope) kept me honest. Amy's own book on Fronto's letters is eagerly anticipated: she and I came to the idea of ancient letters as souvenirs separately, but her work on Fronto long precedes mine on Cicero. Sander Goldberg has enabled me with his encouragement and supportive departmental presence long into a notably industrious emeritude. And I have been lucky too in the graduate students alongside whom I have been privileged to think and learn at UCLA. Elliott Piros, Andres Matlock, Diana Librandi, and Jasmine Akiyama-Kim, to name but a few, have all taught me more than I have taught them, and have introduced me to ideas, texts, and critical theories that I would never have known about without the window they have offered me onto their own interests.

Others in the field of classics have been generous interlocutors throughout the years of this book's gestation: Emily Gowers, Sean Gurd, and Holly Haynes have been my friends and lode stars, setting me an example with their own work and intellectual curiosity—as well as allowing me the optimistic hope of being this book's (ideal) first readers. Members of the UC Santa Barbara Classics department have heard me deliver more sections of this project than any other institution (including my own). I am especially indebted to Bob Morstein-Marx for the occasional lessons I have pestered him to give me on the more recalcitrant details of late republican history. Roy Gibson and Ruth Morello have been the most generous fellow epistolitterateurs, sharing their work and ideas with me, and being open to mine. Joe Howley and Stephanie Frampton have both taught me much about the book technologies that form an important premise of this book's argument.

The Getty Villa provided the ideal *locus amoenus* in which to write this book in the year of leave (frustratingly interrupted by the Covid-19 pandemic) that a generous UC President's Fellowship afforded. I am deeply indebted to Ken Lapatin and Clare Lyons for allowing me to bunker down in the Ranch House as resident hermit in 2019 and then again in 2022, when I resumed the interrupted leave.

My greatest debt of thanks is to my family: to my husband Richard, for his wonderful company and for twelve very funny years of marriage. And to my children, Grace and Walter: this project spans the years of their infancy and early childhood and will always be a memento to me of that sweet, chaotic time. I owe thanks to my mother too, who housed us all for a year during the pandemic, putting up with our late-night zooming to Los Angeles with considerable forbearance (and who continues to house us periodically in our ongoing transatlantic meanderings and to support us with her love).

Finally, this book is dedicated to the treasured memory of my father Dominick, whose death a quarter century ago taught me about loss and longing, themes that lie at its heart.

A slightly modified version of Chapter 1, 'Letters to the Editor' is due to appear in a special issue of *Hermathena* 2024.

Note on the Text

IN QUOTING FROM Cicero's letters, I have used Watt's 1982 OCT edition of both the *Epistulae ad Familiares* and the *Epistulae ad Atticum*, unless otherwise stated. All translations are my own. All abbreviations follow the conventions of *l'Année Philologique*.

Introduction

RECEIVING CICERO'S LETTERS—A BRIEF HISTORY

HOW TO NARRATE the chaos of the end-times? How are these times to be made narratable? To modern readers searching for ways to put form on the experience of contemporary crisis, Cicero's letter collections proffer some suggestive insights. The letters document in real time the final years and months of the Roman Republic—the mode of governance idealized by ancient Romans and later revered by Western polities even after its demise. Organized into collections that put narrative form on this event, the letters' contemporary witness to the dissolution of the Republic is transformed by these collections into a range of accounts that narrate this moment as the end of a historical era, one that takes its name from the political system (the Republic) that had fallen apart. The narratives of historical closure that the collections yield may have been only vaguely discernible as such to the Romans who wrote these letters as they lived through this crisis, not knowing how it would turn out, since the collections took shape only after the event: assembled and published by anonymous editors only after Cicero's death, they make use of the gap that separates the composition of the letters in one era (and under one mode of governance) from their collation and organization in (and under) another in order to lend meaning to the period that had now passed. They demonstrate the various ways in which later readers and reading communities close off and make sense of the past, by reorganizing its archival traces into coherent structural wholes and imposing aesthetic and narrative form on them in answer to their own socio-economic and politico-cultural concerns.

This book is a study of one of the collections—the *Epistulae ad Familiares* (*ad Fam.*)—which packages up Cicero's correspondence to and from a wide range of addressees to produce the most eclectic and complex set of narratives

Souvenirs of Cicero. Francesca K. A. Martelli, Oxford University Press. © Oxford University Press 2024.
DOI: 10.1093/oso/9780197761960.003.0001

about the late Republic of all of Cicero's extant letter collections. The format of this collection is unique: while the other collections transmitted in Cicero's name consist of letters addressed to (and very occasionally from) a single addressee and are organized, for the most part, in chronological order, *ad Fam.*, by contrast, consists of letters written to (and sometimes from) a wide array of correspondents and is organized according to a range of different principles. These unusual aspects of its format present further possibilities for the history of its formation, which constitutes in itself another major source of the collection's interest. For unlike the other extant letter collections, which were likely assembled and published in the format transmitted from antiquity (or something very like it) relatively quickly, *ad Fam.* quite probably took longer to come into formation as a single collection. Its composite sixteen-book structure may well contain the traces of various prior rubrics and incarnations, which bear witness to the shifting/contested meanings that the fall of the Republic held for post-republican readerships as they reorganized the letter books of *ad Fam.* and published them in different groupings and sequences according to their own narrative and ideological prerogatives. The format in which this text was eventually transmitted is still significant, though, if only because it represents a culminating stage in the evolution of this process. In this study, I argue that the structure of the sixteen-book collection, which most scholars have hitherto dismissed as an incidental aspect of the letters' transmission, has much to tell us about what the fall of the Republic meant to imperial (and even, quite possibly, late antique) readerships and about how Cicero was received in this later era. And because of the specifically closural narratives that the collection yields when read in its transmitted form, this is also the format which makes the letters speak most readily to the preoccupations of modern readers too—or, indeed, to any readers grappling with their own political losses.

Yet to read the collection in its transmitted shape is to take up a position against a long-held scholarly orthodoxy that the structure of the collections is little more than an accident of transmission, one that reveals nothing beyond the idiosyncratic interests of the individual editors into whose hands the letters happened to fall. Ever since their rediscovery in the Renaissance, editors have reorganized the letter collections again and again, reshuffling the letters and reordering them according to their own historical interests. The impulse to contest received narratives about the end of the Republic does not stop in antiquity, it seems. In this Introduction, I consider this impulse as it manifests at certain key moments in the history of *ad Fam.*'s

Introduction 3

formation, transmission, and reception, asking why it recurs and what modern readers have to gain by observing or resisting it. Our story begins not in antiquity but at the moment of the letter collections' rediscovery during the Renaissance, when the scholars of this period took up two very different critical positions towards the letters. These positions are instructive because of the different attitudes towards the archive which they reveal so starkly in the near-simultaneous moment of the two major letter collections' discovery.

Petrarch and Salutati in the Archive

In September 1392, Coluccio Salutati wrote to Pasquino Capelli, chancellor of Milan and fellow humanist scholar, to thank him for a remarkable and unexpected gift that the latter had recently sent him.[1] Salutati had petitioned his correspondent to seek out a manuscript of Cicero's *Epistulae ad Atticum* (*ad Att.*), which he believed to be held in the cathedral library at Vercelli. In the course of his searches, however, Capelli had made a 'new' discovery:[2] a codex containing another sixteen-book collection of Cicero's letters, which he had copied and sent to Salutati instead. Less than fifty years after Petrarch's discovery of the *Epistulae ad Atticum* initiated the humanist enterprise of unearthing the lost texts of canonical Latin authors,[3] Salutati marked his identity as heir and guarantor of this legacy with his discovery of a second collection of Cicero's letters in sixteen books.[4]

That the collection which Salutati unearthed would come to be called the *Epistulae ad Familiares*—a title modelled on that of Petrarch's collection

---

1. Salutati 1891, 386–93. Novati offers an extensive discussion of the dating of this letter in the footnote to pp. 386–7.

2. Reeve 1996, 26; and Reeve 1991 on the role played by the discovery of ancient texts in the Renaissance.

3. See Hinds 2005, 50–51 on the significance with which Petrarch himself invests this discovery in *Fam.* 24.3, which becomes, 'a kind of incipit to the Renaissance itself' (despite the fact that Petrarch had embarked on the process of seeking out the lost texts of classical antiquity many years earlier).

4. See Ullman 1963, 39; and Witt 1983, 416 on the crucial role played by Salutati in securing the standing of humanism as a lasting cultural movement following the pioneering efforts of Petrarch (and, to a lesser extent, Boccaccio). Novati 1888, 64 likewise emphasizes Salutati's contribution to the movement, specifying in particular the intimate connection between literature and politics which his particular mode of humanism inaugurated.

of letters to his contemporaries, which was in turn inspired by his own discovery of the 'familiar' letters of Cicero to Atticus—only underscores the secondary status of Salutati's discovery in relation to Petrarch's.[5] Yet Salutati's reaction to the recovery of this 'new' letter collection diverges from Petrarch's response to *his* discovery of *ad Atticum* to a degree which is so marked as to seem like a deliberate attempt to distinguish himself from his predecessor.[6] Where Petrarch had underscored his own disappointment with the Cicero, whom he encountered in *ad Atticum*, by writing to Cicero to tell him of his dismay upon encountering this text's witness to the ancient author's palpably human frailties,[7] Salutati wrote to Capelli to convey his excitement and enthusiasm for the multifarious, multifaceted Cicero whom *he* had encountered in this newly recovered letter collection. 'I saw what sort of man he was in politics, how much he excelled among his friends and indeed among the leading citizens of Rome,' writes Salutati, while also expressing his appreciation of Cicero's rounded humanity: 'I saw how my Cicero was gentle with his family, how he was disappointed with his son, how he could be hopeless when things were bad, fearful when dangers approached, and how, when times were good, he was serene and satisfied.' And, in a dig at the monarchy under which his Milanese correspondent lived and worked (as opposed to the republican independence of his own Florence), 'I saw, thanks to you, the real basis of the civil wars, and what it was that forced Rome, that very capital of the whole world, to move from a popular model of governance to enslavement to monarchy.'[8]

The story of these divergent reactions to the two major collections of Cicero's letters to be discovered in the Renaissance tells us much, no doubt, about the changing prerogatives of successive generations of Renaissance humanism, as told through this era's relationship with the ancient past. For

---

5. The first attestation of *Epistulae ad Familiares* as a title for Cicero's letter collection is first found in the printed 1526 edition of Robertus Stephanus. See Tyrrell and Purser 1904 (vol. 1, 3rd ed.), 72 for discussion. See Hinds 2005, 53 on the likelihood that the title given to Cicero's *Epistulae ad Familiares* is modelled on the title of Petrarch's *Epistulae ad Familiares*—and on the significance for reception studies of this 'splendid instance of reverse-chronological influence'.

6. Schmidt 1983, 43–44 likewise notes the divergence between Petrarch's and Salutati's reactions to their respective discoveries.

7. See Petrarch *Fam.* 24.3 for the fullest account of this reaction; with Hinds 2005, 53–54 on the paradoxical defamiliarizing effect that the discovery of *ad Atticum* has on Petrarch's relationship with Cicero.

8. Salutati 1891, 389. See Stacey 2007, 170; and Celenza 2020, 61 on the contemporary political resonance implied by this account of Cicero's travails for Salutati, proudly living in a free Republic, and Capelli, living (in fear) under the rule of the Visconti family in Milan.

Petrarch, the contemplative, striving to reconcile the ideals of pagan antiquity with his Christian faith, the Cicero of *ad Atticum* is a disappointment. Whereas for the worldly Salutati, an active politician with more secular interests writing a generation later, the Cicero of *ad Fam.* holds up a welcome mirror to his own life and times.[9] But the reactions of Petrarch and Salutati are not peculiar to the Renaissance. Rather, they are representative of a more general set of divergent attitudes towards the function and nature of the archive for which Cicero's letter collections present an extraordinary case study. The divergence stems, in brief, from a view of the archive as the passive receptacle of a past that precedes it—fully formed and closed; or one that sees the past itself as a product of the archive, an archive endlessly open to new accretions, which reframe and remake history accordingly.[10] Petrarch's disappointment stems from the disruption that the letters to Atticus bring to an ideational past formed out of his own deeply invested framing of another archive (namely, the idealized picture of virtue and eloquence found in Cicero's philosophical treatises and in speeches like the *Pro Archia*),[11] which *ad Atticum* refuses to corroborate. Instead of recognizing the revision of this picture that the letters to Atticus insist upon, Petrarch remains attached to his version, and, in addressing Cicero as if he were present and chiding him for shattering this phantasmatic portrait, refuses the multiplicity that the newly recovered letter collection might bring to his view of the ancient author. Salutati, by contrast, welcomes the unexpected appearance of new archival material (we recall that he had been seeking not the letter collection that Capelli sent him but *ad*

---

9. Celenza 2020, 60 summarizes the difference between Petrarch and Salutati along these lines.

10. In this, I follow the two alternative conceptions of the archive that Derrida puts forward in *Archive Fever* (on which, see Earlie 2015, 315–16). In *Archive Fever*, Derrida critiques the uses to which the Jewish historian Yosef Hayim Yerushalmi tries to put the Freudian archive in his book *Freud's Moses* when he (Yerushalmi) goes through Freud's archives in search of evidence that might be used to posit a causal link between Freud's Jewish upbringing and the science of psychoanalysis. Derrida takes issue in particular with Yerushalmi's reliance on a conception of the archive as a place of absolute and singular origin, the return to which promises an illusory moment of presence—in which the past is made identical with itself. This approach to the archive ignores the differential movement of spacing that separates the present from the past, which is evident in the layers of history out of which any archive is built, and which make the potential disclosures of the archive endlessly possible and unpredictable. See esp. Derrida 1996, 36 for the idea that, 'the question of the archive is not a question of the past. It is not the question of a concept dealing with the past that might *already* be at our disposal or not at our disposal, an archivable concept of the archive. It is a question of the future, the question of the future itself, the question of a response, of a promise, and of a responsibility for tomorrow.'

11. See Reeve 1996, 20–23; and McLaughlin 2015, 21 on the significance of Petrarch's discovery of the *Pro Archia* in 1333 (twelve years before his discovery of *ad Atticum* in Verona) for the ideals of the humanist movement.

SOUVENIRS OF CICERO

Atticum) and honours the historical difference between himself and Cicero (his own appreciation of the newly unearthed letter collection is expressed not in a letter to Cicero but to his contemporary, Capelli). Or, to put the difference between them in more explicitly Derridean terms, Petrarch's response is that of the *mal d'archive* (the burning desire for the archive that is simultaneously a compulsion to destroy it),[12] whereas Salutati's speaks to the desire without the death drive (a commitment to the promise of the archive, its infinite potential to disclose the unforeseen).

The polarized responses of Petrarch and Salutati to the unearthing of Cicero's two major letter collections in the Renaissance transcend their historical moment, inaugurating the two chief approaches that have been taken to them since the event of their discovery. There is, on the one hand, the Petrarchan position of 'correcting' the letter collections to make their content answer to modern expectations, an approach that treats the collections themselves as passive receptacles of historical data to be excavated and reorganized according to modern epistemic principles in order to make Cicero and his historical era 'more' present.[13] The alternative approach is to recognize and investigate the layers of context and meaning out of which these archives are built in appreciation of their consequence for the portrait of Cicero (and narratives of late republican history) that the letter collections yield.[14] This book is a study of one of those archives. In it, I explore the *Epistulae ad Familiares*, the letter collection discovered by Salutati, and attempt to follow his lead in recognizing the text's capacity to expand our purview of the past. This commitment entails placing the archive itself to the fore of our reading

---

12. See Derrida 1996, 10–12 on the relationship between the archive and the Freudian death drive; with Telò 2020, 14–19 (and *passim*) for exposition in relation to the death-driven archives of Greek tragedy.

13. Beard 2002, 106–12 traces the attempts by nineteenth-century editors to reorganize Cicero's letter collections on chronological grounds, culminating with the edition of Tyrrell and Purser (published in seven volumes between 1879 and 1901), which disaggregated all of Cicero's letters from their collections and arranged the sum total of them in chronological order. Gibson 2012, 62 traces this impulse back to the seventeenth century with the 1611 edition of *ad Fam.* by Adamus Theodorus Siberus.

14. This approach, inaugurated by Beard 2002, 130–44 (on *Fam.* 16) has subsequently been built on by a number of scholars intent on recuperating the book units of the letter collections as meaningful narrative frames: see e.g., Gunderson 2007 on *Fam.* 14 and 16; Leach 1999 on *Fam.* 9 and 2016 on *Fam.* 3; Grillo 2015a on *Fam.* 1 and 2016 on *Fam.* 1 and *Fam.* 6; Martelli 2016 on *Att.* 12 and 2017 on *Fam.* 15; and Gibson 2017 on *Fam.* 4. See also Henderson 2016 and Martelli 2017 for attempts to recuperate the narrative structure of the collection as a whole (in the case of the *ad Qfr.* and *ad Fam.*, respectively) as a broader meaningful frame for reading the letters and letter books that they contain.

practices and attending to the shape and form that it places on Cicero's letters. It also entails shifting our focus away from the period of history in which Cicero wrote the letters to that later period when the archives themselves took form. Selected and assembled into various collections only after their author's death, Cicero's letters are always already filtered through the lens of subsequent history. And because of the ways in which his death is made to coincide with the fall of the Republic in the Roman cultural imagination,[15] the lens of retrospection that this later era brings to the letters is, more particularly, that mode of rewriting brought to the late republican past by the period of imperial rule that displaced it.[16] The distortions produced by this lens are the subject of this study.

The Archive's Distanced Intimacies

The discovery of Cicero's letters in the Renaissance is a primal scene not just for Petrarch and Salutati but for any scholar of ancient Rome intent on making new discoveries about it. The intimate disclosures of these letter collections make their discovery signify as more than that of just any ancient text: they reveal the background to so many others and deliver a personal connection point for the known historical events of this period. It is not only the unprecedented quantity of contextual information that they provide for the period of history on which they comment,[17] but, above all, the sense they give the modern reader of being made privy to antiquity's secrets. Because we read them over the shoulder of Atticus and Cicero's other *familiares*, they address us later readers as if we occupy a similar position of *familiaritas*, drawing us into Cicero's private confidence. They answer to our desire for intimate knowledge of the ancient world as few other ancient texts can or do. Small wonder, then, that classical scholars have in recent years attempted to recuperate Petrarch's

---

15. The equation drawn between Cicero's death and the end of the Republic begins with the account in Livy 120, which is quoted by the elder Seneca *Suas.* 6.17. Cf. Richlin 1999; and Pierini 2003, 24–26 for discussion. See also Kaster 1998; and Wright 2001 for the way in which the hagiographical tradition surrounding Cicero's death comes into formation. Keeline 2018, 102–95 fills out our picture of this tradition by showing how declamation schools in the early empire made Cicero an object of *controversiae*, balancing their sympathy for the manner of his death with criticism of other moments from and aspects of his life.

16. See Gowing 2005 for an overview of this imperial project.

17. More than 900 letters from or (occasionally) to Cicero survive. See Beard 2015, 22–41 on the significance of Cicero's letters for our ability to reconstruct the history of first-century BCE Rome in such detail.

response to his discovery of *ad Atticum* as a template for the modern reader's engagement with the texts and authors of Greco-Roman antiquity, modelling our desire for intimacy with an ancient past that can feel all too distant on his.[18] In writing back to Cicero, Petrarch replicates the feeling that Cicero's letters generate of bridging the chronological gap between ancient Rome and the post-classical present but in reverse. Petrarch here strives to make the epistolary medium of the letters serve the idea of their 'reception' at a later point in time, reducing the interval that stands between their ancient composition and post-classical reception to the time that it takes for correspondents to send and receive a letter. His letters to the ancients are celebrated accordingly for their way of making these long absent authors present, conjuring a 'virtual community' of spectral authors from ancient Greece and Rome.[19]

As Derrida himself suggests in *Archive Fever*, however, this desire to summon or address the dead is at the same time an attempt to efface them, since the imagined ghost cannot refute or challenge the question asked of them—or, in Cicero's case, cannot send back a reply.[20] What is especially striking in this instance, though, is that in emulating the familiar epistolary mode of Cicero's letters in his own address to Cicero, Petrarch's performance brings together the two facets of the archive that Derrida locates in its etymological derivation from the Greek *archê*: *archê* as origin, and *archê* as command. For even while chiding Cicero for writing *ad Atticum* as he did, Petrarch cannot help but follow the imperative that this archive issues to write in a similar vein. Petrarch's discovery of this letter collection has been hailed as an important moment of rediscovery in the Renaissance for a mode of intimate epistolary communication that would go on to transform styles

---

18. See esp. Güthenke 2020, 54–60. This goal is also a premise of the study of Hinds 2005, which takes its bearings from the pedagogical practice of using Petrarch's 'letters to the ancients' to introduce students to the idea of reading ancient authors as a mode of intimate communication with the distant past.

19. See Hinds 2004 on Petrarch's practice of conjuring a 'virtual community' of poets and authors through the use of allusion in his letters to the ancients.

20. Derrida 1996, 37–41 makes this point with reference to Yerushalmi's decision at the very end of *Freud's Moses: Judaism Terminable and Interminable* to apostrophize Freud with the question of whether psychoanalysis is a Jewish science. As Derrida points out (p. 37): 'By definition, because he is dead, and thus incapable of responding, Freud can only acquiesce. He cannot refuse this community at once proposed and imposed.' Derrida goes on to describe the patriarchal position that Yerushalmi therefore adopts towards Freud, inscribing him into the position of voiceless nursling, and metaphorically repeating the act of circumcision that Jakob Freud had performed on his son (an act that has a crucial significance for the thesis of Yerushalmi's book). Petrarch's apostrophizing of Cicero, I suggest, performs a similar paradoxically patriarchal act in its reversal of the traditional genealogies of literary history.

Introduction 9

of written communication for generations, the legacy of which we still enjoy today every time we write an informal email.[21] In following the imperative that *ad Atticum* issues to espouse Cicero's intimate mode of writing in their own day, later readers honour the way in which this archive continues to shape the future, quite as much as it shapes the past.

The jussive *archê* that *ad Atticum* issues in teaching its post-classical readers how to write intimately is, however, only one of its legacies. Another relates to the *archê* of its origin—or what it tells readers about antiquity. As we have seen, Petrarch and Salutati inaugurate two polarized approaches to this aspect of the letter collections: one intent on correcting their presentation of the past, by reorganizing the letters chronologically, and another content to appraise the collections as they stand. The ground of contestation for these divergent approaches centres on the media used to transmit the letters, in another demonstration of one of Derrida's most compelling insights concerning the archive. *Archive Fever* draws attention to the crucial importance of the archival medium for its content—that is, how the media and technologies of archivization determine the archivable event by creating the very conditions of its possibility.[22] For Cicero's letters, the media that matter are the book roll and codex, the constraints of which shaped the collections' content in antiquity, determining not only which letters were collected but also why and how they were grouped and organized as they were. Yet from the nineteenth century until very recently, scholarship has sought to dismantle the frameworks imposed by these media and reorganize the letters chronologically.[23] Paradoxically, it is *ad Fam.*, the collection that Salutati discovered, that has suffered more from the Petrarchan impulse to correct, for reasons that have to do precisely with the materiality of its archival substrate, and the extent to which this intervenes in the structure of the collection. Because this collection is not primarily organized along

---

21. This is a central thesis of Eden 2012.

22. Derrida 1996, 16–17: 'The technical structure of the archiving archive also determines the structure of the archivable content even in its very coming into existence and in its relationship to the future. The archivization produces as much as it records the event. This is also our political experience of the so-called news media.'

23. Attempts to reorganize Cicero's letters chronologically did not stop with those of Tyrrell and Purser (discussed in Beard 2002, 106–12; see n. 13 above). But their edition represents the most extreme manifestation of this endeavour, in that its reordering amalgamates the letters from all Cicero's letter collections, tessellating them chronologically by dateline. The authoritative modern editions of Shackleton Bailey (1965–70 on *ad Atticum*; 1977 on *ad Fam.*; and 1980 on *ad Qfr.* and *ad Brut.*) also reorganize the letters (largely) chronologically, while respecting the parameters of the discrete collections.

chronological lines (as *ad Atticum.*, by and large, is), it has been more vulnerable to the modern scholarly project of dismantling the structures shaped by its book media than others.[24] The effect of this enterprise is to make *ad Fam.* resemble *ad Atticum* in ways that perpetuate the secondary relationship of the former collection to the latter, a dynamic that, as we shall see, has its roots in antiquity.

The results of this process of chronological reordering have informed modern historians' constructions of 'what actually happened' in the decades of the late Republic, but at some considerable cost to our historical under-standing of the archive from which this information comes—a cost that, in turn, has consequences for the reconstruction of events that modern historians have assembled out of the collections' contents. For one thing, this approach explains little about why we have the information that we do—and lack the information that we lack—for this period: it does nothing to explain the blank areas and blind spots or why we have a surfeit of information for some people, periods, or places, but not for others. Above all, it does nothing to explain the interests determining the delivery (or withholding) of infor-mation, interests that are best understood by considering the many traces of context out of which these archives are built.[25] The alternative approach is to place the archive front and centre of our reading of the letters, on the under-standing that the collections themselves provide essential contextual informa-tion about the letters they contain: they reveal what kind of portrait of Cicero and his society the letters have been marshalled to assemble, and they tell us about how one period of history was received by the readers of a later era, looking back and putting closural form on the letters' first-hand witness to the experience of chaotic upheaval. Reading the letters for the archive means put-ting the letters back into the letter books (for which the book roll is an impor-tant medium) and broader collections (for which the codex is an important technology) in which they were circulated in antiquity and allowing the *form* of these archives to disclose certain possibilities for their historical formation.

Scholars have embarked on the enterprise of recuperating one of these formats—the book roll—on the understanding that it may well be the constraints of this format that determine which of Cicero's letters were

---

24. This is, for example, evident in Shackleton Bailey's 1977 edition of *ad Fam.* See Gibson 2012, 61–64, however, on the exceptional nature of the chronological organization of *ad Atticum.* As he points out, ancient letter collections are usually organized according to different principles (e.g., addressee), principles typified by *ad Fam.*

25. In this, the structure of the epistolary situation, in which letters are addressed and delivered from sender to receiver, models the structure of the contract between editor and reader of the letter collection.

Introduction   11

transmitted: the book units of *ad Fam.*, in particular, produce discernible, self-contained narratives about Cicero and the Republic, and the letters placed within these books have clearly been carefully selected to produce these narratives.[26] But while the logic of this argument extends to the larger archival format within which the individual books are transmitted, scholars rarely submit the whole collection of *ad Fam.* to the same formal analysis that they extend to the individual letter books, put off, no doubt, by how little we know about when the collection came into formation as we have it. Unlike *ad Atticum*, which is attested as a collection consisting of numbered books by Gellius, the books of *ad Fam.* are only ever cited in antiquity by the name of their opening addressee,[27] and they may have circulated either as individual books or in various small groupings, along with the many other books of Cicero's letters that were circulating in antiquity, for some considerable time.[28] We can imagine, for example, the 'Mutina books', which, in our collection comprise *Fam.* 10–12, once circulating as a self-contained three-book

---

26. See n. 14 above for examples of scholarship that has taken this approach to the letter books, analysing the narratives that the letters yield when read in the sequence in which they were transmitted.

27. Gellius is the first ancient author to identify a book of *ad Atticum* by number (e.g., *Noct.* 4.9.6: *Itaque M. Cicero in libro epistularum nono ad Atticum*), a reference that tallies with the numbering of our sixteen-book collection. References to books contained in *ad Fam.* are also first found in Gellius, but he cites them by the name of their first addressee rather than by number (e.g., *Noct.* 1.22.19: *in libro M. Tulli epistularum ad Servium Sulpicium*, i.e., *ad Fam.* 4; or ibid., 1.22.19: *in libro epistularum M. Ciceronis ad L. Plancum et in epistula M. Asini Pollionis ad Ciceronem*, i.e., *ad Fam.* 10.33). The letters that Gellius cites in this way correspond to their location in the books of *ad Fam.* that he mentions (suggesting that these letters were circulating within the books that the manuscript tradition preserved by the end of the second century CE), even if these letter books may not have yet formed a sixteen-book collection. See Beard 2002, 117–18 for discussion.

28. See Nicholson 1998 for discussion of Cicero's 'lost' letter collections (that is, collections of letters addressed to others that we find cited by other ancient authors but which are not extant). These include collections of letters to Caesar, to Pompey, to Octavian, to Q. Axius, to C. Pansa, and to Hirtius. As Beard 2002, 119 n. 51 notes, Nicholson takes a notably skeptical line towards the question of whether these collections were published in any meaningful sense. While I am less skeptical than Nicholson, I do share questions about whether all of these letter collections were in circulation for any extensive length of time. In particular, it is strange to hear tell of collections of letters to Caesar and Pompey when we find letters to these individuals included in *ad Fam.*, since the extant letter collections are remarkably consistent in not 'sharing' addressees. The one exception to this rule is *Fam.* 11.2 and 11.3, which are addressed jointly by Brutus and Cassius to Antony (the correspondence between Cicero and M. Brutus is otherwise contained within the *ad Brutum*), but this can be explained by the co-authorship of these letters (letters between Cassius and Cicero are included in *Fam.* 12 and *Fam.* 15). It seems safe to deduce from this that the publication of *ad Brut.* must predate the sixteen-book version of *ad Fam.* See Boissier 1863, 30–34 for the view (which I share) that the formation of *ad Fam.* postdates all the other extant letter collections and, probably, the non-extant ones too. Boissier

collection, or some (if not all) of the Cilicia books of 51–50 BCE (*Fam.* 2–3, *Fam.* 8, and *Fam.* 15) once circulating as a group.[29] We might equally imagine the domestic books of *Fam.* 14 and 16 once circulating alongside Cicero's non-extant books of letters to his son; or, equally, the letter books to Marcus Junior being grouped together with our *Fam.* 2 (consisting primarily of letters addressed to Curio and Caelius) as part of a series of paternalistic letter books to errant youth. Thus, although it is possible that *ad Fam.* was fixed as an (unnumbered) sixteen-book collection within a generation of Cicero's death, its books may well have circulated in a variety of highly fluid formats until the codex finally arrested this process when it became the dominant textual medium at some point in the fourth or fifth centuries CE.[30] In this study, I attempt to recuperate the format of the sixteen-book collection as a complete, formal unit, on the understanding that just as the constraints of the individual book roll determined which letters were transmitted, so too the constraints of the whole collection determined which books of Cicero's letters were selected for and included within it;[31] that its design therefore has much to tell us about how Cicero and the late republican era that he comes to represent were received in antiquity; and that it also presents, in passing, certain telling scenarios about the processes through which collective memory comes to bring a cultural text such as this one into formation.

However, if we are to celebrate the fluidity of the archive, its metamorphoses and openness to new accretions, we may wonder why we would want to recuperate the form of any one of its incarnations. For doing so might well be taken to arrest the very mobility that is so crucial to its ongoing power to reframe the past. As we have seen, the idea that these collections may have circulated in antiquity in a variety of different formats is a strong possibility

---

believes that *ad Fam.* was formed out of those books that were not incorporated into other letter collections addressed to a single addressee.

29. This latter hypothetical grouping provides us with an especially good opportunity to reflect on the new meanings that these books would take on when removed from such a micro-collection and dispersed into the places they hold across the sixteen-book *ad Fam.*

30. This is the view of Tyrrell and Purser 1904 (vol. 1, 3rd ed.), 71: 'Some time about the fifth century the scattered *libelli* were bound into larger volumes.' The fifth century has presumably been chosen because this was when the codex is thought to have taken over the papyrus roll as the predominant textual medium. Beard 2002, 118 follows Tyrrell and Purser in offering this date as a *terminus post quem* for the formation of the collection, but she is at pains to argue throughout this essay that no evidence precludes the possibility of a much earlier date for the formation of the sixteen-book collection.

31. See pp. 20–21 for the argument that *ad Fam.*'s sixteen-book format is modelled on the sixteen-book collection of *ad Atticum.*

for *ad Fam.*[32] and bears witness to one of the most paradoxical dynamics of the archive: namely, its status as a vehicle for both memory and oblivion at one and the same time. As Derrida realizes, in its attempt to guard against oblivion by consigning objects and records to a physical medium or location, the archive must compromise the very memories that it seeks to preserve.[33] For the physical exteriority of the archive, whether conceived of as place or as graphic medium, is vulnerable to forms of physical erasure—as ancient institutions, such as the library at Alexandria or the medieval palimpsest, are especially well placed to illustrate. A similar combination of archival and anarchival processes can be found at work in Cicero's letter collections, which, in whatever format we read them, contain the traces of all those other formats in which they may once have been read but which are now lost to us: they remind us of all the other books of letters by Cicero that we know were circulating in antiquity but which have not reached the modern era. The dismantling of the collections undertaken by modern scholars might well be taken as an extension of this very process. What do we have to gain, then, by fixing (or fixating) on any one of this letter collection's textual instantiations?

My argument is not that the sixteen-book collection that Capelli and Salutati unearthed was the only format of this text that existed in antiquity: I do not believe that it represents either the earliest format in which the books of this collection circulated or the last.[34] But I do hold that it represents one

---

32. McCutcheon 2016, arguing for a completely fluid text of Cicero's letter collections, views the sixteen-book format of *ad Fam.* that the manuscript Mediceus 49.9 ('M') transmits as somewhat arbitrary. While I am in sympathy with McCutcheon's attempt to dislodge assumptions about the fixity of the sixteen-book collection, I would contest some of the details of his arguments. First, he makes no distinction between the fluidity of the arrangement of letter books within the collection and the state of the letters within the letter books. Yet the fact that letters cited as belonging within particular letter books by Gellius match the contents of the letter books transmitted by M can hardly be a coincidence and suggests that the order of letters within (at least some of) the letter books must have been fixed by the second century, if not before. Furthermore, McCutcheon 2016, 54–55 n. 84 points to our earliest witness to the text of *ad Fam.*, the Turin palimpsest (dated to fifth or sixth century), which, in its single leaf, contained an abridged version of *Fam.* 6.9.1 through *Fam.* 6.10.6, omitting the personal matters that these letters contain and including only their 'official' information, as evidence for the variety of formats in which the collection was circulating at this stage. Yet the fact that despite having their content abridged, these letters still maintain the same sequence that they hold in the version of *Fam.* 6 transmitted in our oldest manuscript M might equally be taken to demonstrate how fixed the order of the letters was in their letter books by this stage.

33. Derrida 1996, 11–12.

34. Some may question whether it has a truly ancient pedigree at all: see Reynolds 1983, 138–39; and Shackleton Bailey 1977, 3–8 for discussion of the fact that the manuscript tradition for this text is divided into two branches—one for the first eight books, and another for the second—and that M numbers the last eight books (as well as the first eight books) from one to eight,

quite definitive stage in the ancient evolution of the collection; and, because of the long interval that stands between the copying and discovery of our earliest manuscript of this text, here is a cardinal moment of arrested fluidity in the life of this archive, which invites our scrutiny because of the magnified glimpse it offers of this long-held, static moment in its history. Attending to the format in which antiquity transmits this text to the modern era presents an opportunity to focus on the differential between past and present—to the meanings that emerge from this gap and to the resonances that cross it. For if this format tells us about how imperial (and late antique readers) organized and consumed the late republican past, shaping the narrative of its closure to meet their own ideological desires and needs, this narrative is also one that speaks to modern readers contending with comparable political losses in quite different historical circumstances. And it is a story told through the collection's transmitted form. The main thesis of this book—that Cicero's letter collections are best read as imperial (and post-imperial) texts, which have as much to say (if not more) about how Cicero was received in the period(s) when they were assembled as they do about the republican era

---

suggesting that these two eight-book collections may have been the formats of the collection that antiquity knew; and that the process of putting these two collections together to make our sixteen-book collection may have been the innovation of M in the eighth century. But while this pair of eight-book collections may predate our earliest manuscript for this collection, they do not necessarily predate the sixteen-book format that we find transmitted in M. Indeed, it is very difficult to see how the two halves of this diptych might have come into formation as separate entities, since the relationship between the two halves is marked. For example, we find letter books that consist of letters by Cicero in Cilicia to correspondents in Rome on both sides of the diptych (in *Fam.* 2 as well as in *Fam.* 15; i.e., symmetrical positions), as if balancing each other out. Furthermore, *Fam.* 13, which consists entirely of letters of introduction, serves as an inventory for the collection as a whole, insofar as it 'introduces' many of the correspondents that we will meet elsewhere—on both sides of the collection (in *Fam.* 1–8, as well as in *Fam.* 9–16). On top of this, the symmetry of two eight-book collections, each one addressed to a plurality of Cicero's friends, seems unlikely to be coincidental, given that all the other multi-book collections of Cicero's letters that we hear were circulating in antiquity addressed a single correspondent (and none of those extant takes an eight-book format). Finally, there is the fact that together these two eight-book halves create a collection that consists of the same number of books as *ad Atticum* (see pp. 20–21 for further discussion of this point). For all these reasons, and others that I will present in the chapters of this study, I believe that a sixteen-book format predates the two eight-book collections, and that these must have come about as a result of dividing the larger collection into half at some point. M would thus be reuniting two halves of a collection that belong together. That *Fam.* 1–8 should be placed (as it is) prior to *Fam.* 9–16 has now been convincingly demonstrated by the recent study of Serena Cammoranesi 2022, which demonstrates a broad chronological movement forward across *ad Fam.*, from the letters of book 1, composed in 56 BCE, to the letters of *Fam.* 10–12, composed right at the end, in 44 to 43 BCE. All these points lead me to conclude that a sixteen-book collection circulated in antiquity in the form that we have it. Accordingly, this sixteen-book text is the object addressed by the present study.

Introduction   15

in which the letters themselves were written—draws on the premise that it is the form of the collection (at both the micro level of book unit and the macro level of complete collection) that delivers these narratives. Before we dismantle these units, and the narratives they construct, and rearrange this archive according to our own epistemic prerogatives, we would do well to scrutinize and attempt to understand the ideological object that we are dismantling.

The idea that the *Epistulae ad Familiares* should be read specifically as an imperial (and/or post-imperial) text should not be a controversial one, since there is a broad scholarly consensus that all of Cicero's letter collections (including the books of *ad Fam.*) were assembled after their author's death.[35] The horizon of this event establishes one very significant frame of meaning for the collection: it invites us to read the letters enclosed within from the vantage point that we derive from looking back to them from across that watershed. Above all, because of the way in which Cicero's death coincides with the 'death' of the Republic, and is frequently read as a synecdoche for that historical juncture from the very start of the imperial period, the republican world depicted in *ad Fam.* is presented to readers as already in the past and already subject to that process of rewriting that is the subsequent era's prerogative.[36] The creation of the books of the *ad Fam.* forms a significant part of that process of rewriting and, along with the publication of Cicero's other letter collections, must have served as a vehicle for articulating the shift from one historical era to another for later Roman readers. For example, many of the books of *ad Fam.* are organized around a particular republican institution, the meaning of which changes radically when read in an imperial

---

35. Arguments for the broad scholarly assumption that the process of collecting and publishing Cicero's letters cannot have been completed until after his death and must, therefore, have been undertaken by others are summarized by White 2010, 31–34. We know from a letter to Atticus (*Att.* 16.5.5), written a year and a half before Cicero's death, that no letter collection existed at this stage, although within this letter Cicero mentions a συναγωγή of seventy letters that Tiro had begun compiling. Among the arguments for believing that someone other than Cicero must have produced the collections after his death are the view that he would not have had the time or occasion to begin sifting through the massive archive of letters until perhaps the last five months of his life, and that this would not have given sufficient time to produce the collections that went into circulation, given the sheer quantity of letters involved (including those from the 'lost' collections). In addition, and more concretely, White 2010, 33–34 notes the number of editorial slips in the collection that Cicero could hardly have made, most of which relate to questions of mistaken identity—e.g., mistaking T. Fadius Gallus (Cicero's ex-quaestor) for M. Fabius Gallus (a wealthy friend), by placing a letter to the former at the end of a sequence of letters to the latter.

36. See the references in n. 15 for discussion.

context.[37] In this book, I show how such given features of Roman life as the freedman, provincial government, the games, and the *familia* resonate differently in the imperial context in which these epistolary narratives were put together and circulated, when compared with the republican context in which the original letters were written. These narratives will have served to reinforce readers' sense of a historical shift taking place between the era of the letters' writing and the era of their reception within the collections. At the same time, though, to call this collection an imperial text may be to blur the boundaries at the other end of its composition process. For if the advent of the codex is responsible for bringing the disparate books of this collection together, then it may be that we should be describing it as a late antique product too.[38] In Chapter 2, 'Enclosing the Collection: Frames of Meaning in *Fam.* 1 and *Fam.* 15', I consider some possible consequences for reading this collection of republican era letters not only when the Republic no longer existed but also when Rome herself was no longer the empire's administrative centre.

Moreover, imagining a relatively late date for the latest phase of the collection's formation does more than impinge on the kinds of contextual resonance that the collection would have found when read in these later historical contexts. For in this instance, it may well be these resonances that determined which of Cicero's many letter books made it into the collection. In other words, the context in which these letter books were read may have determined the shape of the collection itself. Above all, though, this scenario obliges us to relinquish ideas about *ad Fam.* as the product of a single editor working in isolation to promote his (or her) particular vision of Cicero and the late Republic, and invites us to espouse instead a more distributive, democratic model of editorship, one that allows the multiple readers of Cicero's letter books, over a lengthy period of time, a collective agency over the formation of the collection. It is in this sense that *ad Fam.* may be viewed as an important vehicle for collective memory—in that it not only preserves the memory of the late republican social collective who wrote and received the letters but also transcribes the collective memory of imperial readers in the process of remembering their earlier forebears. In taking this view of the

---

37. See Martelli 2017 for an illustration of how this works in the case of the narrative surrounding Cicero's bid for a triumph in *Fam.* 15, the meaning of which changes radically when seen in the imperial context within which this letter book was assembled and published.

38. See Roberts and Skeat 1983; and Harnett 2017 for broad agreement that the codex took over from the book roll as the predominant textual medium in the fourth to fifth centuries CE. I discuss the significance of this event (and its dating) for *ad Fam.* on pp. 12–14.

Introduction 17

dynamics of the collection's genesis, I take my cue from the original letters, which model a form of informational distribution that will prove helpful for understanding how *ad Fam.* came into being *as a collection.*

Cicero's Letters as Residual Media

A popular book by Tom Standage on the long history of social media opens with a close look at Cicero's letters, which, he suggests, offer one of our best witnesses from the ancient world of a social media system in action. As he points out, the letters reveal an informal network of communication, in which information circulated through the exchange of letters and other documents that were copied, commented on, and shared among peers. He goes on to say:[39]

> To modern eyes this all seems strangely familiar. Cicero was, to use today's Internet jargon, participating in a social media system: that is, an environment in which information was passed from one person to another along social connections, to create a distributed discussion or community. The Romans did it with papyrus rolls and messengers; today, hundreds of millions of people do the same things rather more quickly using Facebook, Twitter, blogs, and other Internet tools. The technologies involved are very different; but these two forms of so-cial media, separated by two millennia, share many of the same un-derlying structures and dynamics: they are two-way, conversational environments in which information passes horizontally from one person to another along social networks, rather than being delivered vertically from an impersonal central source.

The letters transmitted to modernity in Cicero's name do not, however, offer a transparent window onto this informational ecosystem, since, as we have seen, they come down to us filtered by the interests and narratives of the collections that contain them, and selected, organized, and published (or so we assume) by anonymous editors. According to this view, the 'authorship' of these letters is therefore distributed along two quite different axes: the hor-izontal one of Cicero's own social network, which operates through the ex-change of letters among peers; and the vertical axis through which the letters

---

39. Standage 2013, 2–3.

were distributed by editors after his death. The convergence of these two axes of distribution is responsible for the highly partial view that the collections give of the networks of exchange that the letters originally participate in, which are filtered entirely through Cicero's relationships and almost entirely through his words.

Yet the vertical model of authorship (or editorship) that takes the singular editor as the primary agent behind the collection is challenged by the possibility that it took decades, and perhaps even centuries, for the collection to assemble out of a multiplicity of letter books that were circulating over this period (much greater in number than those contained by *ad Fam.*). This scenario calls for a model of authorship that approximates to the mode of distribution found in the original letters—a distributive model of assemblage that shares common ground with the participatory dynamics found operating on the Internet, and for which theorists of digital media have some suggestive conceptual tools. 'Spreadable media' is the phrase coined by some of these theorists to describe the way in which content moves through digital media networks, circulated on the basis of its capacity to be 'liked' and 'shared' among peers.[40] This is a horizontal axis of distribution, one that contrasts with the centrally controlled, vertical axis through which mass media such as newspapers, for example, are distributed. It offers an apposite way of thinking about how the books of *ad Fam.* found their way into the collection, included on the basis of their 'collectability'—of *their* capacity to be liked and shared. And it has the advantage of transferring much of the intentional agency behind the shape of the collection away from individual editors and placing it squarely with the collection's multiple readerships, whose interests and biases the editors may be simply reflecting.

In their attempt to understand what kinds of cultural influence disseminate well across the Internet, theorists of new media have recently resuscitated some of the ideas of the Marxist critic Raymond Williams, whose analysis of the variable rates at which culture moves posits four different categories of cultural phenomena: the *emergent*, which set trends for the future; the *dominant*, which reign in the present; and the *residual* and *archaic*, which designate different kinds of material from the past.[41] The category that interests many new media theorists is the residual, which consists of historical material that has not yet been discarded (as would be true of the archaic) but

---

40. See Jenkins, Ford, and Green 2013.

41. Williams 1977, 121–27.

Introduction 19

which is recirculated and reappraised at some point after its original moment of consumption because it represents 'areas of human experience, aspiration and achievement which the dominant culture neglects, undervalues, opposes, represses or even cannot recognize.'[42] Or, as Jenkins, Ford, and Green put it, explaining why residual content lends itself to being spread on the Internet, 'The residual can linger in popular memory, become the object of nostalgic longing, be used as a resource for making sense of one's present life and identity, serve as the basis of a critique of current institutions and practices, and spark conversations. In short, residual content may become a prime candidate for spreadability.'[43] Cicero's letters, documents of a bygone era, which are subsequently collected into letter books that continue to circulate, in a variety of different groupings, perhaps long after their historical moment has passed, answer to this definition of residual media. Many of them are throwaway items—notes and scraps that were never intended to be viewed by more than their original addressee, but which, once preserved, operate as souvenirs of a past era, repositories of nostalgia and longing. We need a category like the residual in order to understand why such material gets preserved and retains a currency beyond the moment of its immediate function.

In seeking to explain what it is that makes residual objects or media linger on beyond their original moment of consumption, Jenkins et al. suggest that it is the value they accrue as objects of nostalgia for the past, and/or as vehicles for critiquing the present, that keeps them in circulation. Yet before these objects take up such positions of longed-for proximity to one era or critical distance from another, they play an important preliminary role in the workings of these processes simply by helping to articulate the idea of the past as past. Will Straw notes how this works on the Internet, when objects from the recent past cluster into groups, a process that, in itself, helps to reassemble the past and to place order, definition, and narrative structure on it. 'On the Internet, the past is produced as a field of ever greater coherence, through the gathering together of disparate artefacts into sets or collections and through the commentary and annotation that cluster around such agglomerations,

---

42. Williams 1977, 124. For examples of how Williams's category of the residual might be applied specifically to media technologies, see the volume of essays assembled in Acland 2007, which consider a number of different types of obsolescent media, from typewriters (or their products) to VHS videos, and assesses the contexts in which they continue to operate beyond the point of having been made redundant by new media forms. See also Reynolds 2011 (esp. pp. 55–128, and pp. 311–61) for discussion of similar forms of residual media operating in the digital music industry under the broad sign of 'retromania'.

43. Jenkins, Ford, and Green 2013, 99.

made possible in part by high-capacity storage mechanisms.'[44] This process is visible in the case of Cicero's letter collections, which deploy the higher-capacity storage mechanisms of book roll and codex in order to regroup individual letters into particular sequences. The earliest phase of this process, when the original letters were first organized into sequence and circulated in book rolls, may have played a role very similar to that which Straw describes, lending coherence to the relatively recent late republican past simply through the very process of assembling letters into various groups. For the letter sequences that emerged from this process cannot help but produce narratives about the period from which the letters come, packaging up these republican documents into sequences that produce a narratable past for the imperial literary consumer.

It is possible that Cicero's letters were regrouped into different sequences and circulated in different book roll formats for some time after their author's death. Equally possible is that after the letters were first organized into sequence for circulation in book rolls they were fixed into these units, but that the book rolls circulated themselves in different groupings for some time after their author's death. It is also conceivable that the letters were fixed into the very book formats *and* collections in which they were eventually transmitted from the earliest phase of their circulation following Cicero's death. Or it may be that we should imagine different scenarios for different collections: while it is easy to imagine a large collection of letters addressed to a single addressee and organized more or less chronologically, like *ad Atticum*, coming into formation in the shape in which it reaches us relatively early on, this may not hold for a more eclectic (and less chronological) collection like *ad Fam*. For this collection, although we know that the letters themselves were fixed into (at least some of) the book units that have been transmitted to us by the mid-second century CE, it may be that that the books of this collection were not fixed either in number or in sequence by this stage, and the evidence certainly allows for the possibility of a more fluid relationship between the different books of this collection. That it ultimately came to crystallize as a sixteen-book collection suggests that at some point in the process of its formation

---

44. Straw 2007, 4. In this essay, Straw shows how the Internet's markets for obsolete items (such as perfumes, in his example of those found on the website Longlostperfume.com) become in themselves repositories of cultural knowledge. Straw demonstrates how the Internet works to reshape cultural time by drawing on the model of the video rental store, which (before this institution itself became obsolescent) both slowed down the commercial obsolescence of films (by giving them a second life in the home-viewing market) while also accelerating films' first-run time in cinemas.

Introduction 21

readers (or a reader) wanted to model this collection on the sixteen-book *ad Atticum* if only in terms of size. Up until this point, though, some of the letter books that eventually found their way into *ad Fam.* may have circulated in smaller groupings, perhaps in combination with other books of Cicero's letters that were not ultimately transmitted.[45] Any theory about the letter collection's formation has to accommodate this speculative scenario, at any rate. Which presses the question: what determined the inclusion of some books over others in the letter collection that eventually became our sixteen-book collection of *Epistulae ad Familiares*?

The category of the residual again helps us answer this question because it demonstrates how objects and media come to accrue new forms of value as they continue to circulate beyond their original moment of consumption. If the letters or letter books of *ad Fam.* were successively reassembled following the first phase of their circulation, then this only demonstrates their continuing currency throughout that later period, and the ongoing interest that people took in using them to frame and reframe the late republican past. Nostalgia may be one factor driving this interest and critique of the imperial political model another. These feelings can only have been exacerbated by the historical break on which the letter collections are premised and may therefore be best explained by the cultural analyses put forward by Derrida in *Spectres of Marx*, which accounts for the retrospective, even spectral, reflexes that take hold following a major historical watershed, such as the fall of the Berlin Wall (or, indeed, the fall of the Republic).

'Hauntology' (or rather, the French, *hantologie*) is the term coined by Derrida to describe the haunting of the present by the past that settles at moments of historical disjunction, when agencies of the virtual act on events without actually existing, or 'haunt' them in the manner of ghosts. Derrida's particular objective in this work was to describe the way in which the spectre of Marx (and of Marxism) continued to haunt the hegemonic neo-liberal order of the late 1990s, which had been acclaimed by some as an 'end of history', but which, as he points out, only qualifies for this description in an ideal sense at best. The memory of Marxism lingers, ghost-like, in the gaps and contradictions that puncture the dominant system, as residual traces of a path that history might have taken, potential sources of regret and nostalgia. The same is true of the memory of the Republic that Cicero's letter collections produce, which address their readers as friends of the Republic whose demise

---

45. Cugusi 1983, 172 also considers this possibility.

Cicero repeatedly laments.[46] Reading over the shoulder of Cicero's friends and associates, we cannot help but be drawn into his melancholia after the civil war about the shift from a republic to a monarchy,[47] and his excitement at the prospect of saving the political situation at the end, despite the fact that we know it to be doomed. As I argue in Chapter 4, 'Ordering the Collection: History and Counter-History in *Fam.* 10–12', the present tense of these letters allows us to linger on the hopes and aspirations for a different historical outcome to the one that eventually transpired, in ways that are unavailable to authors writing about these historical events in retrospect. This emphasis also helps to explain why certain letter books may have been omitted from this collection: books of letters to Octavian, Caesar, and even Pompey (which are attested in antiquity, but which are not now extant) may never have been incorporated into *ad Fam.* because they could not be made to serve its republican nostalgia.[48]

A refrain that recurs throughout *Spectres of Marx* is the phrase that Hamlet utters following the visitation of his father's ghost that 'time is out of joint.' Derrida uses this phrase to articulate the damage done to the experience of time itself at moments of historical disjunction, when a breach intervenes within the present so as to make the experience of present time unavailable to the historical subject.[49] The quality of untimeliness that descends at such moments is one of the factors that contributes to their spectral aura. In his reformation of the Roman calendar, Augustus created just such a breach in the structure of historical time, reorienting the traditional ways of measuring time at Rome, which had hitherto been anchored to the founding of the Republic, around himself.[50] Julius Caesar himself anticipates this process, not so much in his own calendar reforms (which aimed at greater pragmatic

---

46. I have explored the hauntological status of the Republic for the early empire further in the context of Ovid's exile poetry in Martelli 2020, 66–79.

47. These are the narratives of both *Fam.* 4 (on which, see Gibson 2017) and *Fam.* 9.

48. It is also the case that *ad Fam.* does not incorporate multiple books solely addressed to the same addressee: the books of letters to Octavian, Caesar, and Pompey are in each case attested as circulating in the plural.

49. Derrida 1993, 20–33.

50. See Feeney 2007, 172–82 for discussion of the interventions that Augustus made in the consular *Fasti* in an attempt to anchor time around himself. These involved supplementing the list of consular names with periodic reminders of the number of years that had elapsed since the founding of the city by Romulus (his historical alter ego) in 752 BCE, and also from 22 BCE (when Augustus stepped down from holding the consulship himself), annotating the list of consuls for the year with the number of years since he had held tribunician power.

Introduction

accuracy) but in his initiative of pre-appointing consuls during his dictator-ship for the following few years. The experience of temporality that the impe-rial readers of this letter collection know is one that differs profoundly from that experienced by Cicero and his correspondents in *ad Fam.*, whose lives (up until the civil war) we see ordered and organized by the annual consular (and other official) elections.

The chronological significance of these activities goes beyond the fact that the elections were regular annual events. For on top of this, the fact that newly elected consuls took up their office on New Year's Day, and even gave their names to the year in which they served, highlights how integral their election to office was to the structuring and differentiation of time in the republican period that precedes the civil war. Caesar's pre-appointment of consuls, how-ever, effaces the significance of their moment of taking up office. The spectral consequences of this breach in the republican experience of time are visible in *ad Fam.* in a variety of ways. For one thing, the letters themselves provide evidence for Caesar's activities: the rhetoric of Cicero's attempts to persuade Plancus and D. Brutus in *Fam.* 10 and 11 to step up to the task of defending the Republic relies on their pre-appointment by Caesar to the consulship of 42 BCE, and Cicero refers to both men in those books as *consul designatus*. Yet in the build-up to the war with Antony, Caesar's power to predetermine consulships for years in advance is a source of despair for Cicero.[51] Moreover, in the melancholic books that cover the years of Caesar's dictatorship (e.g., *Fam.* 4 and 9), we are made aware of the absence of senatorial electioneering by sheer contrast with the content of the books set before the civil war[52] and by the feeling of time standing still in the absence of these activities.

But the Julian and Augustan calendar reforms are also felt in these letter books every time we find a reference to the months Quintilis and Sextilis—a relatively frequent occurrence, given the common Ciceronian practice of attaching dates to letters.[53] This latter manifestation of the temporal disjunc-tion that comes about as a result of the different experiences of time that

---

51. Cf. esp. *Att.* 14.6.2: 'Is it not lamentable that we should be upholding the very things which made us hate Caesar? Are we even to have Consuls and Tribunes of his choosing for two years to come?' (*Quid enim miserius quam ea nos tueri propter quae illum oderamus? Etiamne consules et tribunos pl. in biennium quos ille voluit?*)

52. Curio's election to the tribunate of 50 BCE is a significant narrative of *Fam.* 2, and Caelius's campaign to be made aedile for 50 BCE is a prominent narrative of both *Fam.* 2 and 8.

53. We see references to the month of Quintilis at, for example, *Fam.* 2.8 and *Fam.* 2.19. In *Att.* 16.1.1, Cicero abhors the recent renaming of Quintilis as Julius.

imperial and republican calendars encode derives from a feature peculiar to the medium of the letter. It draws attention to the forms of residual spectrality that cling to these letter collections as a result of the processes of remediation in which they participate. As the individual letter comes to be remediated by the book roll (which organizes the original letters into sets), and as the book roll is itself remediated by the codex (which organizes the individual book rolls into sets), so each of these new media is haunted by the medium it supersedes, and by the particular historical circumstances in which that medium once circulated. This effect is a signatory feature of modern cultural forms that deliberately embrace the hauntological condition of our current times.[54] Mark Fisher describes the attempt by contemporary practitioners of digital music to capture the patina of time on the sounds that they sample by displaying (and even exaggerating) the surface noise of the original media (e.g., the crackle of vinyl) in digital recordings that are perfectly capable of eliminating such noise but which have deliberately chosen not to.[55] Fisher, continuing the play on Derrida's terms of reference, calls this effect the 'metaphysics of crackle', and suggests (following Derrida) that it is designed to make us hear how time is out of joint.[56] Throughout Cicero's letter collections we find a similar effect at work in those places where the status of the original letters *as letters* is put on display: in the references that Cicero makes to writing in reply to letters that remain invisible to us (which exert their spectral presence in the content of Cicero's replies), and in the complaints that he makes about not having received letters from an addressee; in the enclosures that we find scattered through the collections; in the reference that he makes to duplicate letters; and, above all, in the dates that many of the included letters bear. The latter three features are peculiar to Cicero's letter collections and are not found in collections such as those of the younger Pliny, who irons out such clumsy facets of 'real' correspondence when repurposing his letters for presentation in the book roll as time-free (and therefore, implicitly, timeless) literary artefacts. Cicero's letter collections are, by contrast, haunted by

---

54. See Fisher 2014, 97–182; and Reynolds 2011, 311–61 for extensive analyses of the cultural conditions and various forms taken by musical hauntology.

55. Fisher 2013. See also Reynolds 2011, 350–51 on the hauntologists' interest in preserving the 'hiss' of cassettes.

56. Fisher 2013, 48: 'If the metaphysics of presence rests on the privileging of speech and the here-and-now, then the metaphysics of crackle is about dyschronia and disembodiment. Crackle unsettles the very distinction between surface and depth, between background and foreground. In sonic hauntology, we hear that time is out of joint.'

Introduction 25

the layers of historical past that run through their multiple levels of remediation, marked as such by the traces of functional obsolescence that attach to each medium through the very process of its having been superseded by another. This feature of the collections is what characterizes the letters they preserve as souvenirs: items whose dislocation from their original context is marked in stages by the various forms of remediation that they display when presented to readers in multi-book collections and which engender a desire (or fascination) for that original context correlative with their degree of dislocation from it.

Our sense of what has been lost as a result of reading these letters outside the immediate context for which they were conceived forms only part of their story and only part of their residual appeal. Some of the letter books included in *ad Fam.* speak more directly to the tastes and demographic of the collection's later readerships and thus balance out the original letters' contextual losses against the gains they make by being read in subsequent historical contexts. The inclusion of these letter books may well reflect the expansive period of time it took for this collection to come into formation and demonstrates the role that *ad Fam.* (like all Cicero's letter collections) must have played in producing a collective memory of the late republican past for later imperial (and post-imperial) readers who may have had little (or no) direct contact with its events and personalities. While the majority of letters in *ad Fam.* are addressed to Cicero's senatorial colleagues (and inevitably reflect their interests), the collection hosts narratives that expand its purview beyond the narrow circle of oligarchs at the centre of Roman power and speak to Cicero's contact, both positive and negative, with a broader segment of Roman society. The inclusion of a book of letters to Cicero's ex-slave, Tiro, is one spectacular example of this practice. Another would be the letters of introduction collected in *Fam.* 13, which address governors and other state officials posted across the Roman provinces and Italian mainland in the interest of Cicero's contacts abroad—many of them native provincials, and a number of them freedmen. These narratives can only have appealed to the wider and more socially mobile readerships that the collection would need to attract in the imperial period if it were going to offer a collective memory of the late republican past for this broad demographic, to make of it a historical past that they could claim. Other narratives reflect the interests of the social underclasses in Rome and its outsiders by taking a critical view of Cicero's and his colleagues' dealings with them. We see this in the narrative of Mutina found in *Fam.* 10–12, where the history (or counter-history) of Cicero's aspirations for the historical outcome of this moment is punctured by the perspective of various social groups that we do not expect to see represented in the republican narrative (or the triumviral one, for that matter). This perspective shifts our view of the struggle from being between alternative ideologies (Republic and Empire) to being between factions (*optimates* and *populares*) and classes (elite and non-elite, Roman and non-Roman), and allows us to see how later readerships, accustomed to greater social mobility and ready access to Roman citizenship, might look back at the late Republic in terms more critical than nostalgic.

Book Outline and Chapter Summaries

This book is, then, a study of how the sixteen-book collection of *Epistulae ad Familiares* transforms the letters it contains into souvenirs. It addresses how the constraints of the collection determine how we read the letter books that it comprises, and it considers the various forms of hermeneutic distortion that the collection imposes on the letters when we view the collection as the product of a later era. Although we know little about the closing *terminus ante quem* of the era of this collection's formation (other than that it quite possibly reaches into late antiquity), we do know that it post-dates Cicero's death and the advent of the new age of monarchy in Rome. The collection, then, transforms the letters into souvenirs of a past era and of a lost world and displays the new value that they accrue in their very distance from this original context—as vectors of imperial (and possibly even late antique) longing and nostalgia, as well as critique (of both the past and the present). Because I am interested in the particular lens that the collection imposes on the letter books and letters it contains, my chapters focus on those individual books, or groups of books, which have something to say about the larger corporate structure in which they are transmitted. I have therefore focused on books in the frame (*Fam.* 16, *Fam.* 1 and 15) and centre (*Fam.* 8) of the collection, which help articulate its composite form, as well as letter books (*Fam.* 10–12) which display particularly well the meanings produced by the juxtaposition of certain books alongside one another, or which effect certain kinds of thematic transition for the collection (*Fam.* 13). This study does not, therefore, offer a comprehensive book-by-book reading of *ad Fam.* Many readers will doubtless remain sceptical about my insistence that the form of this sixteen-book collection matters, and almost all the readings that I offer are designed to hold up as readings of individual books. But they are also designed to demonstrate how the whole collection hangs together and how, as a whole, it produces certain narratives about Cicero and the late Republic that reflect

Introduction 27

the retrospective view of these objects taken by later (imperial and late antique) editors and readers. Furthermore, these narratives need not be seen as the work of the lone editor, shaping the collection according to their own idiosyncratic whims; but may rather be the work of multiple editors operating over an extensive period of time, responding to the reactions of Cicero's readerships and to certain agreed narratives about this author to which his long-circulating letter books had given rise. It is perfectly possible that the editors of *ad Fam.* are, at least in part, shaping the collection to reflect these reactions.

I begin with a reading of *Fam.* 16 that takes seriously its location at the very end of the collection, where, I suggest, the paratextual position that it occupies on the outermost frame invites us to reflect on questions pertaining to the editing and transmission of the *Epistulae ad Familiares*. The puzzling question of who (or what) created this collection is given an answer in this book of letters, which consists entirely of letters to or about Cicero's freedman secretary, Tiro—the figure whom many scholars have seen as the likeliest candidate for the role of (first) editor of the individual books of *ad Fam.*, if not for the collection as a whole. While the identity of the editor is something that we are unlikely ever to ascertain, the paratextual position of book 16 invites readers to cast Tiro as editor and to look for insights about the procedures of transmission and dissemination within this book. In Chapter 1, 'Letters to the Editor: Constructing the Editor in *Fam.* 16' I therefore read *Fam.* 16 for the editorial commentary that its paratextual location imposes on its content and offer readings of a number of different narrative threads, most of them related to Tiro's ex-servile status, that lend themselves to this commentary: the story of Tiro's manumission, for example, showcases the role reversal that takes place when Tiro, the servile object, is made a subject and, by extension, when Cicero, the authorial master, is implicitly transformed into the object of his ex-slave's procedures of editorial rewriting. At the same time, Cicero's concern for Tiro's ill health and ardent expressions of love for Tiro express a desire to close the gap between author and editor and to make their identities merge. It is in these expressions of desire, furthermore, that we find the best articulation of the letters' status within the collections as souvenirs, vectors of longing from one historical context to another, and it is here that I set out in detail what it means for us to think of them as such. I conclude with a discussion of the historical significance of casting the freedman as editor in the imperial period, arguing that the narratives of *Fam.* 16 credit the ex-slave with a degree of control over his late master's legacy that may well reflect the more socially mobile demographic of readers in this period (and later), who were

28 SOUVENIRS OF CICERO

accustomed to seeing freedmen take a more prominent role in Roman society than was the case in Cicero's own day.

In Chapter 2, I build on ideas of the frame that the collection, as a fixed sixteen-book entity, implies, which may have come about as a consequence of being assembled by the book technology of the codex. Drawing inspiration from recent bibliographical studies of the Gutenberg revolution, which see the effect of containment or enclosure as one of the printed book's most powerful and wide-reaching consequences, I consider how this effect may be traced back in part to the advent of the codex and put forward *ad Fam.* as a case study for this effect. The paratext of *Fam.* 16 is not the only frame visible in this collection. Rather, frames beget frames, as we can see in the dialogue between *Fam.* 1 and *Fam.* 15, the books that enclose the preceding unit that *Fam.* 16 appends. In this chapter, I consider how these books thematize the very idea of enclosure and containment, which they themselves enact by virtue of their location in the frame of the collection, in the narratives that they generate, both individually and together, about geopolitical space and social exclusion and inclusion. The remarkable symmetry of these two books emerges from the parallel trajectories that the letters they contain traverse between Rome and the province of Cilicia—in 56 BCE, when the majority of letters in book 1 were composed by Cicero in Rome to Lentulus Spinther in Cilicia, and in 51 BCE when the majority of the letters in book 15 were written by Cicero now in Cilicia to a number of senatorial colleagues in Rome. In focusing the reader's attention on the experiences of two proconsuls of Cilicia, shortly before this province was dissolved into other provinces and placed under the administrative power of the emperor, these letter books, which themselves enclose the collection, represent the enclosure of late republican space, and the marking off of the Roman from the non-Roman world at the point in historical time that *ad Fam.* closes off. Yet the spatial concerns of these books are not limited to geopolitical forms of enclosure; they encompass social forms of alienation and inclusion as well, as both Cicero and Lentulus experience their proconsular tenures as forms of exile and/or social exclusion from the factional political scene in Rome. In this chapter, I consider how the act of positioning these books of letters at opposite ends of the collection has the effect of writing Lentulus and Cicero into the mirror image of each other, and I draw on Lacanian theories of subject formation to suggest what is at stake in this specular portrait: an ideal(ized) consular pair that might have been.

Chapter 3, 'Reorienting the Collection: Cicero as Addressee and the Arena of Letters in *Fam.* 8', moves from the frame to the centre of *ad Fam.*, to consider how the structure of the whole collection, and the codex that quite possibly produced it, is thematized in book 8. This book, which is located at the very heart of *ad Fam.*, is unusual because it reverses the pattern of authorship that we find in the other letter books of the collection, which consist largely of letters penned by Cicero to other people: *Fam.* 8 reverses this pattern insofar as it consists entirely of letters penned by someone else to him. In this chapter, I trace what it means to find the other side of a correspondence, and the perspective of someone else within the social media system in which Cicero's letters participate, systematically represented within this central book. I note how the evacuation of the Ciceronian author from this central point in the collection is complemented by a striking metaphor that emerges within book 8: Caelius's repeated references to the games that he is expected to host as a newly elected aedile, and comparison of the feud unfolding between Caesar and Pompey to a spectacle entertainment must evoke, for imperial readers, the (anachronistic) image of the amphitheatre. I argue that this image provides a dominant metaphor for the kinds of spectacle that the letters afford once assembled and published as a collection, which makes the letters available for a wider readership, much as the arena facilitates mass entertainment in the imperial age. If it is the codex that produces the composite sixteen-book letter collection, then the amphitheatre presents an especially apposite image for its organizational effects, in that it represents the capacity of this book technology to impose concrete form on the letter books it contains—much like the permanent amphitheatre, with its fixed, enclosing form and concentric rows of seating within. Above all, the amphitheatre is a building that represents the distinctive modality of power that imperial rule will come to take better than any other and as such prefigures the outcome of the civil war that is presented as a spectacle for the reader's consumption within this central book.

Chapter 4 'Ordering the Collection: History and Counter-History in *Fam.* 10–12' unpacks the linear order that the collection imposes on its assemblage of multiple letter books and explores in particular the narrative significance of plotting certain books of letters into sequence. This feature of the collection gets to the heart of its unique mode of writing historical narrative: when plotting letters and/or letter books into sequence, the editors cast retrospective significance on letters written in the present (and even future) tense. The gaps that open up between the unknowing perspective on events displayed by the letters' writers and the knowing hindsight of the letter collection's editors is the source of extensive irony for the various narrative sequences that the collection contains—whether within individual books or across multiple books, where this effect is magnified. My case study for this effect is the juxtaposition of *Fam.* 10, 11, and 12, where three different books of letters narrate the 'same' set of events from a different set of epistolary perspectives, even as they also reveal a connected meta-historical narrative (with a beginning, middle and end) that cuts across the three books. The events that these three books recount directly precipitate the fall of the Republic, which makes them showcase particularly starkly the ironies that open up in the gap between the (limited) foresight of the letters' writers and the superior hindsight of their editors. In this chapter, I argue that the different viewpoints of the letters' writers from the collection's editors generate competing historical narratives across the three books, as the narrative of sovereign power that the editors understand (that which sees monarchy prevailing over the Republic) is set against a counter-history of this period, written by the letters' authors, whose letters express a desire for a different historical outcome to that which would eventually emerge. I demonstrate how artfully these narratives have been made to intersect and at times swap over with one another, as the dialectical relationship between victor history and its inverse is allowed to play out across *Fam.* 10–12.

In the final chapter, Chapter 5, 'Structures of Feeling: The Household of *Familiaritas* in *Fam.* 13', I address what it means to have, with *ad Fam.*, a letter collection that embraces a multiplicity of addressees. Unlike the other collections of Cicero's letters, which each address a single named individual, the letters in *ad Fam.* write to a host of readers from across a fairly broad cross-section of Roman society, and also include letters written by them to Cicero. The letters' portrait of late republican society invites us to examine how this society resembles or differs from that to which its imperial readership belongs. In this chapter, I home in on a letter book where we see the distribution of late republican society at its widest. *Fam.* 13 consists of eighty-one letters written to twenty-eight different addressees recommending the interests of seventy-six different individuals, many of whom are of notably lower status than the individuals with whom we see Cicero corresponding in other letter books (provincials whom he had encountered during service abroad, for example, including a large number of freedmen). This book expands the purview of *ad Fam.* beyond the narrow circle of oligarchs whose interests take up so much of the rest of the collection and offers a picture of late republican society with which the more socially mobile and geographically expansive readership of the imperial age could more easily identify. Appearing, as it does, between the public letter books (*Fam.* 1–12) and the domestic books (*Fam.* 14–16) that close the collection,[57] *Fam.* 13 provides a transition between the public and private sides of Cicero's social network: its inventory of late republican society offers important social context for the first twelve books, but it is also structured by the image of the domestic household that dominates the collection's close.

In this closing chapter, I argue that the opening letter of *Fam.* 13, with its striking picture of the dilapidated house of Epicurus in Athens, proffers a suggestive image for the structure of late republican society as this is presented in the rest of the book: like the commune of friends housed in Epicurus's former home, Cicero's *familiares* are tied together by bonds of hospitality and by the obligation to protect each other's property (or *res familiaris*), albeit via networks distributed across the expanse of the republican empire, even as traditional social structures were shifting (like Epicurus's crumbling building) with the spread of citizenship in the provinces, for example, and with the rise of freedmen. In this chapter, I also draw on Raymond Williams's account of the emergent feelings that attend cultural and social change (his 'structures of feeling') to argue that the financial terminology that pervades the language of friendship in this book may be understood by contextualization against the backdrop of the redistribution of property that was taking place during Caesar's dictatorship. I consider how it speaks to Cicero's anxieties about broader forms of social and political dispossession. And I ask what an imperial readership might make of these anxieties in light of the novel institution of the *familia Caesaris*, the pervasive imperial household which administered the finances and much of the governance of empire under the Caesars, and which served as a reminder of how far public life had been privatized with the advent of monarchy.

The readings that I offer in these chapters, both of the individual books of *ad Fam.* and of the composite collection that these letter books comprise, are not designed to be definitive—let alone to exhaust the meanings that the collection contains. I would be the first to allow that the narrative meanings of the letter books are as many as (and more than) the range of possible relations between them and have simply focused on those that appear salient to me as I survey the collection from my own twenty-first-century viewpoint. *Ad Fam.* speaks to this modern viewpoint because of the political crisis that the letters cover, a crisis that resonates strongly with the seemingly permanent state of political crisis of our own times. This letter collection puts form, both

---

57. See Martelli 2017 on the exceptional status of *Fam.* 15 within *Fam.* 14–16.

narrative and thematic, on this crisis of the late Republic, and helps to draw a line around it, in ways that are, from our modern vantage point, less comforting than depressing. But the definition that these formal parameters bring to the letters is also what makes the crisis that they have been made to recount legible. The chapters that I offer here are designed to demonstrate how the formal constraints that make this crisis narratable arise, and to suggest what kinds of agency—social, political, and technological—produce them. They seek to show how archives turn letters into souvenirs, vehicles of nostalgia, critique, and historical revisionism that both distance us from the past and enable us to read it.

I

Letters to the Editor

CONSTRUCTING THE EDITOR IN *FAM.* 16

WHOSE CICERO DO we encounter in the letter collections? Who writes the version of this author that we find therein? The self-evident design of these collections, their status as artefacts as much as archives, inevitably confronts us with questions about the artistry, agency, and identity of their editors. Suspecting (as we might) that the editors are people other than Cicero, these are uncomfortable questions, insofar as they challenge our expectation that historical letters should bring us closer to their author. In the case of these letter collections, we realize instead that the intimate portrait of Cicero, The Author, that the letters construct is the creation of (an)other author(s)—anonymous and unknown editors, whose biases and sympathies determine what we see in the collection. Thus the proximity to Cicero that the letters seem to give us is a fiction—mediated, as the letters are, by the editorial hand of another (or of multiple others).

Cicero's letter collections do not obscure their editors' alterity, but rather invite us to reflect on it, since they offer an especially stark display of the transformative power of the editor's art: without needing to change a word that Cicero actually wrote, the editors of these collections have performed a powerful, if barely visible, act of reading and writing (or rewriting) simply by selecting letters from Cicero's vast correspondence and organizing them into various sequences.[1] The authorial work that this activity performs on the text

---

1. As we have seen, this is particularly evident in the case of *ad Fam.*, which brings together books of letters addressed to multiple different correspondents, and which makes use of a variety of structuring principles other than chronology in its organization, thereby rendering the editor's interventions the more visible. But it is no less true of the other letter collections which are organized (more or less) chronologically: for example, the decision to begin *ad Atticum*

Souvenirs of Cicero. Francesca K. A. Martelli, Oxford University Press. © Oxford University Press 2024.
DOI: 10.1093/oso/9780197761960.003.0002

of Cicero's letters invites us to consider the degree of appropriation entailed in publishing as artfully edited books a set of documents not destined for publication as such by their original author. At stake in this process is not only the transformation of letters into literature, and the creation of a new kind of readership from the one originally marked out by the letters' addressees, but the packaging up of an archive of late republican documents into a set of narratives *about* the late Republic to be procured by the imperial (and post-imperial) literary consumer.

But who are these editors, and what is their relationship to Cicero? How close are they to him, or we the readers, in turn, to them? One consequence of the authorial role that the editors of these collections play in shaping the epistolary portrait of Cicero that they proffer is that our desire to get to know the Author behind the letters is displaced, to some extent, onto the editor who 'writes' this version of Cicero. This desire is destined to be frustrated because, in absolute terms, the identity of the editors is unknown and unknowable and can only be broached by being placed on a spectrum of possible degrees of distance from Cicero. In the case of *ad Fam.*, it extends from a maximal point of distance at some point in the fifth century CE when (we assume) the sixteen books must have been assembled into the format that the manuscripts transmit, to a minimal point of distance that identifies the editor as a member of Cicero's household. The former scenario could involve any number of different editors (or readers) assembling the content of *ad Fam.* in any number of different configurations over centuries, whereas the latter sees the collection assembled perhaps just once, by a single individual, within a generation of Cicero's death.

Yet however brief the interval separating the letter collections' editors from the letters' author,[2] it has a transformative effect on the meaning of the

---

where the editor of this collection has chosen to do so has far-reaching consequences for its narrative shape. For discussion of this, see Martelli forthcoming.

2. All that we can say with certainty about the publication dates of *ad Fam.* and *ad Atticum* respectively, is that some of the letters from each collection were circulating in the first century CE: the elder Seneca, for example, quotes from a letter that corresponds to our *Fam.* 15.19 with near accuracy in, for example, *Suas.* 1.5, which is dated to the 30s BCE; while the younger Seneca accurately quotes from a number of Cicero's letters to Atticus. White 2010, 174–75 points to a reference in Quntilian (*Inst.* 6.3.108) to a joke in *Att.* 8.7.2, drawn from a treatise on humour by Domitius Marsus, to argue that letters from *ad Atticum* must have been circulating already by the end of Augustus's reign. See p. 11 n. 27 for discussion of the different ways in which Gellius cites the books of *ad Fam.* and *ad Atticum* and of the testimony this offers for the various formats these two collections may have taken at this stage in the second century CE. See also p. 12 for discussion of why scholars have posited the fourth or fifth centuries CE as the cut-off date by which time *ad Fam.* would likely have been organized into numbered

letters because it necessarily takes in Cicero's death in 43 BCE, and therefore encloses the shift from republican to imperial eras that we are accustomed to locate around this time.[3] Wherever we locate the editors of *ad Fam.* on a spectrum of distance from Cicero, this will always be the interval that matters most, and the editor's proximity to Cicero must always be qualified by this abyssal shift in context. Far from simply documenting this historical transition, the letter collections are in fact complicit in producing it. *Ad Fam.*, in particular, is a tour de force of retrospective rewriting, one that actively exploits the time lag that separates the moment of the letters' composition from their moment of dissemination and draws on the hindsight that we derive from the revolutionary historical events that had arisen in the interim in order to confer new meanings on the letters.[4] By rewriting the letters in this way, its editors reinforce the historical break on which its hermeneutic transformations are premised. They also reinforce their own difference and/or distance from Cicero, whose death at precisely this moment of historical rupture draws an absolute line between his composition of the original letters in the late Republic[5] and their 'rewriting' of them in the subsequent era.

Where scholars have speculated about the identity of the editors of Cicero's letter collections, it has either been to maximize or to minimize this shift. At one end of the spectrum, we meet the theory of Carcopino, who concluded that the picture of Cicero to emerge from *ad Atticum* was of such pettiness and vanity that its publication could only have been overseen by Octavian/Augustus himself, with the aim of posthumously denigrating Cicero.[6] More common are the assumptions made (but seldom investigated in any detail)

---

books. Boissier 1863; Büchner 1939, 1211–23; and more recently Beard 2002, 117–18; and White 2010, 174–75 offer discussion of what we know about the publication history of *ad Fam.* and *ad Atticum* in antiquity.

3. On p. 15 n. 35, I follow the arguments put forward by White 2010, 32–33 for reasons why Cicero cannot be identified as the editor of the letter collections. These include the testimony of Nepos, who towards the end of his life of Atticus, refers to Cicero's letters to Atticus in terms that suggest they were not yet published in any formal sense by the time of Atticus's death (see White 2010, 188 n. 9 for discussion of Nepos *Att.* 16.3). White 2010, 33 also notes a number of editorial 'slips' in the misidentification of individual addressees at certain points in *ad Fam.*, which, he points out, Cicero is unlikely to have made himself.

4. Cf. Martelli 2017 and Gibson 2017 for readings of what this shift in historical context might mean for our interpretation of *Fam.* 15 and *Fam.* 4, respectively.

5. See p. 7 n. 15 above for discussion of the equation drawn by imperial authors (from Livy onward) between Cicero's death and the end of the Republic.

6. Carcopino 1947. Cf. Balsdon 1952 for discussion of the speculative excesses of Carcopino's approach.

at the other end of the scale: that various members of Cicero's *familia* had a hand in the posthumous publishing of his letter collections. Marcus Junior, Atticus, and Tiro all outlived Cicero by enough years to have overseen such a project, and each is mentioned by various scholars as a plausible contender for the role of editor of one, if not more, of the collections.[7] Aside from the plausibility of these candidates, given their ready access to Cicero's archive of documents, there is the additional appeal of casting Cicero's closest proxies as editors of his letter collections in order to minimize the space between author and editor and to allow us to perpetuate the illusion that the letters might still bring us close to Cicero, even if only by bringing us closer to the view of him forged by his closest associates.

Of all these potential editors, the one who would seem to rub up closest is Tiro, the secretarial figure who, as slave (and/or ex-slave), constitutes the 'minimal addition' to his master's presence and person, and hence a means of extending his authorial identity by the shortest possible distance.[8] Although Tiro's identity as editor of Cicero's speeches, and an author in his own right after Cicero's death, was well known to later imperial writers,[9] his identity as editor of any or all of the letter collections is as speculative a possibility as any other. It demands our attention, however, because it is a narrative that one of the collections itself constructs. The closing book of *ad Fam.* consists entirely

---

7. See Nake 1861, 2–3 for the view that Atticus edited both *ad Atticum* and *ad Fam.*; Carcopino 1947, 305–63 regards Atticus as responsible for the formal publication of many of Cicero's works, including *ad Atticum*, while Sommer 1926 maintains that Atticus may have played a role in 'publishing' these works in private circles (but not more widely and not for commercial purposes). Tyrrell and Purser 1979 (vol. 1, 1st ed.) believe that Tiro probably edited *ad Fam.*; Büchner 1939, 1222 contends that Tiro assembled and published *ad Fam.* along with the other major letter collections, with the exception of *ad Atticum*, as a *corpus*. McDermott 1972, 281 suggests that if Tiro were responsible for publishing Cicero's letter collections, he may have been aided in the task by Atticus and Marcus *filius*.

8. Cf. Fitzgerald 2011 for the idea of slave as 'minimal addition'.

9. Quintilian (*Inst.* 10.7.30–31), for example, mentions the *commentarii* that Tiro published on some of Cicero's (otherwise seemingly unpublished) speeches, as well as books of Cicero's witticisms that Tiro may have published (Quint. *Inst.* 6.3.5). Gellius refers to his copy of Cicero's *Verrines* being a 'Tironian book' (*NA* 13.21.6) or crafted with *Tironiana cura* (*NA* 1.7.1), while Fronto likewise mentions Tiro's editions of Cicero's books in a letter to Marcus Aurelius (*ad M. Caes.* 1.7.4). See McDermott 1972, 277–82 for a full discussion of these (and other) references to Tiro's editorial work by later authors. See Zetzel 1973, 231–43; and Hendrickson 2018, 130–32 for discussion of the complex question of whether all these 'Tironian' editions/ copies were 'genuine'.

of letters to or about Tiro. As the culminating book in the collection,[10] it occupies the paratextual position commonly reserved for editorial statements and discussions of publication and transmission. Scholars never explicitly cite the book's position within the collection as a contributing factor to Tiro's identity as editor, and with good reason: for however little we know about the editing of the letters into individual books, we know even less about the organization of the books themselves into a collection. And given that in antiquity the books of *ad Fam.* are cited not by number but by the name of their opening letter's addressee, we might be forgiven for thinking their position within the collection irrelevant—irrelevant, that is, to the task of identifying their original editor and his (or her) prerogatives, let alone getting us any closer to the letters' author.

Nevertheless, however little we may know about the agencies responsible for shaping this collection as we have it, they have answered our desire to identify Tiro as editor by placing the book of letters addressed to him last. In this chapter, I offer a reading of *Fam.* 16 which scrutinizes the editorial pretensions of this book, in light of its paratextual position at the end of the collection, and which attempts to locate the editorial commentary that this position imposes on its content. My argument is not that Tiro should be identified as the historical figure responsible for editing the sixteen books of *ad Fam.* into the collection that we have,[11] but rather that the organization of the collection has cast him as such and that the process of doing so has significant hermeneutic consequences for *ad Fam.* as a whole. As we shall see, Tiro may offer the minimal extension of Cicero's author function, but the interval between them is still enough to accommodate the transformative historical ruptures that took place between Cicero's death and his own some forty years later.[12] Furthermore, far from minimizing the space between Author (Cicero)

---

10. Whether we view the collection as comprising all sixteen books of *ad Fam.* or just the eight-book unit of *Fam.* 9–16, which we know also circulated independently from *Fam.* 1–8. On this, see my discussion on pp. 13–14 n. 34.

11. See pp. 17–21 for my own view of the broader social forces behind the formation of the collection as we have it.

12. The date for Tiro's death is given by Jerome. Under the year equated with 5/4 BCE, Jerome writes (*ad Olymp.* 194.1): 'M. Tullius Tiro, Cicero's freedman, who was the first to invent shorthand, lived out his old age in his estate in Puteoli right up to his hundredth year' (*M. Tullius Tiro, Ciceronis libertus, qui primus notas commentus est, in Puteolano praedio usque ad centesimum annum consenescit*). Cf. McDermott 1972, 277–86 for speculation about Tiro's life and career following Cicero's death. Tiro is an obvious choice for other reasons too, not least because in a letter addressed to Atticus a year and a half before his death Cicero describes Tiro as currently engaged in producing a collection of his master's letters to be published in due

SOUVENIRS OF CICERO

and editor, Tiro's servile (or ex-servile) status opens up a number of narratives that comment on the transformations that the collection exerts on the letters it contains, including the historical shift from Republic to monarchy on which all these transformations are premised.

Author Function

Our text of *Fam.* 16 opens programmatically with a letter that comes from *all* the (male) Cicerones to Tiro (*Fam.* 16.1): *M. T. C. ET CICERO MEUS ET FR. ET FRATRIS FIL. S. P. D. TIRONI.* ('I Tullius, my son Cicero, and my brother and his son, send warmest greetings to Tiro.') This turns out to be a false start, though, because it is one of very few instances in the vulgate text of *ad Fam.* where the numbering of letters does not correspond with the sequence we find in the manuscript tradition, which starts with what the vulgate calls *Fam.* 16.5.[13] Yet this letter too comes from all the male Cicerones, and outdoes *Fam.* 16.1 by marking Tiro out as their own mirror image in *humanitas: TULLIUS ET CICERO ET Q. Q. S. P. D. TIRONI HUMANISS. ET OPT.* ('Tullius, and Cicero, and the two Quinti send warmest greetings to that most human/kindly/erudite and best of men, Tiro.')[14] This opening sends a powerful message to the world about Tiro's participation in the Ciceronian author function, but it also lays bare some of the complex power dynamics running through it. In particular, 'Tullius', the name that all the senders of this letter share, is also born by Marcus Tullius Tiro, even after he has been freed, by virtue of his once having been the possession of this family.[15] At the same time, the Cicerones's characterization of Tiro as *humanissimus* seems

---

course: Cf. *Att.* 16.5.5, where Cicero refers to a συναγωγή of about seventy of his letters of his that Tiro was compiling at the time (44 BCE). Scholars have commonly identified this collection as *Fam.* 13, on the basis of its approximate tally with this book's number of letters.

13. On this strange feature of *Fam.* 16's reorganization, see Beard 2002, 131. By 'vulgate', scholars and editors refer to the *textus receptus* or *consensus editorum* (i.e., the received tradition) of printing *ad Fam.* as it was traditionally printed prior to those editorial interventions that sought to reorganize the collection according to modern editorial prerogatives. While the vulgate text of *ad Fam.* normally corresponds to M, there are places like this where it occasionally diverges.

14. Later on in this opening sequence, in *Fam.* 16.11 (which, in the manuscripts, appears as the tenth letter in *Fam.* 16), we find the Ciceronian name amplified to include the female members of this family as well (*Fam.* 16.11): 'I Tullius and my son Cicero, Terentia and Tullia, my brother Quintus, and his son Quintus send warmest greetings to Tiro' (*M. T. ET C., TERENTIA ET TULLIA, Q. FRATER ET Q. F. S. P. D. TIRONI*).

15. Cf. Mouritsen 2011, 39 for discussion of the procedure whereby a manumitted slave assumed both the gentilicial *nomen* and the *praenomen* of his master once he was freed, as if he had been

designed to compliment his extra-human(e) (and hence pointedly non-servile) qualities, as if to attribute to him a status that enables him to bear the name 'Tullius' on an approximate footing with them.[16]

The ambiguities of Tiro's servile identity contribute to his perfect casting as the editor of this collection from the outset: if the editor is a figure who extends the author, who better to do this than the ex-slave who shares his master's name? Yet this ex-slave is made to function as more than a prosthetic extension of his owner (or ex-owner).[17] The very existence of the letters written to him attests to his capacity to exist outside his immediate proximity to Cicero—and to Cicero's capacity to recognize and respect Tiro's independence.[18] This degree of autonomy is significant for the editorial narrative of *ad Fam.* 16 insofar as it enables the relationship between author (master) and editor (ex-slave) to be cast as differential. The gap that separates Tiro-as-editor from Cicero-as-author creates for readers a plausible hermeneutic interval in which the editor's reappraisals may emerge, as we can imagine him reading and interpreting the author's words and reframing (or rewriting) them accordingly. The spatial distances that separate Tiro from Cicero, and which create the opportunity for epistolary exchange, thus precondition the modes of temporal distance that also stand between them, both within the world of the letters and then beyond it once Cicero is dead and Tiro is imagined living on to secure his master's legacy as editor of his life in letters. Tiro's conspicuous (if minimal) autonomy casts him in *ad Fam.* 16 as more than just an instrument of Cicero's posthumous survival: indeed, as a potential rewriter of Cicero's 'life' and 'letters'.[19]

---

reborn as his child. See also Gunderson 2007, 41 n. 129 for discussion of the play on *suo* in *Fam.* 16.18.1, when Cicero banters with Tiro over the decision to address him *Cicero Tironi suo*.

16. The condescension with which this compliment is delivered ensures that it maintains, rather than closes (as it purports to), the gap in status between them.

17. On the Roman conception of the slave as a prosthetic extension of the master, see Habinek 2005, 385; and Blake 2012.

18. A further manifestation of Tiro's authorial autonomy arises from the references that various correspondents in *ad Fam.* 16 make to letters they have received from Tiro (Cicero refers to them at *Fam.* 16.2, 16.3, 16.5.1, 16.6.2, 16.7, 16.11–14, 16.19, and 16.24.2; Quintus refers to letters from Tiro at *Fam.* 16.16.1 and 16.26.1; and when Marcus Junior writes to Tiro in *Fam.* 16.21 and 16.25, it is in response to letters that Tiro has written to him). Yet it is of course equally significant that no letter by Tiro appears in *Fam.* 16, with the result that the book's portrait of him is drawn through the words of his masters.

19. Howley 2018, 174–90 notes that this very autonomy is a cause of both censure and anxiety for later authors such as Gellius: censure when Tiro is held responsible for errors in his master's manuscripts, and anxiety because Gellius recognizes how dependent he and his peers are on

Yet if the gap that opens up here between Cicero and Tiro is one in which a vertical (or temporal) mode of self-extension emerges, Tiro also serves in *Fam.* 16 as a means of extending Cicero's identity horizontally too. In book 16, Tiro is made to fulfil an important role in defining the broader parameters of the author function that operates under his master's name, by gathering all the other male bearers of that name in the book of letters devoted to him. Cicero's letters to Quintus may have formed a separate collection outside this work, but the only letters written *by* Quintus himself that have been transmitted are preserved in this book of letters, and three of the four are addressed to Tiro. Likewise with Cicero's son, Marcus Junior: again, while Cicero's letters to his son are thought to have once circulated in two (now lost) books of letters,[20] the only letter transmitted in the son's name is preserved in *Fam.* 16, and that letter is addressed not to his father but to Tiro. Tiro, it seems, is the missing link between all the male Cicerones, the glue that binds them together as a family. In this book of letters, they are gathered under the sign of their common name and collectively display the fact that that name belongs not just to Cicero but to a wider author function of which Tiro, the ex-slave, forms an integral part.

Tiro not only finds his way into the authorial sign under which this work is written (or rewritten) but also occupies a privileged position within the letter collection's internal readership of named addressees. His is the lowest status of any figure addressed in this, or any other of Cicero's collections. No other slave or *libertus* is addressed in the extant letters,[21] and *ad Fam.* contains few letters addressed even to *equites*. Instead, the majority of the recipients in this collection are members of the senatorial class. Tiro is a marked exception. Yet the title of this collection, *ad Familiares*, seems designed to promote his presence within it over and above this grander company. Although this particular title was bestowed on the collection in the Renaissance,[22] and so cannot be claimed as the work of the original editor(s), the fact that it

---

the judgment calls of an ex-slave, whose presence as part of the scene of writing he is loth to acknowledge.

20. Cf. Weyssenhoff 1966; and Nicholson 1998, 76–87 on the thirty-nine 'lost' books of correspondence addressed to other *familiares* (including these two to Marcus Junior) that were, according to Nonius Marcellus, circulating in antiquity.

21. Although a number of *liberti* are recommended to addressees in *Fam.* 13. Cf. pp. 139–44 for discussion of the significance of this.

22. Cf. Shackleton Bailey 1977, 23 for discussion. Cf. Hinds 2005, 53 on the likelihood that the title of Cicero's *Epistulae ad Familiares* derives from Petrarch's letter collection of the same name (rather than vice versa).

was given to the collection in the first place, and, more importantly, the fact that it has persisted, is a testament to the magnetic force of Tiro's presence in this collection. The primary meaning of the substantive *familiaris* is 'servant', or at least 'member of one's domestic household', a designation which may be extended to refer to one's close acquaintance.[23] A title has been chosen which enables this slippage between a member of Cicero's domestic staff and the senatorial grandees who make up the majority of his letters' recipients (a large number of whom stretch the category of *familiaris*). At the same time, the term does more to assimilate the latter to Tiro's status than the other way around. Despite the uniqueness of Tiro's status, the title of this collection identifies him not as an outlier but as the yardstick by which all other standards of proximity to Cicero may be measured.

But if Tiro's proximity to Cicero—nominally, temporally, spatially— makes him the perfect candidate for editor, his casting in this role also produces certain paradoxical effects for Cicero's authorial subject position. An inevitable dynamic of the relationship between master and slave to which scholars of ancient slavery have alerted us is its capacity to subvert the expected hierarchies of domination at any time.[24] One of William Fitzgerald's most notable examples of this process is found in the tradition of *envoi* poems, which often portray the book, on the brink of transmission, as a slave more free than its master.[25] This *envoi* tradition resonates strongly with *ad Fam.* 16, when we read this book with an eye to the editorial status that its position on the outermost frame of the collection marks. The dynamic of hierarchical subversion that Fitzgerald identifies at work in the master and slave relationship of author and book spills over in this instance into the relationship between author and editor, as Cicero, author of the letters, becomes the object of his slave-editor's construction. This process of authorial subject becoming object is the theme on which this book of letters riffs, as the book itself provides us with a number of different narratives through which to think through the various implications of this process.

---

23. Cf. Ernout and Meillet 1967 s.v. *famulus* for the etymology of *familiaris*.

24. Cf. Fitzgerald 2000, 13–31.

25. Hor. *Epist.* 1.20; Ov. *Tr.* 1.1; with Fitzgerald 2000, 30–31.

Manumission

At the heart of *Fam.* 16 is the story of Tiro's manumission: letters 13 to 16 make up a run of letters dated to the middle of April 54 or 53 BCE and build up to the topic of Tiro's imminent (and/or recent) freedom. All scholars who turn their attention to this book of letters see this narrative as being somehow central to the book as a whole, and that centrality is marked by these letters' dislocation (despite having been written several years prior to all the other letters contained in this book, they are placed in the middle of it). Various interpretations for the prominence of this sequence have been suggested: that it inverts and comments on the process of enslavement that the Roman state was undergoing at this time,[26] or that it prefigures the rise of freedmen that will become such an important narrative for the imperial period. What, though, are we to make of this story in light of its position in book 16, and, more particularly, in light of the editorial frame through which we might read this book? The narrative of Tiro's manumission provides a negative foil for the process of Cicero's authorial subject becoming the edited collection's object, for it is a narrative of the opposite—of an object turning into a subject.[27] The location of this story in the middle of *Fam.* 16 causes it to operate as a pivot for the book as a whole. Told against the inverse process of Cicero's transformation into 'Cicero', the story helps to explain a series of reversals in the relationship between subject and object, master and slave that arise in the course of this book, and it helps to articulate the way in which Cicero swaps positions with the figure who has been cast as his editor, and who is therefore presented as playing an authorial role over the collection as a whole.

One of the first things Fitzgerald emphasizes about the discourse surrounding slaves is that it operates primarily through imperatives.[28] The slave is an instrument of his (or her) master's will and exists to satisfy the master's desires. The slave exists to be commanded. Cicero's letters to Tiro would appear to obey this logic: in no other book of letters is the imperative so ubiquitous. Yet there is an inverted logic to these commands, which corresponds to Cicero's expressions of desire and longing elsewhere. In Lacanian terms, the imperative is an expression of the paternal metaphor, the *nom-du-père*, which articulates the need that

---

26. Beard 2002, 138–41.

27. See Cliff 1990 for discussion of an analogous process that takes place for Black female artists when they take control of the White narratives about Black cultures and identities that have hitherto been used to objectify them.

28. Fitzgerald 2000, 6.

the subject encounters within the symbolic to renounce a substantive part of his desire.[29] What is strange about the imperatives found in this letter book is that they articulate the renunciation not of Tiro's desire but of Cicero's. Again and again, Cicero orders Tiro to stay put and look after his health at the expense of satisfying his master's pressing desire to see him as soon as possible.[30] In themselves, then, these imperatives convey the strange place that Tiro occupies in relation to Cicero's subject position: instrument of Cicero's will, yet someone whose own well-being is more important than that will. Tiro forces Cicero to confront the need to renounce his desire in the interests of something else.

This impulse makes particular sense when we consider the role in which Tiro is cast as this book's editor, and hence as the extension of Cicero's authorial subject position over time. Many of Cicero's imperatives take on a new meaning when read in this light. The frequent messages of concern for Tiro's health that dominate *Fam.* 16 read in retrospect as injunctions that he should live long enough to survive his master's death and guarantee his authorial position in the long run by getting this letter collection in order. As Gunderson also notes, the command delivered in *Fam.* 16.4, where Cicero tells Tiro to put everything aside and serve the *corpus*, may be taken as a reference to the epistolary *corpus* that this book of letters closes (*Fam.* 16.4.4):[31]

> **Sic habeto**, *mi Tiro, neminem esse qui me amet quin idem te amet; et cum tua et mea maxime interest te valere, tum multis est curae. Adhuc, dum mihi nullo loco deesse vis, numquam te confirmare potuisti; nunc te nihil impedit;* **omnia depone; corpori servi.**

> **Believe me**, my Tiro, that there is nobody who loves me, who does not also love you; and while your health is the highest concern for you and me, it is a matter of concern to many. So far, as a result of never wanting

---

29. On the paternal metaphor, see Lacan 1997, esp. 196–206; 2006, 228–31 and 677–700; and 2015. The second person discourse of Cicero's letters, and the mode of interpellation that this discourse entails, makes them (like all letters) especially amenable to Lacanian analaysis, which has been a major current in the scholarship on Cicero's letters since Leach 1999. For more recent Lacanian approaches to the letters, see Cappello 2016 and Martelli 2016.

30. The gesture appears first in *Fam.* 16.1: 'Above everything, **take care of yourself**. Of the many duties you've performed in my service, this will please me the most.' (**Cura ergo potissimum, ut valeas;** *de tuis innumerabilibus in me officiis erit hoc gratissimum.*) Cf. also *Fam.* 16.10: '**Please be ready to render** due services to our Muses . . . **mind you make a complete recovery.**' (*Tu Musis nostris* **para ut** *operas* **reddas** . . . **fac plane ut valeas.**)

31. Cf. Gunderson 2007, 39. For Cicero's use of the term *corpus* to refer to a whole treatise or literary work (cf. *Fam.* 5.12.4 and *Qfr.* 2.12.4).

44 SOUVENIRS OF CICERO

to fail me in any way, you've never been able to recover your strength. Now nothing stands in your way. **Put everything aside; be the slave of your body.**

The instruction that Cicero delivers to Tiro in *Fam.* 16.20 to organize the books that he has just sent to Tusculum, and to make a list of them, as soon as the doctor allows, may be read in a similar vein:[32] *Sollicitat, ita vivam, me tua, mi Tiro, valetudo. . . .* **Libros compone; indicem,** *cum Metrodoro libebit, quoniam eius arbitratu vivendum est.* ('As I live, Tiro, your health worries me. . . . **Please arrange my books and make a catalogue** of them, as soon as Metrodorus [the doctor] has no objection since you have to live according to his orders.') All these imperatives are expressed in the interests of self-preservation, which makes sense when we view Tiro as an extension of the author's subject position, entrusted with the task of preserving Cicero's literary corpus over time.

If these imperatives are an expression of the paternal metaphor, reformulated here to articulate the master-slave relationship, later on in the book we see a displacement of the terms of this metaphor when Tiro is made to assume something of his master's paternal role in his own right. *Fam.* 16.21, a letter dated to September 44 BCE, is addressed by Marcus Cicero Junior to Tiro from Athens, where the former was studying philosophy at the time (*Fam.* 16.21.1–2):

> *Cum vehementer tabellarios exspectarem cottidie, aliquando venerunt post diem quadragesimum et sextum quam a vobis discesserant. Quorum mihi fuit adventus optatissimus;* **nam cum maximam cepissem laetitiam ex humanissimi et carissimi patris epistula, tum vero iucundissimae tuae litterae cumulum mihi gaudii attulerunt.** *. . . Vehementer igitur gaudeo te meam sine dubitatione accepisse excusationem. Gratos tibi optatosque esse qui de me rumores adferuntur non dubito, mi dulcissime Tiro, praestaboque et enitar ut in dies magis magisque haec nascens de me duplicetur opinio. Qua re quod polliceris te bucinatorem fore existimationis meae, firmo id constantique animo facias licet; tantum enim mihi dolorem cruciatumque attulerunt errata aetatis meae ut non solum animus a factis sed aures quoque a commemoratione abhorreant.*

---

32. Cicero's mention of this new shipment of books to Tusculum picks up on a playful reference to Tiro having no new books to read in *Fam.* 16.18.4 (which seems to have been composed and sent shortly before *Fam.* 16.20). See Shackleton Bailey 1977, 386–87 for discussion.

Although I was anxiously waiting for your letter carriers every day, they only finally arrived forty-six days after they had left you. Their arrival was very welcome. **For although I derived the greatest possible pleasure from my most kindly and beloved father's epistle, still it was your delightful letter that brought me most joy.** . . . So I'm thrilled that you've accepted my excuse without hesitation. I have no doubt, dearest Tiro, that the rumours about me that have come to your ears are pleasing and welcome to you; and I shall try my hardest to ensure that this opinion of me, which is growing more and more every day, becomes twice as good. For that reason, you may with full confidence fulfil your promise of being the trumpeter of my reputation. For the errors of my youth have caused me such grief and agony that not only do my thoughts shrink from what I have done, but my very ears shrink from recalling it.

The letter presents Tiro as a stand-in for the father—and does so all the more urgently because this letter to Tiro is seen by some scholars as a stand-in for the letter that Marcus Junior *should* have written *to* his father, on the basis of a complaint found in a contemporaneous letter from Cicero to Atticus about his son's failure to reply to his last missive.[33] In this letter, then, we see a set of displacements circling around the father-son relationship and introducing Tiro as the new token in the paternal chain.[34]

Ultimately, the letter falls short of identifying Tiro as a father figure. It identifies him rather as a *socius* or ally, someone who will mediate between father and son by trumpeting Marcus Junior's *existimatio* to Marcus Senior. Yet the imperatives that Marcus Jr. has so penitently internalized still issue in part from Tiro; and in the absence of any letters from Marcus to his father in this collection, or, for that matter, from Marcus Senior to his son, this letter allows Tiro to assume the total function of the paternal metaphor. Again, Tiro displaces Cicero in his relationship with the male relatives who share his name. Nor is this where the displacement process ends. The paternal function is obviously best suited to Tiro in his role as preserver and guarantor of Cicero's legacy. In view of this, it is particularly striking that all this letter makes plain, with its open picture of the feckless if well-meaning son, is that

---

33. *Att.* 15.15.4. Cf. McDermott 1972, 276 for discussion.

34. The set of displacements that we encounter when we see Tiro standing in for the father is an appropriate (and inevitable) effect of the paternal metaphor, which, in Lacanian thought, instantiates the mode of substitution that is a prerogative of the symbolic.

this legacy will not reside with Cicero's children—but in the studies that he presents elsewhere as the fruit of his and Tiro's mutual insemination. In *Fam.* 16.10,[35] the affectionate diminutives used to describe the *litterulae*, pining away for their absent parent Tiro, recall the way in which Cicero refers to the beloved (and very definitely un-feckless) daughter, Tullia—or Tulliola—before her death. Here, as elsewhere, Tiro is cast not as Cicero's child but as displacing his master from the role of parent, and thereby absorbing a position that we identify most closely with the authorial subject.[36]

The final two letters of *Fam.* 16 complete this commentary on the reversal in Tiro's position, from object to subject, that we find thematized by the narrative of his manumission. *Fam.* 16 closes with a pair of letters addressed by Cicero's brother Quintus to Tiro, which both open with playful references to the punishment that can only serve to remind the *libertus* of his erstwhile status as the Cicero family's property:

Fam. 16.26 (Quintus to Tiro, Rome, 44 BCE)
Verberavi te cogitationis tacito dumtaxat convicio quod fasciculus alter ad me iam sine tuis litteris perlatus est. non potes effugere huius culpae poenam te patrono. Marcus est adhibendus, isque diu et multis lucubrationibus commentata oratione, vide ut probare possit te non peccasse.... etiamsi quod scribas non habebis, scribito tamen, ne furtum cessationis quaesivisse videaris. Valde enim mi semper et vera et dulcia tuis epistulis nuntiantur.

I've just given you a flogging (as far as I could in a silent reproach), because a second packet has now reached me without a letter from you. You can't escape punishment for this sin—if you undertake your own defence. No, my brother must be called in; and when he's worked over his speech for a long time and many a night by lamplight, let's see if even he can prove your innocence. ... Even if you've nothing to write, write to me anyway, and thus avoid the suspicion of having stolen a day off. I always find the news in your letters as true as it is sweetly told.

---

35. *Fam.* 16.10 (Cumae, April 17, 54/53 BCE): 'My poor little studies (or, if you like, ours) have simply pined away with longing for you. But this letter which Acastus brought me has made them lift up their eyes a little.' (*Litterulae meae sive nostrae tui desiderio oblanguerunt; hac tamen epistula quam Acastus attulit oculos paulum sustulerunt*).

36. Cf., e.g., Ovid *Tr.* 1.1.115, where Ovid explicitly casts himself as the *parens* of his literary works, including the Oedipal *Ars Amatoria*. Cf. Hinds 1985, 13–14 for the pun on *liber* ('bookroll') as 'child' (as well as 'freed slave') in this poem.

Fam. 16.27 (Quintus to Tiro, Rome, late December, 44 BCE)
Mirificam mi verberationem cessationis epistula dedisti; *nam quae parcius frater perscripserat, verecundia videlicet et properatione, ea tu sine adsentatione ut erant ad me scripsisti, et maxime de consulibus designatis, quos ego penitus novi, libidinum et languoris <et> effeminatissimi animi plenos; qui nisi a gubernaculis recesserint, maximum ab universo naufragio periculum est. Incredibile est quae ego illos scio, oppositis Gallorum castris in aestivis fecisse; quos ille latro, nisi aliquid firmius fuerit, societate vitiorum deleniet. Res est aut tribuniciis aut privatis consiliis munienda; nam isti duo vix sunt digni quibus alteri Caesanam, alteri Cossutianarum tabernarum fundamenta credas.*

In your letter you've given me **an amazing beating** for my laziness. For what my brother wrote to me in brief, with clear restraint and in a hurry, you've also written to me, stating the facts without approving them; and especially regarding the consuls designate, who, I know for sure, are consumed with the lusts and weakness of effeminate minds. Unless they resign from the helm, there's the utmost danger of universal shipwreck. You wouldn't believe what I know those men did in summer quarters, when the camp of the Gauls was right opposite them—men whom that bandit, unless firmer measures are taken, will weaken further by making them share in his vices. The state must be fortified either by the tribunes or by private individuals taking counsel together. As for those two, they're hardly fit for you to entrust Caesena to one of them, or the vaults under Cossutius's wine shops to the other.

We can only surmise what effect these jocular reminders of his physical vulnerability to the whims of a master's displeasure would have held for the former slave. But they serve a different function when located in the collection, where they contribute to the editorial commentary that runs through the discussions of Tiro's servile status in *Fam.* 16, all the more pointedly because they are placed at the very end of this book of letters—and of the collection as a whole. For while the penultimate letter of *Fam.* 16 sees Quintus threatening Tiro with a metaphorical flogging, in the final letter he turns the tables on himself, claiming that Tiro has subjected him to a good thrashing, by writing to him at length and thereby reproaching him for his own laziness in failing to write himself. The object of the thrashing is made its agent. Just as the letter from Marcus Junior honours Tiro's gifts as a correspondent, so too this letter from Quintus honours Tiro at the expense of his ex-master. The role reversal offers an eloquent last word on the transformation of Tiro's subject position in relation to Cicero's, and one that fits all too neatly with his characterization as the editor—and hence author—of the collection that this final letter closes.

But there are other reasons that make this letter a powerful point of closure for book 16 and the collection as a whole. The reason Mary Beard adduces is for its portrayal of Mark Antony, identified as the *latro* responsible for Hirtius's and Pansa's descent into effeminate depravity. The letter, as Beard sees it, has been placed here to leave us with a negative image of the man who will order Cicero's death.[37] But Mark Antony is not the only figure who makes this letter a fitting note on which to close the collection. The consuls designate, Hirtius and Pansa, name the year of Cicero's death, and thus close the book with a reminder of the *terminus post quem* for the collection's publication. Quintus's description of them, as too weak-minded and womanish to resist Antony's bad example, does not fit with Cicero's view of these men—nor that of later posterity.[38] Hirtius, in particular, was a friend of Cicero's, and had been persuaded by him to abandon Antony following Julius Caesar's death and to fight against him at Mutina, as Pansa also did.[39] Both consuls were killed defending the Republic against Antony, an event which is presented elsewhere in the collection as a tragedy.[40] The negative view of these men that provides the *ad Fam's* closing image is perhaps less a reflection of them than of the historical moment that their names sign—the year 43 BCE, forever inscribed with their consular names, which marks the death of the Republic, and, as it happens, of Cicero too.[41]

---

37. Beard 2002, 142.

38. Cf. *Fam.* 6.12.2 for Cicero's account of the devotion of a number of Caesar's supporters, including Hirtius and Pansa, to himself at this time. Pansa's upright conduct is singled out for praise elsewhere in *ad Fam.*—in an exchange with Cassius at *Fam.* 15.17.3 (Cicero to Cassius) and *Fam.* 15.19.2 (Cassius to Cicero).

39. Galba provides Cicero with an account of the successful early part of their campaign at Mutina at *Fam.* 10.30. Cf. pp. 128–30 for discussion.

40. Asinius Pollio provides the (secondhand) account of their subsequent defeat and death at *Fam.* 10.33.4. Cf. pp. 128–129 for discussion.

41. On the significance of Cicero's death for the end of the Republic in subsequent Roman memory, cf. Kaster 1998 and Richlin 1999, 203–5 for discussion of the connection that early imperial scholastic texts (e.g., Seneca *Cont.* 7.2 and *Suas.* 6 and 7) drew between Cicero's decapitation and the end of free speech in Rome. Of course, the Roman republic has a staggered death, and could also plausibly be said to come to an end in 42 with the battle of Philippi. See Syme 1939, 201–6; and Osgood 2006, 94–101 on the retrospective significance of Philippi for the end of Roman *libertas*.

On Longing

The historical rupture that we find thematized in the closing letter of book 16 has implications for another major emphasis of *Fam.* 16, which is the longing that Cicero feels for Tiro whenever parted from him. This is a theme that dominates the entire book. We see it emphasized repeatedly in the opening letter of our text of *Fam.* 16 (*Fam.* 16. 1–3):

> *TULLIUS TIRONI SUO SAL. PLUR. DIC. ET CICERO MEUS ET FRATER ET FRATRIS F.*
> *Paulo facilius putavi posse me ferre* **desiderium** *tui, sed plane non fero et, quamquam magni ad honorem nostrum interest quam primum ad urbem me venire, tamen peccasse mihi videor qui a te discesserim. . . . Nos ita te* **desideramus** *ut amemus; amor ut valentem videamus hortatur,* **desiderium** *ut quam primum; illud igitur potius.*

> **I thought I could stand my longing for you a bit more easily**, but clearly I can't. And although I have to reach the city as soon as possible for the sake of my triumph, I still think it was a mistake on my part to have left you. . . . As for me, **I long for you**, as one who loves you; love urges me to see you in good health; **longing** makes me want to see you as soon as possible. The former should come first.

Elsewhere, we see Cicero attempting to project his own longing for Tiro onto Tiro himself, when he describes first his own *desiderium* for Tiro, then Tiro's imagined longing for him (*Fam.* 16.11.1):

> *TULLIUS ET CICERO, TERENTIA, TULLIA, Q. Q. TIRONI SAL. PLURIMUM DIC.*
> *Etsi opportunitatem operae tuae omnibus locis* **desidero**, *tamen non tam mea quam tua causa doleo te non valere. . . .* **Non ignoro quantum ex desiderio labores;** *sed erunt omnia facilia si valebis.*

> Although **I miss your helpful services** at every turn, yet it is not for my own sake as much as it is for yours that your illness worries me. . . . I know how much you are burdened by **your longing to be with us**, but as long as you get better, everything will be easy to bear.

50 SOUVENIRS OF CICERO

Expressions like these persist throughout *Fam.* 16.[42] Where scholars have addressed them, they have tended to focus on the precise degree of intimacy they imply between master and slave,[43] a line of inquiry justified, as Gunderson points out, by earlier scholars' outright disavowal of the very idea of sexual relations between Cicero and Tiro.[44] What, though, are we to make of these traces of desire in light of the editorial framework suggested by the positioning of *Fam.* 16 within the collection?

Susan Stewart's *On Longing* offers a suggestive route into this question. In this work, Stewart analyses a number of different types of narrative in which longing or desire is inscribed in the mechanism by which that particular narrative mode relates to its objects. Stewart treats longing as a symptom of the sign in crisis, an effect produced by the gap between signifier and signified, which generates a nostalgic desire for the original, signified objects that language keeps in abeyance. Narrative, she suggests, is a structure of desire, one that 'both invents and distances its object and thereby inscribes again and again the gap between signifier and signified that is the place of generation for the symbolic'.[45] All the narrative modes that Stewart discusses in *On Longing* are marked by a form of distortion, which emerges as a result of this gap: distortions of scale, for example, in the case of the gigantic and the miniature, are perhaps the most striking. But two other narrative modes are discussed whose effects are produced by the distortions of memory: the souvenir and the collection. The souvenir is described as a trace of authentic experience, which, once removed from its original context, always comes supplemented by a narrative discourse that both attaches it to its origins even as it also mythologizes those origins:[46]

---

42. Cf., e.g., the following letter (*Fam.*16.12.6): 'Since you couldn't be with me **at the very moment when I most longed for your faithful services**, take care not to hurry now, nor to make the mistake of sailing when you're ill, or when the weather's bad. I will never think you've come too late, as long as you're safe and sound when you do come.' (*Tu quoniam eo tempore mecum esse non potuisti quo ego maxime operam et fidelitatem desideravi tuam, cave festines aut committas ut aut aeger aut hieme naviges. Numquam sero te venisse putabo si salvus veneris.*)

43. The speculation is encouraged not just by the striking affective undercurrent that runs through *Fam.* 16 but also by a letter of Pliny's (*Ep.* 7.4.3–6) in which he claims to have come across an erotic poem addressed by Cicero to Tiro. Cf. Beard 2002, 134; and Gunderson 2007, 28–29 for discussion.

44. Cf. esp. Gunderson 2007, 29.

45. Stewart 1993.

46. Stewart 1993, 135.

Through narrative, the souvenir substitutes a context of perpetual consumption for its context of origin. It represents not the lived experience of its maker but the 'secondhand' experience of its possessor/owner. Like the collection, it always displays the romance of contraband, for its scandal is its removal from its natural location. Yet it is only by means of its material relation to that location that it acquires its value.'

It is through the language of longing that the souvenir relates to its context of origin, since its value, Stewart suggests, arises not from its use but from the demands of nostalgia, its affective freight a measure of its residual appeal.[47]

Stewart's account of the souvenir provides a compelling way of understanding the expressions of desire that we encounter in *Fam.* 16, when we read this book through the editorial frame that its paratextual position invites us to construct for it. Viewed within this context, *Fam.* 16 (or its editor) has repurposed the phrases of longing exchanged between Cicero, the original author of the letters, and Tiro, the figure cast as the collection's editor, to make them seem to issue from a desire to close the gap between the letters' context of origin and the new context of consumption that they accrue once collected into books.[48] At the same time, the desire to close this gap only serves to open it—reinforcing and even producing a sense of distinction and rupture between the republican past of the letters' author and the imperial (or post-imperial) present of their reader.[49] Viewed in this light, the expressions of longing that recur throughout *Fam.* 16 as its defining leitmotif also answer to the procedures of 'reflective nostalgia' that Svetlana Boym formulates in her study of the different forms of nostalgia that have accompanied our age of globalization, particularly in the post-communist cities of the former Soviet Union. 'Reflective nostalgia' differs from 'restorative nostalgia' in that it seeks not to reconstruct the past but to dwell on the

---

47. See pp. 19–21 for discussion of the nostalgic currency of Williams's category of the residual, and how Cicero's letter collections might be analysed in light of Williams's taxonomy of the rates of cultural change.

48. *Ad Fam.* thus reverses the view of Tiro that emerges from Gellius's *NA*, where, as Howley 2018, 188–90 points out, it is precisely Tiro's autonomy from Cicero that makes him suspicious to Gellius and his peers.

49. Boym 2001, xvi notes how the nostalgia that is often generated in the aftermath of a revolution lends shape to the period that precedes it. In this instance, *ad Fam.* can be seen as a cultural text that participates in such a process.

mechanisms of longing that distort our view of it and make its recuperation impossible.[50]

Stewart's account, in particular, of how the souvenir mediates between past and present, striving to authenticate a past or otherwise remote experience while simultaneously discrediting or alienating the present, helps to explain what *ad Fam.* becomes when published as a collection in the new historical era that it helps to create. Stewart writes:[51]

> The double function of the souvenir is to authenticate a past or otherwise remote experience and, at the same time, to discredit the present. The present is either too impersonal, too looming, or too alienating compared to the intimate and direct experience of contact which the souvenir has as its referent. This referent is authenticity. What lies between here and there is oblivion, a void marking a radical separation between past and present. The nostalgia of the souvenir plays in the distance between the present and an imagined pre-lapsarian experience, experience as it might be directly lived. The location of authenticity becomes whatever is distant to the present time and space.

The souvenir can only refer to the *idea* of authenticity, or an 'imagined pre-lapsarian experience',[52] which tallies closely with the distortions of nostalgia that govern the editing of *ad Fam.* For while the picture of late republican politics that we find in this collection is hardly a perpetually happy one, it is notable that the periods which engender Cicero's deepest political despair (his exile and the months leading up to and through the civil war) are documented much more fully in the correspondence with Atticus. More significantly, *ad Fam.* encloses a period in which monarchy does not quite have the final word: the latest letter in the collection is dated to 28 July 43 BCE,[53] before senatorial hopes had submitted entirely to the consequences of

---

50. Boym 2001, 41–55. The modern editorial practice of reorganizing Cicero's letters chronologically offers a prime example of 'restorative nostalgia,' one that would do away with the narrative of desire (among other narratives) that we find in the collection of souvenirs that is *Fam.* 16, when we leave this book intact.

51. Stewart 1993, 139–40.

52. Again, Stewart's account here of the phantasmatic status of the souvenir's objects of nostalgia tallies with what Boym 2001, 49–56 has to say about the procedures of reflective nostalgia.

53. *Fam.* 10.24, from Plancus in Gaul to Cicero. The letter presents the fortunes of the Republic on a knife edge, with everything hinging on whether Octavian would choose to join the republican forces or those of Antony and Lepidus.

the second triumvirate. The letter collection therefore produces a (distorted) memory of an era in which the Republic remains viable as a political system. It might well be construed as a site of imagined authenticity, in which letters serve to supplement, or be supplemented by, a political discourse conducted by senators in the forum, rather than to constitute a virtual alternative to that lived reality (the 'Republic of Letters' that comes into its own in the imperial period). Above all, though, by enclosing the late Republic and drawing a line around its ending, *ad Fam.* generates a (distorted) view of this period as a self-contained and sealed off whole.

The figure whom Stewart identifies as collector of souvenirs is the antiquarian—the very role that subsequent authors project onto Tiro, after Cicero's death, on the basis of other works attributed to him.[54] Stewart's account of the antiquarian notably matches the role performed by the editor of *ad Fam.* Unlike the historian, Stewart maintains, the antiquarian's interest in the relationship between past and present is primarily aesthetic; their prerogative, she says, is to 'erase the actual past in order to create an imagined past, which is available for consumption,'[55] and their primary means of producing this imagined past is through the collection. Her account further emphasizes the consequences of serialization, whereby the object accrues value only through its relation to other objects in a series rather than through its use value or context of origin.[56] Or, as William Davies King puts it in his poignant memoir of a lifetime spent collecting discarded food labels, the collection 'finds order in things, virtue in preservation, knowledge in obscurity, and above all it discovers and even creates value.'[57] This effect helps to explain

---

54. Gellius *NA* 13.9.1–3 credits Tiro with writing a *Pandectae*, which seems to have contained material very similar to the antiquarian content of Gellius's own *Noctes Atticae*. Cf. McDermott 1972, 285 for discussion; and Howley 2018, 181–83 for Gellius's own anxieties about the proximity of Tiro's project to his own.

55. Stewart 1993, 142–43: 'The antiquarian seeks to both distance and appropriate the past. In order to entertain an antiquarian sensibility, a rupture in historical consciousness must have occurred, creating a sense that one can make one's own culture other—distant and discontinuous. Time must be seen as concomitant with a loss of understanding, a loss which can be relieved through the reawakening of objects and, thereby, a reawakening of narrative. . . . In contrast to the historian who looks for design and causality, the antiquarian looks for material evidence of the past. Yet at the same time, the antiquarian searches for an internal relation between past and present which is made possible by their absolute disruption. Hence his or her search is primarily an aesthetic one, an attempt to erase the actual past in order to create an imagined past which is available for consumption.'

56. On this, see also Baudrillard 1996, 147–48.

57. King 2008, 7.

54   SOUVENIRS OF CICERO

some of the oddities preserved in *ad Fam.* and to explain the fetishized status
they acquire by being preserved in this new context. The last letter that Cicero
writes to his wife Terentia before divorcing her, for example, is a case in point
(*Fam.* 14.20):

> *In Tusculanum nos venturos putamus aut Nonis aut postridie. Ibi ut sint*
> *omnia parata; plures enim fortasse nobiscum erunt et, ut arbitror, diutius*
> *ibi commorabimur. Labrum si in balineo non est, ut sit; item cetera quae*
> *sunt ad victum et ad valetudinem necessaria. Vale.*

I think I'll arrive at Tusculum either on the Nones or on the day after.
See that everything's ready there. I might have several others with me,
and I expect we'll stay there for some time. If there's no tub in the bathroom, make sure there is one, and likewise with everything else necessary for our sustenance and health. Goodbye.

This letter, with its bald instructions to get the bathroom ready prior to his
arrival at Tusculum seems to exist primarily to display the disproportionate
levels of attention required (on the part of archivists, copyists, and the like) in
order to preserve a message that is almost devoid of content; and to highlight
the imbalance between the original use value of a piece of textual detritus like
this and the (much greater) new value it acquires as an object of consumption
within the collection, where it forms part of a fascinating series of letters that
documents the breakdown of Cicero's relationship with Terentia.

What holds for this letter to Terentia is no less true for all the letters in
Fam. 16, each of which individually begs questions as to why it has been preserved. Simply by virtue of having been addressed to a member of Cicero's
domestic staff and focused on Cicero's dependence on his freedman secretary
(a relationship almost always rendered invisible elsewhere in Latin literature),
these are not texts that obviously address themselves to a public readership
insofar as they seldom touch on narratives of Roman public interest. Yet collectively, as a book of letters, *Fam.* 16 amounts to much more than the sum
of its parts: for the letters, when serialized, connect up to produce all manner
of valuable narratives about Cicero (and his dependence on Tiro), Tiro
(and the literary career of the freed slave), and the identity that they share
as participants in a single author function (including Tiro's role in posthumously extending his master's authorial identity by editing and publishing his
unpublished works). These narratives may not have been seen at the time of
Cicero's writing as anything other than ancillary to the more significant tide

of history, but they have only gained in value for the vistas they open up onto an otherwise unseen dimension of social history. Nowhere is the alchemic effect of collecting more apparent than in the letters of *Fam.* 16, which count today among the most valued of all Cicero's letters, precisely because they render the freed slave visible.

The Servile Editor and the Imperial Roman Reader

In his book on slavery and the Roman imagination, William Fitzgerald invokes Hegel's discussion of the master-and-slave dialectic as a way of construing the symbiotic relationship between these two figures. Hegel's *Phenomenology* uses the relationship to describe the self-cancelling nature of a dialectic based on unequal power relations, where the slave is called upon to recognize the master's subject position but ultimately cannot do so owing to their own subordination. Paradoxically, it is the slave who then achieves some measure of mastery and self-consciousness through the self-confirmation they encounter in the objects of their labour. Thus, while the master becomes enslaved by his dependency on the slave's productivity, and relates to the world solely as consumer, the slave transforms it with their work. Fitzgerald draws on this paradox, only to invert it again, when pointing to the gestures through which a literary author may disavow his social position of mastery and even appropriate the position of slave in order to advertise the mode of workmanship peculiar to his literary vocation.[58] Thus the dynamics of textuality distort and reorient the dynamics of Hegel's dialectical configuration, as authors achieve self-consciousness (and recognition) through the objects of their work and frequently draw on the language or imagery of slavery in order to display this kind of identification.

Ad Fam. adds a further twist to this skein of Hegelian inversions: in casting Tiro as the collection's editor, it identifies the letters contained within as the master's work, transformed here by the slave into an object of consumption for somebody else. This dynamic has consequences for the way in which we view the imperial readership of *ad Fam.* For if consumption is to be treated as a mode of enslavement, then the very status of *ad Fam.* as a collection to be bought and sold, identifies its readership as one enslaved by its dependence on the authorial work of Cicero and his (implied) editor, Marcus Tullius Tiro. The actual status of Tiro as an ex-slave helps to draw out the different forms

---

58. Fitzgerald 2000, 28–29.

of enslavement at the heart of this dialectical relationship between author/ editor and reader/consumer. This casting of the readership of *ad Fam.* as an enslaved public chimes more broadly with the way in which authors of the imperial period characterize Rome's subjects under the Caesars: spectators of, rather than participants in, a public sphere that had become privatized, as much as they were now consumers of a past political discourse that had, in Cicero's day, been free. Yet the enslavement of Roman subjects by the Caesars means loss of freedom, more often than not, for the elite who normally write this narrative.[59] Tiro, the ex-slave, is also a freedman, and hence a member of the very class that is credited by some with helping to bring about the Roman revolution.[60] His casting as editor of *ad Fam.* offers a powerful comment on the forms of control that other members of his class might expect to exert over the narrative of Roman politics and Roman history under the principate.[61]

Tiro's role as editor of *ad Fam.* is a fiction that fits well with other narratives about the Roman Empire and the new classes and categories of person that take over its control. Yet ultimately it is just a fiction, for we do not know who or what created the letter collection in the form that we have it. The very idea that we can reduce the identity of a text's creator (either its author or its editor) to a single individual is itself a premise that the modern reader might wish to call into question. What is significant in the case of *ad Fam.* is that this fiction is produced not by a written account, attributable to the hand of a single individual, but by a more opaque phenomenon: namely, the organization of books within the collection. This process may be the work of a singular editor; but even if it is, it is also quite likely the work of a larger collective: the mass of readers who, over time, marked their preference for some

---

59. As Tacitus makes clear at *Ann.* 1.2 when speaking of the lack of opposition that Augustus faced following his defeat of Antony: 'Without anyone in opposition, when the fiercest had fallen either in battle or by proscription, the **rest of the nobles** were elevated to wealth and honours (each according to how much they were disposed to **slavery**), and thus exalted by revolution, they preferred the safety of the present to the dangers of the past.' (*Nullo adversante, cum ferocissimi per acies aut proscriptione cecidissent,* **ceteri nobilium**, *quanto quis* **servitio** *promptior, opibus et honoribus extollerentur ac novis ex rebus aucti tuta et praesentia quam vetera et periculosa mallent.*) See Lavan 2011 for the self-criticism implied in the application of the slavery metaphor by the elite to themselves, as evinced in Tacitus's *Agricola*, for example.

60. Cf. Treggiari 1969, 229 for this view. See also the famously excoriating appraisal of Syme 1939, 385 (and *passim*). Bell and Ramsby 2012, 17 n.20 highlight how Syme's appraisal of the role played by freedmen in the proscriptions as leeches feasting on the blood of the citizenry (Syme 1939, 195) is indebted to ancient views by, e.g., the elder Pliny *HN* 35.201.

61. On the role that the rise of freedmen played in transforming Roman values in the imperial period, see now McLean 2018.

Letters to the Editor

letters over others, and for some books of letters over others, and in so doing ensured that *this* letter book was included in the collection. What does the inclusion of *Fam.* 16 tell us about the identities or sympathies of these readers?

The model of transmission that I have outlined as one possibility for this collection,[62] whereby letters (and books of letters) circulated and were ultimately transmitted according to their 'spreadability' (that is, their appeal to the tastes of the widest possible readership),[63] may explain the inclusion of this book of letters within *ad Fam.* It may have played a role, too, in the designation of Tiro as editor of the letter collection through the placement of his book of letters last. As Cicero's individual letter books circulated over time, certain consensual assumptions may have emerged about the figure who had most plausibly organized the letters within them into books. Such that when the codex took over as the predominant textual medium, Tiro's imagined role as editor of the individual books of letters was honoured by placing his book of letters last in the collection, a gesture that, whether by accident or design, also cast him (anachronistically) as editor of the collection as a whole. Readers did not have to select Tiro for this role.[64] That they did so (if they did so) may speak to the changing demographic of readers in the imperial period, which, as it grew, moved ever further away from the elite status of the letters' original circle of addressees.[65] Tiro-as-editor may be a fiction, but it is a fiction likely to appeal to a post-republican readership for whom Marcus Tullius Tiro, an ex-slave, would be an editorial figure with whom a greater number of readers could relate—a figure who could make the idea of the Ciceronian author accessible.

---

62. See my discussion on pp. 18–21 of the Introduction.

63. For the concept of 'spreadable media', a participatory model of circulation whereby media content is shared and circulated thanks to bottom-up forces rather than as a result of more centralized mechanisms of distribution, see Jenkins, Ford, and Green 2013 (with my discussion on pp. 18–19 of the Introduction).

64. Marcus Junior would have been another plausible candidate, but the two books of letters written to him were not included in *ad Fam.*, and if they once made up a mini-collection of their own, it has not been transmitted.

65. In this, I follow a number of recent studies that seek to highlight the important presence of slaves and ex-slaves as readers of imperial literature: for arguments that the readers of Xenophon of Ephesus and Chariton included literate ex-slaves, see Owens 2020; for arguments that the author of the *Historia Augusta* wrote this text for a learned reading community of *grammatici*, who may have also included freed slaves among their number, see Rohrbacher 2016. On this question, the forthcoming work of Joseph Howley on the Roman book slave is vital: whatever one can and cannot say about which groups of people read which categories of text in ancient Rome, the one social group that we know read all of it was slaves (because they were reading it to their masters).

2

Enclosing the Collection

FRAMES OF MEANING IN *FAM.* 1 AND *FAM.* 15

WHAT ARE THE effects of reading a text in a particular book format? My argument that it is the codex that brings a letter collection like *ad Fam.* into formation assumes that this is also the format in which we need to read this text in order to locate its narrative structures and meanings (as many of us still do—though many more will read *ad Fam.* online). The recent rise of book history within the study of Greco-Roman literary cultures has taught modern readers to notice how and why the physical form of the ancient book matters.[1] Studies of the codex frequently emphasize its higher capacity, its compressed size, and its concomitant portability, or they focus on why it took so long for this more convenient medium to take over from the book roll and what role the rise of Christianity played in this shift.[2] These are all important aspects of the codex that help explain why and how it came to shape the formation of the collection, but they shed little light on how this particular book format impinges on our experience of reading it. In this chapter, I follow the lead of ancient book historians by drawing on insights taken from bibliographical studies of the Gutenberg revolution in order to consider one particular feature that the codex produces for our experience of reading *ad Fam.*: the framing effect that comes about as a result of enclosing the world of the late Republic between its covers. This effect, I argue, has far-reaching consequences for how

---

1. Important recent studies in ancient Greco-Roman book history include Johnson 2004 and 2010, Howley 2018, and Frampton 2019.

2. See Harnett 2017 for a recent survey of these aspects of the codex, and for a reappraisal of why it took so long for the codex to take over from the book roll as the predominant textual medium in Greco-Roman antiquity.

Souvenirs of Cicero. Francesca K. A. Martelli, Oxford University Press. © Oxford University Press 2024.
DOI: 10.1093/oso/9780197761960.003.0003

we construe the boundaries of this world, both spatial and temporal, as the collection describes them.

In an article written under the auspices of The Gutenberg Parenthesis, a research group dedicated to exploring the commonalities between digital media and those oral modes of communication that preceded the advent of the printing press, Thomas Pettit offers a comprehensive account of the cognitive and cultural consequences of the printed book over the period of its hegemony as a written medium.[3] His article articulates the effect of the book across a vast array of cultural developments that coincided with its rise, and identifies this effect, broadly speaking, as one of containment: as printing has the effect of containing its verbal messages within the covers of a book, so contemporaneous developments in other art forms, such as painting and drama, are marked by similar forms of enclosure, from the framed canvas to the play composed for performance in a purpose-built theatre.[4] And this mode of containment is not confined to artistic media: Pettit also relates deeper cognitive shifts, such as the growing sense of individual identity, and perceptions of the body as bounded, to the same phenomenon, even as he extends this idea beyond the body to the human relationship with space more generally. The shift in spatial awareness that is marked by the rise of cartography and, subsequently, by the enclosure of common land, belongs, he argues, to the same move towards containment to which the Gutenberg revolution gives rise.[5]

Whether or not we accept the full extent of the magnetic pull that Pettit adduces to the printed book's cognitive effects, his argument is a suggestive one, and provides a salutary reminder of one of the book's most distinctive powers. The effect of containment tends to get passed over by many recent studies of early modern bibliography, which focus more on dismantling the idea of the book as a fixed entity and revealing the fluid processes of its composition and re-composition over time.[6] Yet as Pettit's article highlights, the book's capacity to enclose its textual content is one of its most determining properties and speaks to its most powerful ability to shape and organize the world. Implied in the ideas of enclosure and containment is nothing less than the dialectic of inside and outside, a division which Gaston Bachelard

---

3. Pettit 2009.

4. Ibid., 6 and 8–9.

5. Ibid., 12–14 on the rise of the idea of the body as bounded; and ibid., 15–17 on the development of the idea of environment as a form of enclosure.

6. See McKenzie 1999 for an especially influential work in this vein.

describes as possessing a geometry that is so obvious as to be blinding—the decisive sharpness of the dialectics of being and non-being, or of *yes* and *no*:[7] and so it is in the case of the book, whose acts of enclosure are also inevitably acts of exclusion. Yet, as with other types of frames, the book does not simply separate the internal content from its exterior, but rather serves to mediate the relationship between them, a relationship that is constantly shifting according to the context within which it is being read.

Mapping the Gutenberg revolution onto earlier shifts in book history that took place, for example, in antiquity is in many ways a perverse enterprise. For the shifts that scholars like Pettit identify with the emergence of the printing press are specifically aimed at drawing a line between this moment and the 'pre-parenthetical' book, relegating the complex history of the book prior to Gutenberg to an undifferentiated past. Yet for anyone interested in tracing the history of the book back to antiquity, it is fairly clear that the shifts to which the Gutenberg revolution gave rise do not have the monopoly on ideas of enclosure and containment. In particular, the emergence of the codex, with its novel ability to contain a multibook work within its covers, matches and anticipates the work of enclosure that the printed book performs, insofar as it draws a line around a series of textual units which may, up until this point, have been circulating discretely. We cannot say whether the transition to the codex was accompanied by the same cognitive shifts that Pettit identifies with the Gutenberg revolution because we know too little about when precisely the codex came to overtake the book roll as the dominant medium for textual dissemination, and the probable coexistence of these two media over an extended period of time would seem to soften the cognitive impact.[8] One thing we can say, however, is that the forms of enclosure that we can expect the codex, on the model of the printed book, to impose may be extensive, ramifying far beyond the question of the book's literal contents to touch on the larger dialectics of inside and outside that are the prerogative of such a framing device.

Ad Fam. presents a fascinating case study for the codex's power of containment, one that extends beyond the literal act of enclosure it performs by uniting between its covers a number of otherwise disparate books, to address

---

7. Bachelard 1994, 211–30.

8. Harnett 2017, 211–217 nuances the timeline for the scale of adoption of the codex, relative to the book roll, put forward by Roberts and Skeat 1983, 45–76 but both these studies view these two media as overlapping, to varying degrees, from the first to the sixth centuries CE, with the codex becoming the predominant medium in the first half of the fourth century.

Enclosing the Collection 61

larger questions about what it means for such content to be enclosed and closed off. As discussed in the Introduction, although we know very little in concrete terms about the process by which this letter collection became a collection, it is possible that the codex played a formative role in this process, bringing together books that had been circulating separately or in smaller groupings and fixing them into numbered sequence. In this case, the codex's act of enclosure also involves additional processes of ordination and organization and is responsible for the various narratives that the juxtaposition and relative positioning of books within the overall sequence produces for the work as a whole. Nowhere is the artful effect of this organization more visible than in the frame, as the relative positioning of books at either end of the collection works to reinforce our sense of the outermost material frame enclosing the collection as a whole.

The most noticeable frame imposed on *ad Fam.* is the paratextual one that we have already considered: *Fam.* 16, the book of letters addressed to Tiro, closes off the collection with an epistolary portrait of the figure who is cast as having crafted it as a collection. And within the book itself we find a number of narratives that speak not only to the editorial commentary that the book's position invites us to locate here but also, more specifically, to some extremely significant effects of enclosure that this book performs for the collection. But frames beget frames, as John Frow points out in his study of the aesthetics of the literary frame,[9] such that the enclosure of the codex by its covers is replicated through further internal frames constructed by the books within the collection in ever-diminishing concentric circles. *Ad Fam.* provides a good example of this, enclosed, as it is, by at least two frames, each of which speaks directly to quite different (and complementary) dimensions of the world it seeks to close off. For if we bracket off the paratext of book 16, and consider the preceding collection on which it comments, we encounter another striking frame in the books that open and close the structure that remains. Books 1 and 15 possess a remarkable symmetry, composed as they are of letters exchanged between Rome and the province of Cilicia: book 1 consists almost entirely of letters composed in 56 BCE by Cicero in Rome to Lentulus Spinther, who was then proconsul of Cilicia; while book 15 consists largely of letters composed by Cicero during *his* proconsular tenure of Cilicia in 51

---

9. Frow 1982, 25: 'Since the frame is not simply a material fact, it can be multiple—the frame of a painting, for example, may be reinforced by the broader frame of the museum—and we could think of the "edge" of the work as a series of concentric waves in which the aesthetic space is enclosed.'

BCE to a variety of senatorial grandees in Rome. If the frame that book 16 constructs speaks to the enclosure of time, this one returns to the more immediate implications of the metaphor, in dealing with the framing and enclosure of space (more particularly, with a geopolitical boundary of Roman provincial governance and the marking off of the 'Roman' from the 'non-Roman' world at the point in historical time that the collection closes off).[10]

What considerations does this distinctive spatial frame hold for the collection's reader? One consideration concerns the space of textual circulation: the exchange of letters between Rome and Cilicia models the space of circulation for the collection as a whole and advertises the scope of its geographical ambitions. But the books' representation of space is not limited to perspectives on the distances negotiated by various kinds of text. These books also open a window onto the relationship between Rome and her provinces and on related questions of foreign policy in the decade immediately prior to the civil war. This too is a narrative that gains its significance, in part, from that sense of rupture with the period of empire that follows, a rupture, which, as we have seen, the formation of the letter collection as a collection plays its part in creating.

Books 1 and 15 cast a spotlight on the relatively new province of Cilicia, a province which no longer existed by the time of Cicero's death, having been absorbed first into the province of Syria in 44 BCE and subsequently partitioned off and incorporated into the imperial province of Galatia by 25 BCE.[11] Unremarkable, perhaps, given the territorial shifts that marked Roman provincial possession and administration in the build-up to and aftermath of the transition to monarchy.[12] And yet *Fam.* 1 and 15 depict a geopolitical region that no longer existed, and a mode of senatorial governance in the provinces that no longer held for this area, by the time that the letters were published, when the management of Galatia was under the direct

---

10. At the time that Lentulus Spinther and Cicero were governors of Cilicia (from 56 to 50 BCE), the province was bordered on two sides by Roman provinces (Asia and Syria) but by the client kingdoms of Galatia and Cappadocia to the north. Syme 1939b, 301–2 offers a description of the parameters of Cilicia from 56 to 50 BCE, noting the broad interior region that it encompassed (including the dioceses of Laodicea, Apamea, and Synnada—on the evidence of cistophori of Lentulus Spinther, Ap. Claudius Pulcher, and Cicero coined at Apamea and Laodicea).

11. See Syme 1939b, 322–32 for a useful survey of these transformations.

12. See Lintott 1993, 121–26 for an overview of the changes to provincial administration that the advent of monarchy brought with it, with its creation of imperial and senatorial provinces.

Enclosing the Collection

control of the emperor.[13] Yet the picture that emerges of this lost world is less than idealized. The busy traffic of communication between Rome and Cilicia that we read in *ad Fam.* 1 and 15 reveals the self-interests served by proconsular office in the late Republic, as Lentulus and Cicero carry out their duties as governors with a constant eye on how their performances will affect their careers back in Rome: the focus of the correspondence for much of book 1 is on Lentulus's chances of being appointed to the potentially lucrative commission of restoring Ptolemy Auletes to the throne following his tenure of office in Cilicia;[14] the focus in *Fam.* 15 is on Cicero's chances of being awarded a *supplicatio*, and thereafter a triumph, for his questionable military success over a band of Parthians.[15] And if these narratives characterize the respective proconsuls as self-promoting and self-obsessed, the books also highlight the negligence and blindness of the senate, too preoccupied with the problem of Caesar to heed Cicero's warnings about the vulnerability of this eastern frontier to attacks from Parthia without reinforcements.[16] Pliny's letters to Trajan from Pontus tell an instructive counternarrative of idealized imperial administration, as Greg Woolf has shown, where, in his words, 'emperor and senator work together, supported by an excellent cast of smaller players, and the provincials are enriched, protected and cherished by the cooperative efforts of their rulers.'[17] Woolf neatly suggests that Pliny has constructed his book of letters to Trajan from Pontus with Cicero's own proconsular correspondence in mind, as if to play up the improved conditions for provincial administration under the principate, through implicit contrast with the dysfunctional senatorial governance that we witness in Cicero's correspondence to and from Cilicia.[18] If one effect of the formation of this collection *as* a collection is to produce a contrast between Republic and Empire, that contrast is not drawn in wholly nostalgic terms.

---

13. Ramsay 1922, 151–53 for insights as to why Galatia was made an imperial province.

14. This is the explicit focus of the first seven letters of *Fam.* 1 (with the exception of *Fam.* 1.3, a letter of recommendation). See Grillo 2015a, 658 and 660 for discussion of this motif in *Fam.* 1 (and how the emphasis on it fades towards the end of the book). Shackleton Bailey 1977, 293 provides a useful summary of the historical background to this affair.

15. Cf. esp. *Fam.* 15.1–13; with Martelli 2017.

16. This topic is programmatically introduced in *Fam.* 15.1.1 and remains a key concern throughout the first four letters of *Fam.* 15.

17. Woolf 2006, 102.

18. Ibid., 102–3.

Yet there is a more complex set of negotiations at work in the spatial forms of enclosure that we find foregrounded in *ad Fam.*'s frame. When we look to the narrative emphases of these two books, both separately and as a pair, we find the spatial metaphor of inside/outside, which their position in the frame imposes, playing out first and foremost in social terms. The geographical distance between Rome and Cilicia, which might have seemed at first the most obvious manifestation of this spatial metaphor, is more importantly put into the service of questions of social integration or alienation, as distance from Rome brings with it the threat of various forms of social distancing too. The symmetry drawn between books 1 and 15 on the basis of the parallel positions in which they cast Lentulus and Cicero, respectively, in the role of governor of Cilicia, invites us to observe further symmetries between these two figures and, as ever in these cases, to spot the differences between them as well. As a choice for the projection of Cicero's mirror image, Lentulus could not have furnished the editor(s) with a better example of the kind of social insider and paragon of traditional optimate values whom we might expect Cicero would want to emulate; in choosing him for this role, the editor has replicated in the frame of the collection a dynamic of many of the letters contained within it. Unlike *ad Atticum*, or the *ad Quintum fratrem*, letter collections addressed to Cicero's social equals (or even inferiors),[19] *ad Fam.* is addressed for the most part to members of the senatorial elite, many of whom can lay claim to the inheritance of political power and social position that Cicero cannot. Scholars have noted the effect that this potential disparity of address may have on the dialectical processes of subject formation that are an inevitable consequence of letter writing.[20] In Cicero's case, the letters in *ad Fam.*, which are addressed to some of the core members of Rome's social and political aristocracy, enable Cicero to project a variety of idealized versions of himself in the mirror image of his socially (and, sometimes, ethically) superior friends. Lentulus Spinther provides a prime and, coming first, programmatic example of this. In social terms, Lentulus is the perfect insider. Purely by virtue of his family's social prestige, he stands at the centre of the Roman senatorial elite among whom Cicero will spend his career trying to earn a place by graft and talent rather

---

19. On the dynamics produced by Cicero's unequal relationship with Quintus (his younger and non-consular brother) in the *ad Qfr.*, see Henderson 2016; and with Atticus (an equestrian) in *ad Atticum*, see Martelli forthcoming.

20. See esp. Leach 1999, 165–68 and Gunderson 2016, 527–38 for discussions of this dynamic as it plays out in Cicero's self-positioning with respect to Varro in *Fam.* 9.

Enclosing the Collection

than by birth.[21] Lentulus's social status as prime insider alongside and against whom Cicero's own desires to make it into Rome's political inner circle are measured invites us to think through the social dimensions of the dialectic of inside and outside, which, as we have seen, the position of this book in the frame of the collection imposes.

Tellingly, however, Cicero's only direct references to Lentulus's social position in *ad Fam.* are gestures of disavowal. In a letter in book 3 addressed to Appius Claudius Pulcher, another proconsul of Cilicia to have an entire book of letters devoted to him, Cicero alludes to Appius's and Lentulus's inherited nobility by referring to their *Appietas* and *Lentulitas*, only to claim that such things do not matter to him.[22] What matters most, he maintains, is the honour conferred by the demonstration of *virtus*, and in this Cicero can claim to be Appius's and Lentulus's equal.[23] He goes on to point out that this is a view shared by no lesser individuals than Pompey and Lentulus, men whom Cicero regards as possessed of a *virtus* that exceeds everyone else, including himself.[24] Lentulus's high birth is here made to yield to his ethical

---

21. On the aristocratic prestige of Lentulus Spinther and his family, see Gruen 1974, 144–45; and Deniaux 1993, 399–401, who notes the special influence this family had towards the end of the Republic, with five of its members elected to the consulship between 72 and 49 BCE.

22. *Fam.* 3.7.5: 'Pausanias also kept telling me that you said: "Why, of course! An Appius went to meet a Lentulus, and a Lentulus an Appius: but a Cicero—no, he wouldn't go to meet an Appius?" (*Illud idem Pausania dicebat te dixisse: 'quidni? Appius Lentulo, Lentulus †Ampio† processit obviam, Cicero Appio noluit?'*). Now, I ask you, talking of these absurdities, do you of all people—a man in my view of the greatest common sense, and so erudite too, and with extensive experience in public affairs—I might add to this your urbanity also, which the Stoics rightly consider a virtue—do you, I ask, suppose that any Appiism or Lentulism in the world matters more to me than the distinctions conferred by virtue?' (*Quaeso, etiamne tu has ineptias, homo mea sententia summa prudentia, multa etiam doctrina, plurimo rerum usu, addo urbanitatem, quae est virtus, ut Stoici rectissime putant? ullam Appietatem aut Lentulitatem valere apud me plus quam ornamenta virtutis existimas?*) See Leach 2016, 509 on the mapping of consular prestige that we see represented in spatial terms in this passage.

23. *Fam.* 3.7.5: 'Before I had even attained the honours which count for most in the eyes of men, I was never in awe of your names; it was the men who bequeathed them to you that I thought great.' (*Cum ea consecutus nondum eram quae sunt hominum opinionibus amplissima, tamen ista vestra nomina numquam sum admiratus: viros eos qui ea vobis reliquissent magnos arbitrabar.*) 'Afterwards, when I had received and administered the highest offices of the empire so as to feel that I had obtained all I desired in the way of both distinction and glory, I hoped that I had become, never, indeed, your superior, but at least your peer.' (*Postea vero quam ita et cepi et gessi maxima imperia ut mihi nihil neque ad honorem neque ad gloriam adquirendum putarem, superiorem quidem numquam sed parem vobis me speravi esse factum.*)

24. *Fam.* 3.7.5: 'And I swear that I never noticed that any different opinion was held either by Cn. Pompey, whom I consider a better man than anyone who's ever lived, or by Lentulus, whom I consider a better man than myself.' (*Nec mehercule aliter vidi existimare vel Cn. Pompeium, quem omnibus qui umquam fuerunt, vel P. Lentulum, quem mihi ipsi antepono*).

superiority, as Cicero constructs an idealized socio-political sphere in which *virtus* rather than breeding makes you an insider. The subtext to Cicero's redrawing of a new circle of virtuous elite is, of course, the efforts made by these named individuals, Pompey and Lentulus, to recall him from exile.[25] Appius's pointed exclusion from this circle may well be traced back to his resistance to this action.[26] The contrast with Lentulus, who as consul in 57 BCE had vigorously and successfully petitioned for Cicero's recall, could not be more striking.[27] It is this that makes him an ideal mirror image for Cicero, one that can be counted on to reflect back to Cicero his own most cherished impressions of himself. And it is for this reason that we find him represented in the collection's frame, rather than, say, Appius, that other proconsul of Cilicia, who presents more of a foil for the virtues of Lentulus than an alter ego for Cicero. Sure enough, Cicero's correspondence with Lentulus in *Fam.* 1 is full of reminders of his indebtedness to Lentulus for this service. Indeed, the whole point of this letter sequence is presented as being motivated by Cicero's desire to repay Lentulus for the loyalty of his friendship at that time by demonstrating his own loyalty to Lentulus during *his* absence from Rome.[28] Here we see the socio-political dimensions of the inside/outside dialectic reconfigured, as the tenure of proconsular office, and its enforcement of absence from Rome, is implicitly likened to exile, as if to draw further parallels between Cicero's and Lentulus's situations and careers. Each of these figures is cast as the insider to the other's outsider, when exile or provincial administration sends them out of Rome and makes them rely on trusted friends within the city to negotiate their most successful and prestigious return. This parallel

---

25. Shackleton Bailey 1977, 293 notes with reference to Cicero's mention of the *pietas* that he owes to Lentulus Spinther in the opening line of *Fam.* 1.1 that, following his return to Rome from exile, he reserves this sentiment for the architects of his restoration (Lentulus, Pompey, and Milo).

26. Gruen 1969, 88 on Ap. Claudius's resistance to Pompey's efforts to recall Cicero in 57. Ap. Claudius's hostility towards Cicero was also owed to his fraternal relationship to Cicero's arch enemy, P. Clodius Pulcher: see Hall 2009a, 139–40 on this background to the relationship between Cicero and Appius and to the efforts that *Fam.* 3 reveal towards patching things up; and White 2010, 52–53 on how Cicero's letter sequence to Appius in *Fam.* 3 has been shaped to occlude their past hostilities.

27. Outside this letter sequence, Cicero's debt to Lentulus Spinther is recorded in similarly laudatory terms at *post Red. in Sen.* 8, *post Red. ad Quir.* 11, and *Sest.* 144.

28. See Grillo 2015a, 661–63 on the theme of Cicero's *fides* to Lentulus (and the related theme of others' *perfidia*) throughout the letter sequence in *Fam.* 1.

Enclosing the Collection 67

is only made more explicit once Cicero is himself made proconsul of Cilicia and repeatedly describes this experience as akin to a second exile.[29]

In *Fam.* 1, it is Cicero who is cast as the insider to Lentulus's outsider, in a reversal of their relative positioning to one another during the days of Cicero's exile. Cicero spends most of *Fam.* 1 filling Lentulus in on events and debates taking place in the senate, particularly as they pertain to the question of Lentulus's appointment to the task of restoring Ptolemy Auletes to the throne in Egypt and offering him advice about what to do regarding the machinations made by various members of the senate to remove this appointment from him. Despite being cast as the ostensible insider within the epistolary relationship here, Cicero's own sense of alienation from the rest of the senate is palpable in this book of letters and emerges gradually from the mutual ground that he identifies as sharing with Lentulus, as common targets of invidious senatorial enmity, past and present.[30] The senate's hostility to Lentulus's proposed appointment is a theme throughout the book, but as the book develops this becomes a point of solidarity between them, as Cicero identifies his own recent experience of senatorial hostility with Lentulus's current trials and thereby uses Lentulus's misfortune as a means of locating his own mirror image in the figure of his addressee. In *Fam.* 1.6, Cicero speaks explicitly of finding in Lentulus's present circumstances an *imago* of his own recent woes, without specifying exactly wherein the reflection lies (*Fam.* 1.6.2):

> *Facile secundo loco me consolatur recordatio meorum temporum,* **quorum imaginem video in rebus tuis**; *nam etsi minore in re violatur tua dignitas quam mea adflicta est,* **tamen est tanta similitudo** *ut sperem te mihi ignoscere si ea non timuerim quae ne tu quidem umquam timenda duxisti.*

> In the second place, I'm easily consoled by recalling the dangers in my own life, **a reflection of which I can see in your present circumstances**; for although your position is attacked in a less important matter than that in which mine was damaged, **still the resemblance is so close**,

---

29. Cf. esp. *Fam.* 2.11.1, *Fam.* 2.12.2, and *Fam.* 2.13.4 for various formulations of Cicero's *desiderium* for Rome while posted in Cilicia; and *Att.* 5.1–11 for similar expressions of his longing for Rome, and exhortations to Atticus to help prevent the extension of his provincial tenure beyond a year.

30. Grillo 2015a, 659–60 on the *perfidia* of other senators against which Cicero's *fides* towards Lentulus (in exchange for the loyalty that Lentulus formerly showed him) is set; and pp. 661–64 on the common cause that Cicero establishes with Lentulus as a result of their sharing the same enemies in the senate.

68 SOUVENIRS OF CICERO

that I hope you may forgive me if I have shown no fear of what even you yourself have never considered worth fearing.

But in the following letter, he is more precise, suggesting that it is the jealousy felt by others towards them that makes their cases similar (cf. *Fam.* 1.7.2):

Quod scire vis qua quisque in te fide sit et voluntate, difficile dictu est de singulis. Unum illud audeo, quod antea tibi saepe significavi, nunc quoque re perspecta et cognita scribere, vehementer quosdam homines, et eos maxime qui te et maxime debuerunt et plurimum iuvare potuerunt, **invidisse dignitati tuae, simillimamque in re dissimili tui temporis nunc et nostri quondam fuisse rationem,** *ut quos tu rei publicae causa laeseras palam te oppugnarent, quorum auctoritatem dignitatem voluntatemque defenderas non tam memores essent virtutis tuae quam laudis inimici.*

As to the fact that you want to know how each man stands in terms of his loyalty and goodwill towards you—well, it's hard to single out individuals. There is one thing, though, which I've often hinted at before, and which I venture to write now that everything's out in the open and has been laid bare, and that is **that certain men, and especially those who ought to have supported you most, and who were most able to do so, have come to envy your position, and that, although the cases are different, a close analogy has appeared between your present crisis and my past one**; for while the men you had fallen out with because of state affairs, attacked you openly, those whose authority, position and policy you had defended, were not so much mindful of your virtue, as resentful of your renown.

Suddenly the parallels between Cicero's exile and Lentulus's secondment to Cilicia start to seem more urgent, as the patent differences between these two modes of absence from Rome are somehow diminished by the reminder of the senatorial hostility that accompanied each of these absences. What comfort Lentulus might draw from the comparison that Cicero makes between their respective situations is uncertain. But Cicero must have found the comparison a self-affirming one.

Later on in *Fam.* 1.7, Cicero returns to the question of Lentulus's high birth with another gesture of disavowal, one that is again designed to diminish any margin of social difference between them, when he tells Lentulus that the parallels between their respective situations have made him realize that the

Enclosing the Collection

enmity that drove him to exile need not have been motivated by hostility towards his position as a social outsider (*Fam.* 1.7.8):

Quod eo liberius ad te scribo quia non solum temporibus his, quae per te sum adeptus, sed iam olim nascenti prope nostrae laudi dignitatique favisti, simulque quod video non, ut antehac putabam, novitati esse invisum meae; in te enim, homine omnium nobilissimo, similia invidorum vitia perspexi, quem tamen illi esse in principibus facile sunt passi, evolare altius certe noluerunt. Gaudeo tuam dissimilem fuisse fortunam; multum enim interest utrum laus imminuatur an salus deseratur. Me meae tamen ne nimis paeniteret tua virtute perfectum est; curasti enim ut plus additum ad memoriam nominis nostri quam demptum de fortuna videretur.

I write this to you all the more frankly because you've supported not only my position today, which I've only attained through your help, but also what was practically the birth of my reputation and position in days gone by; **and at the same time because I now see that it wasn't my status as a newcomer that set men against me, as I've always assumed; for against you too (and you're the crème de la crème) I've noticed a similar kind of enmity from envious men, for while they were quite prepared to tolerate your being one of our leading men, they certainly didn't want you to fly any higher.** I'm happy that your fortune differed from mine; for it is one thing to have your renown diminished, and quite another to have your personal safety deserted. It was thanks to your virtue that I was not overwhelmed with grief at my change of fortune; **for you saw to it that the memory of my name seemed to gain more than my fortune lost.**

The jealousy of others acts as a leveller between Lentulus and Cicero, effacing one of the more obvious factors that might be said to differentiate them: the distinction of birth. Again, Cicero mentions this difference only to disavow it. Having raised this issue, he then uses it as a means of advancing his own claim to prestige. Starting by congratulating Lentulus on having suffered less misfortune at the hands of these jealous detractors than he himself had, Cicero then draws attention to the fact that the fame that subsequently attached to his own name stands in direct correlation to the scale of the misfortune he suffered at this time. Lentulus's support is credited with assisting in this process. But Lentulus himself is implicitly excluded from the process of renown-conferring misfortune since his own misfortunes are less severe.[31] Here we see Cicero trying to compensate for the lack of a famous inherited *nomen* by reminding Lentulus of the fame his own name has won on account of his exceptional actions and sufferings. Alternative sources of prestige are being weighed up against each other in order to help Cicero locate his reflection in Lentulus's mirror image and to hunt around for modes of equivalence when the obvious sources of such are lacking.

The story of the optimate enmity and jealousy that *Fam.* 1 spins culminates in *Fam.* 1.9, which is the letter that orients the entire book for other reasons too. In this letter, we hear Cicero's lengthy justification for the extraordinary volte-face he made some time in April/May of 56 BCE, when having previously (and quite recently) attacked Caesar in an attempt to drive a wedge between him and Pompey, he suddenly came out in support of the triumviral arrangements drawn up at Luca in his speech defending the renewal of Caesar's tenure in Gaul.[32] *Fam.* 1.9 is written some two years after this event

---

31. Grillo 2015a, 662 likewise notes how Cicero places himself above Lentulus in this passage by virtue of his greater sufferings.

32. See Grillo 2015b, 9–10 for an excellent summary of the historical background to the shifting alliances of 56 BCE, both up to and following the conference at Luca; Gruen 1969 for a broader picture of Pompey's loss of standing among the optimates, and consequently in the eyes of the other triumvirs, in the years and months leading up to Luca, which made this conference necessary; and Lintott 2008, 202–5 for an admirable attempt to untangle the evidence for Cicero's and Pompey's ambiguous motivations in this period. The key events that are held to mark Cicero's changing position towards Caesar are: his attack on Caesar's adherent Vatinius in his defence speech for Sestius and subsequently in the senate in February (yet opinions differ as to whether or not this speech should be seen as a direct attack on Caesar: see Gruen 1969, 91 n. 94 for arguments for and Mitchell 1969, 308–12 for arguments against); a meeting of the senate on April 5, where Cicero's proposal to fix a date (of May 15) to discuss (and perhaps modify) Caesar's bill of 59 BCE, concerning the redistribution of Campanian land, was voted through (see Gruen 1969, 91 for the possibility that Cicero may have been acting on Pompey's initiative, but Mitchell 1969, 299–306 for a different emphasis—on the limited scope that any discussion of laws passed during Caesar's consulship could have on repealing them, and for arguments downplaying the role that either Cicero or Pompey played in the debate of April 5); the meeting of the triumvirs at Luca in mid-April, in which they renewed the terms of their compact (the details of which Cicero does not mention in any contemporaneous letter, and for which we therefore rely on other sources: Plut. *Caes.* 21.5; *Pomp.* 51.4; and *App. BCiv.* 2.17.62); the senate meeting of May 15 to discuss the issue of the Campanian land, which Cicero (who had originally proposed the quorate meeting, but was now apparently under pressure from Pompey to reverse his earlier stance and come out in support of Caesar) skipped (see Lintott 2008, 203 for discussion of the corrupt passage in *ad Qfr* 2.7.1–2, where Cicero informs Quintus of his absence from this meeting, and for the suggestion that his absence from this event corroborates the view that his role in the debate of April 5 may have been marginal); and the senate meeting at which Cicero, again apparently under pressure from Pompey to express his support for his triumviral colleagues, argued in the speech published as *de provinciis consularibus*, that Caesar should be confirmed in his retention of Gaul (see Grillo 2015b, 12–13 for discussion of the date of this meeting, which he locates between mid-June and mid-July).

and sees Cicero offering further justification for the even more spectacular switch of loyalties demonstrated in his defence of Vatinius on charges of electoral bribery.[33] As Luca Grillo argues in his reading of *Fam.* 1, Cicero's self-defence in *Fam.* 1.9 gains a considerable amount of exonerating context by being placed at the end of the sequence of letters that precedes it.[34] Here Cicero explains that his newfound support for Caesar is conditioned by the fact that the optimates, who have been consistently criticized for their jealousy and treachery in the preceding run of letters, have lost their identity and no longer represent the interests that they once stood for. It is notable that the only times when they *are* said to have represented these interests are during the consulships of himself and Lentulus (*Fam.* 1.9.17):

> *Hic meae vitae cursus offendit eos fortasse qui splendorem et speciem huius vitae intuentur, sollicitudinem autem et laborem perspicere non possunt; illud vero non obscure queruntur, in meis sententiis quibus ornem Caesarem quasi desciscere me <a> pristina causa. Ego autem cum illa sequor quae paulo ante proposui tum hoc non in postremis de quo coeperam exponere. Non offendes eundem bonorum sensum, Lentule, quem reliquisti; **qui confirmatus consulatu nostro, <non> numquam postea interruptus, adflictus ante te consulem, recreatus abs te, totus est nunc ab iis a quibus tuendus fuerat derelictus;** idque non solum fronte atque vultu, quibus simulatio facillime sustinetur, declarant ii qui tum <in> nostro illo statu optimates nominabantur, sed etiam sententiis saepe iam tabellaque docuerunt.*

> This course of life perhaps offends those who fix their eyes on the glitter and show of my public position but cannot discern its anxieties and troubles; but about one thing they are open in their criticism—that in any of my opinions honouring Caesar, I am, as it were, betraying my old

---

Both Mitchell 1991, 170–72; and Lintott 2008, downplay the idea of a breach between Pompey and Caesar in advance of the conference at Luca, and point to the likely incidental nature of Cicero's participation in the debate on the Campanian land on April 5 to suggest that Cicero's own change of heart towards Caesar was more gradual than some have suggested. Much of the confusion lies in the way in which Cicero retrospectively exaggerates his role in this debate in *Fam.* 1.9 in a face-saving attempt to present his position on this occasion as a gallant last stand in defence of the *res publica* before submitting to the demands of *utilitas*.

33. Mitchell 1969, 318–20 emphasizes how unreliable *Fam.* 1.9 is as a source for the conference at Luca, and the events leading up to it, given the gloss on these events that Cicero's retrospective self-justification is likely to bring to them, especially to a correspondent like Lentulus Spinther.

34. Grillo 2015a, 663–66.

political cause. Now I'm influenced not only by what I mentioned to you a little while ago, but also, and not least, by what I had begun to explain; and that is, my dear Lentulus, that you will not find the feelings of the *boni* the same as you left behind. **Those feelings, confirmed by my consulship, afterwards occasionally broken apart, utterly damaged before your consulship, but revived by you, have now been completely abandoned by those who should have cultivated them;** and those who in the earlier days of our constitution were called optimates, show clearly that this is so not only by their demeanour and expression, through which it's very easy to keep up a pretence, but have even now often demonstrated it by their actual votes in the senate and as jurymen.

Again, Cicero and Lentulus are made to resemble one another by standing apart from their political peers and representing the interests that, Cicero argues, the optimates have historically stood for but which they have given up on in recent times. Thus far the resemblance between them seems to be based on a common sense of alienation resulting from what social scientists might call a state of *anomie*, or normlessness, in Roman political culture at the time.[35] But Cicero casts a more narcissistic light on this relationship of resemblance when he goes on to describe the further property that they share in common: a magnetic power to attract their wayward group of optimates into their way of thinking when placed in the position of supreme power as consul, and an equally marked propensity to become targets of misunderstanding and abuse when removed from this position. The mirroring effect that Lentulus and Cicero have on one another is thus shown to have a remit that extends far beyond themselves when they find themselves cast at the centre of Roman politics: as leaders they can consolidate the identity of the optimates around themselves; as rank and file, they may only end up identifying with each other. What we are presented with here is a counterfactual model of Roman politics and history in which, between them, Lentulus and Cicero are shown to be capable of perpetuating the old model of republican politics had they been allowed to stay on in power or had there been a sufficient number of consular candidates like them. Cicero's belief that only he and Lentulus are fit to lead the senate makes his position look barely different from the triumvirs' desire to monopolize the prime positions of power. Yet the reflection that he

---

35. The concept of anomie was popularized by Durkheim 1893, 343–66, and further developed in his 1897 study of suicide.

Enclosing the Collection

keeps looking for and finding in Lentulus, on so many levels, inflects his own aspirations for power with a dualism that resembles the dyadic power structure of the consulship. What readers are presented with in this book of letters is an ideal pair of consuls, who reflect their own traditional optimate values back at each other and who are shown capable of mobilizing the rest of the senate behind them in these values too. This is Cicero's (or *Fam.* 1's) answer to the question of how the Republic could have remained, even as this letter's ostensible narrative deals with explaining the necessary change of allegiance that finds Cicero coming out in support of the triumvirate.

So much for the opening book. How does *Fam.* 15, the other side of the collection's frame, either reaffirm or distort the mirror image of Cicero that he had located in Lentulus in *Fam.* 1? Lentulus is neither mentioned nor addressed in *Fam.* 15, yet the position of this book of letters from Cilicia at the close of the collection invites us to read it against the opening book of letters addressed to this province and consider whether the mirroring of Cicero and Lentulus that we found thematized within that opening book still holds for the larger symmetry at work in the frame. Several narratives in *Fam.* 15 replicate narratives that run through *Fam.* 1 and transform those narratives in certain significant ways. For one thing, we find Cicero at pains to reconcile himself with representative members of the group of optimates that gets such a severe drumming in *Fam.* 1. Barely any of Lentulus's enemies, or of Cicero's, are identified by name in book 1. The one exception to this rule is C. Porcius Cato, a cousin of M. Porcius Cato and tribune for 56 BCE,[36] whose resistance to the prospect of Lentulus being given the commission to restore Ptolemy to the throne is shown to be extreme.[37] C. Cato's politics do not align with those of his cousin or with the rest of Cato's supporters, who are implicitly impugned as the architects of hostility towards Lentulus, Pompey, and Cicero throughout *Fam.* 1. Yet by virtue of his familial relationship to this group, so clearly marked by his own name, and by virtue of the absence of any other named *inimici* within book 1, he comes to stand in for the political faction that takes its identity from the name that he happens to share with his cousin. Graded shades of difference between *inimici* are less important than the fact that a Cato is identified by name as Lentulus's chief enemy in book 1.

---

36. Gruen 1974, 100 and 182, notes how little this Cato had in common with his more famous cousin, approximating more to the model of populist tribune typified by Clodius.

37. At *Fam.* 1.5a.2, for example, Cicero mentions a *nefaria promulgatio* proposed by Cato to strip Lentulus of his proconsulship in Cilicia in order to make him ineligible for the Egypt commission.

74   SOUVENIRS OF CICERO

But this book also reveals the cost of this faction's polemical position on this, as on other matters. In *Fam.* 1.9 an unnamed *inimicus* is presented as an example of the kind of isolation and loss of *dignitas* incumbent on those who lash out at their friends, when Cicero writes (*Fam.* 1.9.2):

> *Quamquam ille perennis inimicus amicorum suorum, qui tuis maximis beneficiis ornatus in te potissimum fractam illam et debilitatam vim suam contulit, nostram vicem ultus est ipse sese; ea est enim conatus quibus patefactis nullam sibi in posterum non modo dignitatis sed ne libertatis quidem partem reliquit.*

Although that unfailing enemy of his own friends, who, though you honoured him with the greatest kindnesses, bore against you above all others his broken and enfeebled attempts at violence, has done our work for us and punished himself; for he attempted such awful things that their disclosure has left him without a scrap not only of dignity, but even of independence for the rest of his life.

Though earlier editors take this figure to be C. Cato, the one enemy already named, Shackleton Bailey shows that this cannot be the case, and he argues that Cicero is in fact referring to Domitius Ahenobarbus, who, together with his consular colleague, Ap. Claudius, had been caught in a bribery pact with Memmius and Calvinus, candidates for the consulship of the coming year. Domitius was related by marriage to M. Porcius Cato and was one of his chief supporters throughout the 50s BCE. If we mistake him for a Cato, then, that is perhaps the point. Either way, the overall picture that we form of this unnamed member of the Catonian faction is deeply negative.

Fam. 15 offers an overwhelming corrective to this view of 'Cato', and the political faction that that name stands in for. It contains the only two letters to the true representative of this group, M. Porcius Cato, included in Cicero's correspondence, along with this Cato's reply to the first of these two letters, which is, fascinatingly, the only document in Cato's hand transmitted at all from antiquity. These letters, along with most of those contained in *Fam.* 15, deal primarily with Cicero's campaign to have his military success in Cilicia recognized by the vote of a *supplicatio*, the normal preliminary to a triumph. Cato's letter explains his own refusal to vote for this honour, and it is normally taken as an example of the curmudgeonly churlishness for which his name was a byword at this time (although, as we shall see, they take on a different complexion within the context of the published letter book).[38] But Cicero's letters *to* Cato demonstrate Cicero's urgent desire to persuade Cato of the importance of supporting the vote for his *supplicatio* and undermine the suggestion that he made to Lentulus in *Fam.* 1.9 that his enemies' polemical posturing had ultimately cost them any lasting political standing. *Fam.* 15.4, the letter in which Cicero first writes to Cato about his military success, is the longest letter in the collection after 1.9 and is notable for the formality and respectful tone of its address.[39] The striking contrast with *Fam.* 1.9 invites us to consider how much has changed since Cicero wrote that letter and to consider how Cicero, when placed at a distance from Rome, finds himself striving to rally the optimates around him. The other letters in the book are addressed to Caesar's staunchest enemies: Marcus and Gaius Marcellus and their relatives, men whose consulships in 51 and 50 BCE would play a critical role in ramping up hostilities with Caesar and precipitating civil war,[40] along with Cassius and Trebonius, two of Caesar's eventual assassins, and the only tyrannicides to be addressed in *ad Fam.*[41] This book gathers together some of the most prominent enemies of Caesar to be addressed in the entirety of Cicero's correspondence and unites them around the idea of the *supplicatio*— the vote of thanksgiving that Cicero hoped that the senate would hold in his honour.[42] Book 15 thus stands as something of a corrective to the narrative that we encountered in *Fam.* 1, with its justification for coming out in support of Caesar—a remarkable feat of editorial rewriting, especially given that Cicero's position with regard to Caesar had not yet formally changed. The outsider has become an insider, using his position of distance from Rome

---

38. Beard 2007, 193 cites Tyrrell and Purser 1914 (vol. 3, 2nd ed.), xxxiii; and Rawson 1975, 170 for this appraisal.

39. See esp. the opening of this letter, *Fam.* 15.4.1: 'Your supreme influence and my own steadfast opinion of your exceptional virtue have given me the impression that it is greatly in my interest that you should be aware not only of my past achievements but also of the fair dealing and integrity with which I have protected our allies and administered this province.' (*Summa tua auctoritas fecit meumque perpetuum de tua singulari virtute iudicium ut magni mea interesse putarem et res eas quas gessissem tibi notas esse et non ignorari a te qua aequitate et continentia tuerer socios provinciamque administrarem*).

40. *Fam.* 15.7–11.

41. *Fam.* 15.14–21.

42. On the significance of these addressees in *Fam.* 15 as enemies of Caesar from different moments in his career as a unifying theme of the book, and on how their identity as such produces a (distorted) picture of Cicero as the cornerstone of Caesarean resistance, a position that he did not historically occupy at any point in his own lifetime, see Martelli 2017, 112–13.

as an opportunity to appeal to the group of optimates from whom he had seemed so estranged in book 1.

And there are other, more specific ways in which we see the editor(s) capitalizing on the contrast with Lentulus, Cicero's forerunner in Cilicia, whose book of letters, at the opposite end of the collection, so clearly invites comparison. One narrative in *Fam.* 15 that picks up on certain threads in *Fam.* 1, showcases Cicero's exemplary handling of client kings and reminds us of the less-than-edifying spectacle we witnessed in *Fam.* 1 of various members of the senate, including Lentulus, vying with one another for the lucrative commission of putting one client king, Ptolemy Auletes, back on the throne. In *Fam.* 1, we rarely hear of Lentulus's experiences in Cilicia—the main focus of the correspondence is on the Egyptian commission that he hoped to see tacked onto the end of his proconsulship, as if his time in Cilicia were simply a passport to this other more self-advancing post. In *Fam.* 15, by contrast, Cicero's dealings with client kings form an integral part of his proconsular mandate. Early on in his letter to Cato, Cicero tells Cato of how he rescued Ariobarzanes III, the king of Cappadocia, from a plot on his life and secured his position by enforcing the withdrawal of certain negative influences from his court, and the recall of leading partisans who had been driven into exile by the king's scheming mother.[43] Cicero stresses that in supporting the young king like this, he is acting on the authority of the senate[44]—a point which solicits from Sherwin-White the tart comment that 'it is characteristic of the

---

43. *Fam.* 15.4.6. See also *Fam.* 15.2.6 for Cicero's account to the senate of how the king (and Cicero) learned about this plot.

44. *Fam.* 15.4.6: 'I delivered King Ariobarzanes, whose safety had been entrusted to me by the senate at your insistence, from an imminent plot of which he was not aware. . . .' (*Regem Ariobarzanem, cuius salutem a senatu te auctore commendatam habebam, praesentibus insidiis necopinantem liberavi. . . .*). Magie 1950, 1251 n. 55 notes the emphasis here on Cato's role in instigating the senatorial decree. That decree receives even more emphasis at *Fam.* 15.2.4: 'For since you had intervened with a resolution that I should protect King Ariobarzanes, entitled "The dutiful" and "Lover of Rome," and defend that monarch's personal safety and the stability of his realm, and be a safeguard to both king and kingdom, and since you had added that the safety of that king was a matter of great concern for the people and senate—a decree which had never been passed by our body in reference to any other king—I decided that I ought to report your pronouncement to the king and promise him my protection and loyalty and devotion, so that, since his personal security and the stability of his kingdom had been entrusted by you to me, he might tell me if he wishes to have anything done.' (*Cum enim vestra auctoritas intercessisset ut ego regem Ariobarzanem Eusebem et Philorhomaeum tuerer eiusque regis salutem et incolumitatem regnumque defenderem, regi regnoque praesidio essem, adiunxissetisque salutem eius regis populo senatuique magnae curae esse, quod nullo umquam de rege decretum esset a nostro ordine, existimavi me iudicium vestrum ad regem deferre debere eique praesidium meum et fidem et diligentiam polliceri, ut, quoniam salus ipsius, incolumitas regni mihi commendata esset a vobis, diceret si quid vellet.*).

Senate's management of the east at this time that the sole matter on which it gave explicit advice concerned the treatment of a king.'[45] The reader recalls here the affair of Ptolemy Auletes in which they took such a vested and jealous interest in *Fam.* 1.

But we are also alerted to the differences between that affair and this, and to the ways in which those differences allow for certain forms of one-upmanship in the reflection that the structure of *ad Fam.* allows us to see operating between its portraits of Cicero and Lentulus. Again, these differences take on a new significance in light of that sense of rupture between Republic and Empire which this letter collection (*as* a collection) plays its part in creating. It is not only that Cicero's support for Ariobarzanes III sees him acting on the senate's authority, thus revealing a perfect alignment between proconsular action and senatorial will,[46] as Lentulus's case does not. For another thing, the Cappadocian king is a young, defenceless individual, heavily dependent on Roman support, whose kingdom would eventually be easily (and gratefully) absorbed into the Roman imperial province of Galatia. The contrast with Egypt could not be more striking: Ptolemy Auletes was father to Ptolemy Philopator, who, in his youth and susceptibility to being influenced and dominated by scheming advisors with agendas of their own, both resembles Ariobarzanes and provides a negative foil for the characterization of that other young king. He was also, of course, the father of Cleopatra, whose reign in Egypt would end up posing more of a threat to Roman security than any other foreign force for some time. The decision to open *ad Fam.* with the story of the commission to restore Ptolemy Auletes to the throne is presumably informed by the ironies that entail from knowing what damage his progeny would try to inflict on Rome within the following quarter century that follows the composition of the letters contained in this book. The positioning of book 15 at the other end of the letter collection, by contrast, closes its narrative of late republican politics with the positive image of Cicero's successful proconsular governance and reassuring dealings with non-threatening kings—an idealized (if, admittedly, unlikely) image of what might have been had late republican foreign policy been left in his hands.[47]

---

45. Sherwin-White 1984, 293.

46. See esp. *Fam.* 15.2.4, quoted in n. 44 above, for Cicero's emphasis on his acting on the senate's authority.

47. See Magie 1950, 391–99 for an extensive overview of Cicero's compassionate governance of Cilicia in 51–50 BCE (albeit one drawn primarily from the evidence that Cicero himself provides in his letters from this period).

SOUVENIRS OF CICERO

It is in light of this retrospective gloss on events, and the view of Cicero that this narrative promotes, that Cato's reply to *Fam.* 15.4 must be read, since it too takes on a very different set of meanings when considered in the context of events that took place after its composition. As we have already noted, Cato's reply, in which he explains to Cicero his reasons for refusing to vote for the *supplicatio* that Cicero was after, is normally simply treated as an example of the curmudgeonly behaviour for which his name was a byword at the time of the letter's composition. Yet it takes on a very different set of meanings in its published context, following the event of Cato's death, when the quality of stubborn recalcitrance which had been such a headache for Cicero and his peers throughout the 50s BCE, becomes in retrospect an essential part of his posthumous hagiography (*Fam.* 15.5.1–3):

M. CATO S. D. M. CICERONI IMP.

Quod et res publica me et nostra amicitia hortatur libenter facio, ut tuam **virtutem innocentiam diligentiam,** *cognitam in maximis rebus domi togati, armati foris pari industria administrare gaudeam. Itaque, quod pro meo iudicio facere potui, ut* **innocentia consilioque** *tuo defensam provinciam, servatum Ariobarzanis cum ipso rege regnum, sociorum revocatam ad studium imperi nostri voluntatem sententia mea et decreto laudarem, feci. Supplicationem decretam, si tu, qua in re nihil fortuito* **sed summa tua ratione et continentia** *rei publicae provisum est, dis immortalibus gratulari nos quam tibi referre acceptum mavis, gaudeo; quod si triumphi praerogativam putas supplicationem et idcirco casum potius quam te laudari mavis, neque supplicationem sequitur semper triumphus et triumpho multo clarius est senatum iudicare potius mansuetudine et innocentia imperatoris provinciam quam vi militum aut benignitate deorum retentam atque conservatam esse; quod ego mea sententia censebam. atque haec ego idcirco ad te contra consuetudinem meam pluribus scripsi ut, quod maxime volo, existimes me laborare ut tibi persuadeam me et voluisse de tua maiestate quod amplissimum sim arbitratus et quod tu maluisti factum esse gaudere. Vale et nos dilige et instituto itinere* **severitatem diligentiamque** *sociis et rei publicae praesta.*

Both the Republic and our friendship urge me to rejoice, as I freely do, that your **virtue**, **integrity**, *and* **conscientiousness**, already proven as a civilian in momentous events at home, are no less actively at work in arms abroad. Accordingly, I did what my judgment allowed me to do: that is to say, I paid you tribute with my voice and vote for defending your province by your integrity and wisdom, for saving Ariobarzanes's

Enclosing the Collection

throne and person, and for winning back the hearts of our subjects to the support of Roman rule. As for the decree of a *supplicatio*, if you prefer us to render thanks to the immortal gods in respect of provision taken for the public good **by your own admirable policy and administrative rectitude**, not at all the result of chance, rather than put it down to your own credit—why, I am very glad of it. If, however, you regard a *supplicatio* as the guarantee of a triumph, and on that account prefer the praise to go to accident rather than to yourself, then a triumph does not invariably follow a *supplicatio*; and the senate's judgment that a province has been held and preserved by its governor's mild and upright administration rather than by the swords of an army or the favour of the gods is a far greater distinction than a triumph; and that is what I proposed to the senate. I have written to you at some length on this subject (contrary to my normal habit) so that you may realize, as I most earnestly hope you will, my anxiety to convince you of two things: firstly, as regards your prestige, I desired what I conceived to be most complimentary to yourself; secondly, I am very glad that what you preferred has come to pass. Goodbye, remember me kindly, and follow your chosen course, rendering to our subjects and to the state their due of a **rigorous and conscientious** administration.

The personal differences between Cicero and Cato, which Cicero tries desperately hard to plaster over in his letter to Cato,[48] are unflinchingly exposed by Cato's reply: not only does he refuse Cicero's request, but the short length of his reply in comparison with Cicero's letter to him—an imbalance witheringly underscored by the claim (at *Fam.* 15.5.3) that he has written at greater length than usual—displays the stark polarity between the ways in which these two figures express themselves in pursuit of their respective political goals. Moreover, Cato's pointed remark about the true recipient of a *supplicatio* being the gods, rather than the Roman generals in whose name this vote of thanksgiving was decreed, brings out a particularly difficult point of difference. It reminds us of the role that Cicero had himself played in transforming the form and function of the *supplicatio* to accommodate the honorific demands of Rome's leading generals in the preceding years.[49] Given the state of crisis to which these two generals' competition for

---

48. See esp. *Fam.* 15.4.16; with Martelli 2017, 94–98.

49. Cf. Hickson-Hahn 2000, 249–54 on *Prov. cons.* 25–27, where Cicero advertises the prominent role that he himself has played in inflating the honours bestowed by the *supplicatio* on

honours had brought politics at Rome at the time of writing, Cato's remark about the true beneficiaries of the *supplicatio* being the gods may be read as an open accusation to Cicero for his role in precipitating this crisis. At first sight, this letter reinforces the divisions that set Cato and his supporters against Cicero and the dynasts, divisions to which *Fam.* 1 (and especially *Fam.* 1.9) first introduced us.

Yet the barbed accusations that seem to dominate this letter when viewed in the context of its compositional moment are not necessarily its most prevailing features when read with the benefit of a few years' hindsight. Viewed from this retrospective position, it is the letter's kinder appraisals that begin to stand out. In the course of explaining why he chose not to vote for the *supplicatio*, Cato praises Cicero for the various virtues that he has displayed during his proconsular tenure and claims that the reason for his refusal lies in the fact that he prefers to give Cicero the credit for his upright conduct rather than thanking the gods for them. Extremely significant here are the virtues with which Cato accredits Cicero: *virtus, innocentia* (twice), *diligentia* (twice), *ratio* and *continentia*, and most tellingly, perhaps, at the very close of the letter, *severitas*. Cato here attempts to write Cicero into the terms of his own self-fashioning, accrediting his addressee with all the virtues that he himself had displayed when sent out to oversee the annexation of Cyprus in 58 BCE, a post that (we are told by Plutarch) he had accepted not for military glory or financial gain but as an opportunity to show by his upright behaviour the responsibilities of empire.[50]

But the virtues that Cato prizes meant very different things to his contemporaries before and after the civil war. A point nowhere better illustrated than by Cicero's own evaluation of them. In a letter to Atticus written in January 60 BCE, we find Cicero descrying the nexus of qualities that led Cato to act obstructively in the senate (*Att.* 1.18.7):[51] *Unus est qui curet,* **constantia magis et integritate** *quam, ut mihi videtur, consilio aut ingenio,*

---

both Pompey and Caesar: in Pompey's case, Cicero had first, as consul, instigated the proposal to double the number of days for the *supplicatio* voted for by the senate following Mithridates's death in 63 BCE, and then proposed an unparalleled second *supplicatio* for the same military achievement (along with Pompey's other military successes against the pirates) in the following year.

50. Plut. *Cat. Min.* 35–38 provides the ancient account of Cato's commission to Cyprus, with an emphasis on his scrupulous administration of this office. Cf. Badian 1965 for an economic explanation as to why Clodius needed to appoint the upright Cato to this commission; and Oost 1955 for a more skeptical appraisal of Cato's conduct in Cyprus.

51. In this instance, tormenting the equestrian tax-farmers by refusing their request to reduce the terms of their contract for the province of Asia Minor and thereby preventing the completion of any other senatorial business. See Stem 2006, 223–27 for discussion of how Cicero's

Cato. ('The one man who cares [for the *res publica*] **with more resolution and integrity**, it seems to me, than judgment or intelligence, is Cato.') Yet after the civil war, it is precisely this nexus of qualities that Cicero explains to Atticus he cannot afford to ignore when composing his eulogy of Cato, the pamphlet that helped transform Cato into a republican martyr in the immediate aftermath of his death (*Att.* 12.4.2):

> *Sed de Catone, προβλημα Άρχιμήδειον est. non adsequor ut scribam quod tui convivae non modo libenter sed etiam aequo animo legere possint; quin etiam si a sententiis eius dictis, si ab omni voluntate consiliisque quae de republica habuit recedam ψιλωσque velim* **gravitatem constantiamque eius laudare**, *hoc ipsum tamen istis odiosum άχουσμα sit. sed vere laudari ille vir non potest nisi haec ornata sint, quod ille ea quae nunc sunt et futura viderit et ne fierent contenderit et facta ne videret vitam reliquerit.*

Now about the Cato: it's like trying to square a circle. I can't work out how to write anything that your dinner companions could read with pleasure or at least without losing their temper. Even if I were to steer clear of his votes in the senate, his whole political outlook and his public opinions and choose simply to praise his **seriousness of purpose and steadfastness**, even this would grate on their ears. But no genuine eulogy of that remarkable man is possible without paying tribute to the way he foresaw our present situation and tried to avert it and abandoned his life rather than witness its materialization.

These, then, are the very qualities that would identify Cato as the staunch optimate defender of the Republic after his death, even if they were viewed very differently in the years that led up to that moment. By including *Fam.* 15.5, in which Cato attributes to Cicero the range of qualities for which he himself would be posthumously lionized, the editor of *ad Fam.* has found an opportunity to identify Cicero as a prime exemplar of Catonian virtues. So that despite Cato's refusal to comply with Cicero's request, and despite the provocative dig with which he concludes when claiming that he has a better idea than Cicero of what is good for his (Cicero's) *maiestas*, all these gestures pale into insignificance beside the litany of Catonian virtues that Cicero is commemorated as possessing by their most authoritative exponent. In a

---

characterization of Cato in this letter fits the portrait of Cato's intransigent idealism that we derive from elsewhere in his oeuvre.

reversal of the enmity that we find staged throughout *Fam.* 1, *Fam.* 15 crowns Cicero as an optimate possessed of all those virtues, which in retrospect (and, for Cicero, perhaps *only* in retrospect) made them deserve the label *boni*.[52]

This transformation of the qualities that Cato prizes (and embodies), before and after his death, is a subtext to the published letter book of *Fam.* 15— as well as to the dialogue that it generates with *Fam.* 1 when placed within the sixteen-book collection: Cato's posthumous reputation enhances the value of the (highly Catonian) compliments that he pays Cicero in *Fam.* 15.5, which, when seen within the collection, reverse the picture of optimate enmity that we drew from *Fam.* 1 and suggest that Cicero has been brought into the fold of optimate approval through this recognition of his unimpeachable record of public service abroad. Thus the narrative of *Fam.* 15, which already makes use of the time lag that separates the moment of the letters' composition and the moment of their publication within the individual letter book (and, in particular, the re-evaluation of Cato that had taken place in the interim), is subsequently made part of a more complex narrative when placed by the editor(s) of the sixteen-book collection in dialogue with *Fam.* 1. Narratives of social exclusion are converted into narratives of social acceptance and integration in the very books that frame the collection, and thus they invite our reflection on what it means to be inside or outside in the world of the late Republic.

Conclusion

These narratives are the work of an editor who may or may not have been in full control of the implications involved in placing these particular books (*Fam.* 1 and *Fam.* 15) at either end of the collection. My argument that the reception of Cicero in the imperial period may have influenced editors in determining where to place the books in the collection is designed to take some intentional

---

52. See Martelli 2017, 101–2 on how Cicero's posthumous eulogy of Cato remains an important unspoken intertext throughout *Fam.* 15, and especially so in the following letter (*Fam.* 15.6), in which Cicero muses testily over the question of what one man's praise of another might mean, clearly piqued by Cato's high-handed treatment of himself. This letter is itself in close dialogue with *Fam.* 5.12.7, where, in this famous letter to Lucceius inviting the latter to write a history of his (Cicero's) consulship, Cicero reflects on the *dignitas* that Lucceius would confer on him by doing so, not just because of his famous literary talents but also because of the *dignitas* of his own standing in public life. The dialogue between this letter and *Fam.* 15.6 is lent new significance by Cicero's posthumous eulogy of Cato, which itself exemplifies the *dignitas* that one honoured public figure (Cicero) can lend another (Cato) by praising their life and career, demonstrating the mutual benefits of *laudator* and *laudandus* that *Fam.* 15.5 also illustrates in light of Cato's honourable death.

Enclosing the Collection 83

agency away from the individual editors and attribute it to a broader, less-visible collective, although ultimately all I can be said to be describing is the effect of their editorial decisions, rather than the intentions behind them. But there is a further, more impersonal factor driving the need to look for books that would work well in the frame, one that has consequences for how we read the narrative that we find there. For as we have seen, the editors may have been compelled to enclose and combine the books of *ad Fam.* in the order in which we have them by the arrival of the codex. The process of editorial rewriting that comes about as a result of the positioning of these books in the collection may therefore be driven in this instance not just by the reception of Cicero at some (or various) unknown point(s) in the imperial period but also quite possibly by the formal constraints and horizons made available by a new textual medium (even if this is, of course, something that we will never likely know for certain). What difference does it make to our reading of *ad Fam.* to envisage the codex as responsible for its organization into a fixed (and enframed) sequence of books?

The effects of enclosure and containment are not exclusive to the medium of the book or codex. Rather, these media make especially visible an effect that belongs to all forms and modes of textuality, as Pettit would be the first to allow. In many ways, the fixed ordering of books within the collection simply replicates a principle that is already at work within the individual books themselves. Likewise, the meaningful juxtapositions that we find operating in the collection as a whole may have been available at a more local level when the books were circulating as papyrus rolls, particularly if the papyrus roll was capable of containing more than one book of letters, as is possible, from the earliest moment of the letters' circulation *as* books;[53] or, if they circulated in smaller groupings, that were numbered on *sillyba*.[54] Frames beget frames, and this principle works outwards as well as inwards, such that a demand for a larger framing principle for the assemblage of books in larger

---

53. *Fam.* 14 (the shortest letter book) is less than a quarter of the length of *Fam.* 13 (the longest). See Johnson 2004, 64 on the variable lengths of papyrus roll; and Hunt, Smith, and Stok 2017, 29–30 for the view that the book length of literary works is not driven in any absolute sense by the constraints of the papyrus roll.

54. See Kenyon 1932, 59–60 for discussion of the practice of labelling book rolls with *sillyba*. Houston 2014, 9–10 notes that it is unclear how widespread the use of *sillyba* was. Furthermore, it seems quite possible in light of Gellius's testimony (on which see p. 11 n. 27), that if *sillyba* were attached to the books of *ad Fam.*, either as a sixteen-book collection of papyrus rolls or in smaller groupings, they would have identified the books by the name of their first addressee rather than by number, leaving readers at liberty to read them in any order.

84 SOUVENIRS OF CICERO

groupings may be driven by the existence of smaller-framed book units. In fixing the number and sequence of letter books and transforming them into a collection, the codex may have realized this demand and made its effect more visible and more absolute.

But the possibility that it is the codex that is responsible for creating the sixteen-book collection, with the symmetries and enframing effects that this organizational unit produces, raises further questions of dating and periodization that have a particular bearing on the narrative dialogue between *Fam.* 1 and *Fam.* 15. As we have seen, the creation of these books in the imperial period, when the province of Cilicia no longer existed, and had been incorporated into a province that was now under imperial rather than senatorial administration, means that individually these books tell the story of a world that no longer existed. Even if these particular narratives are not inflected with a nostalgia for the province of Cilicia, or its republican mode of senatorial governance, the obsolescence of this particular administrative unit by the time that either of these letter books was first published means that this is a narrative that serves to close off the world of the letters from the world of the letter books. It reinforces that sense of historical rupture between Cicero's time and the period in which his letters were published in book rolls. This sense of rupture is only increased when we view the sixteen-book collection, and the enframing narrative between these two books that the collection produces, as a consequence of the emergence of the codex, which only became the predominant textual medium in the fourth or fifth century CE. The consequences of reading the collection as a whole as the product of late antiquity impinge on the meanings of all the letter books that it comprises.[55] But they are felt especially in the dialogue between *Fam.* 1 and 15, with their narratives of absence and exclusion from Rome, if this narrative is read in a context when Rome was no longer the administrative centre of the empire. Each stage of the letters' remediation, by book roll and codex, not only showcases the obsolescence of the medium that precedes it but also inscribes other forms of cultural, institutional, and geopolitical obsolescence along with it. Cicero's longing for Rome articulates a feeling with which late antique readers might well have identified.

---

55. See Nicholson 1998, 103–4 on the widely scattered references to Cicero's correspondence in Late Antique authors, from Ausonius to Ammianus Marcellinus.

3

Reorienting the Collection

CICERO AS ADDRESSEE AND THE ARENA OF LETTERS
IN *FAM.* 8

THE DOUBLE ROLE that Cicero plays in the letter collections, as author of the letters and as object of the editors' rewriting, makes him encompass the reversibility that is a key feature of epistolary exchange: correspondents write letters in the hope of eliciting a reply from their addressee and hence of becoming an addressee in turn. In the case of Cicero's letters, this dynamic is performed multiple times: firstly, between Cicero and his original addressees, whose replies to his letters are occasionally included within *ad Fam.*;[1] and subsequently, between Cicero and his editors, who 'write back' to his letters by organizing them into collections that amount to a form of reply in themselves. Cicero as addressee is, more specifically, the *indirect* object of their address and rewriting, and as such occupies a significant position for a specifically ideological reading of *ad Fam.* In Lacanian psychoanalysis, the letter (as token for the symbolic) determines the subject, by positioning her in a network of intersubjective relations, regardless of its content: 'The letter always reaches its destination', writes Lacan, because, even when it gets waylaid and ends up in the wrong hands, it construes its recipient as addressee,[2] an idea that underpins Althusser's theorization of ideology, in which subjects are constituted by procedures of interpellation—that is, by being hailed as

---

1. Of all Cicero's letter collections, *ad Fam.* is unique in this respect. For an overarching discussion of the 'other voices' in this collection, see Morello 2017.

2. Lacan 2006, 30. With Johnson 1988, 248; and Zizek 1992, 9–23.

Souvenirs of Cicero. Francesca K. A. Martelli, Oxford University Press. © Oxford University Press 2024.
DOI: 10.1093/oso/9780197761960.003.0004

SOUVENIRS OF CICERO

subjects by state apparatuses that construe them as such.[3] Throughout this book, I consider what kind of destination Cicero's letters reach in the hands of those who organized them into collections, how his letters hail these readers and editors as ideological subjects, and how they in turn do the same to him.

At the heart of *ad Fam.*,[4] we find a book of letters that is uniquely well placed to reflect on these questions, in that it is composed entirely of letters written by someone else to Cicero and hails him as their addressee throughout: in *Fam.* 8, Marcus Caelius Rufus, a younger friend of Cicero's, writes to him when he (Cicero) was stationed as governor of the far-distant province of Cilicia in the year 51–50 BCE. The authorship of this book of letters is a unique phenomenon: while letters by others are occasionally transmitted within this collection, they are a rare occurrence in the first seven books of the collection, and we seldom see more than one letter composed by someone else transmitted in sequence in the entirety of *ad Fam.* The existence of this book-long letter sequence, composed exclusively by a letter writer other than Cicero, raises a host of unanswerable questions about the mechanics of Cicero's author function: it makes us ask whether Cicero's team of secretaries archived (and copied down) *all* the letters that Cicero received, as well as those that he sent; and if so, why more of these have not been transmitted.[5]

But it also raises more answerable questions about the effect that the authorship of this book of letters has on the portrait of Cicero that *ad Fam.* produces—on Cicero as (indirect) object, referent, and addressee. What does it mean to find the normal authorial perspective reversed in this book? For yet again, far from situating Cicero within his wider social network, and allowing

---

3. Althusser 2014, 232–72. For the Lacanian foundations of Althusser's theory of ideology, see Pêcheux 1982, 92–114.

4. If we construe *Fam.* 16 as the collection's editorial paratext, as I try to do in Chapter 1, 'Letters to the Editor: Constructing the Editor in *Fam.* 16', *Fam.* 8 emerges as its central book. See my discussion on pp. 13–14 n. 34 above about the division in the manuscript traditions, which variously place *Fam.* 8 as it stands in the vulgate at the heart of the collection, or as the closing book of a collection comprising *Fam.* 1–8.

5. Cicero says little about this process himself, such that we can only infer, because we have them in such large numbers, that his own letters were systematically reduplicated and archived at home. See Garland 1992, 166–67 for the observation that Cicero's *librarii* must have been few in number (consistent with the modest total number of slaves that Cicero owned) on the grounds that they are seen undertaking a variety of non-specialist tasks, including non-secretarial ones. Atticus's household of slaves seems to have been much bigger: See Garland 1992, 168; and Treggiari 1969b, 203 for discussion of those letters in *ad Atticum* (e.g., *Att.* 13.44 and *Att.* 4.4) and *ad Fam.* (*Fam.* 16.22), where we see Cicero making use of his friend's more sizeable team of *librarii* to copy and disseminate his works. See Blake 2012 and Moss 2023, 23–24 and 40 for discussion of the invisibility of these book slaves.

Reorienting the Collection

us a transparent view of that network in all its sprawling breadth, the new perspective that we are given in *Fam.* 8 is a very narrow one: the letters of a single individual, separated (as so often) from their correspondent's replies (all the more conspicuously, in this case, because a number of Cicero's replies to Caelius happen to have been transmitted for us in *Fam.* 2). The isolation of the non-Ciceronian author is clearly the point of this letter book and again highlights the conspicuous intervention of later editors: both in compiling Caelius's letters into their own self-contained book and in subsequently choosing to place a book of letters written by someone else at the heart of a sixteen-book collection transmitted in Cicero's name. For although 'Cicero' is evacuated from this letter book, he is not effaced. Rather, as the implied reader of Caelius's information and opinions, his presence hovers over this book of letters as a conspicuous absence, one that defines the contours of the information it contains in virtual, if not actual, terms, like a hologram. Cicero as the implied or virtual addressee, rather than an actual one, becomes a site of transference—the face given to the symbolic space of the Republic, whose ideals are betrayed by Caelius and others of his generation in *Fam.* 8, even as this book also highlights how their record will be shaped forever by the republican interests of Cicero's author function.

Yet there is another aspect to this authorial reversal, one that emerges as an inevitable facet of the historical fulcrum that *Fam.* 8 represents, a turning point which the central position of this book within the collection underscores. In terms of their outlook (if not their biographical outcomes), Caelius and Cicero sit on different sides of this historical divide, the one characterized by his youth and foresight,[6] and the other by his attachment to the past. My reading of *Fam.* 8 will suggest that the reversible reflexes involved in the letters' authorship are designed to comment on how Cicero is addressed or hailed by this letter collection, following the processes of remediation that the original letters undergo as a result of the different book technologies involved in their

---

6. Caelius was in fact probably 36 or 37 years old in 51 BCE when most of these letters were written, if we disregard the evidence of Pliny *HN* 7. 165, who places his birthdate in 82 BCE and instead follow those scholars (e.g., Wegehaupt 1878, 5–7; and Sumner 1971, 247–8) who estimate that he must have been born in 87 or 88 BCE if he were aedile in 50. However, see Lintott 2008, 431 for the possibility that he may have been allowed to run for election early because of his successful prosecution of C. Antonius in 59 BCE (the latter defended by Cicero himself). See Wiseman 1985, 62 n.41; and Dyck 2013, 4 n.19 for discussion. Even if we allow Pliny's evidence, a birthdate in 82 BCE would make him 31 at the time of these letters, thus a far cry from the *adulescens* that Cicero portrays him as in the *Pro Caelio.* My argument in this chapter is that this book of letters sustains the characterization of him as the feckless (but lovable) youth that Cicero portrays him as in that defence speech.

transmission. Caelius's authorship stands in for that of the later editors, who address Cicero through the words of one who articulates, in his own strong sense of the generational divide between himself and his addressee, the new world order that awaits the outcome of civil war, the event that this book of letters anticipates. This editorial narrative is reinforced by an elaborate metaphor that emerges in the course of *Fam.* 8 for the new contexts and conditions for viewing the letters that the new book formats bring with them, and which happens to comment in passing on the new ideological circumstances that accompany them. In this chapter, I dwell at length on the significance of this metaphor, with the aim of tracing a poetics of remediation for *ad Fam.*

Caelius/Cicero: The Generational Divide

The letters in *Fam.* 8 are composed by Marcus Caelius Rufus, a younger friend and erstwhile protégé of Cicero, while the latter was stationed away from Rome on proconsular duty in Cilicia in 51–50 BCE. Caelius is, of course, best known to later readers because of Cicero's defence speech on his behalf, in which the famous orator took up the cause of his young friend at the trial of 56 BCE in which Caelius had been accused *de vi* by his notorious ex-lover, Clodia. Cicero's defence strategy for this *cause célèbre*, which took place on the Megalensia when the jurors should have been at the theatre, was to play up his own paternalistic role towards Caelius and to cast the latter as the wayward but harmless *adulescens* of Roman comedy.[7] Dealing as it does with relations between mentors and protégés, it is hardly surprising to discover that the *Pro Caelio* was recognized in antiquity for its educational value: the speech was mined by Quintilian for the ethical and rhetorical tropes worth teaching a young orator.[8] And this aspect of the speech remains an enduring part of its appeal in the modern era, having been used as a school text for teaching generations of school and university students Latin throughout the twentieth

---

7. On the comedic aspects of the *Pro Caelio* (and the strategy behind them), see Geffcken 1973, Arcellaschi 1997, and Leigh 2004. See Henderson 2002, 210 on the paternal/patronizing attitude that Cicero takes up in the *Pro Caelio*—not just towards Caelius but towards the seventeen-year-old prosecuting counsel, Atratinus, as well.

8. Austin 1951, 41 opens his commentary on the speech with the observation that Quintilian admired the exordium to the *Pro Caelio* and cites Quint. *Inst.* 4.1.31, 4.1.39, and 9.2.39 to illustrate how frequently the imperial schoolteacher drew on this part of the speech to illustrate certain rhetorical principles. Dyck 2013, 27–28 notes that Quintilian cites the speech twenty-one times. See Henderson 2002, 211–12 on the paternal relationship that Austin constructs between Quint. *Inst.* 12 and the *Pro Caelio* as a result of his 1948 and (originally) 1933 commentaries on these texts.

century.[9] The generational difference between Cicero and Caelius,[10] already underscored for rhetorical purposes within the speech, is reinforced by the pedagogical uses to which this text has so often been put.

Fam. 8 reinforces this sense of generational disparity at every turn: not just in the different political views that Caelius espouses, but in the mode of self-presentation and language that he uses throughout, in letters which seem to have been chosen to corroborate the *Pro Caelio's* portrait of him as the louche but lovable young libertine. When we open *Fam.* 8, we are conscious of being addressed in a very different tone and manner to that which we have seen thus far in the letter collection. Caelius speaks in the opening letter of *Fam.* 8 about being the laziest of letter writers (*ad litteras sribendas . . . pigerrimo*), a characterization that Cicero teasingly rebukes him for in *Fam.* 2, and which contrasts pointedly with the epistolary industry of his addressee, to which the first seven books of *ad Fam.* are, in themselves, a formidable testament. But it is above all Caelius's satirical descriptions of political figures, and the general political scene in Rome, the language that he uses to conjure this world, and his humorous enjoyment of it that convey the younger man's attitude. The linguistic data police may tell us that we cannot classify words like *subrostrani* and *embaineticam* as colloquialisms.[11] Yet the abundant unusual words and

---

9. For Henderson 2002, 208–13, this was the case in the anglophone world, at least, because of Austin's exemplary commentary. The broader point of Henderson's study is to show how the paternal/patronal relationship between Cicero and Caelius is replicated by Austin between the different editions of his commentary, which not only pits his more mature scholarly self against his younger one (in a spirit of self-criticism) but also attends to the shifting needs and expectations of students between the 1933 and 1951 (reissued in 1960) editions.

10. If Caelius were born in 87 or 88 BCE, there would still be a generational divide between himself and Cicero, albeit one exaggerated considerably by Cicero's rhetorical strategies in the *Pro Caelio*.

11. These two hapax legomena are both found in the same paragraph of the opening letter of *Fam.* 8. *Oxford Latin Dictionary* (*OLD*) accommodates Caelius's tone and personality in its translation of *subrostrani* as 'loafers about the forum', but views *embaineticam* as corrupt. But Shackleton Bailey 1977, 384 notes that it is a derivative of ἐμβαίνω ('I embark') and suggests that it must therefore relate to the building or hiring of boats. Pinkster 2010, 191 believes that both these terms may be Caelius's inventions, observing, however, that it is of course impossible to know for sure. Throughout this essay, Pinkster shies away from calling them, or any other feature of Caelius's style 'colloquialisms', by which he is specifically referring to features of oral as opposed to written language. Colloquialism, by this hyper-literal definition, may not be quite the right term or line of approach. One of Pinkster's arguments (p. 190) against seeing anything remarkable in Caelius's distinctive vocabulary is that we see a similar number of hapax legomena in Cicero's letters to him (in e.g., *Fam.* 2.8.1: *compilatio* for 'burglary' and *gladiatorum compositiones* for 'pairs of gladiators'). But this ignores the strong possibility that Cicero may be quoting Caelius here—or, alternatively, trying to match the improvised style of his hip young (or, at any rate, younger) friend.

90 SOUVENIRS OF CICERO

other colourful phrases,[12] along with the caricatures of politicians of all different stripes,[13] combine to conjure a slang or idiom of youth that we would need an urban dictionary (rather than just comparative linguistic data) to decode.

The humour with which Caelius draws up these amusing vignettes of Roman politics in the early letters of *Fam.* 8 for Cicero's entertainment makes them his answer to the comedic qualities of the *Pro Caelio* and was clearly shared by Cicero despite their difference in age.[14] But the perspicacity that Caelius's political sketches reveal are part and parcel of what made Cicero identify him as the very correspondent to keep him informed about the political scene in Rome while he was away in Cilicia. In the opening letter of the sequence of letters addressed to Caelius in book 2, Cicero writes (*Fam.* 2.8.1): *Scribent alii, multi nuntiabunt, perferet multa etiam ipse rumor. Qua re ego nec praeterita nec praesentia abs te sed, ut ab homine longe in posterum prospiciente, futura exspecto.* ('Others will write, many will bring news, much too will reach me by way of rumour. That is why I don't look to you to inform me about the past or present, but, as is fitting for one who sees so far into the future, about what is going to happen.') It is this idea of foresight, as the

---

12. See *Fam.* 8.5.2: *incile*, 'ditch', 'trough' (*sane tamquam in quodam incili iam omnia adhaeserunt*, 'everything's stuck in a kind of ditch'). Lebek 1970, 134 lists fourteen words that Caelius uses which are not found in Cicero, any of his other correspondents, or even in the works of Caesar.

13. For example, Caelius' description of Pompey at *Fam.* 8.1.3: 'For he generally thinks one thing and says another, but isn't quite clever enough to disguise what he really wants.'(*Solet enim aliud sentire et loqui neque tantum valere ingenio ut non appareat quid cupiat.*); and of Domitius Ahenobarbus's conspicuous show of secrecy about Caesar's fortunes in Gaul at *Fam.* 8.1.4: 'But Domitius puts his fingers to his lips before he speaks!' (*At Domitius cum manus ad os apposuit!*) See also Caelius' characterization of M. Octavius and C. Hirrus, his competitors in the elections for aedile, at *Fam.* 8.2.2: 'I have standing against me a real toff and an aspiring one.' (*Ego incidi in competitorem nobilem et nobilem agentem.*)

14. See *Fam.* 8.3.1 for Caelius's description to Cicero of the comedic value of his running in the elections for aedile: 'But this would be so delicious—if it happens, we won't be short of a laugh for the rest of our lives' (*Sed hoc usque eo suave est ut, si acciderit, tota vita risus nobis deesse non possit.*) Cicero himself answers this call for laughter upon hearing of Caelius's success at being elected at *Fam.* 2.9.1: 'I both congratulate you and I also cannot find words to thank you for the manner of your election, which has given us, as you write to me, something to laugh about for the rest of our lives.' (*Et cum gratulor tum vero quibus verbis tibi gratias agam non reperio, quod ita factus sis ut dederis nobis, quem ad modum scripseras ad me, quod semper ridere possemus.*) The chief butt of their shared laughter appears to be Hirrus, Caelius's unsuccessful rival in the election to be aedile, whose affectations and speech impediment Cicero mocks mercilessly in subsequent sections of *Fam.* 2.9 and also in *Fam.* 2.10, referring to him as *'ille'* (sc. *'illus'* for Hirrus) throughout. See also *Fam.* 2.12.1 and *Fam.* 2.13.3 for Cicero's expressions of regret at not being able to laugh about events in Rome with Caelius, despite the gravity of the situation there (the latter example provoked by Curio's transfer of loyalties to Caesar, which Cicero had predicted).

special prerogative of Caelius's youthful (or, at any rate, younger) outlook, that we must single out as a guiding idea behind the narrative that *Fam.* 8 yields, when we read this letter book in the context of the sixteen-book collection; this, along with Cicero's relative senescence, and inability to read the future because of his commitment to dated ideals, which emerges by way of contrast with the prescience of his young friend. These two correspondents, who belong to different sides of a generational divide, look at politics—and history—in different directions: one forward, one backward.[15] It is this difference in age and outlook that underpins the meaning of the central metaphor of *Fam.* 8.

The Arena of Letters in Fam. *8*

Caelius's letters to Cicero are primarily taken up with his reports about the debates that took place in the senate while Cicero was away in Cilicia, which dealt with the contentious business of recalling Julius Caesar from Gaul. These debates were to play a significant role in the precipitation of civil war, such that the removal of Cicero's authorial voice from *Fam.* 8 may be designed, in part, to have an exonerating function: to underscore his absence from the debates that would end up tearing the Roman Republic apart and to absolve him of any responsibility for them. But the absence of Cicero's replies from the sequence of letters, and his casting as the recipient throughout, has a more profound effect on the drawing of Cicero that the letter collection produces, one that emerges in tandem with the central metaphor of book 8, as the hollow shape that the absent Ciceronian author takes at the heart of the collection finds expression in concrete form.

Amid Caelius's faithful reporting of the major political (and juridical) events in Rome that would be of interest to Cicero, and the banter that cuts through his side of their exchange, is a request that he makes repeatedly of his addressee to get hold of some panthers from his exotic province and send them to Rome for him to use in the games that he was expected to put on that year as a newly elected aedile. We first hear about these ambitions in

---

15. Dettenhofer 1992, 3–6 and 131–37 likewise maintains that those individuals (including Caelius) who represent the generation of *perdita iuventus*, who were born between 87 and 80 BCE and died either in the conflict between Caesar and Pompey or in the subsequent showdown with Antony, shared a political outlook.

92   SOUVENIRS OF CICERO

the second letter of *Fam.* 8, when Caelius had not yet even been elected;[16] and they are still on his mind in the fourth letter, by which time he had been elected.[17] They receive a mention in *Fam.* 8.6, dated to February 50 BCE,[18] and they start to sound more shrill in *Fam.* 8.8,[19] which is dated prior to *Fam.* 8.6, as is *Fam.* 8.9 (which is dated even further back, prior to *Fam.* 8.8), where Caelius's preoccupation with the panthers reaches its climax (*Fam.* 8.9.3):[20]

> *Fere litteris omnibus tibi de pantheris scripsi. Turpe tibi erit Patiscum Curioni decem pantheras misisse, te non multis partibus pluris; quas ipsas Curio mihi et alias Africanas decem donavit, ne putes illum tantum praedia rustica dare scire. Tu si modo memoria tenueris et Cibyratas arcessieris itemque in Pamphyliam litteras miseris (nam ibi plures capi aiunt), quod voles efficies. Hoc vehementius laboro nunc quod seorsus a conlega puto mihi omnia paranda. Amabo te, impera tibi hoc. Curare soles libenter, ut ego maiorem partem nihil curare. In hoc negotio nulla tua nisi loquendi cura est, hoc est imperandi et mandandi; nam simul atque erunt captae, qui alant eas et deportent habes eos quos ad Sittianam*

---

16. *Fam.* 8.2.2: 'Anyhow, as soon as you hear that I'm appointed, can you please take care of the matter of the panthers.' (*Tu tamen simul ac me designatum audieris, ut tibi curae sit, quod <ad> pantheras attinet, rogo*).

17. *Fam.* 8.4.5: 'I keep reminding you again and again about Sittius's bond; for I'm anxious that you should understand how exceedingly important that matter is to me. Also about the panthers, that you should send for some men from Cibyra, and see that the animals are shipped to me.' (*Saepius te admoneo de syngrapha Sittiana—cupio enim te intelligere eam rem ad me valde pertinere—; item de pantheris, ut Cibyratas accersas curesque, ut mihi vehantur*).

18. *Fam.* 8.6.5: 'It will be a disgrace to you if I have to go without any Greek panthers.' (*Turpe tibi erit pantheras Graecas me non habere*). Caelius is here distinguishing between the panthers that Cicero can provide (from the Hellenized East) and the African ones that Curio has already offered him. Throughout these letters, Caelius's need to outdo Curio in the games the latter put on for his father earlier in 50 BCE, and, in particular, to outnumber the panthers that Curio featured at those games, is marked. See Shackleton Bailey 1977, 414 for discussion of the date.

19. *Fam.* 8.8.10: 'For myself, Curio treats me generously, and has made me a somewhat onerous present in the shape of the African panthers that were imported for his games. Had he not done that, I might have let mine go.' (*Me tractat liberaliter Curio et mihi suo munere negotium imposuit; nam si mihi non dedisset eas quae ad ludos ei advectae erant Africanae, potuit supersederi.*) 'As it is, since I must give them, I would be glad if you would take the trouble to let me have a few beasts from your part of the world. (I have been constantly begging you this favour.' (*Nunc, quoniam dare necesse est, velim tibi curae sit, quod a te semper petii, ut aliquid istinc bestiarum habeamus.*) See Shackleton Bailey 1977, 397 for the dating of this letter to the month of October.

20. *Fam.* 8.9 is dated to September 2 by Caelius himself at *Fam.* 8.9.2, where he mentions sending this letter on the fourth day before the September Nones.

syngrapham misi. Puto etiam, si ullam spem mihi litteris ostenderis, me isto missurum alios.

In almost all my letters, I've mentioned the panthers to you. It will be of little credit to you that Patiscus has sent Curio ten panthers and that you have failed to send many more. Curio has given me those same animals, and another ten from Africa—in case you imagine that landed estates are the only presents he knows how to give! If you only keep this in mind, and send for some hunters from Cibyra, and also send letters to Pamphylia (for they tell me that more of them are caught there), you'll achieve what you want. I'm labouring over this point all the more anxiously now because I think that I'll have to provide everything myself, without any help from my colleague. For love's sake, take this on! You're usually as painstaking, as I'm lackadaisical. In this matter, you need do nothing except to say a few words—that is, give orders and instructions. For as soon as the animals are caught, you have the men I sent to deal with Sittius's bond available to feed them and ship them to Rome. I also think that if you hold out any hopes to me in your letter, I'll send you some more men.

The request, though issued repeatedly, seems to have been taken none too seriously by the letters' addressee, as we can see from the playful tone of a reply that Cicero writes to Caelius at this time.[21] Yet the way in which these letters are organized within *Fam.* 8, upending chronological sequence, while slowly building up to a fever pitch of panther frenzy, suggests the centrality of this motif to the meaning of the book as a whole.

It speaks, no doubt, to the pressure that Romans who held the office of aedile were under at this time to boost their own popularity by putting on ever-more-spectacular games in the city of Rome.[22] This, at least, is how scholars

---

21. *Fam.* 2.11: 'About the panthers, the business is being carefully conducted under my orders by those who hunt them regularly.' (*De pantheris per eos qui venari solent agitur mandatu meo diligenter.*) 'But it's surprising how few panthers there are; and they tell me that those that do exist complain bitterly that no traps are set in my province for any other animal apart from themselves.' (*Sed mira paucitas est, et eas quae sunt valde aiunt queri quod nihil cuiquam insidiarum in mea provincia nisi sibi fiat.*) 'And so it's said that they've decided to emigrate from this province into Caria.' (*Itaque constituisse dicuntur in Cariam ex nostra provincia decedere.*) 'But the matter is being busily attended to, and by nobody more diligently than Patiscus. Any animal caught will be yours; but how many there are, I don't know.' (*Sed tamen sedulo fit et in primis a Patisco. Quicquid erit, tibi erit; sed quid esset plane nesciebamus.*)

22. One of the best analyses of the republican politics of the Roman games, and the competition among aediles and other magistrates competing to outdo one another by putting on ever

SOUVENIRS OF CICERO

have inclined to interpret Caelius's preoccupation within the context of the moment of his writing. But the motif has a new currency when the letters are read in the specific context of the larger letter collection, formed and enclosed by the codex. This is the context of the Roman Empire, during which period games stopped being held in makeshift structures assembled for a particular event or festival and came to be held in permanent arenas, built out of concrete, marble, and stone.[23] So rapidly did this distinctive edifice spread across the Roman Empire during the imperial period, and so uniquely Roman (and uniquely violent) a form of entertainment did it represent, that it is seen by many as a symbol of Romanization and an emblem, perhaps, of the brutal inexorability of Roman power at this time.[24] When Caelius speaks about panthers for his games, this is the structure that many readers of the letter collection will have in mind, even though it is a structure that post-dates the writing of the original letters. It is an edifice that belongs to the later era of the codex—which happens to start being used as a new book format around the same time that the Flavian amphitheatre was built.[25]

More than this, though, it is a structure that resembles the codex, and provides a suggestive metaphor for the kinds of spectacle that the letters afford once assembled and published in this new medium. Like the codex, the arena is a form that encloses.[26] Located in book 8, at the very heart of the

---

more lavish spectacles for them, is found in Futrell 2006, 11–29 (who quotes and commentates on much of the evidence for this competition found in Cicero's letters).

23. There were, of course, some permanent stone amphitheatres outside Rome—mainly in Campania, but also in other regions, both inside and outside Italy—before this period: on which, see esp. Welch 2007, 72–100; also Bomgardner 2000, 39–60 for a more restricted focus on the amphitheatre at Pompeii. The first permanent, free-standing, stone amphitheatre in Rome was erected in 30 BCE by Statilius Taurus. See Welch 2007, 108–26 for discussion of the significance of this monumental building—including its use by the emperors Augustus, Tiberius, and Caligula—and the history of the amphitheatre in Rome.

24. Futrell 1997, 53–76 offers a probing analysis of the variety of reasons for which amphitheatres spread in the western provinces: whether because they were following military bases (as on the northern frontier), or arose because of a local expression of loyalty to the emperor, or whether the impetus came from the natives (as suggested by the existence of a number of rural amphitheatres in Gaul), the amphitheatre as symbol of Romanization was clearly a complex phenomenon.

25. Our first evidence for the use of the codex comes from Martial (on which, see Fowler 1995). Martial is also the poet who commemorates the inauguration of the Flavian amphitheatre in 80 CE with the *Liber Spectaculorum*. The fact that the same (poetic) source attests the advent of these two new media makes their historical coincidence all the more striking.

26. See Golvin 2012, 21–32 on the origins of (and reasons for) the elliptical form of the amphitheatre building type.

collection, the arena metaphor speaks to the enclosing form that the codex imposes on the collection from without, containing the books held inside in concentric circles, like the rows of ranked seating in an amphitheatre, and imposing a concrete form upon them. The metaphor makes of this central book the hollow space at the centre of this edifice, and in this, purely formal sense, speaks to the evacuation of the Ciceronian author at this central point in the letter collection, whose presence is felt here as a void. But the arena also provides the setting for a spectacle, a public show for mass viewing and mass entertainment. In this sense, too, it provides a good analogy for the work of the codex, which makes available these personal letters, and the historical narrative that they construct, to a wider readership. And it points to this book, at the centre of the collection, as the focal point of its spectacle.

The point of this image is confirmed by a letter that culminates the sequence that Caelius writes to Cicero in the year 51–50 BCE, which explicitly presents the political disaster unfolding before them as a spectacle worthy of the arena (*Fam.* 8.14.4):[27]

> *Ad summam (quaeris quid putem futurum), si alter uter eorum ad Parthicum bellum non eat, video magnas impendere discordias, quas ferrum et vis iudicabit; uterque et animo et copiis est paratus. Si sine summo periculo fieri posset, **magnum et iucundum tibi Fortuna spectaculum parabat.***

> To sum up, you want to know what I think will happen: Unless one of them [i.e., Caesar or Pompey] goes to fight the Parthians, I see a mighty feud descending, which only weapons and force will decide. Each of the two is well prepared in spirit and in resources. If only it could take place without the utmost danger to yourself, **a great and entertaining spectacle is being staged by Fortune for you.**

The idea that the events narrated in this book of letters constitute a spectacle to be enjoyed and consumed speaks presciently to the effect that remediation will have on the letters: the historical events that the letters record will become a narrative for consumption, repackaged first by the book roll and then by the

---

27. It is tempting to read the spectacle presented to us by Caelius in this book as an answer to the underwhelming spectacle of Pompey's games that Cicero describes in his letter to Marius in *Fam.* 7.1.

codex to answer to the demands of readerly entertainment, much like the historical re-enactments that the arena will come to stage.[28] Without ever explicitly mentioning an amphitheatre (how could he, since this architectural form did not yet exist in Rome in any permanent sense),[29] this is the metaphorical structure that Caelius's book of letters yields, one that presents the political drama that the letters narrate as material for a bloody show. And this metaphorical structure answers quite neatly to the phrasing of the request that we have already seen Cicero making at the very outset of their correspondence—that Caelius's letters offer a forecast of the political shape of things to come, specifically by giving Cicero a sense *of the kind of building to expect* on his return to Rome (*Fam.* 2.8.1):

> *Scribent alii, multi nuntiabunt, perferet multa etiam ipse rumor. Qua re ego nec praeterita nec praesentia abs te sed, ut ab homine longe in posterum prospiciente, futura exspecto, ut ex tuis litteris cum formam rei publicae viderim quale aedificium futurum sit scire possim.*

> Others will write, many will bring me news, much too will reach me even by way of rumour. That is why I don't look to you to inform me about the past or present, but as is fitting for one who sees so far into the future, about what is going to happen, so that when your letters have explained to me the general political design, I may be in a position to know what sort of a building to expect.

The amphitheatre, which is the answer that Caelius's book of letters yields to this question, also sums up the generational difference between himself and Cicero, whose preferred analogy for the spectacle of public life had always been, by contrast, that most republican of cultural institutions: the theatre.[30]

---

28. As Coleman 1990, 64 notes, the majority of fatal charades that Martial describes in the *Liber Spectaculorum* are mythological re-enactments, although he does mention an arena re-enactment of the historical legend of Mucius Scaevola in Mart. *Ep.* 8.30 and 10.25; and of the near-contemporary story of the bandit leader Laureolus in *Lib. Spect.* 7. Presumably these were not the only ones. On the historical re-enactment of naval battles in the Flavian amphitheatre and other venues, see Coleman 1993.

29. Even if it did exist in locations outside Rome (see p. 62 n. 23 above for discussion).

30. The analogy that Cicero makes between the theatre and public life is one that pervades his career: see, e.g., *Brut.* 290 (with Vasaly 1985, 1–2), where Cicero explicitly compares the performance of the orator in a court of law to that of Roscius Amerinus on stage; *Orat.* 70–74 for a broad conceptualization of oratory as drama; and *de Orat.* 2.338 and *Am.* 97 for Cicero's specific characterization of the *contio* as a *scaena* (with Hölkeskamp 1995; and Bell 1997, 18). I owe this insight about Cicero's frequent recourse to theatrical metaphor, and the different generational outlook that it reveals when compared to Caelius's, to Sander Goldberg.

The amphitheatre not only symbolizes the effects of these letters' remediation but also speaks more concretely to the ultimate outcome of the events that the letters stage. For the reader of the letter collection, who possesses the benefit of hindsight and knows that these decisive events will lead to civil war and subsequently a new monarchical system of government in Rome, the arena is an appropriate answer to give to Cicero's query about what kind of political edifice to expect, in that it is a space that provides one of the best demonstrations available of the distinctive modality of power that imperial rule will come to take. Unlike the games of Cicero and Caelius's day, where public entertainments gave the individual who took charge of them an opportunity to boost his chances of election to a higher political office later on, in imperial Rome the games that took place in the arena had a quite different function in that they were sponsored by the emperor. The arena was one of very few spaces in which he and his subjects came into sight of one another. It provided an opportunity for the ruler to display his munificence to the ruled and for them to reveal to him their appreciation or (occasionally) disapproval of his governance and person in turn.[31] The carefully regulated seating requirements that Augustus stipulated for theatrical shows as well as spectacles in the arena, whereby audience members were grouped by class and gender, made the amphitheatre a space in which subjects could observe their position in the social and symbolic order of imperial Rome and map out where they stood in relation to the centre of Roman power.[32] Gunderson describes the ideological consequences of the observational relations that the arena establishes for Roman citizens' subject positions both inside and outside the arena as follows:[33]

---

31. See Veyne 1976, 685–89; and Millar 1977, 368–75 for slightly different appraisals of the encounter between ruler and subjects that took place in the amphitheatre.

32. Suet. *Aug.* 44 is our source for the Augustan reforms to theatre seating arrangements. See Rawson 1987 on the significance of these seating arrangements and the rule of diminishing importance that she draws out of the observation that (a disproportionate number of) senators would sit ringside, followed by *equites*, then the *plebs*, and lastly (i.e., farthest away) women. And Gunderson 1997, 125 (and *passim*) on the ideological significance of this regime: 'The seating at the arena can be seen as an ideological map of the social structure of the Roman state, a map first laid out in general by the Republican *nobiles* and favorably biased in its representation of themselves, a map later drawn in further and extreme detail by Augustus.'

33. Gunderson 1997, 115–16. I diverge from Gunderson insofar as he views the arena as an organ of surveillance, analogous to Foucault's panopticon, the invisible but all-seeing eye trained on the incarcerated in order to make them internalize the forms of surveillance to which they are subject and conform spontaneously to the requirements of power. This analogy seems to me to be an imperfect one: as an instrument that is designed to enable the few to watch the many, it fails to capture the specific dynamics of observation at work in the arena, where everyone—(a

The arena can thus be taken as an apparatus which not only looks in upon a spectacle, but one which in its organization and structure reproduces the relations subsisting between observer and observed. The arena thus becomes a mapping of a technology of power whose consequences are felt beyond the arena as a mere festive institution. I would then propose that there is no radical outside to the arena and that when a Roman takes up a position on the sand, in the seats or outside the building, the apparatus of the arena serves to structure the truths of those positions. Indeed, the spectacle of the arena has a specular effect which makes a new spectacle of its own observers, revealing and determining them through their relationship to the image of themselves produced by their relationship to the arena.

On top of (or as part of) the ideological relations between emperor and subjects that Gunderson's reading of the arena draws out, his appraisal also captures the remediating effect that the arena has on the Roman games—specifically, its capacity to reproduce the relations between observer and observed on a different plane. When we view the medium as the message,[34] the bloody spectacle staged on the sand (the ostensible object of our gaze) is a lure designed to distract us from the true content of the arena, which is the spectacle of the audience in the seating—that aspect of the amphitheatre which invites us to map the difference between the Roman games of Caelius and Cicero's day and those of the imperial reader's present.

This specular dimension of the arena carries over into its appearance as a metaphor within book 8, where it helps swivel the reader's gaze away from the information which the letters place at the centre, as it were, and around onto Caelius and Cicero, and the relationship between them. For when Caelius casts the two of them as would-be viewers of the unfolding spectacle, he directs us to the true spectacle that *Fam.* 8 stages, which is the drama of gazes generated between the two of them, looking not at some object placed between them but at each other. The information that this book of letters promises to deliver is a lure designed to distract us from this view. This much is made clear in the opening letter of book 8, which openly tells us how little

---

few of) the many and (too many of) the few—watches everyone else and observes themselves being watched at the same time. Furthermore, Foucault explicitly presents the panopticon, and panopticism, as a replacement for the kinds of open spectacle that we find in societies like ancient Rome—and which are well exemplified by the arena.

34. McLuhan 1964.

of the information that we later readers are being told about will actually be made available to us (*Fam.* 8.1):

> *Quod tibi discedens pollicitus sum me omnis res urbanas diligentissime tibi perscripturum, data opera paravi qui sic omnia persequeretur ut verear ne tibi nimium arguta haec sedulitas videatur. . . . Tamen in hoc te deprecor ne meum hoc officium adrogantiae condemnes quod hunc laborem alteri delegavi, non quin mihi suavissimum sit et occupato et ad litteras scribendas, ut tu nosti, pigerrimo tuae memoriae dare operam, **sed ipsum volumen quod tibi misi facile, ut ego arbitror, me excusat. Nescio cuius oti esset non modo perscribere haec sed omnino animadvertere; omnia enim sunt ibi senatus consulta edicta, fabulae rumores.** Quod exemplum si forte minus te delectarit, ne molestiam tibi cum impensa mea exhibeam, fac me certiorem. Si quid in re publica maius actum erit, quod isti operarii minus commode persequi possint, et quem ad modum actum sit et quae existimatio secuta quaeque de eo spes sit diligenter tibi perscribemus.*

As I was leaving, I promised to write to you assiduously about everything that happened in the city; so I've taken pains to get hold of someone who would report to you everything—in such minute detail, that I fear you'll view his efforts as long-windedness. . . . I beg you don't condemn this way of fulfilling my duty as a mark of arrogance, simply because I've delegated the task to another. Not that it wouldn't be a pleasure to give up my own time to remembering you, busy though I am and, as you know, the laziest of writers. **But the packet I'm sending you makes my excuse for me, I think. I don't know how much leisure it would take, not only to write all this out, but even just to observe it. Decrees of the senate, edicts, gossip, rumours— they are all there.** If you're not completely thrilled with this sample, please let me know, so that I can spare your patience and my purse at the same time! If anything of political importance takes place, which those scribes of mine can't explain properly, I'll write you a very thorough account of how it was done, what was thought of it afterwards, and what hopes it's aroused.

The packet of other documents that this letter is said to accompany might be viewed as the original letter's content. However, it is not transmitted in the collection, where its pointed withholding tells us precisely how little information we can expect to glean from these letters when they are remediated by this new book context.

This opening act of suppression has programmatic implications for the rest of the book, in that it replicates a similar procedure of frustration at work within the narrative of events of 51—50 BCE. For the frustration of our gaze in the opening letter is subsequently shown to anticipate a similar procedure of frustration surrounding the emergence of new information throughout book 8, as the information that Caelius does deliver to Cicero is presented as a series of obstructions, refusals, and delays. The repeatedly deferred question that preoccupies these letters is that of Caesar's recall from Gaul and the appointment of successors to his province: Marcellus, one of the consuls for 51 BCE, had moved that, in light of Caesar's success in suppressing the Great Revolt of 52 BCE, and the exceptionally long period of thanksgiving decreed to mark this victory, it was time to bring the general and his army home, even if that did mean cutting short the term of his command as determined by the *lex Pompeia Licinia*.[35] Caelius's letters in *Fam.* 8 chart the frustration of Marcellus's attempts to bring discussion of this issue in the senate to a head, as a result of widespread senatorial reluctance to precipitate a rift with Caesar: in *Fam.* 8.1 itself, dated to late May 51 BCE, we hear of Marcellus putting off discussion of the Gallic succession until June 1;[36] and in *Fam.* 8.4, Caelius prefaces his account of a meeting of the senate in July 51 BCE, at which it was decided that no discussion of the issue should take place until Pompey was able to discuss the matter in person, with the comment (*Fam.* 8.4.4): *De re*

---

35. Suet. *Iul.* 28.2 is our source for Marcellus's arguments to this effect. Both Suetonius and Hirt. *BGall.* 8.53.1 stress the fact that Marcellus was bringing the issue of Caesar's successor to a head before time. Although the year 51 BCE is clearly premature, it is not known when exactly the five-year extension of Caesar's command, granted by the *lex Pompeia* in 55, was due to end: see Morstein-Marx 2021, 266–69 for a clear summary of the problem. As he points out (p. 267), it is not known whether the *lex Pompeia Licinia*, which extended the five-year term set by the *lex Vatinia* by another five years, was meant to come into effect as soon as the term of the earlier law lapsed, whether it was meant to overlap with it, or whether it was separated from it by an interval. Morstein-Marx here follows Pelling 2011, 286 (with n. 10) in viewing the terminal date of Caesar's command as an imprecise matter, one that was meant to be decided in the process of appointing his successor.

36. *Fam.* 8.1.2: 'Furthermore, Marcellus still hasn't referred the question of appointing new governors in the Gallic provinces to the senate, and has put it off, as he told me himself, until the Kalends of June, has certainly elicited the same kind of talk as was going around about him when we were in Rome.' (*Praeterea Marcellus, quod adhuc nihil rettulit de successione provinciarum Galliarum et in Kal. Iun., ut mihi ipse dixit, eam distulit relationem, sane quam eos sermones expressit qui de eo tum fuerant cum Romae nos essemus.*) While Caelius speaks here of Marcellus making no formal motion before June 1, Gruen 1974, 462 n. 45 suggests that the consul must have publicized his intentions before this point.

Reorienting the Collection 101

publica iam novi quidquam exspectare desieramus. ('In politics, we had stopped expecting anything new.')[37] In the following letter, dated shortly afterwards to August 51 BCE, the obstructions to making any progress in the senate about these questions appear to have become routine (*Fam.* 8.5.2 and 8.5.3):

> *Nosti enim haec tralaticia: de Galliis constituetur; erit qui intercedat; deinde alius exsistet qui, nisi libere liceat de omnibus provinciis decernere senatui, reliquas impediat. Sic multum ac diu ludetur, atque ita diu ut plus biennium in his tricis moretur.*

You know the deal. There'll be a decision about Gaul. Somebody will come along with a veto. Then somebody else will stand up and stop any move about the other provinces, unless the senate has free license to pass decrees on all of them. So we shall play a long, elaborate game—so long that a couple of years or more may drag by in these manoeuvres.

Caelius goes on to explain that everything is stuck in a kind of trough (*sane tamquam in quodam incili iam omnia adhaeserunt*) as a result of Marcellus's inability to muster a quorum to support his motion about bringing the question of the Gallic succession to a head.[38] He reiterates this point at *Fam.*

---

37. This meeting took place outside the pomerium, in the temple of Apollo, so that Pompey (who held *imperium* at the time and was about to depart to join his army at Rimini) could participate.

38. *Fam.* 8.5.3: 'If I had anything fresh to tell you about the political situation, I'd follow my usual habit of describing in detail both what happened and what consequences I expect to follow. The fact is that everything is stuck in a kind of trough.' (*Si quid novi de re publica quod tibi scriberem haberem, usus essem mea consuetudine, ut diligenter et quid actum esset et quid ex eo futurum sperarem perscriberem. Sane tamquam in quodam incili iam omnia adhaeserunt.*) 'Marcellus still goes on pressing his point about the provinces, but so far has not succeeded in getting a muster of the senate. But if by the end of this year Curio is tribune, and the same performance about the provinces will come on the boards, you don't need me to tell you how easy it will be then to hold everything up, and how Caesar and those who care nothing for the state are counting on this.' (*Marcellus idem illud de provinciis urget [et] neque adhuc frequentiam senatus efficere potuit. Hoc sic praeterito anno Curio tribunus <erit> et eadem actio de provinciis introierit, quam facile tunc sit omnia impedire, et quam hoc Caesari<ique> qui sua causa rem publicam non curent sperent, non te fallit.*) Throughout these letters, Caelius vacillates between believing that Marcellus's inaction had to do with his inability to convene a sufficient number of supporters (as here, and at *Fam.* 8.2.2, where he allows Marcellus's patience to be strategic); or that it had to do with his own inefficiency—as at *Fam.* 8.10.3: *Nosti Marcellum, quam tardus et parum efficax sit, itemque Servius quam cunctator.* ('You know Marcellus, how slow and ineffective he is, and Servius too—a born procrastinator.') See also *Fam.* 8.1.2 (n. 36 above) for a similar implication.

8.9.2,[39] where the prosecution of Marcellus's cousin, C. Marcellus, consul-elect for the coming year, is holding up the timetable for debating the Gallic provinces even further,[40] and Cicero is told to prepare himself for the eventuality that he may not be able to hand over his province to a successor, since the fate of his own provincial command is being tied to Caesar's in Gaul.[41] Caelius suggests that any discussion of Caesar's successor may have to wait until the following year.[42]

But the process of delay reaches perhaps its most spectacular anticlimax in the centrepiece of book 8: the eighth letter, dated to early October 51 BCE, in which Caelius opens his discussion of politics with the alluring promise of new information. A resolution concerning the provinces has passed and is transcribed for us, along with three *senatus auctoritates* (the motions that failed because they were vetoed), within the letter (*Fam.* 8.8.4):[43]

> *Quod ad rem publicam pertinet, omnino multis diebus exspectatione Galliarum actum nihil est; aliquando tamen, saepe re dilata et graviter acta et plane perspecta Cn. Pompei voluntate in eam partem ut eum decedere post Kal. Mart. placeret, senatus consultum quod tibi misi factum est auctoritatesque perscriptae.*

---

39. This letter, dated to September 2 by Caelius himself (at *Fam.* 8.9.2, see p. 60 n. 20 below), falls chronologically after *Fam.* 8.8, which was sent after September 29, when the debate in the senate at which the *senatus consultum* (transcribed within *Fam.* 8.8) was drafted took place.

40. *Fam.* 8.9.2: 'I told you earlier that there would be a debate on the provinces on the Ides of August, but Consul-Elect Marcellus's trial has upset this timetable. The matter was put off to the Kalends. They'd not even been able to muster a quorum.' (*De provinciis quod tibi scripseram Id. Sext. actum iri, interpellárat iudicium Marcelli, consulis designati. In Kal. <res> reiecta est; ne frequentiam quidem efficere potuerant.*)

41. *Fam.* 8.9.2: 'There is no way clear to the appointment of a successor, because the Gauls, for which a veto is in readiness, are being linked with the other provinces. I am sure of this. That is another reason why I'm writing to you, so that you prepare yourself for this outcome.' (*Nam non expeditur successio, quoniam Galliae, quae habent intercessorum, in eandem condicionem quam ceterae provinciae vocantur. Hoc mihi non est dubium; quo tibi magis scripsi ut ad hunc eventum te parares.*)

42. *Fam.* 8.9.2: 'I'm despatching this letter on September 2, and up to that date nothing substantial accomplished. It looks to me as though the entire question will be relegated to next year....' (*Has litteras a. d. IIII Non. Sept. dedi, cum ad eam diem ne profligatum quidem quicquam erat. Ut video, causa haec integra in proximum annum transferetur....*)

43. Lintott 2008, 269 notes how unusual it is to find the transcription of a *senatus consultum* in a letter. Both O'Brien Moore 1935, 804–8; and Schiller 1978, 451 note that the usual practice of depositing *senatus consulta* in an archive in the *aerarium Saturni* was not generally accompanied by the official publication of these texts; and that while their contents were occasionally communicated to interested parties (as here), this occurrence was exceptional.

Reorienting the Collection

Senatus Consultum, auctoritates:

'Prid. Kal. Oct. in aede Apollinis. Scrib. adfuerunt L. Domitius Cn. f. Fab. Ahenobarbus, Q. Caecilius Q. f. Fab. Metellus Pius Scipio, L. Villius L. f. Pom. Annalis, C. Septimius T. f. Quir., C. Lucilius C. f. Pup. Hirrus, C. Scribonius C. f. Pom. Curio, L. Ateius L. f. An. Capito, M. Eppius M. f. Ter. [sal.]

Quod M. Marcellus cos. v. f. de provinciis consularibus, d. e. r. i. c.,[44] *uti L. Paulus C. Marcellus cos., cum magistratum inissent, [a. d.] ex [X] Kal. Mart. quae in suo magistratu futurae essent de consularibus provinciis ad senatum referrent, neve quid prius ex Kal. Mart. ad senatum referrent, neve quid coniunctim [de ea re referrentur a consiliis], utique eius rei causa per dies comitialis senatum haberent senatusque cons. facerent et, cum de ea re ad senatum referretur, a consuliis, qui eorum in CCC iudicibus essent, s. f. s.*[45] *adducere liceret; si quid d. e. r. ad populum pl. ve lato opus esset, uti Ser. Sulpicius M. Marcellus cos., praetores, tr. q. pl., quibus eorum videretur, ad populum pl. ve ferrent; quod <si> ii non tulissent, uti quicumque deinceps essent ad populum pl. ve ferrent. C.*[46]

As far as politics go, absolutely nothing was done for many days, pending a decision about the Gallic provinces. At last, however, after several postponements, and serious discussions, and when it seemed clear that Pompey was in favour of Caesar quitting his province after March 1, a decree of the senate was passed, which I'm sending you, and the following resolutions that were recorded.

Decree of the Senate. Resolutions. 'On this 29th day of September, in the temple of Apollo. Present at the drafting of the decree: L. Domitius Ahenobarbus, son of Gnaeus, of the tribe Fabia; Q. Caecilius Metellus Pius Scipio, son of Quintus, of the tribe Fabia; L. Villius Annalis, son

---

44. Shackleton Bailey 1977, 403 explicates the abbreviation v.f. as *verba fecit* and d.e.r.i.c. as *de ea re ita censuere*.

45. See Shackleton Bailey 1977, 403 on s.f.s as *sine fraude sua*.

46. Both Watt 1982, 243 and Shackleton Bailey 1977, 165 follow Mommsen in printing 'C.' at the close of this resolution rather than the anomalous letters 'i. u.', which the MSS transmit. See Shackleton Bailey 1977, 403 for discussion of various attempts to make sense of the mysterious abbreviation, which some other editors convert to i.n.: *intercessit nemo*, 'no one vetoed'. He notes that seven of the *senatus consulta* collected in Bruns 1909 end with the abbreviation 'C.' (*censuere*, 'they proposed/moved/voted').

104   SOUVENIRS OF CICERO

of Lucius, of the tribe Pomptina; C. Septimius, son of Titus, of the tribe Quirina; C. Lucilius Hirrus, son of Gaius, of the tribe Pupinia; C. Scribonius Curio, son of Gaius, of the tribe Pomptina; L. Ateius Capito, son of Lucius, of the tribe Aniensis; M. Eppius, son of Marcus, of the tribe Teretina.

Inasmuch as the consul Marcellus has addressed the question of the consular provinces, it was thus resolved that: Lucius Paullus and Gaius Marcellus, the consuls, when they have entered their office, on or after the kalends of March that shall fall within their year of office, should bring the matter of the consular provinces before the senate, and should not give precedence to any other motion after the Kalends of March, or to any other motion in combination with that one; further, that they may hold a meeting of the senate, and pass a decree of the senate, for this purpose on comitial days. And that in bringing this matter before the senate, it shall be lawful to call in those senators who are on the roll of the 300 jurors without their incurring a penalty. Further, if there be need for proposals touching this matter to be brought before the people or plebs, that the Consuls Ser. Sulpicius and M. Marcellus, the praetors, and tribunes of the plebs, whosoever of them see fit, bring such proposals before people or plebs; and that, if they do not do so, then their successors bring such proposals before people or plebs.'
They voted for it.

Here, finally, we encounter the transcript of a decree, one of those enclosures that Caelius mentioned in the opening letter but which we so seldom see, and the promise of significant news that we expect such enclosures to bring. Yet this opening resolution, stipulating that the consuls of 50 BCE should prioritize reopening a general discussion about the reallocation of consular provinces from March 1, 50 BCE, was the only measure that passed. And the significance of its passage is all but cancelled out by the vetoing of the subsequent three motions, which aimed at reinforcing the application of the original resolution to the specific case of Caesar in Gaul and which Caelius also proceeds to transcribe in full: first stating that no veto be allowed to block a resolution concerning the provinces when discussion of their reassignment reopened on March 1; next that soldiers wishing to be discharged from Caesar's army be allowed to make their case before the senate; and finally that almost all the provinces *apart from Caesar's* be assigned to ex-praetors, so as to prioritize discussion of Gaul when the general discussion about the reallocation of consular provinces reopened on March 1.[47] The solemn transcription of each of these measures, along with the record of their being vetoed by tribunes working in Caesar's interests,[48] makes clear that whatever the resolution that passed may stipulate about the reassignment of consular provinces having to be discussed after March 1, its application to Caesar's province was moot.[49] Such that despite the pomp of its official language, and the layers of textual and verbal packaging that heighten our expectation of significant news emerging, the decree itself turns out to be an empty lure, one that stipulates only that the question of the Gallic succession, which has been repeatedly deferred throughout this book of letters, is to be definitively deferred again until March 1 (and quite possibly for even longer, in light of the vetoing of those measures that were designed to reinforce the application of its opening resolution to Caesar and Gaul). The significant information contained within this letter turns out to be not so much the decree itself but Pompey's reaction to it:[50] having previously refused to be drawn into definitive statements about the Gallic succession,[51] on this meeting he did allow himself to take up a position, claiming that while he could not in justice make

---

47. The fourth resolution (*Fam.* 8.8.8) set aside the eight praetorian provinces (Sicily, Sardinia, Africa, Macedonia, Asia, Bithynia, Crete, and Cyrene) as well as Cilicia to be assigned to praetors, leaving only Syria and the Gauls for discussion (since Pompey's command in Spain had already been renewed). See Shackleton Bailey 1977, 405–6 for discussion of why the decree lists eight praetorian provinces, when Crete and Cyrene are widely held to be administered jointly (his suggestion is that they were in fact governed separately by this stage).

48. Gruen 1974, 464 describes the latter three resolutions as 'transparently anti-Caesarian', and hence their vetoing by tribunes on Caesar's side.

49. For the blocking of motion two meant that any resolution unfavourable to Caesar's interests might well be vetoed, and the failure of motion four meant that Caesar's province might again be exempted from the discussion anyway. On this, see Morstein-Marx 2021, 270–71. But see Bonnefond-Coudry 1989, 566–7 on the significance of the motions vetoed—that is, the importance of their transcription for registering the will of the senate.

50. It is for this reason that van den Bruwaene 1953 sees Pompey as the force behind the decree's anti-Caesarian resolutions.

51. Earlier in *Fam.* 8, Pompey had resisted such attempts to goad him into making definitive statements about Caesar, relying on the platitudes that Caelius presents in *Fam.* 8.1.3 as his trademark: see *Fam.* 8.4.4: 'For in the course of the discussion, Pompey let fall the remark that it was every man's duty to render obedience to the senate.' (*Nam in disputando coniecit illam vocem Cn. Pompeius, omnis oportere senatui dicto audientis esse.*) See Morstein Marx 2021, 271 n. 36 for discussion of the reasons for his shift position in *Fam.* 8.8, including the fact that with Caesar about to spend a second consecutive winter in Gaul the two men had had little opportunity to consult one another; and Gruen 1974, 464–5 for the difficult course Pompey was trying to tread at this time between serving his compact with Caesar and cultivating his aristocratic friends.

a decision about Caesar's provinces before March 1,[52] he would not hesitate to act after this date.[53]

If the information that we have been after turns out to be an empty promise, leading us towards the ever-receding prospect of a decision about Caesar's recall, wherein lies the spectacle in this book? Reading instead for the medium *as* the message, we turn away from the elusive information that the letters put off yielding,[54] to the correspondents who communicate it. Book 8 narrates the story of their relationship against the backdrop of an imminent and then current civil war, by organizing their letters from this period into a (more-or-less) chronological sequence. The story that this narrative gives us is one of old friends and alliances shifting as they take sides in the civil conflict underway. This is a story of the social network in a state of radical realignment. Caelius is our chief exemplar of this process, and his makes for

---

52. As Shackleton Bailey 1977, 406 reminds us, intervening before this date would contravene the terms of the *lex Pompeia Licinia*.

53. Caelius follows up his summary of this statement with an account of Pompey's subsequent exchanges with senators who were evidently trying to provoke the general into a more definitive stance (*Fam.* 8.8.9): 'When asked how he would react if someone attempted to veto a decision, Pompey replied that it would make no difference whether Caesar refused to obey the senate or put someone up to obstruct its decrees (*dixit hoc nihil interesse, utrum C. Caesar senatui dicto audiens futurus non esset an pararet qui senatum decernere non pateretur*), and when asked what if Caesar should become consul and keep his army at the same time, Pompey replied, "What if my own son should be minded to lay his stick across my shoulders (*Quid si filius meus fustem mihi impingere volet*)?"' Caelius suggests that these statements led people to suspect that a breach had arisen between Pompey and Caesar, while at the same time refraining from committing himself to the belief that this was necessarily Pompey's intention. See *Fam.* 8.1.3 (and also *Fam.* 8.9.5) for Caelius's view about the gap between Pompey's words and thoughts and his inability to disguise his real desires in spite of such deliberately obscure pronouncements. For more examples of Pompey's vague platitudes elsewhere in Cicero's letters, and discussion, see Gruen 1974, 464 (with n. 54).

54. Although the later letters in *Fam.* 8 do tell us of subsequent developments in the senate that served to exacerbate tensions in 50 BCE, they are frequently so embedded in Caelius's preoccupation with other affairs that the significant information is difficult to extract: thus in *Fam.* 8.11.3 (composed in April 50 BCE), we do hear of the senate's attempt to fix a deadline of the Ides of November 50 for Caesar to leave his province, along with Pompey's support for this new deadline (see Morstein Marx 2021, 279 for discussion). However, the two long opening sections of this letter are taken up with discussion of the votes for Cicero's *supplicatio*. Likewise, at *Fam.* 8.13, we hear of M. Marcellus's (utterly abortive) attempt to end the deadlock caused by Curio's proposal that both Caesar and Pompey give up their commands, by moving that the consuls apply pressure on tribunes to withdraw their veto—but this time, the information is briefly tagged on to Caelius's congratulations to Cicero about Tullia's betrothal to Dolabella; and we hear again of this deadlock in *Fam.* 8.14.2, where it is tagged onto gossip about Domitius Ahenobarbus's failure to be elected to the college of augurs. Caelius's repeated habit of appending discussion of the *res publica* onto matters of personal interest for Cicero may be construed as reckless levity, on the one hand or as charming *familiaritas* on the other.

Reorienting the Collection 107

a spectacular case study. Fittingly, the letters that matter most for the story of his and Cicero's friendship and fallout are found, arena-like, in the frame of book 8.

Theirs is a friendship that begins in deep affection at the start of the book—as witnessed above all in Caelius's boast at the start of *Fam.* 8.3 about having fulfilled his promise to write to Cicero regularly, and subsequently in his description of the hole that Cicero's absence has left in Rome (*Fam.* 8.3.1):

> *Estne? vici et tibi saepe, quod negaras discedens curaturum tibi, litteras mitto? Est, si quidem perferuntur quas do. Atque hoc ego diligentius facio quod, cum otiosus sum, plane ubi delectem otiolum[55] meum non habeo. Tu cum Romae eras, hoc mihi certum ac iucundissimum vacanti negotium erat, tecum id oti tempus consumere; idque non mediocriter desidero, ut mihi non modo solus esse sed Romae te profecto solitudo videatur facta.*

> Is it so? Have I won? And do I constantly send you letters, a thing you declared on leaving Rome that I would never bother to do for you? It is so, provided, of course, that the letters I'm sending reach you. And I do so all the more diligently because, when I'm at liberty, I have simply nowhere to enjoy my scrap of leisure. When you were at Rome, it used to be the greatest pleasure of my idle hours to spend that leisure time with you. And I miss it so badly, that not only do I seem solitary to myself, but your departure seems to have brought about a general solitude in Rome.

Caelius's reference to his habit of spending time in Cicero's company reminds us of the close relationship between them that Cicero gestures towards at the start of the *Pro Caelio*, when trying to establish Caelius's *pudicitia* by reminding the jurors of his *tirocinium* under Cicero.[56] *Fam.* 8.3 updates this picture to show that in latter years the obligations of youth have become the voluntary habits of fond friendship.[57] Later on in this letter, when Caelius

---

55. Both Watt 1982, 233 and Shackleton Bailey 1977, 387 print *otium*, the latter despite claiming to be 'reluctant to follow Sjögren in discarding *otiolum*' (the reading of Victorius, correcting *otiosum* as transmitted in M). While following Watt's text elsewhere, I print *otiolum* as it seems too Caelian to resist.

56. Cf. Cic. *Cael.* 9 for Cicero's claim that as soon as Caelius assumed the *toga virilis* his father entrusted him to Cicero's care for the *tirocinium fori*, and that Caelius was thereafter only ever seen in the company either of his father or of Cicero or of Crassus.

57. The feeling was evidently mutual. In describing how much he misses Rome to Caelius in *Fam.* 2, Cicero singles out Caelius's company as the thing he misses most. See esp. *Fam.*

asks Cicero to write and dedicate a σύνταγμα to himself, we are reminded again of the *Pro Caelio*, which, as a published text answers most readily to Caelius's specific request that the tribute Cicero should dedicate to him be of an educational character.[58] Yet for the reader of *ad Fam.*, there is another possible candidate for this tribute: none other than *Fam.* 8 itself, a book of letters that becomes authorized by Cicero once it works its way into his letter collection and which possesses an educational profile of its own. However, the choice between these two texts is a poignant one. For whereas the *Pro Caelio* casts Caelius as the wayward *adulescens* of Roman comedy, and its educational message is a concomitantly light-hearted one, in *Fam.* 8 Caelius's waywardness has dangerous and tragic consequences: the educational value of this portrait (drawn from the negative *exemplum* that the end of his life and career present) is at the cost of Caelius's life. Given the deep affection that it outlines between Cicero and Caelius at the start, and the souring of their relationship that it subsequently tracks, this book is an open wound at the heart of *ad Fam.*—the fatal gut thrust that we readers witness in the civil war arena sketched out for us at the core of this collection.

The affection of *Fam.* 8.3 transitions from the jokey banter and levity that characterizes Caelius's accounts of the unfolding drama in the senate in subsequent letters, to concern, once civil war begins, as the two friends adopt different courses. In *Fam.* 8.16, composed in April 49 BCE, Caelius, who has by this stage sided with Caesar,[59] warns Cicero of the danger of abandoning his current position of neutrality and joining the anti-Caesarian opposition.[60]

2.11.1: 'You cannot believe how much I yearn for Rome, and particularly for you.' (*Mirum me desiderium tenet urbis, incredibile meorum atque in primis tui.*); and *Fam.* 2.12.2: 'All the profits of a province are not to be compared with a single little stroll, a single chat with you.' (*Cum una mehercule ambulatiuncula atque uno sermone nostro omnis fructus provinciae non confero.*)

58. *Fam.* 8.3.3: 'My wish is that among all your many literary monuments, there should be one that hands down to posterity the memory of our friendship.' (*<Volo> aliquod ex tam multis tuis monumentis exstare quod nostrae amicitiae memoriam posteris quoque prodat.*) 'I suppose you'll ask what kind of thing I want. You'll think of something most suitable sooner than I (acquainted as you are with every kind of learning). But let it be, while especially relevant to myself, of such a generally educational character as to have a wide circulation.' (*Cuiusmodi velim, puto, quaeris. Tu citius, qui omnem nosti disciplinam, quod maxime convenit excogitabis, genere tamen quod et ad nos pertineat et διδασκαλίαν quandam, ut versetur inter manus, habeat.*)

59. Dettenhofer 1992, 94–98 identifies the personal enmities (against certain Pompeians) driving Caelius's decision to side with Caesar.

60. *Fam.* 8.16.1 and 8.16.5: 'In the name of your own life chances and your children, I beg and beseech you, Cicero, to take no step to the serious detriment of your safety and assured position.' (*Per fortunas tuas, Cicero, per liberos te oro et obsecro ne quid gravius de salute et incolumitate tua consulas.*) 'If you imagine that Caesar's policy will be the same as before as regards letting

Reorienting the Collection

The tone turns finally to acrimony, when Caelius grows disillusioned with the side that he has chosen and recriminates Cicero for not having given him better advice earlier.[61] The final letter in book 8 (composed early in the year 48 BCE, after Caelius had become praetor) offers hints of the course that he would subsequently come to take, joining a breakaway rebellion against Caesar when the latter refused to support his proposed program of debt relief.[62] Caelius was killed when Caesar crushed the rebellion later on that year.[63] Notably, the onset of the anti-Caesarian stance that is revealed in this letter does not seem to have brought him any closer to Cicero (*Fam.* 8.17.1):

> *Ergo me potius in Hispania fuisse tum quam Formiis cum tu profectus es ad Pompeium! quod utinam aut Appius Claudius in <hac aut in> ista parte C. Curio, cuius amicitia me paulatim in hanc perditam causam imposuit! nam mihi sentio bonam mentem iracundia et amore ablatam.* **Tu [tu] porro, cum ad te, proficiscens Ariminum noctu venissem, dum mihi pacis mandata das ad Caesarem et mirificum civem agis, amici officium neglexisti neque mi consuluisti.**

---

his opponents off and proposing terms of peace, you are mistaken. His intentions, and even his expression of them, are grim and pitiless.' (*Si existimas eandem rationem fore Caesaris in dimittendis adversariis et condicionibus ferendis, erras; nihil nisi atrox et saevum cogitat atque etiam loquitur.*) 'Think it over again and again, Cicero, so as not to bring utter ruin on yourself and your friends, or knowingly and with your eyes open let yourself sink to that place from where you will not be able to see a way out.' (*Etiam atque etiam, Cicero, cogita, ne te tuosque omnis funditus evertas; ne te sciens prudensque eo demittas, unde exitum vides nullum esse.*) In his reply to this letter, *Fam.* 2.16 (Cicero's last transmitted letter to Caelius in *Fam.* 2), Cicero takes offence at Caelius's charge of improvidence (but manages some jokes at the end of the letter in an attempt to close on a lighter note).

61. Strasburger 1968, 36, following Caelius's suggestion to Cicero in *Fam.* 8.14.3 (before the outbreak of civil war) that Caesar's was the stronger side, rather than the better side, views Cicero's ultimate desertion from Caesar's camp as evidence of reluctant support for Caesar all along. Morstein-Marx 2021, 366–67 notes that such a view is at odds with the mercurial character of Caelius that emerges from his letters in *Fam.* 8; and follows Dio's suggestion that Caelius's desertion was caused by pique at Caesar's preferential treatment of the other praetor, Trebonius. Morstein-Marx also observes that Caelius's desertion comes after the death of Curio at Utica, whose own Caesarian allegiance had evidently influenced Caelius in his initial decision. It is notable that elsewhere *ad Fam.* groups Caelius and Curio together (Cicero's correspondence with these two figures makes up the bulk of *Fam.* 2, in which *Fam.* 2.1–7 are addressed to Curio, and *Fam.* 2.8–16 are addressed to Caelius).

62. Our main source for Caelius's activities as praetor is Caes. *BC.* 3.20.1; and Dio 42.22.2. See Dettenhofer 1992, 156–65 for discussion. Caesar's own proposals for debt relief (outlined at Caes. *BC.* 3.1) had been far more moderate: see *Att.* 7.1.1 and 7.7 for Cicero's reaction.

63. Caes. *BC.* 3.20–22; and Dio 42.22–5 provide the ancient accounts. See Gelzer 1968, 227–28 for discussion.

So I was in Spain instead of at Formiae when you set out to join Pompey! I only wish either that Appius Claudius were on our side, or that C. Curio were on yours; for it was my friendship with the latter that gradually persuaded me to join this lost cause. Indeed, I'm aware that I was robbed of my better judgment by anger on the one hand and affection on the other. **You too, when I came to see you on the eve of my departure for Rimini, while you were giving me messages of peace for Caesar, and playing quite the admirable citizen, yet you overlooked the duties of a friend, and failed to advise me properly.**

In this way, the book stages before our eyes the social consequences of civil war, wherein fathers and sons—or, in Cicero and Caelius's case, substitute fathers and proxy sons—fall out with each other when they take opposing sides.

The one-sided presentation of their correspondence in this book of letters serves this narrative, insofar as it forms part of the narrative performance of civil war, which has to be written from one side or another, and which requires us, as readers, to take sides too. In the event, both Caelius and Cicero end up changing sides in this civil conflict, albeit in different directions. Yet despite the fact that we are only ever ostensibly given Caelius's perspective in this book, we do not side with him: letters like this one reveal the petty motives driving his shifting allegiances, as a matter of purely personal affinities and rifts, and have been selected so as to show him taking a series of missteps, while the compromises and indecision that we know from other sources that Cicero displayed at this time are not revealed to us. This is the consequence of having one's letters transmitted in a letter collection that ultimately belongs to Cicero.

Conclusion

The blinkered perspective on events that this book of letters stages may serve the particular historical situation of civil war, but it has more far-reaching implications for the workings of social media systems in general. From this perspective, it is tempting to view the one-sided presentation of the correspondence as a comment on the constraints that social media systems place on our view of events as a result of their tendency to filter these events through our own interests and to see the fallout between Caelius and Cicero as a consequence of their exclusive communication channel. Admittedly, it is hard to square the image of the amphitheatre with this conclusion: this is a structure that offers the illusion at least of a 360-degree view of events (even if spectators could only ever take up a single viewpoint within this circular structure). The arena perhaps speaks best to the illusion of extraordinary viewing possibilities that social media systems bring with them. So let us conclude with an image that speaks more closely to the reality. It is an image that is directly brought to the reader's mind in this book of letters, with the mention of a particular character, Curio, who has promised to lend Caelius some panthers for his games, and whose own games, held shortly beforehand, we hear Caelius is at pains to try to surpass.[64] What the letters do not mention, but which many readers both contemporaneous with Caelius and Cicero and in later Roman history would have known, was that for the games that Curio staged to honour his dead father in 52 BCE, he devised a temporary amphitheatre for this purpose. This was an ingenious construction that provides perhaps one of our best examples from ancient Rome of a reversible technology of spectacle.

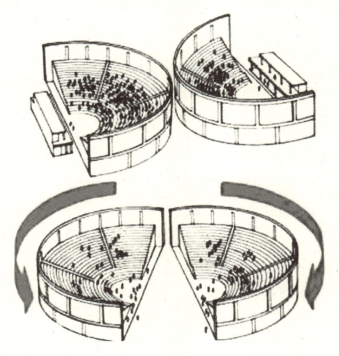

---

64. Besides the reference that Caelius makes to Curio's games at *Fam.* 8.8.10 and 8.9.3, readers of the collection are already primed for Curio's games by Cicero's letter to Curio at *Fam.* 2.3, in which he writes to Curio to tell him to exercise his *virtus* upon returning to Rome, rather than trying to curry favour by laying on spectacular shows to honour his recently deceased father. Futrell 2006, 16–18 brings out the optimate nuances of this letter.

SOUVENIRS OF CICERO

This reversible amphitheatre consisted of two semicircular theatres, which could rotate on a pivot to form an arena, so that the audience could use it to watch theatrical shows in the morning and gladiatorial games in the afternoon.[65] The striking sight of two theatres back to back, offering their respective audiences different perspectives on different shows, is an image that captures the effect of the presentation of correspondence in this letter collection. Additionally, it comments on the dynamics of social media systems more generally: the multiple different perspectives that they open onto events, but also the blind spots and forms of invisibility that they invariably produce as well.

---

65. Pliny *HN* 36.15.117–20 is our source for Curio's remarkable temporary (amphi)theatre. See Golvin 2012, 33 for discussion of the significance of this construction; and Futrell 2006, 57–58 for a more sceptical attitude as to whether ancient engineering was able to construct such a mechanism.

4

Ordering the Collection

HISTORY AND COUNTER-HISTORY IN *FAM.* 10–12

THE END OF the Republic, and emergence of a new system of governance, transforms the meanings of the letters included in *ad Fam.*, investing them with a significance that derives from the changes that took place at this turning point and in the era that followed. But that ending is also narrated within this letter collection, in ways that draw attention to its transformative significance for our interpretation of the collection as a whole. In *Fam.* 10–12, we encounter three books of letters, each of which narrates from a different viewpoint (or set of viewpoints) the events of 44–43 BCE, from after Caesar's death through to the battles of Mutina and their aftermath, in which it became increasingly clear that the republican cause was a lost one. Cicero's death before the Battle of Philippi means that the letter collection does not bear witness to the definitive defeat of republican hopes with the outcome of that battle. But that defeat is anticipated by the turn that events took in the spring and early summer of 43 BCE, which these books do recount: the battles of Mutina, in which both consuls died, thus prefigure the final showdown at Philippi, which killed off Brutus and Cassius. The 'end of the Republic' is thus incorporated into this letter collection, not just as a historical backstory that conditions the new meanings that all the letters take on when amassed in the collection but also as the *telos* towards which one of its major narratives moves. Cicero's prominent role in this story, and death because of it, anticipates (or, quite probably, reflects) the equation that Livy (and subsequent authors) draws between his (Cicero's) life and that of the

Souvenirs of Cicero. Francesca K. A. Martelli, Oxford University Press. © Oxford University Press 2024.
DOI: 10.1093/oso/9780197761960.003.0005

114   SOUVENIRS OF CICERO

Republic herself.[1] It does so all the more authoritatively by being delivered (posthumously) in Cicero's own words.

Of all the narratives that we have considered so far within *ad Fam.*, this one stands out because it is sustained across three adjacent books. This is another place where the organization of the collection intervenes in the narrative meanings that it generates, not through the positioning of books in the frame or centre of the collection but through their juxtaposition alongside one another. The fact that each of the three books covers the same period, and the same events, but from different perspectives, invites us to read them as a trilogy, one that offers a distinctly historiographical account, insofar as it plots events into discernible sequence. Yet as historical narratives go, this one is highly unusual. For one thing, its chronology does not span the three books, but the narrative is instead repeated anew, from a different perspective, in each one. These multiple perspectives have a destabilizing effect on our expectations of historical narrative and on our desire, in particular, to see events plotted into a single storyline, as we are instead made to see that it all happened differently, and at different times, for people located in different parts of the Roman world. Even the dating of the letters, rather than anchoring the chronology of events to precise dates, only emphasizes the gaps that open up between the sending and receiving of information.[2]

But as a historiographical narrative, *Fam.* 10–12 stands out above all because it is written by the losers. Historiographical accounts are normally written in retrospect by those who have survived periods of conflict, either because they were on the winning side or because they arrived at an accommodation with the victors. The narrative of *Fam.* 10–12 is unusual because it is written in large part by the resistance: by those who had most to lose and who did *not*, in large part, survive. Cicero and the majority of his correspondents were hoping for a different historical outcome to the one that finally emerged, and their letters, when placed in sequence, tell the story of the collapse of the Republic *despite* the hopes and desires that they harboured for an alternative historical outcome, one in which the Republic would be restored in some

---

1. In Livy's case, this equation underpins the very structure of his history, which culminates its history of the Republic with the death of Cicero. The influence of Livy's account (and Cicero's own word, esp. *Phil.* 2) on Sen. *Suas.* 6 reveals the extent to which this closural scene of Roman republican history was enshrined as such in the early empire by the declamation schools. On which see, Keeline 2018, 111–18. See also p. 7 n. 15 for additional scholarship on the equation drawn by these (and other) imperial authors between Cicero's death and the death of the Republic.

2. See my discussion on pp. 128–132.

shape or form. The repeated frustration of these hopes is one story that these letter books recount. But the desire for an alternative future is another, no less significant. Tension between these two narrative drives makes this historical account answer to the criteria of what we might call a 'counter-history', because of the negative effect that the republicans' aspirations for an alternative outcome has on the account that *Fam.* 10–12 give us of what did finally occur.

Counter-history, according to the distinct but parallel formulations of Amos Funkenstein and Michel Foucault, constitutes a genre of history writing in which the traditional master narratives of sovereign or religious power are dialectically inverted in order to allow the histories of the peoples that such power represses to emerge. Each of these historians situates the counter-history within a different tradition. For Funkenstein, the counter-history belongs to a polemical tradition of religious history writing, one that begins in the hostile targeting of the Biblical history of the Jews by other peoples in antiquity, and which is subsequently co-opted by the Jewish tradition in their hostile histories of Christianity.[3] Foucault, by contrast, sees the counter-history arising in the critical histories of nation states that emerge in sixteenth-century France and England, when political institutions and also institutions of knowledge, such as historiography, become instruments for the kinds of warfare that had previously been conducted by civilian armies.[4] For both historians, the counter-history is characterized by its systematic inversion of the values and judgments that are embedded in histories of the reigning hegemony and its recuperation of all that those histories exclude or negate.[5] In this sense, they are of a piece with Walter Benjamin's famous

---

3. Funkenstein 1986, 273–76 pursues this polemical religious tradition into the Reformation in his analysis of Protestant histories of the church at this time, in which heretics were reevaluated as the only true vestiges of Christianity in the time of its decay. Funkenstein 1993, 32–50 rounds out his earlier discussion of counter-history in the ancient and early modern periods by pursuing it into (secular) modernity: in Marx's history of capital as the history of the exploited underclasses and in the revisionist histories of the Jew that began emerging at the end of the nineteenth century. Funkenstein's idea of counter-history is indebted to the work of his student David Biale (esp. Biale 1979), who, however, takes a somewhat different view of its dynamics. See Biale 1999 for discussion.

4. Foucault 2003, esp. 65–84. Foucault's theory of the emergence of the counter-history does, however, share with Funkenstein's a strong sense of this being a racial discourse—specifically, a discourse about the struggle between races (which he sees taking place *within* the nation state).

5. Funkenstein 1986, 273 defines the counter-history as follows: 'The systematic exploitation of the adversary's most trusted sources against their overt intent: in the fortunate phrase of Walter Benjamin, counter-histories "comb the sources against the grain," as Marxist historiography indeed does to reconstruct the history of the victim rather than that of the victors.' Foucault 2003, 70, defining the counter-history against histories of national sovereignty that

insight from the seventh of his *Theses on the Philosophy of History* that there is no document of civilization which is not at the same time a document of barbarism.[6] Whether or not they are prepared to trace the counter-historical impulse back to antiquity (as Funkenstein does), or see it emerging for the first time in the sixteenth century (as Foucault does), for both these thinkers, as for Benjamin, the counter-history is the negative flipside of the dominant historical imaginary, and unfolds in dialectical relation to that imaginary's narrative of power.

Fam. 10–12 offers us a counter-history of the events of 44–43 BCE because its account of the developments that took place at Rome in this period are presented through the growing dismay of Cicero and his allies, as their hopes for an alternative historical outcome are gradually confounded. The historical narrative that these books give us is no triumphalist account of the birth of the principate, the form of sovereignty that would hold sway for centuries, and which, for Foucault, determines the historical discourse of 'the West' through to the end of the medieval period as its justification for and reinforcement of monarchical power.[7] What we are given instead is the precise opposite of this: an account not of the rise of the principate but of the fall of the Republic, one that sees events through their negative manifestation in the eyes of the victims. More precisely, the history of the victors and the counter-history of their victims coexist and interact with one another throughout these letter books in a reflection of the dialectical conflict between these two

---

seek to unify and subjugate, writes: 'Not only does this counter-history break up the unity of the sovereign law that imposes obligations; it also breaks the continuity of glory, into the bargain. It reveals that the light—the famous dazzling effect of power—is not something that petrifies, solidifies and immobilizes the entire social body, and thus keeps it in order; it is in fact a divisive light that illuminates one side of the social body but leaves the other side in shadow or casts it into darkness.'

6. While Funkenstein 1986, 273 acknowledges his debt to Benjamin, it is also worth highlighting that Benjamin himself belongs to the same Judaeo-Hebraic tradition that Funkenstein and others (e.g.. Biale 1979) identify with the counter-history. Foucault 2003, 71 also notably identifies counter-history as 'much closer to the mythico-religious discourse of the Jews than to the politico-legendary history of the Romans . . . at least from the Middle Ages onward, the Bible was the great form for the articulation of religious, moral and political protests against the power of kings and the despotism of the church.'

7. Cf. Foucault 2003, 66–69 for an account of the 'Jupiterian' history of sovereignty, which he regards as taking hold in the Roman period and dominating historiographical discourse up until the emergence of the counter-history in the sixteenth century. Foucault's survey of Roman historiography is notably partial: the examples that he cites are Livy and the early annalists.

narratives that extends well into the principate:[8] in the twin historiographical traditions that either celebrate Brutus and Cassius as liberators or damn them as *latrones* and *parricidae*, for example;[9] or in the historiographical tradition of Lucan and Tacitus, who use narrative forms such as epic and annalistic history that traditionally celebrate Rome's sovereign power, only to critique the new power structure of monarchy that had come to occupy the republican institutions that those narrative forms traditionally celebrated.[10]

The coexistence within *Fam.* 10–12 of two histories, the history of the victors and the counter-history of their victims, comes about, in part, as a result of superimposing one temporal perspective over another. For while the individual letters within each book are written in the present tense, without knowing how the story in which they participate will unfold, collectively, their narrative assemblage is informed by a retrospective knowledge and understanding of the final shape of that story. The tension between these different temporal perspectives pervades these three books of letters, where it is frequently expressed in the gap between expectation and outcome, as correspondents write letters anticipating a particular outcome only to find it met by an alternative reality in the letter placed after it. In this sense, the history that we find in *Fam.* 10–12 runs directly counter to the tradition of teleological historiography that Duncan Kennedy sees represented, above all, by the *Aeneid*, in which the past only gains meaning from a future that is known to the narrator (and his readers). As Kennedy puts it:[11]

> For there to be a shape or order to history, the 'future' (seen from whatever constitutes the narrative's 'present') must, at some level, be *known.*

---

8. This dialectic well illustrates the dynamic that Gallagher and Greenblatt 2000, 52 identify as key to the life of the counter-history as Funkenstein formulates it: namely, that the counter-history has no independent existence apart from 'mainstream' historical narratives; rather, the two coexist in a constant process of substitution and exchange, as narratives of sovereign power are replaced by the counter-histories of those whom that power suppresses only for these to become the dominant narratives in turn and so on.

9. See Rawson 1986 for an overview of those traditions. Rawson 1986, 101 notes that the very terms *latrones* and *parricidae* used by later writers to describe Brutus and Cassius are themselves a reflection of the rhetoric used in the civil war, in which both sides used the same terms of abuse to condemn the other.

10. Willis 2017 draws on the subversive counter-history of Lucan's *Bellum Civile* to counter the claim made by Foucault 2003, 68 that all ancient Roman history is the 'Jupiterian' history of sovereignty (see p. 84 n. 7). Lucan's epic, however, belongs to a larger Roman counter-historical tradition.

11. Kennedy 1999, 29.

'How it was' always involves 'how-it-was-to-be': we are asked not only to look back to a point in the past, when that point was the 'present', but also to look forward from that point to the *telos* of the moment which is the focus for the interests and desires which motivate the narrative act, and which the narrative act seeks to satisfy. It is from this shuttle, simultaneously backwards and forwards, that historical representations derive their sense of closure and fulfilment.

The historical narrative that *Fam.* 10–12 yields differs from this model of historiography precisely because the authors of the letters that make up this history do not know the future, whereas those who organize them into sequence do. The different historical perspectives possessed by these two sets of narrators—the letter writers on the one hand, and the editors or compilers on the other—is the source of this narrative's many ironies, as readers share the editor-narrators' hindsight and superior understanding of how the events that the letter-writers are caught up in would subsequently unfold.

Or do they? For this view of the narrative of *Fam.* 10–12 assumes that the narrative *telos*, from the perspective of our moment of reading, is definitively foreclosed. Against this view, we might consider the residual currency that this letter collection retains in the imperial period and beyond as a remnant of a time that the period of monarchy cannot entirely repress. From this perspective, the narrative *telos* of this history is not completely closed, and the potential for a different outcome that Cicero and many of his correspondents hope for remains to some degree open in the minds of readers. This openness speaks to the resistance that monarchical rule continues to inspire in Rome for some time and in the efforts that subsequent emperors periodically took to hand certain forms of power back to the senate. According to this view, it is not the foreclosure of history that strikes the reader when reading *Fam.* 10–12, but the hopes for an alternative outcome that precede it. Again and again, the reader is presented with the alternative narrative desires that the historical actors involved in this story harboured in their experiential present before these were cancelled by the path that history actually took. It is these alternative historical possibilities that are missing, or that are at least much scarcer, in a straightforward historical narrative written purely in the preterite.[12] The

---

12. This is a point emphasized by Osgood 2006, 27 in his discussion of the value of reading Cicero's letters to Atticus as a source for the period immediately after Julius Caesar's assassination: 'Later historical narratives tend to clarify these months by describing separately the actions of Antony and the man who would become his chief rival, Octavian. They judge these actions from hindsight. . . . Cicero's letters, by contrast, suggest other courses events could have

letters give us access to the present tense, and to the uncertain (and unclosed) future, of historical time, the residual possibilities of which may continue to haunt the moment of the letters' compilation and the subsequent moments of their reading—right up to our own time.

But the dialectical inversion of victor history that these books of letters present entails a further set of inversions or negations for the victims who are implicitly raised to the position of victors through the status that they acquire as martyrs. For however much Cicero and most of his correspondents might seek to present themselves as the obverse of their opponents, the collection affords us glimpses of alternative viewpoints from where they are seen as all too similar to the enemy. These are moments where the conflict is presented as one between parties and social classes, rather than ideologies, and where the resemblances between the two factions involved are seen as stronger than any differences. The perspectives that produce these views inevitably come from below the social echelons of Cicero's epistolary peers and from outside the Roman state: from the soldiers fighting on the ground and from those foreign peoples who stand outside Roman *imperium*. In this sense, *Fam.* 10–12 offers a counter-history that answers more precisely to Benjamin's idea of brushing history against the grain, because it incorporates the critical viewpoint of Rome's social underclasses and of those who stand outside her polity.

Profectio et Reversio *(i): Dialectical History in* Fam. *10*

The counter-historical status of this narrative is impressed on readers at a glance at the names of the correspondents who feature most prominently in the first two books. Book 10 is dominated by a sequence of letters exchanged between Cicero and L. Munatius Plancus,[13] book 11 by a correspondence between Cicero and Decimus Brutus.[14] These two men had been pre-appointed by Caesar to take up the consulship together in 42 BCE, a future event that

---

taken, and are thereby truer to the total uncertainty of the period.' See also White 2010, 139 on the value of reading *Fam.* 10–12 as a historical resource: 'Cicero was reacting and contributing to events before they had been emplotted into the historical narrative that we know, and with a less informed idea than we have of the direction in which events were moving.'

13. *Fam.* 10.1–24.

14. *Fam.* 11.4–26.

Cicero anticipates with anxious hope in the opening letter of *Fam.* 10,[15] but which, as we know, will never actually materialize: D. Brutus will be killed before the year 43 ends, trying to escape Italy to join his cousin Marcus in Macedonia;[16] and Plancus will switch to the other side,[17] sharing the consulship of 42 BCE with one of the triumvirs (Lepidus).[18] The hypothetical scenario that Cicero can barely bring himself to articulate in his opening letter to Plancus—that Plancus's consulship will take place in a *res publica* that is only one in name[19]—is the historical outcome that will materialize outside the parameters of this letter book, which we read with the benefit of this hindsight, knowing the extent to which history will swerve away from its desired course.[20]

---

15. *Fam.* 10.1.1: 'But what concerns me is my country, and in particular, dear Plancus, the anxious anticipation of your consulship, which is so distant that we can only hope that we can carry on breathing until the Republic reaches that day.' (*Sed me patria sollicitat in primisque, mi Plance, exspectatio consulatus tui, quae ita longa est ut optandum <vix> sit ut possimus ad id tempus rei publicae spiritum ducere*). Morello 2017, 172 notes the irony of this passage: Cicero, who dies in December 43 BCE, would not be able to keep breathing until the year of Plancus's consulship.

16. D. Brutus's death, at the treacherous hands of Camilus, a Gallic chieftan known to him, here acting on Antony's orders, receives a particularly colourful account in App. *B. Civ.* 3.97–98.

17. App. *B. Civ.* 3.97.

18. Lepidus's consulship was decided along with the pre-appointment of many other magistracies for the following five years at the triumvirs' conference at Bononia in November 43 BCE (see App. *B. Civ.* 4.2–4). Morello 2017, 172–73 notes how it is *this* consular pair that gives form to book 10, which opens and closes with letters either to or from Plancus and Lepidus respectively.

19. *Fam.* 10.1.1: 'For what hope can there possibly be in a republic in which everything has been demolished by the armed force of one so violent and extreme, in which neither the senate nor the people have any power, in which there are neither laws nor law courts, nor any semblance or trace of a state?' (*Quae potest enim spes esse in ea re publica in qua hominis impotentissimi atque intemperantissimi armis oppressa sunt omnia, et in qua nec senatus nec populus vim habet ullam nec leges ullae sunt nec iudicia nec omnino simulacrum aliquod ac vestigium civitatis?*).

20. That swerve is made to appear all the more dramatic because of the overt narrative parallelism between the letter sequences of Cicero and Plancus in *Fam.* 10 and of Cicero and D. Brutus in *Fam.* 11: both sets of correspondence open with Plancus and Decimus Brutus campaigning in their respective provinces in Gaul, and seeking honours for military successes there (*Fam.* 10.2; *Fam.* 11.4), track the events leading up to and following the battle(s) of Mutina with a series of letters that see Cicero exhorting the two men to resist Antony at all costs (cf. esp. the parallel refrain to each of these men to make their ending match their beginning by finishing Antony off in *Fam.* 10.13.2 and *Fam.* 11.5.3), and close with the two men joining forces with one another, each in a spirit of despondence (*Fam.* 10.13; and *Fam.* 11.26). The parallel movement of these narratives is captured particularly eloquently by Decimus Brutus's final letter to Cicero, which sees him marching north to join Plancus, whose narrative in the collection precedes his own, the spatial trajectory of D. Brutus's journey neatly complementing the narrative trajectory of his story.

The sequence of letters in *Fam.* 10 anticipates that swerve away from this preordained plan, in that it is dominated by letters to and from a number of protagonists who changed sides: men who professed loyalty (with varying degrees of credibility) to the republican cause up until a certain point before betraying the Republic to side with Antony (and, at a later stage, Octavian). The correspondence with Plancus is followed by an exchange between Cicero and Lepidus (who publicly defected from the republican side in mid-May),[21] which is in turn interspersed with a sequence of letters addressed to Cicero by Asinius Pollio (who defected later that summer).[22] While neither Plancus's nor Pollio's defections are recounted within this (or any other) book of letters, they are anticipated by the spectacular moment of Lepidus's transfer of loyalties in the closing letter of this book,[23] an action that confers meaning retrospectively on all the letters that precede it. Yet even as this book of letters anticipates the transfer of loyalties that will help to bring down the republican cause, its main focus is an alternative narrative, one in which Cicero will manage to persuade these men of wavering loyalty to stay on the republican side. In containing these two narratives, *Fam.* 10 provides a perfect introduction to the counter-historical dialectic of *Fam.* 10–12 as a whole, insofar as it stages the interaction of history and counter-history as a narrative movement in which certain protagonists transfer from the side of the losers to the side of the winners.[24] If the chief task of counter-history is to tell the story of the victims or losers, while that of 'sovereign history' is to tell the story of the victors, this book of letters stages the interaction between these two narrative poles by focusing on figures who move from one side to the other.

But if the historical narrative that this book of letters recounts is shadowed by a counter-history in which the possibility of things turning out otherwise is maintained, and vice versa, it is not just the three turncoats who embody this dialectical movement. Cicero himself is presented to us from the outset as a figure who has also changed course. This is made clear to readers

---

21. *Fam.* 10.27, *Fam.* 10.34a, and *Fam.* 10.34b are addressed by Lepidus to Cicero.

22. *Fam.* 10.31–33 are all addressed by Asinius Pollio to Cicero.

23. *Fam.* 10.35 (an official despatch addressed to the senate and people of Rome). Lepidus's excuse was that his army were threatening mutiny. See Osgood 2006, 57 for the credibility of Lepidus's claim: other letters in *Fam.* 10 (e.g., *Fam.* 10.11.2 and *Fam.* 10.15.3) attest the disaffection of Lepidus's army, especially after the slaughter of Forum Gallorum.

24. Syme 1939, 180 captures the counter-historical logic of this shift in his acerbic comment: 'Plancus joined the side of the 'parricides' and 'brigands', as he had so recently termed them.'

in the hopeful endorsement that he gives (or seems to give) to Caesar's pre-appointment of Plancus as consul in the opening letter of book 10, which marks a conspicuous departure from his former disapproval of the dictator's practice of pre-appointing (or even just appointing) magistrates.[25] But it is above all represented in an abortive trip to Greece that he makes shortly before the correspondence of *Fam.* 10 begins, which is highlighted at the start of the book and comes to symbolize all his subsequent prevarications. Indeed, his guilt about this episode is presented as a driving factor behind his attempts to persuade Plancus and the others to stay on the republican side. The process of changing sides may distance Lepidus, Pollio, and Plancus from Cicero, but it also turns out to be a point of resemblance between them and him, a preliminary demonstration that there is less to choose between the two sides than Cicero might prefer to think.[26]

The opening letter of book 10 introduces the resemblance that Plancus and Cicero share on the basis of their vacillatory behaviour with programmatic urgency. Written in early September, following the trip to Greece that Cicero had embarked upon but cut short upon hearing of certain measures of resistance to Antony in the senate, and shortly after his delivery in the senate of *Philippics* 1, which it echoes throughout, *Fam.* 10.1 tells us that the narrative of this book (and of the two that follow it) is also the story of the *Philippics*.[27] These fourteen speeches, in which Cicero managed to galvanize the senate against Antony, were delivered at a series of senate meetings (and the occasional *contio*) that took place from early September 44 to late April 43 BCE, and thus span

---

25. This disapproval emerges above all in *Att.* 14.6.2: 'Is it not lamentable that we should be upholding the very things which made us hate Caesar? Are we even to have Consuls and Tribunes of his choosing for two years to come?' See also *Att.* 14.9.2 for similar feelings. Cicero clearly did, however, see the expediency of publicly supporting the proposal to ratify Caesar's *acta*, including his pre-appointment of consuls and other magistracies (see *Phil.* 1.16–17). And, as Watkins 1997, 79 notes, Cicero's change of position on this score is marked above all in *Philippic* 3 (originally delivered on December 20 44 BCE), which closes with the motion that the senate confirm D. Brutus and Plancus, specifically identified as consul-designates, in their respective provinces. See esp. *Phil.* 3.38 for the senate's instructions.

26. One of the most notable instances of Cicero changing course in the period that these letter books cover is his initial recruitment to participate in the second embassy to negotiate peace terms with Antony—and his subsequent refusal to do so (justified in *Phil.* 12.5–6,12.17, and subsequently in *Phil.* 13.47–8). It is striking that this particular change of course is never mentioned within the narrative of *Fam.* 10–12 (although, like all his vacillatory behaviour, it is arguably present under erasure in the examples of his tergiversation that these books do record).

27. Morello 2017, 171 describes *Fam.* 10 as 'the behind-the-scenes companion piece to the *Philippics*'.

Ordering the Collection 123

the same period that the letters of *Fam.* 10–12 cover, even if the letters extend beyond late April into May and even a little later.[28] The *Philippics* famously depict Cicero at the high point of his career[29]—at a moment of political influence not seen since his consulship—and stop before his hopes of conquering Antony fell away. In extending the narrative beyond the point of *Philippics* 14, the letters narrate part of the story of how and why the *Philippics* failed. But the opening letter of *Fam.* 10 also offers insights into the intentions behind Cicero's decision to deliver and publish the *Philippics* in the first place—insights that go some way towards destabilizing their perlocutionary force.

Fam. 10.1 opens with strong reminiscences of the language of *Philippics* 1, which plunge the reader directly into the discourse that that speech instantiates.[30] Like *Philippics* 1, the letter that opens book 10 begins by reminding its addressee of Cicero's decision to abandon his departure for Greece and return to Rome in answer to the call of the *res publica*. Yet while the reference to these movements holds across the two texts, the phrasing shifts in ways that stagger the alignment between them. *Philippics* 1 begins by presenting Cicero's rationale for his abortive sojourn to and early return from Greece as a preface to what he has to say about the state of the *res publica* in a striking temporal clause (*Phil.* 1.1):

> **Antequam de republica, patres conscripti, dicam ea, quae dicenda hoc tempore arbitror, exponam vobis breviter consilium et profectionis et reversionis meae.** *Ego cum sperarem aliquando ad vestrum consilium auctoritatemque rem publicam esse* **revocatam,** *manendum mihi statuebam, quasi in vigilia quadam consulari ac senatoria.*

> **Before I say what I think needs to be said about the state at this time, I shall briefly set out for you the plan behind my departure and return.** As long as I held out hope that the state had been **recalled** to your guidance and authority, I decided that I ought to stay, as if in a kind of vigil—one fitting for a man of consular and even senatorial rank.

---

28. *Fam.* 10.24 (the latest dated letter within *ad Fam.*) is dated to July 43 BCE; *Fam.* 11.14–15, 21, and 24–26 are dated to June 43; as are *Fam.* 12.8–10, along with *Fam.* 12.13, 15, and 30.

29. Mitchell 1991 is an example of this view. But see Bishop 2020, 216–17 for the paradox that this appraisal comes in spite of the *Philippics'* failure to produce any lasting persuasive effect (a failure that Cicero recognizes in *Fam.* 11.14, on which see my discussion on pp. 114–15).

30. Morello 2017, 171–72 also emphasizes the clear relationship between these two texts.

SOUVENIRS OF CICERO

Fam. 10.1 likewise opens its account of Cicero's departure and return in a temporal clause, but one that emphasizes the events and reactions that came after his departure and return from Greece:

> *Et afui proficiscens in Graeciam et,* **postea quam** *de medio cursu rei publicae sum voce* **revocatus,** *numquam per M. Antonium quietus fui.*

> **Ever since I was recalled** by the voice of the Republic from the middle of my journey, while I was away and on my way to Greece, never have I been left in peace by M. Antonius.

The temporal shift marked by the conversion of the conjunction *antequam* into *posteaquam* has the effect of positioning this letter, whether by accident or design, after *Philippics* 1—even, perhaps, after the verbal onslaught from Antony that that speech may have generated.[31] The slight shift in temporal movement across these two parallel texts draws our attention to a procedure that will prove programmatic for *Fam.* 10 as a whole: temporal inconcinnities between the letters and the *Philippics*, as well as between individual letters within the book, reveal (or produce) shifts in intention that undermine the performative authority of Cicero's position, and reproduce in miniature the larger *profectio et reversio* of which he speaks here. This shift is also exemplified in the subtle modification of ideas across these two passages. In the *Philippics* opening, the term *reversio* is used to refer to Cicero's return to Rome following his abortive attempt to leave for Greece earlier that summer,[32] while the verb *revocare* describes the return, or 'recall', of the state to the senate following Julius Caesar's death. Whereas, in *Fam.* 10.1, the verb *revocare* is used to refer to Cicero's recent return (or 'recall') to Rome, in a phrase that conflates this return with his description of the restoration of the Republic to the senate following Julius Caesar's death at the outset of the *Philippics*.[33]

---

31. See Shackleton Bailey 1977, 479 for discussion of the dating of this letter, and, in particular, his endorsement of the view put forward by Nake 1866, 5–6 that *Fam.* 10.1 was written after Antony's violent rejoinder (delivered in the senate on September 19) to the first *Philippic* (which had been delivered on September 2).

32. *Reversio* is the term that Cicero uses somewhat pointedly (against the term *reditus*) to describe his turning back in response to Atticus's (and Brutus's) criticisms at *Att.* 16.7.5–6.

33. As John Henderson points out to me *per litteras*, this opening account of Cicero's *reversio* is programmatic for the larger narrative of *Fam.* 10–12, which never reaches its desired *telos*, but proceeds instead through procedures of repetition and cancellation, for which the term *reversio* may be seen as emblematic.

Yet if Cicero's attempt to identify himself with the Republic might seem like a tactic designed to enhance his own authority, there is an anxiety underpinning this manoeuvre. Cicero's own *profectio et reversio* had been the target of criticism from a number of different quarters, as readers familiar with the narrative of this period assembled in *ad Atticum* 14–16 would know.[34] Cicero begins airing his ideas to Atticus of a trip to Greece to visit his son in *Att.* 14, the book of letters to Atticus that picks up their correspondence, after a gap of three of four months, a few weeks after Caesar's assassination. *Att.* 14–15 trace Cicero's internal conflict about this trip, torn between his desire to absent himself from Italy while Antony remained consul and his concerns about the seemliness of abandoning Rome in her hour of need.[35] The disapproval that met Cicero's eventual departure formed part of his reason for turning back in the middle of his journey, as he himself reports to Atticus in a letter dated to August 19, written in response to a letter that he had received from Atticus, who was adding his own voice to those criticizing Cicero for his decision to leave.[36] In the course of his astonished reply, Cicero picks up on a suggestion that Atticus makes about how he might atone for his contentious trip abroad by publishing a defence of his recent actions (*Att.* 16.7.3):

> *Graviora quae restant: 'velim σχόλιον aliquod elimes ad me, oportuisse te istuc facere.' itane, mi Attice? defensione eget meum factum, praesertim apud te qui id mirabiliter adprobasti? ego vero istum ἀπολογισμὸν συντάξομαι, sed ad eorum aliquem quibus invitis et dissuadentibus profectus sum.*

Worse was the following: 'I'd like you to polish up a little treatise for me, showing that it was your duty to do it.' Really, Atticus? Do my actions require a defence, and to you of all people, who heartily endorsed them? Yet I certainly shall compose such an *apologia*, but I'll address it to one of those who was against my leaving and tried to dissuade me from going.

---

34. Cf. p. xix and xxix for arguments that the publication of *ad Atticum* predates the publication of *ad Fam.* (as a whole collection) by some way.

35. Cf. esp. *Att.* 14.13.3, *Att.* 14.16.3, *Att.* 14.19, *Att.* 15.23, and *Att.* 15.25 for the evolving terms in which Cicero frames his intended journey to Greece and for his persistent state of indecision about undertaking this journey.

36. Cf. *Att.* 16.7.5 for Cicero's account of Brutus's silent reproach.

126   SOUVENIRS OF CICERO

This promise to write an apologia for his untimely departure will be fulfilled
by the lengthy justification for his sojourn at the start of *Philippics* 1. Viewing
this preface as Cicero's apologia for abandoning Italy in her hour of need
transforms our understanding of the motives behind the *Philippics* as a whole,
which now seem to have been delivered and published in order to persuade
his critics (both actual and potential) of his own loyalty to the *res publica*
in the wake of censorious reactions to his trip to Greece. It also transforms
the way in which we view Cicero's correspondence with Plancus, which now
seems haunted in advance by the feeling that Cicero is intent on steering
Plancus away from the model of his own behaviour.

Yet Plancus's actions in *Fam.* 10 are precisely (and repeatedly) encapsulated
by the double movement of *profectio et reversio* that describes Cicero's actions
at the outset of *Philippics* 1. His major contributions to the action of this
book consist, firstly, of joining Lepidus to sue for peace with Antony, before
backtracking and claiming that this had been a ruse designed to wrongfoot the
legions;[37] and second, of marching to join Lepidus, before retreating when he
discovered that Lepidus had already joined forces with Antony.[38] And these

---

37. We hear about this double message in *Fam.* 10.6, in which Cicero recounts to Plancus
the meeting of the senate at which Plancus's letter suing for peace was read out only to be
contradicted by the oral report of his legate Furnius claiming that the letter was a subterfuge.
See also *Phil.* 13 for Cicero's response in the senate to the Gallic commanders' call for peace at
this time (Shackleton Bailey 1977, 509 follows Streng 1885, 99 in believing that Cicero edited
out any mention of Plancus's letter when it came to revising *Phil.* 13 for publication, once he
was again reassured of Plancus's loyalty). Watkins 1997, 92 argues that the discrepancy between
Plancus's letter and Furnius's oral message comes about because, at so far a distance from Rome,
Plancus had not been able to read how far the former appetite for a peaceful solution had
shifted, in the wake of the senate's failed embassy to Antony. Furnius, upon arriving in Rome,
improvized by delivering a message that differed from Plancus's written message of peace. As
White 2010, 154 points out, Plancus's pacific letter to the senate would have been the more
alarming because it came in response to their official summons (issued in February) to come
and help fight Antony in Italy. Mitchell 2019, 172 notes further that this was in fact the first
the senate had heard from him since issuing its declaration on December 20 confirming that
the proconsuls should keep their provinces. Both White 2010, 154; and Mitchell 2019, 173 note
that Cicero's irritation with Plancus comes from the knowledge that Antony was exploiting
the possibility that he might be a supporter in order to win others over. Plancus would later
defend his earlier secrecy (cf. *Fam.* 10.8.4–7), on the grounds that he had been making sure he
could deliver on any promise of loyalty to the senate (as D. Brutus had not been able to) by
strengthening his army.

38. Plancus's decision to abandon his former position of neutrality and move south to help the
republican war effort against Antony comes after the conclusion of the battles of Mutina and
the deaths of the two consuls: in *Fam.* 10.9, dated to April 27, he first writes to Cicero reporting
his march across the Rhone. In his subsequent letters to Cicero (in *Fam.* 10.15, *Fam.* 10.17, and
Fam. 10.18) we hear of his own gradual advance into Lepidus's province, as well as of the movement of Antony's and Ventidius's legions into closer proximity with Lepidus's. Plancus finally
recounts his discovery of Lepidus's transfer of loyalties over to Antony, driven by the fact that

Ordering the Collection 127

actions stand in for the broader volte-face that Plancus performed in this period but which is never explicitly recorded within the parameters of Cicero's letter books: that of supporting the republican side for a certain period of time before finally turning away from it to side with Antony, Octavian, and Lepidus when the time came. This action is, however, anticipated and feared by others, including Cicero himself, throughout this period.[39] The correspondence in *Fam.* 10 begins by describing the actions of Cicero's own immediate past in terms that resonate with the actions that Plancus himself will subsequently take both within this book and after its narrative closes. Plancus's prevarication not only speaks to Cicero's failure to align his addressee's intentions with his own but also mirrors certain inconsistencies between speech and action in the performance of his (Cicero's) own duties. For all their different loyalties, the narrative of *Fam.* 10 suggests that there may be little to choose between Cicero and Plancus—or the different historical narratives that they end up representing.

Profectio et Reversio *(ii): Untimeliness in* Fam. *10*

The resemblance that Cicero and Plancus share as a result of their mutual, and mutually determining, inconsistency is partly an effect of the counter-history's untimeliness, which draws both these figures' actions into its emplotment of

---

he had lost control of his army thanks to days of fraternization with Antony's troops, in *Fam.* 10.21.1, and subsequently in *Fam.* 10.23 (Lepidus's own account of this event is found in his official despatch to the senate at *Fam.* 10.35). In *Fam.* 10.21, Plancus reports his suspicion that Lepidus was luring him into a trap, intent on winning his army over before he could join forces with D. Brutus, and his decision to retreat back across the Isara before Lepidus's disloyal troops could corrupt his own. Syme 1939, 179 assumes that Plancus knew all along that Lepidus would change sides, and was marching south with the intention of doing the same (and of luring D. Brutus into a similar trap himself). But see Mitchell 2019, 175 for the important observation that Plancus only abandoned D. Brutus after Octavian became consul, and established the Pedian court to convict Caesar's assassins, making it impossible for Plancus to support D. Brutus any longer. Watkins 1997, 95 also argues that it is too easy to assume that Plancus, Lepidus, and Pollio intended to abandon the republican cause all along. It is, no doubt, a sign of the success of the editors' retrospective spin on this narrative that modern readers readily make this assumption.

39. Though never explicitly acknowledged, this anxiety subtends the entirety of Cicero's letter exchange with Plancus in *Fam.* 10, and is not least apparent in the excessive praise he heaps on Plancus for any word or show of loyalty to the republican side. D. Brutus reveals explicit doubts about Plancus's commitment to the republican cause in *Fam.* 11.9.2. In *Fam.* 11.11.1 (dated May 6), D. Brutus reports having intercepted letters from Antony to Plancus trying to win Plancus over.

belatedness and prematurity.[40] The republican counter-history manifests across these books of letters in the form of victories declared too soon,[41] and news received too late, forms of untimeliness which some of the actors in *Fam.* 10 exploit, some despair over, and some simply try to keep track of in the hope of personal survival. These moments bring home the hauntological status of the republican narrative, which emerges as a series of lost futures—narrated through the very process of their being lost or cancelled. *Fam* 10.32, the remarkable eyewitness account of Forum Gallorum, composed by Servius Sulpicius Galba, who had fought in this grim battle, a few days after it had ended, concludes with the formulaic euphemism for declaring victory: *res bene gesta est* ('the operation was a success'). Yet the Cicero/Plancus sequence that precedes this letter in the letter book has already revealed to readers that this victory was not destined to last very long.[42] Still, in case the prematurity of this declared victory were lost on readers, it is spelled out for us in the following letter in *Fam.* 10, written from Spain in early June by Asinius Pollio, who has the advantage of a degree of temporal and spatial distance from the battle that Galba did not (*Fam.* 10.33.4):

> *Nunc haec mihi scribuntur ex Gallia Lepidi et nuntiantur: Pansae exercitum concisum esse, Pansam ex vulneribus mortuum, eodem proelio Martiam legionem interisse et L. Fabatum et C. Peducaeum et D. Carfulenum; Hirtiano autem proelio et quartam legionem et omnis peraeque Antoni caesas, item Hirti, quartam vero, cum castra quoque Antoni cepisset, a quinta legione concisam esse; ibi Hirtium quoque perisse et Pontium Aquilam; dici etiam Octavianum cecidisse (quae si, quod di prohibeant, vera sunt, non mediocriter doleo); Antonium turpiter Mutinae obsessionem reliquisse, sed habere equitum <V>, legiones sub signis armatas tris et P. Bagienni unam, inermis bene multos; Ventidium quoque se cum legione VII, VIII, VIIII coniunxisse; si nihil in Lepido*

---

40. As Mitchell 2019, 175 puts it: 'Plancus did not change sides—the sides changed around him.'

41. The prematurity of the republican side's victory at Mutina receives particular emphasis in the letters exchanged between Cicero and D. Brutus in the immediate aftermath of the two battles, at *Fam.* 11.12–14. See especially *Fam.* 11.13a.1–2 for D. Brutus's account of the unfortunate confluence of events that conspired to prevent him finishing off Antony's army after declaring victory, his disappointment about this window of opportunity closing summed up in the closing phrase: *Hic dies hoc modo abiit.* ('And so the day passed away.')

42. Even the date on the letter belies its optimistic verdict: *XII Kal. Mai* (or April 20), by which time the wounds that Pansa had received in the battle five days earlier (and which would prove fatal to him three days later) must have been known to Galba. The prematurity of Galba's verdict is inscribed into the letter itself.

*spei sit, descensurum ad extrema et non modo nationes, sed etiam servitia
concitaturum; Parmam direptam; L. Antonium Alpis occupasse.*

Just now the written and oral reports I'm getting from Lepidus's Gaul
are these: that Pansa's army has been cut to pieces; that Pansa has died
from his wounds; that in the same battle the Martian legion was lost,
including L. Fabatus, C. Peducaeus, and D. Carfulenus; but that in
the battle fought by Hirtius, both the Fourth legion and all Antony's
were equally cut down, as also was Hirtius's; that the Fourth legion
was cut to pieces by the Fifth after it had captured Antony's camp;
that Hirtius also and Pontius Aquila died there; that even Octavian is
said to have died (if—heaven forbid—these things are true, then I am
deeply grieved); that Antony has disgracefully abandoned the siege of
Mutina, but that he still has five thousand cavalry, three legions fully
armed under their standards, and one under Popillius of the Bagienni,
and a good number of unarmed men besides; that Ventidius too has
joined him with the Seventh, Eighth and Ninth legions; that if he has
no grounds for hopes in Lepidus, he will stoop to desperate measures,
and rouse not only foreign tribes but also slaves against us; that Parma
has been sacked, and the Alps taken by L. Antonius.

Pollio's report is pieced together from snippets of rumour and hearsay, and
it comes after the considerable delay imposed on epistolary and other communications by enemy sabotage.[43] The letter begins with an explanation as
to why it took him so long to be informed of the events at Mutina (*Fam.*
10.33.1): *Quo tardius certior fierem de proeliis apud Mutinam factis Lepidus
effecit, qui meos tabellarios novem dies retinuit.* ('Lepidus saw to it that I was
informed about the battles fought near Mutina later than I should have been,
having held up my letter carriers for nine days.') The nine-day delay imposed
by Lepidus's scouts comes on top of the forty days that it already takes to bring
letters from Italy to Spain, as Pollio takes particular care to remind Cicero at
the letter's close.[44] These prominent emphases on the length of time that it

---

43. It is striking that this letter, which, along with the other two by Pollio that immediately
follow this one in book 10, amounts to the most sizable portion of extant text that we can as-
sign to the hand of Pollio, is notable for its pointed refusal of the celebrated autopsy that the
later literary tradition took to be the distinctive hallmark of his (non-extant) historiographical
works. On this aspect of the later construction of Pollio, see Morgan 2000.

44. Pollio closes the letter (*Fam.* 10.33.5): 'What grieves me the most, however, is that I can only
be reached by a route so long and dangerous that all news only reaches me forty days after it's

takes for him to receive information from the outside world frame an elaborate raft of excuses that he proffers in the rest of the letter for not having intervened in events from which he resides at too great and difficult a distance to be able to do so in a timely manner.[45] But the hearsay report that he offers demonstrates the advantages that this delay brings to an understanding of what Mutina signifies, even just a month or two later, when the initial republican victory had been converted into something more like failure. The juxtaposition of Pollio's letter alongside Galba's starkly highlights the prematurity of the declared victory over Mutina, as this particular counter-historical future is cancelled and superseded by the ultimately victorious narrative of the other side. Pollio's position of distance from the event models the perspective of the editors of this letter book and of later readers, who read these letters within the context of the later hegemony that we witness here in the process of taking over the republican narrative; while Galba's too-proximate proximity to the action models the myopia of the historical actors in the thick of it, insisting on their present tense.

The forms of untimeliness that characterize the republican counter-history that we see plotted in *Fam.* 10 stand out because they undermine a central message of Cicero's throughout this period: in the *Philippics*, in *Fam.* 10–12, and in other writings of this period too, Cicero stresses the importance of timely action as critical to a victory for the republican side.[46] Yet *Fam.* 10

---

happened—or even later.' (*Maxime tamen doleo adeo et longo et infesto itinere ad me veniri ut die quadragesimo post aut ultra etiam quam facta sunt omnia nuntientur.*)

45. Cf. esp. *Fam.* 10.33.2–3 for the series of hypotheticals explaining what Pollio would have been able to achieve for the Republic had he not been beset by communication issues. See Fletcher 2016 for a broad assessment of the late republican 'expanded field' of communication to which Pollio's letters from Spain bear witness.

46. The control of time is a major theme not only of the letters of this period, but also of the *Philippics*, where the timeliness of intervention is repeatedly presented as critical to the senate's hopes of success. Cf. esp. *Phil.* 3.1–2, *Phil.* 5.30, and *Phil.* 10.1. Cicero conveys his disappointment about the failure of timely action on the senate's part to Brutus in a number of letters to him (programmatically in the opening letter of book 2 of the *ad Brutum*: 'For you don't need me to tell you how much turns on time in politics, and what a difference it makes to the same policy, whether one is ahead or behind in laying it down, taking it in hand, and carrying it into effect.' (*Non enim ignoras quanta momenta sint in re publica temporum et quid intersit idem illud utrum ante an post decernatur, suscipiatur, agatur.*) Brutus himself is the target of a number of Cicero's reproaches for untimeliness in *ad Brut.* and elsewhere—both for his failure to finish off Antony after Caesar's assassination, and for his refusal to bring his army to Italy in support of D. Brutus. But see *ad Brut.* 1.4.2–3 for Brutus's own charge of untimeliness on Cicero's part—specifically the prematurity of his decision either to condemn or to give his whole-hearted support to certain individuals. Cicero's prematurity is also a theme of *Fam.* 10 (see discussion below).

Ordering the Collection 131

shows readers how far the timing of events and communications lies outside his control and how he himself becomes implicated in the various forms of untimeliness that structure its counter-history. As *Fam.* 10.33 shows, this is in part due to the spatial distances that stand between the different actors involved in this historical drama and the temporal discrepancies that open up as a result of the necessity of epistolary communication.[47] In these books of letters, more than in any others of Cicero's correspondence, the hazards of postal communication are presented to us in very concrete terms.[48] Letters fall into the wrong hands, and information is received by those who were not its intended recipients.[49] Communication fails because letter couriers are blocked, a situation which in turn supplies people of uncertain loyalties with an excuse not to send a letter in the first place.[50] Duplicate letters attest to certain parties' loyalty, in their assiduous attempt to keep correspondents informed.[51] Above all, the publication of letters along with their recipients' replies reveals the delay between sending and receiving letters in Rome and her imperial outposts, and the concomitant difficulty of organizing the letters (and the narrative that they constitute) into chronological sequence: one historical actor's present (or future) may already be their correspondent's past—or may be past by the time the letter reaches them.[52] All these factors highlight how the untimeliness of this counter-history is to some extent a consequence of its

---

47. Plancus himself draws attention to this predicament early on in his correspondence with Cicero in a statement that seems in retrospect to be programmatic (*Fam.* 10.4.3): 'I am not unaware of your feelings: **and if I had been able to opportune myself of your presence, which I certainly long for, I would never disagree with your policies**; and even now, I shall not put it in your power to rebuke any deed of mine with good cause.' (*Non est ignotus mihi sensus tuus; neque, si facultas optabilis mihi quidem tui praesentis esset, umquam a tuis consiliis discreparem nec nunc committam ut ullum meum factum reprehendere iure possis.*)

48. In this, they offer a literal manifestation of the symbolic use to which Derrida 1987 puts the hazards of the postal service as a means of demonstrating the hermeneutic uncertainties that govern all communication.

49. In *Fam.* 11.11.1, for example, D. Brutus reports having intercepted some *libelli* of Antony's that reveal his designs on winning over Lepidus, Plancus, and Pollio.

50. This is the situation that Pollio exploits in *Fam.* 10.33.

51. See D. Brutus's reference to receiving duplicate letters from Cicero in *Fam.* 11.11.1 and Cicero's receipt of duplicate letters from Plancus in *Fam.* 10.5.1.

52. The so-called 'epistolary' tenses are a prominent feature of the letters in these books, and convey precisely how letter writers anticipate the temporal distance between themselves and their addressees: see Shackleton Bailey 1977, 528 on *Fam.* 11.11.1 (*scripsi . . . scribebat*), *Fam.* 11.18.1 (*videbantur*), and *Fam.* 12.5.2 (*erupisset*).

epistolary narrative medium, since the delays in communication by post are a real cause of its failure.

Yet the untimeliness is also an effect of deliberate actions taken by the historical actors involved, some of whom take a quite different view from Cicero to the question of what timely action means, but whom Cicero is drawn into satisfying and (unwittingly) resembling. This is especially true of Plancus, the notorious 'time-server', whose record of service under Caesar reveals a talent for moving with the times (in his own, quite different, take on the question of timeliness)—one that does not square with Cicero's exhortation to stand firmly with the republican cause.[53] Plancus's actions throughout *Fam.* 10 are characterized by the forms of untimeliness—prematurity and belatedness—that structure the republican counter-history and make it visible within this letter book. His major contribution to the action of this book is marked by the act of intervening too late:[54] having thought that he had persuaded Lepidus to abandon the policy of making peace (and joining forces) with Antony, and having marched south to join forces with him himself, Plancus is forced to retreat when he finds that he has been pre-empted by Antony, who has already managed to persuade (or coerce) Lepidus into siding with him. Plancus retreats and then waits for others to act.[55] Yet for all these critical acts of (deliberate) belatedness, Cicero is just as preoccupied with the premature aspirations of his addressee throughout *Fam.* 10—and ends up mirroring Plancus's prematurity, by acting (prematurely) on those very aspirations.

---

53. Cf. *Fam.* 10.3.3 for Cicero's famous reference to Plancus being someone who 'serves the times too much', the label that sticks with him in later history. See Mitchell 2019, 163–65 for discussion of the subsequent history of this phrase in later appraisals of Plancus, and for a reconsideration of what the phrase means in the context of Caesar's dictatorship. For Watkins 1997, 79, the phrase says more about Cicero's strategies of polarization than about Plancus himself, who (he believes) was primarily acting, like others, to avoid the escalation of civil war.

54. White 2010, 154 notes that despite having been bidden to help with the fighting in Italy in February, Plancus did not move from his province until five days after the fighting at Mutina was over (see *Fam.* 10.9.3, where he reports having crossed the Rhone on April 26). See *Fam.* 10.33 for Pollio's mention of a decree summoning Plancus and Lepidus to this effect; Dio 46.29.6 dates this decree to the meeting of the senate on February 2 (the occasion on which *Phil.* 8 was delivered).

55. White 2010, 155–56, suspending judgment about Plancus's intentions (which are impossible to reconstruct) throughout these manoeuvres, attempts to make his actions speak for themselves: 'Two striking facts about his behaviour are that it took him more than three times as long to march 140 miles south from the Isara as it did to march back, and that, for all his marching, he never came within a spear's throw of either Lepidus or Antony.' Watkins 1997, 98–99, however, also notes the length of time that it took him for him to make this journey, but he argues that this was a strategy designed to protect his own troops.

Plancus's pre-appointment by Caesar to the consulship in two years' time, which Cicero mentions in the opening letter, establishes the theme of premature honours from the very outset of their correspondence. Yet as Cicero himself points out in the letter that he writes to him following the delivery of Plancus's letter to the senate suing for peace with Antony, badges of office and distinction are meaningless unless they are preceded by a performance that justifies the honour or station named (*Fam.* 10.6.2):[56]

> *Crede igitur mihi, Plance, omnis quos adhuc gradus dignitatis consecutus sis (es autem adeptus amplissimos) eos honorum vocabula habituros, non dignitatis insignia, nisi te cum libertate populi Romani et cum senatus auctoritate coniunxeris.*

> Believe me, Plancus, that all those steps of rank that you have climbed thus far (and you have achieved the most important of them) will be viewed as titles of public office rather than as badges of merit, unless you side with the freedom of the Roman people and with the authority of the senate.

Cicero's strategy is to persuade Plancus that he needs to earn public honours before receiving them, in an attempt to reverse the convoluted temporality that now governs the most significant magistracy at Rome, which is now predetermined several years in advance and has been divorced from any semblance of personal merit.[57] But again, it is a strategy riven with inconsistencies and hypocrisy on Cicero's part. For throughout this book of letters, we are reminded repeatedly of the prominent role that Cicero himself plays in offering public honours to the protagonists of the unfolding drama whose loyalties were as yet uncertain, in an attempt to coerce them into siding with the senate. In the two letters that immediately follow this one, which arrive in Rome together to reveal Plancus's 'true' position regarding Antony on the

---

56. Indeed, it was the logic of this very position that had provided Cicero with the basis of his contentious claim in *Philippic* 3 that Decimus Brutus's challenge to Antony should be supported by the senate because Antony had not lived up to the office of consul that he held in name. Here Cicero warns Plancus that the same fate may await him. He goes on to make it clear that this danger hangs particularly heavily over Plancus because of his status as one of the consuls-elect pre-appointed by Caesar.

57. One of the anonymous referees for OUP offers the brilliant insight that there may be a play on Plancus's name (meaning 'flat-footed') with the reference to the *gradus* or steps of rank that he is attempting to climb up here.

134 SOUVENIRS OF CICERO

one hand and the senate on the other, we are informed of the honours that had already been paid (prematurely) to Lepidus and Octavian through the filter of Plancus's pique about having not yet received similar honours himself.[58] And shortly after the sequence of letters exchanged between Cicero and Plancus ends, we hear more directly of the honours awarded to Lepidus when Cicero prefaces the letter that he writes by way of reprimand to Lepidus for promoting peace with Antony with a comment noting Lepidus's ingratitude for the honours that the senate had paid him.[59] Clearly, on some occasions, the performative coercion of awarding senatorial honours to certain figures failed to have its effect.[60]

Above all, this letter book provides the evidence that the *Philippics* does not for the honours that Cicero tried to persuade the senate to vote for Plancus in the face of considerable resistance from some of its members, a resistance that hinged precisely on how premature such honours would be.[61] The published text of the *Philippics* does not include the speech that Cicero gave at the meetings of the senate on April 8 and 9 when he attempted to persuade its members to recognize Plancus's loyalty, a lacuna that most scholars put down to the embarrassment that Cicero may have felt about this proposal

---

58. *Fam.* 10.7.2: 'By god, I have felt sorely aggrieved when others seemed to be snatching their claim to glory.' (*Non me dius fidius mediocri dolore adficiebar cum alii occupare possessionem laudis viderentur.*)

Plancus was presumably referring to the honours that Cicero persuaded the senate to vote for Lepidus on January 1, 43 BCE (an honorary decree and a gilt equestrian statue of him to be placed in the forum, on which see *Phil.* 5.38–41). On the same occasion, Cicero also moved the senate to vote D. Brutus an honorary decree (*Phil.* 5.35–7), and to make Octavian (still a *privatus*) propraetor (*Phil.* 5.42–52). Cicero's habit of promoting honours for some seems to generate resentment from others later on in this narrative: Syme 1939, 176 notes how, after the (premature) victory at Mutina, Octavian was clearly annoyed that D. Brutus received the lion's share of the glory (receiving a triumph and the legions of the dead consuls, whereas Octavian received only an *ovatio*). White 2010, 146 emphasizes how little role D. Brutus and his troops seem to have played in the fighting at Mutina (despite Cicero's reference to his *clara . . . eruptio* at *Fam.* 11.14.1).

59. *Fam.* 10.27: 'So great is my goodwill towards you that I have a deep concern for your being elevated to the very highest position, and am therefore distressed at your having paid no thanks to the senate when that body had honoured you with the highest distinctions.'

60. As Cicero himself acknowledges at *Phil.* 13.43; and to Brutus at *ad Brut.* 1.12.2 and *ad Brut.* 1.15.9.

61. It is unknown what exactly the honours were that Cicero was seeking for Plancus. White 2010, 219 n. 52 notes that it is also unclear from *Fam.* 10.12 (and even from Plancus's reply, *Fam.* 10.11) whether or not Cicero was successful in securing these honours. It is not clear whether the *senatus consultum* mentioned in *Fam.* 10.13 refers to the same event. The emphasis placed in *Fam.* 10 on Plancus's quest for (and Cicero's granting of) honours at this juncture is the more striking because of how shadowy these honours are.

Ordering the Collection

at the time, especially in light of how his decision to award Lepidus similar honours had turned out.[62] But in *Fam.* 10.12, written in reply to *Fam.* 10.7 and 10.8, Cicero responds to the proofs that Plancus has just given him of his loyalty by describing his efforts to fight down Plancus's detractors in the senate and win the argument for voting him an honorary decree. The jocular tone of Cicero's account of his decisive victory in the senate, and his insistence that the senate and people of Rome are unified in their support of Plancus, cannot erase readers' memory of his position about the prematurity of decorating Plancus with public honours in *Fam.* 10.10, a letter sent to Plancus before the letters affirming his loyalty (*Fam.* 10.7 and 10.8) had reached Rome. Responding to a (now lost) letter in which, it seems, Plancus reiterated to Cicero his loyalty to the senate, Cicero takes the opportunity to tell him why it is too soon for Plancus to expect any formal recognition from the senate for his services to the state: (*Fam.* 10.10.1):

> *Itaque, si consulem Romae habuissemus, declaratum esset ab senatu cum tuis magnis honoribus quam gratus esset conatus et apparatus tuus: Cuius rei non modo non praeteriit tempus sed ne maturum quidem etiam nunc meo quidem iudicio fuit; is enim denique honos mihi videri solet qui non propter spem futuri benefici sed propter magna merita claris viris defertur et datur.*

> So if we had had a consul at Rome, the senate would have declared how grateful it was for your efforts and preparations by awarding you great honours. But the time for such things has not only not yet passed, but is, in my view, not even now ripe. For the only true distinction seems to me to be the one which is conferred on and given to distinguished men not in the hope of future services but for services already rendered.

Yet twelve days later, Cicero was writing to Plancus to tell him about the honours that he had tried to persuade the senate to vote him. Between *Fam.* 10.10 and *Fam.* 10.12, little of substance had changed, beyond the arrival of Plancus's official despatch to the senate corroborating Furnius's message that the earlier letter advocating peace with Antony was a ruse. By the time *Fam.*

---

62. See Crawford 1984, 259 on these lost orations. Manuwald 2007, 74 notes the discomfiture that Cicero would have experienced in encountering P. Servilius Isauricus's opposition on this matter. If Cicero's proposal was unsuccessful, it is possible too that this is the reason why the speeches were not included within the transmitted text of the *Philippics*.

10.12 was written, there was still no consul in Rome, and Plancus had hardly achieved the kind of *magna merita* that Cicero speaks of as a prerequisite for receiving public honours in *Fam.* 10.10; the honorary recognition (whatever it was) that Cicero advocates was clearly designed to keep Plancus on the republican side rather than to recognize any completed performance of his services to the state. What *Fam.* 10.12 reveals, then, is that Cicero's earlier message in *Fam.* 10.10 about the prematurity of Plancus's expectation of public honours was itself premature. Yet again, in Cicero's own handling of the question of honours for Plancus, he is drawn into the convoluted temporality of his addressee, whose premature honours will be superseded by events and actions that cancel the meaning of those honours, in another example of the republican counter-history's lost futures. And this is, above all significant, because it stands in for Cicero's more critical act of premature support for the honours of another at this time: the decision to support Octavian's quest for the consulship is never mentioned by Cicero in any letter included within *ad Fam.*, yet this too was premature for many reasons,[63] and would soon turn out to put paid to any hope of the republican counter-history prevailing. In emphasizing Cicero's hypocritical stance towards Plancus's premature aspirations, the editor of *Fam.* 10 charges him implicitly with this more definitive act of premature self-cancellation.

Profectio et Reversio *(iii): Doubles in* Fam. *10*

The relation of resemblance that Cicero is drawn into with Plancus is not an isolated example within *Fam.* 10, which not only reveals such resemblances but also makes the idea of the double its theme.[64] Other oppositional pairs within this book are likewise drawn into relations of similitude by virtue of the dialectical structure of the narrative that they find themselves caught up in. Pollio's three letters to Cicero (*Fam.* 10.31 through 10.33) are sandwiched

---

63. Not least because of Octavian's age, as well as his untested loyalties. See *ad Brut.* 1. 4a. 2–3 and *ad Brut.* 1. 16. 4–7 for M. Brutus's objections to the prematurity of Cicero's championing of Octavian.

64. This is apparent early on in *Fam.* 10, in Cicero's description of Plancus's envoy Furnius in *Fam.* 10.2 as a faithful replica of Plancus ('Though I was very pleased to see Furnius for his own sake, I was the more so, because in listening to him, I seemed to be listening to you.'), a detail that gains in significance when Furnius is subsequently made the bearer of an oral message to the senate from Plancus that says the precise opposite of his (Plancus's) written despatch (see *Fam.* 10.6 for the details). On this occasion, Furnius's version of Plancus's intentions transpires to be the correct one. Yet Cicero's initial insistence on Furnius's fidelity to the character of Plancus in itself sows doubts about Plancus's consistency—doubts that are subsequently corroborated by the turn of events both within *Fam.* 10 (cf., e.g., *Fam.* 10.6) and outside it.

Ordering the Collection

between Cicero's letter to Lepidus (*Fam.* 10.27) and the letters that Lepidus writes to Cicero first asserting his loyalty to the republican side (*Fam.* 10.34a through 10.34b) and then spectacularly reneging on that promise when he writes to admit having joined forces with Antony after the event in the final letter of book 10 (*Fam.* 10.35). Enclosed within Cicero's correspondence with Lepidus, Pollio's own assertions of loyalty to the senate in these letters are invested with the irony of knowing that he too will change sides to join forces with Lepidus and Antony in due course.[65] And within Pollio's letter sequence, the idea of doubling is prominently thematized by the uncertain identity of an enemy mentioned in the first of his three letters included within *Fam.* 10, which is resolved for us in the memorable portrait he provides of his quaestor, Balbus, in the second.[66] When Pollio first introduces this figure in *Fam.* 10.31, without naming him, his damning description offers so suggestive a portrait of Antony that commentators feel beholden to explain that it cannot in fact be Antony, with whom Pollio is known to have been on friendly terms.[67] But the double-take that readers experience upon reading about this Antonian avatar at large in the province of Spain is a significant and perhaps deliberate effect that this book of letters produces. It allows later readers to experience for themselves that feeling of epistemic uncertainty that *Fam.* 10 presents as the prevailing reality for the historical actors involved in the events of this period, when distance, conflict, and uncertain loyalties contributed to the difficulty of knowing who was on what side, what was happening where, and what any of it meant for the fortunes of the Republic.

That this structure of uncertainty should manifest in *Fam.* 10.31 in the uncertain identity of a particular individual, within a letter sequence that is organized to highlight the resemblances between two other historical actors (Lepidus and Pollio), provides a fitting closural comment on the book as a whole. The resemblance between Plancus and Cicero, for example, which is established

---

65. Pollio's expressions of loyalty are reiterated at *Fam.* 10.31.5 and *Fam.* 10.32.5.

66. *Fam.* 10.31.2: 'There's no danger of my being afflicted by the talk of one whom no one wants to see—although men don't hate him as much as he deserves. I loathe him so intensely that I view with disgust anything I have to do alongside him' (*Ne movear eius sermonibus, quem tametsi nemo est qui videre velit, tamen nequaquam proinde ac dignus est oderunt homines, periculum non est; adeo est enim invisus mihi ut nihil non acerbum putem quod commune cum illo sit.*) This figure, who remains unnamed in this letter, is identified by name and post in the opening words of the following one (*Fam.* 10.32.1: 'Balbus quaestor'), which proceeds to elaborate on his rapacious behaviour towards the provincials. See Fletcher 2016 for further discussion of the relationship between these two letters.

67. Shackleton Bailey 1977, 507.

138 SOUVENIRS OF CICERO

in the opening letter, is sustained to the end of their letter sequence, where it culminates by challenging the reader's ability to recognize which of the two is being described. In the closing three letters of this sequence, all three penned by Plancus, one sentiment stands out for its prominent expression: *pudor*. The appearance of this motif across the three adjacent letters is made the more striking by the fact that they are written at some distance apart: *Fam.* 10.21, which is dated to mid-May and recounts Plancus's discovery of Lepidus's imminent treachery and his own decision to retreat from the overtures that he had already made to join forces with Lepidus, opens by describing Plancus's *pudor* at sending Cicero inconsistent messages, even as it attempts to excuse that inconsistency by attributing it to Lepidus's own behaviour (*Fam.* 10.21.1):

> **Puderet** *me inconstantiae mearum litterarum si non haec ex aliena levitate penderent.*

> **I would be ashamed** of the inconsistency of my letters if these did not hang on the flightiness of another.

The next letter by Plancus in the book, written in early June after Lepidus had actually joined forces with Antony, and Plancus had beaten a hasty retreat, opens by describing the regrets he harbours (or not) for the intentions behind his recent actions.[68] It was, he goes on to explain, *pudor* rather than *temeritas* that placed him in danger, leading him to intervene in the war to fend off charges of inaction (*Fam.* 10.23.1):

> *Sed ego non hoc vitio paene sum deceptus; Lepidum enim pulchre noram. Quid ergo est?* **Pudor** *me, qui in bello maxime est periculosus, hunc casum coegit subire.*

> It was not this fault, however, that nearly betrayed me, for I knew Lepidus only too well. So what was it? **It was my desire for approval**, which is most dangerous in war, that forced me to undergo this perilous course.

The final letter in their correspondence, both in date and in sequence, likewise opens with an expression of the *pudor* Plancus feels in thanking Cicero

---

68. (*Fam.* 10.23.1): 'Never, I swear, dear Cicero, will I regret undergoing the greatest dangers on behalf of the republic, as long as, if anything happens to me, I escape the charge of rashness.' (*Numquam mehercules, mi Cicero, me paenitebit maxima pericula pro patria subire dum, si quid acciderit mihi, a reprehensione temeritatis absim.*)

Ordering the Collection

in words—when deeds, he implies, would offer a better form of repayment (*Fam.* 10.24.1):

> *Facere non possum quin in singulas res meritaque tua tibi gratias agam, sed mehercules facio cum **pudore**.*

> I cannot thank you without singling out every one of your services. But still, I do so with a **sense of shame**.

This letter, written in late July, is the latest securely dated letter within *ad Fam.* In it, Plancus, who has now joined forces with D. Brutus, complains about the impasse they find themselves in and places the blame for this situation squarely on Octavian.[69] Within the published book, at least, this letter is met by a resounding silence.

Whether or not it was intended as a reproach, Plancus's complaints about Octavian certainly read like one to readers who possess the benefit of hindsight.[70] Readers, in particular, who have read *ad Brutum* (a letter collection which must predate *ad Fam.*)[71] will know that this was Brutus's chief complaint about Cicero: that his championing of Octavian was excessive and misdirected,[72] no better than his promotion of any other individual (including Antony) with a claim to be Caesar's heir would have been at this time.[73] The *pudor* that Plancus emphasizes in his last three letters to Cicero

---

69. Cf. esp. *Fam.* 10.24.6: 'But—and whatever I write to you, I swear I do so more in grief than in enmity: the fact that Antony is alive today, that Lepidus is with him, that their armies are not to be sneered at, that they have hopes and ambitions of success, all this they can put down to Caesar.' (*Sed (quicquid tibi scribo, dolenter mehercules magis quam inimice facio) quod vivit Antonius hodie, quod Lepidus una est, quod exercitus habent non contemnendos [habent], quod sperant, quod audent, omne Caesari acceptum referre possunt.*) See Whitton 2017, 211 for discussion of the significance of this criticism of Octavian at this point in *ad Fam.* and how it may relate to the last dated letters in *ad Brut.* (*ad Brut.* 1. 16–17, if these letters are authentic).

70. Morello 2017, 181–82 also notes the implicit reproach to Cicero in this letter for his support of Octavian, whose hastily grabbed consulship has pre-empted Plancus's own and served as a distraction from concluding the war against Antony.

71. I assume that the *ad Brutum* was published as a collection before *ad Fam.* was assembled, as otherwise we would expect to find letters to and from him within this narrative block in *Fam.* 10–12 (as we find letters to and from Cassius, for example).

72. Cf. *ad Brut.* 1.4a.2–3.

73. Indeed, as the author of *ad Brut.* 16 and 17 makes clear, Cicero's championing of Octavian was especially awkward, since Octavian had already made clear to D. Brutus that he could never make political cause with his uncle's assassins.

names the feeling that readers of the collection may feel inclined to read into Cicero's silence following the last of Plancus's letters to him, projecting that feeling onto Cicero himself for the role that he played in bringing this story to the concluding point that we arrive at, with Plancus, in July 43 BCE. By the end of their letter sequence, Cicero and Plancus have become interchangeable, not least in the guilt they share for creating this crisis.

Into the Void: Writing the Siege in Fam. *11*

Fam. 11 is the book in the middle of this three-book narrative, and its position at the centre reverberates through the structure and the theme of the book, as Cicero's letter exchange with D. Brutus, the man who finds himself at the centre of the crisis, is itself placed inside a ring of letters that serve to contextualize the correspondence at its core.[74] D. Brutus is also placed quite literally at the heart of this conflict, when he finds himself besieged by Antony within the city of Mutina. In letters to others, and also within the *Philippics*, Cicero repeatedly refers to the moment of the siege as a *discrimen* or turning point for the *res publica*, a term that he never uses explicitly in letters to D. Brutus or to anyone else in *Fam.* 11.[75] But the book itself enacts this turning point in the structure of its narrative, as Cicero's correspondence with D. Brutus is enclosed by letters to and from others that invite readers to compare this event and its outcome with crises from the recent past. This book of letters focuses our attention, above all, on the *form* of the counter-history: the siege that determines the content of these letters inspires the enclosing form that governs their organization within *Fam.* 11; yet the siege itself also blocks communication, such that its effects can only be felt in advance or in retrospect, enforcing the book's enframing form as a matter of historical necessity. In these quite disparate ways, *Fam.* 11 disrupts the conventions of historiographical narrative representation: by making use, on the one hand, of the events it recounts in order to structure its organization; but also, on the other hand, by drawing on the letters' contact with the historical real in order to reproduce

---

74. *Fam.* 11.4–26, the letters exchanged between D. Brutus and Cicero, are enclosed between *Fam.* 11.1–3, letters by three of the tyrannicides (D. Brutus, M. Brutus, and Cassius), and *Fam.* 11.27–29, Cicero's exchanges Matius and Oppius.

75. Cf. *Phil.* 3.29, 5.39, 6.19, 7.1 and 7.12, 8.29, 9.6, 10.14, and 14.3. Cicero also repeatedly uses this word in his frantic attempts to summon M. Brutus over from Macedonia (see *ad Brut.* 1.12.1, 2.1.1, and 2.2.2), as well as in his letters to Cassius (*Fam.* 12.5 and 12.6).

Ordering the Collection 141

the blockages, gaps, and lacunae of history and represent them as spaces of narrative suppression.[76]

The opening of *Fam.* 11 takes us back to a point in the story before the narrative of *Fam.* 10 begins: a dramatic moment shortly after Caesar's assassination, when D. Brutus, who had participated in that assassination, writes to M. Brutus and Cassius to offer his perspective on how the political landscape lies in the aftermath of Caesar's death. His description of the vacuum that Caesar's death has produced at Rome, given the absence of any individual possessed of the necessary financial and military resources for the republicans to rally around, provides an important prelude to the way in which the crisis is staged in the rest of the book (*Fam.* 11.1.4):

> *Succurret fortasse hoc loco alicui vestrum cur novissimum tempus exspectemus potius quam nunc aliquid moliamur.* **Quia, ubi consistamus non habemus** *praeter Sex. Pompeium et Bassum Caecilium; qui mihi videntur hoc nuntio de Caesare adlato firmiores futuri. Satis tempore ad eos accedemus ubi quid valeant scierimus.*

> Perhaps it will occur to one of you at this point to ask why we should wait for that last stage rather than strive for something now? **Because we have nowhere where we can take a stand**, except for Sextus Pompeius and Caecilius Bassus, who, it seems to me, will be more firmly established when this news about Caesar has reached them. There will be time enough for us to join them once we've discovered what their strength is.

The power vacuum described here will be further elaborated for us in the subsequent exchange of letters with Cicero, as D. Brutus himself steps into this vacuum, and is unwittingly made the rallying point for the republican cause that he himself describes as lacking in the opening letter. Yet this vacuum poses a problem for narrative representation—even for verbal description, as D. Brutus's syntactical

---

76. One of the most eloquent examples of this effect is *Fam.* 11.13b, of which we only have the incipit preserved in the index to M, which runs: 'The residents of Parma, poor wretches...' (*Parmenses miserrimos...*), and evidently introduces D. Brutus's account of L. Antonius' brutal treatment of this town, following his brother's army's escape from Mutina. The erasure of the letter seems to comment all the more eloquently on the destruction of the people it evidently would have described, as readers are made fleetingly aware of the destructive events that barely make it into the historical record, but are forced to supply the details of the victims' suffering from the resources of their own imagination.

periphrasis eloquently suggests. In *Fam.* 11, the periphrastic formulation of this vacuum, seen first in the opening letter, is conveyed in part by the structure of the book, as letters in the enclosing frame demonstrate the social and political consequences of this crisis by comparing it to the earlier one of 49 BCE.[77]

The letters that make up this frame stand out immediately for the diverse political affiliations of the correspondents involved: the tyrannicides, Cassius and M. Brutus, at one end of the book, and two Caesarean friends of Cicero, Matius and Oppius, at the other.[78] Yet between them, these letters work together to contextualize the correspondence in the middle by producing an implicit comparison between the current situation and the crisis of five years earlier. Matius and Oppius, a familiar pair from elsewhere in Cicero's correspondence where they are called on to illustrate two slightly different models of Caesarean loyalty,[79] are brought together at the end of *Fam.* 11 to highlight what they share in common: a capacity (demonstrated at the time of the crisis in 49 BCE and in the years since then) to balance loyalty to Caesar with a genuine concern for Cicero's best interests, despite the misalignment between Cicero and Caesar at this time. The pair of letters exchanged between Cicero and Matius in the autumn of 44 BCE in which Cicero responds to Matius's concern that he had publicly criticized his loyalty to Caesar's memory after his death, provides Cicero with the opportunity to rehearse Matius's many kindnesses to him and his family, both during the civil war and afterwards, when Cicero was navigating his position under the dictatorship.[80] The closing letter to Oppius produces a similar picture of friendship, in which political affiliations and personal regard for the welfare of friends are capable of being separated out:[81] Cicero thanks Oppius for helping him come to a decision about his imminent departure for Greece, and contextualizes this assistance

---

77. Cf. *Fam.* 9.9.3 for a similarly periphrastic description of the political vacuum of 49/48 BCE in Dolabella's letter to Cicero in May 48 BCE, attempting to persuade him to change sides and support the Caesarean faction: 'It remains for us to be there where the new *res publica* is, rather than to be in none while we pursue the old one.' (*Reliquum est, ubi nunc est res publica, ibi simus potius quam, dum illam veterem sequamur, simus in nulla.*)

78. *Fam.* 11.1 is composed by D. Brutus to Cassius and M. Brutus a few days after the assassination of Caesar, and *Fam.* 11.2–3 are both addressed by Cassius and M. Brutus (jointly) to Antony in June; while *Fam.* 11.27–9 are Cicero's exchanges with Matius and Oppius.

79. See *Att.* 14.1.1 for the contrast that Cicero draws between Matius and Oppius on the grounds of their different reactions to Caesar's death: one, Matius, reveals a die-hard devotion to Caesar, while the other, Oppius, is more restrained.

80. These are enumerated at length at *Fam.* 11.27.2–5.

81. Hall 2009a, 62 notes the similarity of tone between Cicero's letter to Matius (*Fam.* 11.27) and his letter to Oppius (*Fam.* 11.29).

Ordering the Collection 143

by comparing it to the advice that Oppius gave him in 49 BCE, when he advised Cicero, uncertain whether to join Pompey or stay in Italy, to consider his *dignitas*, by joining the republican forces abroad. Like Matius, Oppius has a track record of separating out his loyalties and of distinguishing personal feeling from his views about the political good, having done this for Cicero at the time of the earlier crisis, in 49 BCE.

The letters to Matius and Oppius contrast instructively with the picture of hardening animosity in the aftermath of Caesar's death that the early letters within this book convey. In the opening letter of *Fam.* 11, D. Brutus expresses strong doubts about Antony's intentions at this time[82]—doubts that are only corroborated by the following letter, penned by Cassius and M. Brutus to Antony, in which we hear of Antony's plans to assemble veterans in Rome for the senate meeting on the kalends of June.[83] And in Brutus and Cassius's second letter to Antony, written after Antony had refused their appeal to be relieved of the corn commission, we are reminded of how far the new crisis that these historical actors find themselves in diverges from the old one: the hostilities that this letter records are decisive and irreversible, and relationships between the figures involved will not be restored.[84] The letters in the frame of the book contextualize the *discrimen* that Mutina represents by reminding readers of the extent to which it differs from the earlier turning point of 49 BCE. Figures like Matius and Oppius will not be the norm in this new crisis; their ability to separate out loyalties belongs to the past.

The structure of *Fam.* 11 also gives D. Brutus's narrative two beginnings: the assassination of Caesar, evoked in *Fam.* 11.1, marks one starting point; and the subsequent provocation that he presents to Antony when refusing to hand over his province, charted from the start of his letter exchange with Cicero, marks another. Cicero argues that the two actions build on each other— that the decision to defy Antony is the logical consequence of assassinating

---

82. At the outset of *Fam.* 11.1.1, D. Brutus describes Antony's *mens* (intentions) as *pessima scilicet et infidelissima* ('utterly depraved, to be sure, and treacherous'): Antony, he claims, was engineering to take D. Brutus's province for himself, and to remove the tyrannicides from Rome, for fear of the danger their potential popularity in the city might pose to himself.

83. Cf. *Fam.* 11.2.1.

84. *Fam.* 11.3.1 opens with Brutus and Cassius describing a letter that Antony has sent them, along with a public edict to the same effect, as 'insulting, intimidating, and hardly a worthy letter for you [Antony] to have addressed to us' (*contumeliosas, minacis, minime dignas quae a te nobis mitterentur*). Antony's letter and edict appear to be responding not only to their appeal to be relieved of the corn commission but to rumours that they were trying to take over the command of armies in the east (as they eventually did).

Caesar,[85] and that between them these two actions generate a momentum of republican resistance that cannot be rolled back.[86] Yet from another perspective, they cancel each other out, lending a further nuance to the idea of the vacuum into which D. Brutus steps. For D. Brutus's refusal to hand over his province was an illegal act, no less than the action that Caesar had taken at the start of the earlier civil war in leading his army over the Rubicon into Italy. The memories of the crisis of 49 BCE that surface in the frame of this book of letters directly invite this comparison with Caesar; *Fam.* 11 reveals how one of Caesar's leading assassins was encouraged to act in a way that resembles Caesar's own criminal actions. The published text of *Philippics* 3 had revealed the ingenious but highly contentious arguments that Cicero had used to persuade the senate at its meeting on December 20 to support D. Brutus's illegal position.[87] The correspondence of *Fam.* 11 builds on this to reveal the leading role that Cicero himself had played in persuading D. Brutus to adopt this position in the first place. Readers familiar with the events of that meeting from the *Philippics* may not have known, for example, that D. Brutus's public opposition to Antony, proclaimed in the despatch that Cicero suggests in *Fam.* 11.6a prompted him to attend the senate meeting that day,[88] was preceded by a personal letter (*Fam.* 11.5) from Cicero encouraging him to take this stand.[89]

---

85. Cf. esp. *Fam.* 11.5.2–3: 'If you recall day and night (as I know that you do) how much you have already achieved, you certainly won't forget how much even now remains for you to achieve. . . . And that's why I beg you with the same prayers used by the Senate and people of Rome that you will set the Republic free for all time from the tyranny of a king, and make your ending agree with your beginning.' (*Tu si dies noctesque memineris, quod te facere certo scio, quantam rem gesseris, non obliviscere profecto quantae tibi etiam nunc gerendae sint. . . . Quamobrem te obsecro, isdem precibus quibus senatus populusque Romanus, ut in perpetuum rem publicam dominatu regio liberes, ut principiis consentiant exitus.*) Cicero's strategy is to present Antony as an extension of Caesar, ignoring the extent to which D. Brutus's actions made him look like a version of Caesar himself.

86. White 2010, 145 argues that the reason why Cicero emphasizes D. Brutus's assassination of Caesar repeatedly in his early letters to him is to sidle around the objection that if he refused to hand over his province to Antony he would be acting illegally, by reminding him that, in killing Caesar, he had already placed himself outside the law.

87. See Galinsky 1996, 51 for discussion of how Cicero get around the question of the legality of D. Brutus's actions at *Phil.* 3.12. Manuwald 2007, 98–101 contextualizes Cicero's appeal to a higher law at this point in the speech by considering this kind of appeal as part a career-long strategy.

88. Sternkopf 1901 explains why this letter should be separated from *Fam.* 11.6, which he dates to September.

89. *Fam.* 11.5 (part of which is quoted in n. 85 above) is dated to around (or shortly after) December 9 on the basis of a reference to Cicero's arrival in Rome on the fifth day before the Ides.

Nor will they have known that Cicero himself wrote a letter (*Fam.* 11.7) to D. Brutus shortly before the senate meeting of December 20,[90] telling him to ignore the senate if it did not vote to support his stance.[91] Postponed to the position that it holds after the later letter of *Fam.* 11.6, this letter (*Fam.* 11.7) caps the series of illegal measures that Cicero urges D. Brutus to take in this early part of their letter sequence, where his advice amounts to a formula for action that looks increasingly like Caesar's five years earlier.

The difficulty of narrating, representing, or even naming the political vacuum of which D. Brutus speaks in the opening letter of *Fam.* 11 is further compounded by the narrative consequences of the position that he finds himself in when he is placed at the centre of this vacuum and targeted accordingly. The confrontation with Antony that Cicero helped bring to a head results in the besieging of D. Brutus at Mutina, a standoff that lasted three months, during which the letter sequence is suspended, because (we assume) letters could neither get in nor out. This is a remarkable moment where historical realities and their representation in the letter book's narrative coincide (and even feed into one another): the siege blocks epistolary communication, while, at the same time, the narrative lacuna produced within *Fam.* 11 by the lack of letters offers a fitting representation of the siege, which is, above all, a blockade imposed on a city by its military enclosure. When the correspondence resumes in late April, it is largely to communicate the fact that the opportunities that once were have been lost, swept up in the epistolary lacuna of the siege, such that the additional hole that this lacuna now expresses is the narrative gap—familiar from *Fam.* 10—between expectation and outcome: a space in which future possibilities have already been overtaken (and cancelled) by an alternative historical narrative.[92]

---

90. See Sternkopf 1901, 282 ff. on the dating of this letter (which he places before *Fam.* 11.6a).

91. *Fam.* 11.7.2: 'But the main point is this . . . that in preserving the liberty and welfare of the Roman people you should not wait for the sanction of a senate which is still enslaved.' (*Caput autem est hoc . . . ut ne in libertate et salute populi Romani conservanda auctoritatem senatus exspectes nondum liberi.*) See Sternkopf 1901 for discussion of the significance of this letter for the events of December 44 BCE and January 43 BCE. The advice to ignore the senate here, on the grounds that, in its currently enslaved state, it was not free to vote according to its natural wishes, conforms with advice we also see Cicero offering Plancus elsewhere in this narrative not to wait for senatorial authorization but 'to be a senate unto yourself' (*Fam.* 10.16.2: *ipse tibi sis senatus*). On this occasion, though, Cicero also emphasizes his concern for Octavian, whose mustering of veterans was in defiance of Antony.

92. This point is emphasized by the speed and frequency with which historical events are voided by subsequent events that displace or nullify their significance at this stage in the narrative of *Fam.* 11: see esp. *Fam.* 11.12, in which Cicero acknowledges his receipt of three letters from D. Brutus, after the siege is lifted, which report the latter's movements in pursuit of Antony

146 SOUVENIRS OF CICERO

D. Brutus's opening letter to Cicero after the siege, written on April 29, eight days after the second battle, emphasizes this with particular force. It begins by describing how much has been lost with the death of Pansa, the second consul to die in the conflict.[93] The sudden coincidence of the two consuls' deaths will go on to dismantle the proper functioning of the senate and will bring to a close the strategy of effective speech that Cicero had pursued with the *Philippics*, by removing the context in which speech might be weaponized. Reflecting on this in retrospect, Cicero comments (*Fam.* 11.14.1):

> *Plane iam, Brute, frigeo; ὄργανον enim erat meum senatus; id iam est dissolutum. Tantam spem attulerat exploratae victoriae tua praeclara Mutina eruptio, fuga Antoni conciso exercitu, ut omnium animi relaxati sint meaeque illae vehementes contentiones tamquam σκιαμαχίαι esse videantur.*

> Right now, Brutus, I'm completely paralysed. My tool was the senate, and that tool is now in pieces. Your brilliant sally out of Mutina, and Antony's flight once his army had been cut down, had brought such high hopes of a definitive victory that now our nerves are all in tatters; and those furious diatribes of mine seem like shadow-boxing.

The death of Pansa, and with him, the proper functioning of the senate, cancels a future for Cicero, as he reckons with the prospect of no longer being able to intervene in the conflict as he had done. More than this, his description of his speeches as 'shadow-boxing' cancels the past too—or rather comments on how past futures, which is to say, the intentions and aspirations of the past, have now been voided.[94] The *Philippics* themselves, now emptied

---

in the aftermath of the battle, and successively build up a picture of Antony's rapid recovery. The rapid series of events that swiftly eliminates D. Brutus's best expectations is matched by the synchronous delivery of his previous three letters, which are brought to Cicero all at once, confounding narrative chronology and compounding the disappointment that they deliver.

93. *Fam.* 11.9 begins: 'It cannot escape your notice how great a blow the republic has received with the loss of Pansa.' (*Pansa amisso quantum detrimenti res publica acceperit non te praeterit.*)

94. *Fam.* 11.14.3: 'For when the victory was announced on your birthday, we caught a glimpse of an independent Republic that might last many generations. These new fears cancel your earlier successes.' (*Nam die tuo natali victoria nuntiata in multa saecula videbamus rem publicam liberatam; hi novi timores retexunt superiora.*) Cicero notably stops short of celebrating the victory at Mutina as a fait accompli in *Phil.* 14.1–5, but he does look forward to receiving the news of it.

Ordering the Collection 147

of all performative effect and effectiveness, are here presented as the ghostly script of a (counter-)history that never was.

Counter-history and the Anecdote in Fam. 11

The siege-like arrangement of letters in *Fam.* 11, which is so distinctive a feature of its organization and form, is part and parcel of its interest in testing the limits and possibilities of historical representation, and in finding alternative ways of conveying the counter-history's (counter)effects. But the book contains other formal means of producing these effects: among the later letters exchanged between D. Brutus and Cicero, two in particular stand out for their presentation of a narrative (or anti-narrative) form—the anecdote—that is also held to disrupt narrative history.

This anecdote, in particular, is worth dwelling on because it challenges the dominating counter-historical narrative within these letter books and opens up alternative narrative vistas, shedding new light on Cicero's intentions throughout this period and opening up a channel for critical voices from below the elite republican narrative to be heard.

The sovereign histories against which counter-histories run are characteristically teleological narratives, which impose a familiar narrative form on the events of which they write, transforming disparate happenstances into meaningful events by relating them in a sequence that builds up to (and explains) a narrative finale. Yet, as Hayden White points out, this mode of narrativity stands in some degree of tension with the historical content of a historical narrative: the events that took place in real time, which (we assume) precede their representation in narrative, and belong to a different order of reality.[95] A characteristic technique of the counter-history is to attempt to puncture the representational veneer of a given historical narrative by disrupting its narrative flow and introducing elements that seem to give us direct access to the historical realities that precede their narrative representation. The anecdote is singled out by historians as a historeme that performs this disruptive function particularly well, puncturing the grand narratives of history by introducing a 'wrinkle' or opening into their

---

95. Cf. White 1987, 1–25. However impossible it may be to access this reality, some historiographical records do come closer to it, documenting events without imposing obvious narrative form on them: White's example in this chapter is the medieval chronicle, which lists the years in sequence, offering entries of events (including such items as crop yields etc) for some years and keeping some years empty.

148

SOUVENIRS OF CICERO

totalizing scope.[96] These openings may be counter-historical simply by running against the grain of common historical narrative explanation. But they are also frequently found to offer a more socially targeted form of counter-history by providing a channel for the suppressed voices of history to be heard.[97]

Towards the end of *Fam.* 11, after the siege and the battles, and after Decimus had failed either to capture Antony or to reconcile Octavian to joining forces with one of his uncle's assassins, we encounter an anecdote that conforms to both these counter-historical ends: it introduces a view of Cicero's about Octavian that we do not hear from him elsewhere in the transmitted corpus of letters, and which even runs directly against sentiments that we hear him expressing earlier on in his correspondence with D. Brutus.[98] It also provides a channel for the otherwise-muted voices of a non-elite group of historical actors to be heard, albeit in the act of quoting Cicero back at himself. Most importantly, perhaps, it forces us to confront the tension between representation and reality which *this* historical narrative raises with particular urgency as a result of being composed out of letters—that is, tokens of the reality of the events that the letter books also describe in narrative form. If, as Hayden White would have it, historical discourse is marked by a tension between the incompatible demands of historical reality on the one hand and of narrative representation on the other, then in some ways the historical narrative that *Fam.* 10–12 presents displays these tensions with particular clarity. The letter as token of reality, or fragment of historical memory, has here been assembled into a structure that parades as its opposite: that is, the historical narrative—a representation of history.[99] When readers experience the puncturing effect of the anecdote in *Fam.* 11.20 and 11.21, they are reminded of the narrative status of the letter sequence that they have been reading so far.

In *Fam.* 11.20, D. Brutus writes to Cicero to relay to him an anecdote passed on to him by an apparently notorious gossip, Labeo Segulius, which

---

96. Cf. Fineman 1989, 61; and Greenblatt and Gallagher 2000, 51–52.

97. Greenblatt and Gallagher 2000, 52: 'The anecdote could be conceived as a tool with which to rub literary texts against the grain of received notions about their determinants, revealing the fingerprints of the accidental, suppressed, defeated, uncanny, abjected, or exotic—in short, the non-surviving—even if only fleetingly.' Greenblatt and Gallagher emphasize the culturalist imprint of the anecdote by presenting the works of E. P. Thompson and Raymond Williams as their main examples of its counter-historical currency.

98. Cf. *Fam.* 11.7 for Cicero's expressions of concern for Octavian's safety.

99. At the same time, though, these letters were always already narrative, linguistic, and, indeed, textual forms, and therefore highlight the extent to which the events of history can hardly be extricated from the media that communicate them. In this sense, the letter book is an extension of a procedure already underway in the letter.

Ordering the Collection

homes in on a saying of Cicero's about Octavian that was currently circulating around Rome (*Fam.* 11.20.1):[100]

> *Saepe enim mihi cum esset dictum neque a me contemptum, novissime Labeo Segulius, homo sui simillimus, narrat mihi apud Caesarem se fuisse multumque sermonem de te habitum esse; ipsum Caesarem nihil sane de te questum nisi dictum quod diceret te dixisse, laudandum adulescentem, ornandum, tollendum; se non esse commissurum ut tolli posset. Hoc ego Labeonem credo illi rettulisse aut finxisse dictum, non ab adulescente prolatum.*

Although I had often been told the story, and hadn't dismissed it, recently Labeo Segulius (and it's so like him) told me that he'd been with Caesar [Octavian], and that there'd been much talk of you; that Caesar himself had made no complaint at all about you except about the remark which he said you'd made to the effect that 'the young man should be praised, honoured, and removed,' adding that he had no intention of being removed.[101] For my part, I believe that it was Labeo who reported the remark to him, or made it up himself, and that it was not brought up by the young man.

D. Brutus goes on to report that the veterans were circulating Cicero's line noisily among themselves with the aim of intimidating Cicero into rewarding them with land and money in his capacity as one of the newly appointed decemvirs tasked with investigating the validity of Antony's *acta*.[102]

---

100. This *bon mot* of Cicero's is also attested by Vell. Pat. 2.62.6 and Suet. *Aug.* 12. Many modern historians lift this anecdote out of context and use it to disclose Cicero's true feelings and intentions about Octavian in this period. While I would be the first to allow that it is the formal prerogative of the anecdote to be circulated out of its original context, my own interest is on its place within the narrative of *Fam.* 10–12.

101. Shackleton Bailey 1977, 541 does not credit the double meaning that most have read into *tollere* here (meaning 'to praise' as well as 'to remove'), arguing that *aliquem tollere* meaning 'to praise' is otherwise unattested without the qualifying phrase *in caelum.* But it is hard to see the point of the quotation without the *double entendre.*

102. Cf. *Fam.* 11.20.1–2: 'But as for the veterans, Labeo would have me believe that they are using the worst kind of language, that you are in danger from that quarter, and that they're especially indignant because neither Caesar nor I are to be found among the ten commissioners, and that everything's been given over to the arbitration of you and your friends.... Regarding your own danger, believe me—what they're hoping is that, once you've been thoroughly frightened and the young man provoked to anger by their careless language and threats of danger,

The embedding of this anecdote within multiple layers of reported speech, and the doubts that D. Brutus himself casts on who said what, creates a halo effect around the saying, as if to highlight the hole that it punctures into *Fam.* 11's narrative of events. But the status of this hole is a strange one. Far from disrupting the representational screen of a historical narrative with an opening that allows readers to make contact with the real, this anecdote is itself hedged with queries about the authenticity of the quotation that stands at its heart. Nevertheless, the puncturing effect remains, and feels all the more scandalous precisely because the narrative that it disrupts is composed out of letters, which, the reader assumes, give us access to Cicero's true feelings and intentions. This anecdote places a wrinkle or opening in that narrative, by revealing Cicero's true sentiments about Octavian, sentiments that remain hidden behind a screen of official policy in the rest of the letters to D. Brutus and others in *Fam.* 10–12. The 'prick of the real' that the anecdote brings to this narrative is the realization that alongside the circulation of the letters and the speeches to which readers of these letter books have been made privy, Cicero's unofficial spoken words, which were also circulating widely but to which we are seldom given access, may tell a quite different story. Joel Fineman argues that the anecdote's disruptive effect comes from the way in which it allows contingency into a narrative, establishing an event as an event both within and also outside its frame.[103] That contingency is brought home by D. Brutus's emphasis on the alternative narrative world that the circulation of Cicero's saying opens up—not only quoted in a conversation between Octavian and Segulius but also doing the wider rounds at Rome (he himself claims to have heard it circulating some time beforehand, even as he also points to its continuing dissemination among veteran soldiers). The anecdote opens up a parallel world and a parallel history within *Fam.* 11's narrative of events, which both

---

handsome rewards may follow; and that the whole point of circulating that jingle of yours is to get as much money as they can.' (*Veteranos vero pessime loqui volebat Labeo me credere et tibi ab iis instare periculum, maximeque indignari quod in decem viris neque Caesar neque ego habiti essemus atque omnia ad vestrum arbitrium essent conlata. . . . nam de tuo periculo, crede mihi iactatione verborum et denuntiatione periculi sperare eos te pertimefacto, adolescente impulso, posse magna consequi praemia, et totam istam cantilenam ex hoc pendere, ut quam plurimum lucri faciant.*)

103. Fineman 1989, 61: 'The anecdote is the literary form that uniquely lets history happen by virtue of the way it introduces an opening into the teleological, and therefore timeless, narration of beginning, middle, and end. The anecdote produces the effect of the real, the occurrence of contingency, by establishing an event as an event within and yet without the framing context of historical successivity, i.e. it does so only insofar as its narration both comprises and refracts the narration it reports.'

Ordering the Collection 151

contains it and is also intersected and even exceeded by it, in that the fears that it reports Cicero harbouring about the danger that Octavian poses to the state will be vindicated by the eventual outcome of events. The hole that it punctures into the narrative of this book is one that will expand to become the history that replaces or swallows up the counter-history that we have been reading so far.

But this story also carries the additional social freight that historians see as part of the counter-historical potential of the anecdote. The ostensible aim of D. Brutus's letter is to warn Cicero of the dangers that the rampant circulation of his saying poses for him, not just in the (relatively) enclosed context of Octavian's conversation with Segulius but more particularly among veterans seeking to intimidate him by quoting it noisily in Octavian's hearing. This narrative—about Cicero's conflict with Caesar's legions—is taken by at least one later historian as disclosing the true balance of power at this time.[104] The account given in *Fam.* 10–12 confirms this view to some extent, highlighting the determining role that the veteran soldiers play in the narrative of events in this period: we hear of them mustering in Rome, at Antony's bidding, to intimidate his political opponents at the senate meeting of June 2, 44 BCE, in *Fam.* 11.2, when the provinces were reallocated; we see Cicero trying to protect those veterans who subsequently abandoned Antony to side with Octavian in *Fam.* 11.7; we hear of the ruthless efficiency with which veteran armies on both sides slaughtered one another at the battle of Forum Gallorum;[105] and we hear that Antony's eventual comeback, following his defeat in this battle, was reliant on the veteran armies that his allies managed to supply for him in Gaul.[106] Yet nowhere within this narrative do we hear the voices of these soldiers speaking. This anecdote allows us to hear, for a fleeting instant, the words that they spoke and, more importantly, the way in which they might

---

104. See App. *B. Civ.* 3.90–93 with Magnino 1984, 195–6; and Gabba 1956, 173–4. Cicero's battle with the loyalties and wishes of the legions is made clear at times in the *Philippics* (e.g., *Phil.* 10.19): 'If the views of this body [the senate] are to be governed by a nod from the veterans and all we say and do is subject to their wishes, then death is to be desired.' (*Si veteranorum nutu mentes huius ordinis gubernantur omniaque ad eorum voluntatem nostra dicta, facta referuntur, optanda mors est.*) Both Syme 1939, 180–81; and Osgood 2006, 43–61 emphasize the role played by the veterans in the events of this period.

105. Cf. *Fam.* 10.30. Osgood 2006, 52 notes how the Martian legion and two praetorian cohorts undertook all the fighting for the republican side at Forum Gallorum, fearing that Pansa's recruits would only confuse things with their inexperience.

106. Cf. *Fam.* 11.10.4 and *Fam.* 11.13a.3 for the swelling of Antony's depleted army with Ventidius's legions.

use speech to push the senatorial class into action (even if those words were simply quoting Cicero back at himself).

Endgames in Fam. *12: Resistance in the Mirror of the* Res Publica

After the claustrophobia of events in Gallia Cisalpina and northern Italy, reported in *Fam.* 10 and 11, we turn, in *Fam.* 12, to the east—and to the future. This book is divided into two groups of letters. The first half is taken up with Cicero's letter sequence with Cassius in Syria,[107] and with other republicans stationed nearby.[108] The latter half consists of letters to Quintus Cornificius, then proconsul of Africa Vetus.[109] The coherence of the book belongs to the chronological significance of these two regions in events that postdate the period covered by the letter collection: while the letters in *Fam.* 12 cover the same period as the letters in *Fam.* 10–11, they turn our gaze towards those parts of the world that will provide some form of historical closure to the period of turbulence that Mutina catalysed in the years that followed Cicero's death. Cassius will remain in the east, eventually joining Brutus to bring the conflict with Antony to one conclusion at Philippi. But the tensions between the triumvirs continue beyond this endpoint in the allocation of provinces after Philippi. Cornificius would die in one of the most complex of these struggles,[110] which was resolved in the provisional settlement that saw Africa awarded to Lepidus, the western provinces to Octavian and the eastern ones to Antony. The geographical movement of *Fam.* 10–12, from correspondents in Gallia Comata, Gallia Narbonensis, and Spain in *Fam.* 10, to Gallia Cisalpina in *Fam.* 11, to the eastern provinces and Africa in *Fam.* 12, takes the reader clockwise through the provincial divisions that would be formally distributed among the triumvirs with the Pact of Brundisium in 40 BCE. Gallia Cisalpina, which was dissolved in 42 BCE and made part of Italia, was the one region that the two leading triumvirs retained in common, and appropriately finds its narrative space in the central book (*Fam.* 11) of the three-book narrative.

---

107. *Fam.* 12.1–12.

108. *Fam.* 12.13 (from Cassius Parmensis, stationed on Cyprus) and *Fam.* 12.14–15 (from Lentulus Spinther in Asia).

109. *Fam.* 12.17–30.

110. Fishwick 1993, 61.

Fam. 12 fills in and recaps the story we have already been told twice over in the preceding books, even as it turns our attention to the story of simultaneous happenings in the east and their consequences beyond the chronological parameters of this letter collection. While much of this eastern story is new, it has been anticipated in earlier books by letters that address or mention its protagonists. Letters exchanged between D. Brutus and Cicero in *Fam.* 11 speak with increasing desperation about the need to send for his cousin M. Brutus,[111] a refrain that Cicero echoes in his letters to Cassius in *Fam.* 12, where he reiterates the idea that all hopes for saving the Republic lie with Brutus and Cassius.[112] The refrain anticipates the showdown at Philippi that will provide this story with one of its narrative endings. But a crisis such as this one, which clusters multiple narrative threads together, has multiple endings, and *Fam.* 12 points readers in the direction of a number of them. Philippi will be one ending, Brundisium another, and Actium and the death of Antony yet another. The extensive treatment of Antony's behaviour in Cicero's early letters to Cassius and the narrative resolution that a letter by Trebonius provides to the reproach that Cicero issues in a letter to him in *Fam.* 10 for not killing Antony at the time of Julius Caesar's assassination combine to focus our attention on the ending that awaits Antony, including the work that will be done to deface his memory after death.[113] Other letter sequences within this book

---

111. Cf. *Fam.* 11.14.2, *Fam.* 11.25.2, and *Fam.* 11.26.

112. Cf. esp. *Fam.* 12.6.2 and *Fam.* 12.10.4.

113. *Fam.* 12.16, written by Trebonius to Cicero towards the end of May 44 BCE, describes a meeting that he held with Cicero's son in Athens, while en route to Asia, and stands out both for its complimentary treatment of Marcus Junior and for the marked contrast in tone it presents to the tetchy letter that Cicero himself writes to Trebonius eight months later, which is included in *Fam.* 10. In that letter, Cicero complains of the role that Trebonius had played in the assassination plot, leading Antony outside the senate house, when (Cicero suggests) it would have been better if he had had him killed too. *Fam.* 12.16 provides an answer to this charge: in the course of praising Cicero's son, Trebonius mentions the hopes that Marcus Junior had expressed to him of visiting him in Asia, hopes that Trebonius says that he encouraged. Cicero's son would eventually leave Athens, not to visit Trebonius but to serve under Brutus in Macedonia, where (we hear in *Philippics* 10) he took over the legion that had been in the command of Antony's legate, Lucius Piso. This marked the beginning of Cicero Minor's public career, a career that was characterized by opposition to Antony throughout. He would go on to fight for the liberators at Philippi, and then sail with the republican survivors of Philippi to Sicily to join forces with Sextus Pompeius, before turning to Octavian in the amnesty of 39 BCE and fighting for him at Actium. As Plutarch relates in the closing sentences of his life of Cicero (Plut. *Cic.* 49.4), Marcus Junior would go on to become consul in 30 BCE, when he was charged with the task of reading out the news of Antony's suicide to the senate, overseeing the removal of Antony's statues from Rome, nullifying his decrees and, in a personal tribute to his father, stipulating that no Antonius could ever again bear the *praenomen* Marcus. This narrative takes place well outside the parameters of *ad Fam.*, but its potential is contained like

154 SOUVENIRS OF CICERO

sketch broader lines of narrative closure—for the Republic as a political entity and for the generation of Romans that this letter collection represents.[114]

But at the heart of *Fam.* 12, we encounter a brief run of letters (*Fam.* 12.13–15) that similarly anticipate the end of the Republic, but which do so by turning the poles of this republican counter-history on their head. The documents are composed by two republican loyalists stationed in Asia (Cassius Parmensis and P. Lentulus Spinther), who offer an extensive report of the war that Cassius and others were waging against Dolabella in the east from late May to mid-June 43 BCE. History would vindicate these authors' expectations of success: Dolabella would go on to commit suicide, after Cassius invaded the town of Laodicea, where he had holed up, cutting him off from supplies and means of escape. Yet for all that the republicans' campaign against Dolabella would be successful, all three of these letters draw attention to various sites of resistance to the republican cause in the midst of this war. One, in particular, holds up a mirror to the Republic and offers a prelude of its eventual downfall.

The first letter in the sequence, written by a kinsman of Cassius, Cassius Parmensis, comes chronologically last and details the start of the final showdown between Dolabella and Cassius at Laodicea in Syria.[115] Cassius Parmensis had participated in the attempt to prevent the fleet that Dolabella had assembled in Asia from reaching Syria. Having pursued the fleet as far as Corycus, on the coast of Cilicia, where it was forced to take refuge, Cassius Parmensis proceeded to Cyprus, from where he wrote this letter, with the aim of passing on to Cicero news that he had heard of the standoff between Dolabella and Cassius in Syria. Towards the end of the letter, Cassius correctly

---

a time capsule within *Fam.* 12.16, in which Trebonius praises the younger Marcus extensively, alludes to his ambitions to look beyond private study and learn something about public service abroad, and anticipates the various forms of revenge that Marcus Junior will eventually take on Antony in the elaborate description that Trebonius offers of a pamphlet that he himself had written attacking Antony in unusually biting terms (*Fam.* 12.16.3).

114. *Fam.* 12.17–30, the letters from Cicero to Quintus Cornificius, close the narrative of *Fam.* 10–12 with a reminder not just of the situation in Africa Vetus, where Cornificius was being urged to resist the takeover of his province first by Gaius Calvisius Sabinus, and subsequently by Titus Sextius, but also of the last generation of Romans for whom Cornificius stands, who combine culture, learning, and good company (on which see esp. *Fam.* 12.17.2, *Fam.* 12.18.2, and *Fam.* 12.20) with a career of public service. The cultured portrait of Cornificius that *Fam.* 12.17–30 yield corroborates the little we know of him from other sources (mainly, that he was a member of Catullus's circle of friends, as seen from the cameo appearance he makes in *Catullus* 38).

115. See App. *B. Civ.* 4.65–73 (with Gowing 1992, 171–72) for the full account of Cassius's final confrontation with Dolabella.

Ordering the Collection

surmises that Dolabella would not be able to withstand the threats of famine and desertion that awaited him as a result of his relative's tactic of penning him into the town and cutting him off from supplies. But before reassuring Cicero of his kinsman's inevitable victory, he alludes in passing to the support that Dolabella had mustered in Laodicea, and before that in Tarsus, recruiting an army from the manpower provided by these two free states (*Fam.* 12.13.4):[116]

> *Dolabellam ut Tarsenses, pessimi socii, ita Laodiceni multo **amentiores** ultro arcessierunt; ex quibus utrisque civitatibus Graecorum militum numero speciem exercitus effecit.*

Like the citizens of Tarsus, our worst allies, so now the Laodiceans, **who are much more insane**, have furthermore sent for Dolabella; and he has managed to produce the semblance of an army out of a rabble of Greek soldiers from both of those states.

The language used here to describe the Laodiceans infatuation with Dolabella is shared by Lentulus Spinther in his description of another eastern state sympathetic to Dolabella in the following letter. The free state of Rhodes had demonstrated its independence by refusing entry to both Dolabella and Lentulus Spinther, when each man came to seek their help for his side.[117] The Rhodians had, however, agreed to provide Dolabella with ships for his fleet, while refusing assistance to the republican side,[118] a decision that Lentulus Spinther takes as a sign of their having sided with Dolabella and a mark of their *amentia* (*Fam.* 12.14.3):

> *Rhodii nos et rem publicam quam valde speraverint ex litteris quas publice misi cognosces. Et quidem multo parcius scripsi quam re vera furere eos inveni. Quod vero aliquid de iis scripsi mirari noli; mira est eorum **amentia**. Nec me meae ullae privatim iniuriae umquam <moverunt>; malus animus*

---

116. See App. *B. Civ.* 4.64; and Dio 47.31.1 for accounts of this episode. Appian, in particular, emphasizes Cassius's brutal treatment of the inhabitants of Tarsus for their fluctuating loyalties towards himself and Dolabella, punishing them with fines that necessitated their melting down temple offerings, confiscating private property, and selling free-born persons into slavery.

117. Magie 1950, 423–26; and Osgood 2006, 89–92 provide further historical and cultural context for this episode.

118. See Dio 77.33.1; and App. *B. Civ.* 4.61. With Magie 1950, 423.

eorum in nostram salutem, cupiditas partium aliarum, perseverantia in contemptione optimi cuiusque ferenda mihi non fuit.

What desperate expectations the Rhodians have of us and the Republic, you will learn from my public despatch. And I have written even more sparingly than my actual experience of their madness deserved. Don't be amazed about the fact that I have written something about them: **their insanity** is astonishing. Nor was it a matter to me of personal injuries. It was their ill feeling towards our very security, their desire for the other side, their persistent contempt for every optimate—all that was more than I could bear.

Yet underpinning Lentulus's description of the enmity driving the Rhodians to act against the interests he represents is an anxiety about what this says about where the *res publica* resides—with his side or with Dolabella's. As Lentulus reminds the senate in his despatch to them, the key term of Rhodes's treaty of alliance with Rome was an agreement to share the same enemies in common.[119] Lentulus is amazed to discover that his understanding of who those enemies are is not shared by the Rhodians, when confronted with a civil war that required them to take sides with one of the two factions dividing Roman rule. The senate might have tried to single out Dolabella and Antony by branding them *hostes*, but Lentulus's letter reveals the Rhodians' desire to plot the divisions along party lines, when he refers to their scorn for the *optimi*. And Lentulus himself more or less confirms the factional nature of the divisions in his public despatch, when he describes the Rhodians' tendency to discredit the position of the *boni* and their inversion of all the truths that he holds dear as a consequence of this (*Fam.* 12.15.3):

> *Rhodios autem tanta in pravitate animadverti ut omnis firmiores putarent quam bonos, ut hanc concordiam et conspirationem omnium ordinum ad defendendam libertatem propense non crederent esse factam, ut patientiam senatus et optimi cuiusque manere etiam nunc confiderent nec potuisse audere quemquam Dolabellam hostem iudicare, ut denique omnia quae improbi fingebant magis vera existimarent quam quae vere facta erant et a nobis docebantur.*

---

119. See *Fam.* 12.15.2 for the details.

I observed that the Rhodians were so utterly sunk in depravity as to think that everyone was in a position of greater strength than the *boni*; to disbelieve the existence of this spirit of harmony and unanimity among all orders in the defence of freedom; to trust that the patience of the senate and of every optimate endured even now, and that no one could have dared judge Dolabella a public enemy; in short, to judge that everything which our enemies were inventing was more true than what was actually happening and I was telling them.

The disbelief that Lentulus experiences in confronting a view of this war that casts his side as the enemy stems from the anomaly of encountering a state that resides outside Roman *imperium*, one that was capable of judging for itself which factions within Rome represented the *res publica* that it wanted to recognize.[120] It takes an encounter with this external viewpoint to reveal the counter-historical perspective of the other side. Or, rather, to reveal the viewpoint that otherwise overwhelms this book of letters (that of Cicero, Cassius Longinus, Cassius Parmensis, and Lentulus) to be counter-historical insofar as it represents the losing side.

But Rhodes would later suffer for this show of independence. Both Appian and Dio record the measures that Cassius and Brutus determined to take against Rhodes and the free states of Lycia in the spring of 42 BCE in return for their having refused to aid their cause in the conflict with Dolabella the year before. Cassius attacked Rhodes in two naval battles, which he won decisively, before confiscating all the gold and silver in the city as part of his peace terms. Brutus led an army into Lycia, and, defeating the forces sent to meet him by the Lycian federation, encountered a more stubborn resistance when he proceeded to attack the city of Xanthus, the comprehensive destruction of which served as an example to the other Lycian cities, which surrendered more quickly.[121] The later sources that report these struggles are divided as to the extent to which these free states suffered at the hands of Brutus and Cassius, or were rather treated sparingly by them, in line with divisions within the broader historiographical and cultural tradition that commemorated

---

120. Osgood 2006, 92 notes how decades later Dio Chryostom (*Or.* 31.66) described the war in which the Rhodians had suffered so much not as a civil war but as 'the war of the Romans', in a comment on the factional nature of this war—as it appeared to outsiders.

121. See App. *B. Civ.* 4.76–80; and Dio 47.34; with Magie 1950, 527–9 for accounts of this episode. A number of the Greek letters attributed to Brutus make reference to his brutal treatment of the Xanthians (see esp. letters 17 and 19). With Jones 2015 for a recent discussion (and attempt to recuperate) the authenticity of these letters.

Brutus and Cassius as either liberators or bandits. Both the triumviral narrative as well as its republican counter-history take ownership of the legacy of Brutus and Cassius, and each co-opts the other's terms of praise and abuse for its own ends.

But cutting across these divisions is a sense of the extent to which Brutus and Cassius recognized (or ought to recognize) these free states in the very acts of resistance that they undertook against them in the name of freedom. Appian's account of Cassius's campaign against the Rhodians includes a lengthy exchange between Cassius and Archelaus, his erstwhile teacher at Rhodes, who formed part of the embassy sent to plead with him to spare the island state.[122] In Appian's rendering of this scene, Archelaus argues that in sparing the Rhodians the Romans would be honouring their commitment to the very same ideal of liberty that was driving the republicans to fight for Rome.[123] Archelaus's words, Appian tells us, made Cassius blush.[124] And Appian likewise records Brutus's admiration for the Xanthians' love of freedom. He notes the pains that Brutus took to prevent their mass suicide when, preferring death to conquest, they threw themselves into the flames of

---

122. Appian *B. Civ.* 4.66–74. With Rawson 1986, 111; and Magie 1950, 423–24.

123. Appian *B. Civ.* 4.67: 'Nevertheless, they still sent an ambassador to Cassius in the shape of Archelaus, who had taught him Greek on Rhodes, to make him a more polished appeal. This he did, taking Cassius's hand in a familiar manner: "As a man who loves Greece, do not destroy a Greek city. **As a man who loves freedom, do not destroy Rhodes** (μὴ πόλιν ἀναστήσῃς Ἑλληνίδα φιλέλλην ἀνήρ, μὴ Ῥόδον φιλελεύθερος ἀνήρ). Do not bring shame on the reputation of our Dorian state which has remained undefeated from its first existence, and do not forget the proud history you learnt in Rhodes and in Rome—in Rhodes, the great exploits of the Rhodian cities even against kings, above all Demetrius and Mithridates, who appeared completely irresistible, **and how these exploits were performed in the name of the same liberty by which you too justify your efforts** (ὑπὲρ ἐλευθερίας ἔπραξαν, ὑπὲρ ἧς δὴ καὶ σὺ φῂς τάδε κάμνειν), and in Rome where you possess inscriptions in our honour, you learnt how much we assisted you in fighting against Antiochus and others. I will say no more of our descent and reputation, **or of the fact that we have never so far lost our freedom** (καὶ τύχης ἐς τὸ νῦν ἀδουλώτου), or of our alliance and goodwill towards you, Romans." ' Osgood 2006, 91 n. 99 notes that Lentulus's letter lends credence to Appian's account. My own view is that (depending on whether one views Appian's account being written prior to the assembling of *Fam.* 12, or vice versa) Appian may either be picking up on the implicit criticism of the republican narrative that is already there in the narrative of *Fam.* 12 or that the narrative of *Fam.* 12 may have been put together influenced by Appian's anti-republican bias, in which case the letters of Lentulus Spinther and Cassius Parmensis will have been chosen because of how well they serve this bias.

124. Gabba 1956, 182–84 regards Appian's account of this episode as steeped in Augustan propaganda (though he does not specify the source).

Ordering the Collection　159

their burning city rather than accepting any terms of surrender.[125] The self-cancelling nature of the resemblance between the liberators of Rome and the free states that were intent on resisting their predations encapsulates many of the paradoxes of counter-history. All the more so because, in retrospect, the defeat of these foreign free states at the hands of the liberators seems to prelude the defeat that the liberators will themselves suffer in due course, and the loss of their own free state to the triumvirs, who will, in turn, restore to Rhodes and the cities of Lycia their former status and privileges. As in Appian's narrative, the letters in *Fam.* 12 encourage us to see the defenders of the Republic and the representatives of these other free states or cities as both opponents and as mirror images of one another, as the counter-historical perspective slides for a moment from the former to the latter. And in that moment, the reader is made to question the counter-historical status of the republican narrative, which appears, from this external viewpoint, as just another exercise in the discourse of Roman sovereign power, little different (and possibly even worse) than its triumviral counterpart. We might expect to find this kind critical view expressed in a source like Appian or, indeed, Josephus (and we do);[126] what is striking is to find it incorporated into the narrative that is penned (at least in part) by the republican loyalists themselves.

Conclusion

We might assume that the decision to include letters such as *Fam.* 12.13 through 12.15 within the narrative of *Fam.* 12 is a sign of the editors' desire to denigrate the republican figures involved, exposing their hypocrisy and blindness. And this must be so, at least in part. But this is not the whole story, as the vast majority of letters in this narrative encourage the reader's sympathy for

---

125. Appian *B. Civ.* 4.80: 'Now that the town was taken, the Xanthians ran home and put their loved ones to death, a fate they willingly endured. Cries of anguish arose, and Brutus, thinking that it was pillage, had heralds order the army to stop. **When he found out what was happening, he took pity on the independent spirit of the Xanthians and offered a truce** (ὡς δὲ ἔγνω τὸ γιγνόμενον, ᾤκτειρεν ἀνδρῶν φρόνημα φιλελεύθερον καὶ σπονδὰς περιέπεμπεν), **but they hurled missiles at the messengers.** They took all their possessions, piled them on pyres which had been previously heaped up inside their houses, and after setting light to the pyres committed suicide on top of them. Brutus saved what he could of the sacred property, but the only prisoners he took from Xanthus were slaves and, of the free population, a few women and not as many as 150 men in all. This was the third occasion on which the Xanthians perished by their own hands in the name of freedom.' See Rawson 1986, 111; and Magie 1950, 528–29 for discussion.

126. See Jos. *AJ* 14.272 and *BJ* 1.220 for a very different account of Cassius's military success in Judaea (including his financial predations of the locals and enslavement of resistant towns) to

the republican plight. Whatever positions our schoolroom training may have taught us to take up with regard to Cicero, Brutus, or Cassius, it would be hard to read this narrative without feeling regret for the fates of Hirtius and Pansa in *Fam.* 10, shock at the behaviour of Lepidus, anxiety for D. Brutus and his troops in *Fam.* 11, when he writes to tell Cicero that his men are starving because he does not have the money to feed them,[127] and dismay at the brutal torturing of Trebonius by Dolabella that we hear about in *Fam.* 12.[128] And it would be hard too to read *Fam.* 12 and feel immune to the pleasure of Quintus Cornificius's company, whom we only ever meet as the addressee of Cicero's letters to him, in one of the collection's one-sided letter sequences that make us long to hear the voice of the muted correspondent all the more.

It is possible to see these sympathies marshalled squarely against Cicero, who holds considerable responsibility for precipitating the conflict that we find narrated in these books: certainly, the letters do not do much to exonerate him, and in fact they contribute certain details about his role in the crisis that it is hard to imagine would otherwise be known to history.[129] But because Cicero is our portal into the social media network from which these letters come, we only ever see this world through the lens of his hopes and desires (hopes and desires that are very difficult to eliminate). When, in the opening letter of *Fam.* 10, Cicero expresses his fears and concerns for a Republic that may soon exist only in name (*Fam.* 10.1.1),[130] it is worth pondering how an imperial reader would experience these sentiments—reading them at a time when the Republic *did* exist only in name. The critical lens that is occasionally cast on Cicero and the other republicans cannot cancel the residual currency

---

that which we find in Cassius's letters to Cicero at *Fam.* 12.11–12. With Osgood 2006, 88–89. And see Osgood 2006, 92 n. 102 on the traces of a critical attitude towards Cassius in Appius's account of Archelaus speech to him at *B. Civ.* 4.67–68. For a further example of Appian's critical attitude towards Cicero, see Winterbottom 1981, 239 on Appian's treatment of Cicero's handling of the Catilinarian crisis at *B. Civ.* 2.3, where Appian incorporates a perspective (which must have its roots in the propaganda against Cicero that circulated in the immediate aftermath of his consulship) that saw his consulship as the cause of the conspiracy.

127. *Fam.* 11.10.5.

128. This event is reported in *Fam.* 12.12.1, *Fam.* 12.14.5, and *Fam.* 12.15.4. It is also the central topic of *Phil.* 11, in which Cicero argued that Cassius should be appointed proconsul of Syria with the task of pursuing Dolabella.

129. See esp. my discussion (with Sternkopf 1901) of the letters to D. Brutus before the senate meeting of December 20 on pp. 144–45 above. See also pp. 134–36 above for discussion of Cicero's promotion of honours for Plancus in *Fam.* 10.10–13, which appear to offer the only historical record of such.

130. See p. 120 n. 19 for discussion of the phrasing of these concerns.

of their narrative. Furthermore, the larger structure of the collection in which we find the narrative of *Fam.* 10–12 located suggests motives for Cicero's polemical stance with which it is hard not to sympathize: coming immediately after *Fam.* 9, a letter book pervaded with Cicero's despair at the outcome of the civil war, when his own attempts at peace-making had failed, and he is left marooned by the political transformations taking place under Caesar's dictatorship, the decision to risk all in the standoff with Antony is given a certain amount of explanatory context.

What is striking about the narrative of *Fam.* 10–12 is that this critical viewpoint comes not from the leaders of the faction on the other side (whose criticism would doubtless reinforce our sympathy for the republicans) but from those whose voices (and perspectives) are generally excluded from both the triumviral narrative and its republican counterpart (excluded, that is, from both the history and the counter-history). The republican counter-history ceases to become 'counter' once it becomes the dominant narrative (as it does in *Fam.* 10–12), and we are made aware of the resemblances between this account of events and the triumviral narrative for which it is meant to provide the negative imprint. Yet the structure of the counter-history forces us to search for counter-effects somewhere, and we find these in the perspectives of those whose voices are seldom heard in either of these histories. These voices slip through the cracks of the narrative in *Fam.* 10–12 and open up a new counter-historical vista on this period, one that comes from below the senatorial elite whose voices otherwise predominate and from outside the controlling reach of Roman imperium. The inclusion within the collection of *Fam.* 10–12, with these particular critical voices, may well reflect the interests and demographic of later imperial readerships, whose greater social mobility and cosmopolitanism might well incline them to sympathize with these very viewpoints.

5

Structures of Feeling

THE HOUSEHOLD OF *FAMILIARITAS* IN *FAM.* 13

WHAT PICTURE OF republican society does *ad Fam.* leave us with? For this is surely one of its most striking effects. Unlike the other letter collections transmitted under Cicero's name, which consist of letters addressed by Cicero to a single individual, the letters in *ad Fam.* address a plurality of readers from across a fairly broad cross-section of Roman society and also include letters written by them to Cicero. The social distribution of the letters themselves makes the collection to which they belong amount to a portrait of this social collective. But, as we have seen, *ad Fam.* is also quite likely the work of another social collective which leaves its own traces on its picture of Roman society: not just the community of late republican social actors who receive and write the letters, but the imperial readerships that the letter books subsequently attract, which display their own cultural prerogatives as another broad social collective in the way in which they select and organize these books into a collection. The portrait of late republican society that we find in *ad Fam.* has been pieced together from the partial memory of these later imperial readerships on the basis of perceived resemblances with their own. This letter collection is, therefore, a portrait of their society too.

The most visible record that we have within *ad Fam.* of the broad distribution of Cicero's original social circle comes in book 13, which amasses a large number of letters of recommendation—the so-called *litterae commendaticiae*—to a particularly large number of addressees: eighty-one letters in total, written to twenty-eight different addressees, recommending the interests of seventy-six other named individuals. Of all the books that seem designed to introduce us to late republican society as a whole, this one seems to do so especially programmatically because its letters of recommendation

Souvenirs of Cicero. Francesca K. A. Martelli, Oxford University Press. © Oxford University Press 2024.
DOI: 10.1093/oso/9780197761960.003.0006

Structures of Feeling 163

are also letters of introduction: Cicero writes to proconsuls and other government agents posted both in the provinces and on the Italian peninsula in order to introduce them to the friends of his who are placed in their vicinity. Taken together, these letters of introduction make the book as a whole serve as a directory for *ad Fam.*, since a number of the people either addressed or mentioned in them appear again within letter sequences elsewhere in the collection as actors in other narratives.[1]

However, the book carries a broader significance for its imperial readerships as an inventory of late republican society, insofar as it holds up a mirror to imperial society and asks its readers if they recognize their own social collective in the reflection of this one. In light of this, it must be significant that the people whom Cicero recommends in this book come from all over the republican empire: from bankers in Asia to hoteliers in Patras, this is a book of cosmopolitan memory-making, one that expands the purview of *ad Fam.* beyond the narrow circle of oligarchs at the centre of late republican power, whose interests take up so much of the rest of the collection. If this letter collection provides a memory of late republican society that an imperial Roman readership could buy into, it may in part be because the farthest reaches of the Roman Empire find representatives in this book of letters.[2]

What unites the people recommended in *Fam.* 13 is the degree of *familiaritas* that connects them to Cicero. The term *familiaris*, used either as an adjective or as a noun, and its variants (including the abstraction *familiaritas*, and

---

1. To name just some of the figures who play a prominent role in other narratives within the collection: Servius Sulpicius Rufus, the addressee of *Fam.* 13.17–27, is also the author and recipient of letters to Cicero in *Fam.* 4.2–6; M. Brutus, whose correspondence with Cicero forms a separate collection but whose letters (co-signed with Cassius) to Antony are included in *Fam.* 11.1–2, is also addressed as governor of Cisalpine Gaul at *Fam.* 13.10–14; Julius Caesar, addressed in *Fam.* 13.15–16, is also addressed in *Fam.* 7.5–6 (and is a ubiquitous topic of conversation throughout the letters contained in *ad Fam.*); Lyso and Asclapo, mentioned respectively in *Fam.* 13.19 and 13.20, also appear as part of the story of Tiro's stay of ill health in Patras in *Fam.* 16.4, 16.5, and 16.9; as does Manius Curius, whose interests are represented in *Fam.* 13.17 and 13.50, and who appears again in *Fam.* 7.28 through 7.29, as well as in *Fam.* 16.4, 16.5, 16.9, and 16.11; L. Munatius Plancus, Cicero's chief correspondent in *Fam.* 10, receives a letter in *Fam.* 13.29; and L. Lucceius, to whom Cicero writes in *Fam.* 5.12, to try to persuade him to write an account of the Catilinarian conspiracy, is recommended by Cicero in *Fam.* 13.41 and 13.42. Many others in *Fam.* 13 are introduced as relatives or close friends of figures who play a prominent role elsewhere in the collection.

2. Although the organization of *Fam.* 13 can seem random, in that it does not follow chronological order, for example, it has a clear spatial organization, in that the letter sequences are organized by addressee, who are identified for the most part as governors and other state officials stationed abroad. Since Cicero's dealings with the peoples of each province is generally determined by the time he spent there at one or other point in his life/career, the book also commemorates the different periods of time that Cicero spent abroad.

adverbs *familiariter* or *familiarissime*) arise seventy-four times in the course of the book—and hence with a prevalence hitherto unseen in this letter collection. But what does this term, or family of terms, mean? It is easy to assume that we know this all too well. It was, of course, precisely the idea of *familiaritas* that so struck Renaissance readers when they unearthed Cicero's letter collections in the fourteenth century that they made it the defining quality of the discourse that they saw exemplified in the letters and singled this quality out as a central object of emulation for their own humanistic enterprise. In doing so, however, they separated off the quality of discourse that the letters display from the structure of social relationships that generated it. A *familiaris* in ancient Rome covers a range of social relationships, from slaves to would-be monarchs (like Julius Caesar), that would not be available to a Renaissance reader, such as Petrarch. The mode of discourse that he finds encapsulated by the 'familiar' (or intimate) style of Cicero's letters, and that seeks to replicate in his own letters to friends, is a Renaissance confection of his own making, informed by the social structures of his own time and place.

How, then, is the range of relationships covered by the term *familiaris* parsed in *Fam.* 13? The very position of the book, between the first twelve letter books addressed to Cicero's senatorial friends and the domestic books that close the collection,[3] invites us to ask this question. What does the inclusion (and position) of this book within the collection tell us about how imperial readers forged their memory of the social relationships that structured late republican society? For Renaissance readers, at least, the term carries with it an affective valence—intimacy—that is at least as important as the social relationships it describes. What are the feelings generated by the range of relationships that Cicero covers with the term *familiaris* in *Fam.* 13? If any book of letters can tell us something about what the relational structures of late republican society felt like, it is this one. Yet the question of how we access that feeling, mediated as it is by the imperial hermeneutic frame of the collection within which it resides, remains a difficult one.

In his analysis of the different rates at which culture moves, Raymond Williams uses the phrase 'structures of feeling' to describe that category of consciousness or affective experience which exerts social pressure but which has not yet crystallized into known social forms.[4] Cultural change, Williams

---

3. *Fam.* 14 and 16 are addressed to the women and ex-slave/freedman secretary in Cicero's household, respectively. For the exceptional status of *Fam.* 15 within this block, see Martelli 2017, 92–94.

4. Williams 1977, 128–36.

Structures of Feeling   165

observes, takes place at variable rates, with the result that the dominant or hegemonic elements of that culture coexist with elements from the past (the archaic and the residual) along with elements that have not yet but will become dominant in the future (the emergent). Epochal history has a tendency to seize upon cultural processes and convert them into systems with determinate features. But the reality of cultural change is that the emergent elements, and the feelings that attend them, evade these known forms and establish alternative structures of their own, at the very edge of semantic availability, which may eventually crystallize into the institutions and formations of the future hegemony.

'Structures of feeling', this tenet of Williams's theorization of culture, has been critiqued from many different angles.[5] But Williams's broader attempt to distinguish between the different rates of cultural change is, as we have seen, very useful for unpacking the multiple cultural and historical layers of which *ad Fam.* is composed.[6] As a central component of this procedure, 'structures of feeling' is an idea worth resuscitating for the insight it may bring to the social feelings that attend the revolutionary changes transforming society in late republican Rome and to the way in which such feelings are subsequently converted into some of the most characteristic institutions and formations of imperial rule.

Fam. 13 stages for us the process by which the structure of feelings in which *familiaritas* participates becomes a fixed structure—a discernible, semantic form that preserves the memory of the originally emergent feeling. The materialist framework of Williams's approach is especially apposite for this book because the major theme that runs through it, in relation to which *familiaritas* forges its emergent structure, centres on questions of property: in this book, we see Cicero, the eternal defender of private property and of the propertied classes,[7] promoting the financial interests of his friends to various state officials against a backdrop of great economic upheaval, particularly in the years 46 and 45 BCE, the period in which most of the letters within it

---

5. Gallagher and Greenblatt 2000, 62–4 offer a helpful summary of the various objections that scholars have lodged against Williams's formulation of this idea.

6. See my discussion in the Introduction on pp. 18–21.

7. One of Cicero's most representative statements to this effect comes in *Att.* 1.19.4 in the context of a discussion of the distribution of the public land in and around Volterra (on which, see my further discussion on pp. 154–56): 'But I, with the considerable gratitude of the landowners, confirmed all the owners in their rights over their *possessiones*. For this, as you know, is my army: the men of property.' (*Ego autem magna cum agrariorum gratia confirmabam omnium privatorum possessiones; is enim est noster exercitus, hominum, ut tute scis, locupletium.*) See Walcot 1975 on Cicero's career-long defence of the rights and interests of private property: from his condemnation of Sulla's confiscations to his resistance to agrarian reform to his

166   SOUVENIRS OF CICERO

were written, when property was going through another wave of redistribution under Caesar, as it had done recently under Sulla. The expressions of *familiaritas* that we see in the letters of book 13 appear in connection with these changes and are accompanied by the expectation that a *familiaris* is someone whose property (or *res familiaris*) one has a duty to protect.

Epicurus and the Household of Friends

The most famous letter in *Fam.* 13 is undoubtedly the first in the book. In *Fam.* 13.1, Cicero writes to Gaius Memmius, well known to modern readers as the addressee of Lucretius's *de Rerum Natura*,[8] and currently living in exile in Athens,[9] to plead with him on behalf of his friend Atticus to give back to the Epicureans the house of Epicurus that he (Memmius) had recently purchased, now that he has abandoned his plans to rebuild on the site. The letter is normally isolated from the rest of *Fam.* 13 and scrutinized for the evidence that it may or may not yield about Memmius's feelings for Epicureanism.[10] My interest in this letter is rather in the position that it holds at the very start of *Fam.* 13 and in the concrete image of a house—and, furthermore, a household—that it presents to readers as this book's opening image.[11]

---

theorization of the foremost duties of a statesman (i.e., to protect private property) in the *de Officiis* (see esp. *Off.* 2.78).

8. Although Hutchinson 2001, 158–9 argues that the addressee of *DRN* may be identified as another C. Memmius, the tribune for 54 BCE, whose handling of the case against Gabinius in this year was praised by Cicero (*ad Qfr.* 3.2.1), most scholars assume the Memmius of *DRN* to be the same figure addressed by Cicero here.

9. The exiled Memmius had been indicted *de ambitu* for his role in the consular elections for 53 BCE, the details of which Cicero lays out in a sequence of contemporaneous letters to Atticus (*Att.* 4.15–18). See Gruen 1969 for discussion of this election.

10. Cf. Morgan and Taylor 2017; Griffin 1995, 33 n. 36; Griffin 1989, 16–17; and Stearns 1931 for discussion.

11. Most discussions of Epicurus's house focus on the question of its separation from the famous garden, which Diogenes Laertius tells us in his discussion of Epicurus' will (Diog. Laert. 10.16–21) was situated outside the Dipylon Gate on the way to the Academy (the house was some distance away in the deme of Melite), and which is commonly identified as the focus of Epicurean observance (and of the Epicurean community) in subsequent sources. See Clay 2009 for discussion of the traditional identification of Epicureanism with the 'retreat' of the garden. Cicero does know of this tradition (see *ND* 1.93, where he refers to the garden disparagingly as a site of *tantum licentiae*), but he chooses to emphasize the house as the locus of the Epicurean community in Torquatus's discussion of the value that Epicureans place on friendship at *Fin.* 1.65 (see p. 168 for discussion).

Structures of Feeling   167

The property itself appears to be a conspicuous wreck—described by Cicero as *nescio quid illud Epicuri parietinarum* ('some dilapidated house of Epicurus').[12] Yet Cicero's plea conjures a list of abstract properties dear to the community of Epicureans that he suggests will be preserved (*tueri*) along with the safekeeping of this crumbling building. Writing to Memmius that he need not remind him of these, since the details of Patro's petition will be well known to him, Cicero proceeds to rehearse them (*Fam.* 13.1.4): *Honorem, officium, testamentorum ius, Epicuri auctoritatem, Phaedri obtestationem, sedem, domicilium, vestigia summorum hominum sibi tuenda esse dicit.* ('He [Patro] says that honour, duty, the sanctity of wills, the authority of Epicurus's name, the solemn plea of Phaedrus, the residence, domicile and reliquaries of great men must be safeguarded by him.') Cicero goes on to comment (*Fam.* 13.1.4): *Totam hominis viam rationemque quam sequitur in philosophia derideamus licet si hanc eius contentionem volumus reprehendere.* ('If we're inclined to find fault with his goal, we may as well be mocking the whole lifestyle and the principles that he follows in his philosophy.') As this aside implies, it is above all the community of Epicureans which will be preserved with the safekeeping of Epicurus's house. The concrete building, which once housed a circle of friends living in commune with the figure of Epicurus, is a tangible symbol of the way of life that unites the community of Epicureans following his death.

What work does this letter do for book 13, placed as it is at its very outset? On the one hand, in recommending the property interests of a group of people to a member of his acquaintance, the letter is typical of many other letters in the book. And in recommending them as a favour to a friend, it is also of a piece with them.[13] But in other respects, the letter is a striking anomaly. Memmius is no empowered state official, but instead is a disgraced Roman citizen, living abroad in exile; and the Epicureans as a group can never inspire Cicero's wholehearted support given his views about Epicureanism.[14] The recommendation stands out from all the others in this book of letters for

---

12. *Fam.* 13.1.3: 'This Patro sent a letter to me at Rome, asking me to make his peace with you and beg you to yield possession to him of some dilapidated house, which once belonged to Epicurus; but I wrote nothing to you because I didn't want your building plans to be impeded by any recommendation of mine.' (*Is igitur Patro cum ad me Romam litteras misisset uti te sibi placarem peteremque ut nescio quid illud Epicuri parietinarum sibi concederes, nihil scripsi ad te ob eam rem quod aedificationis tuae consilium commendatione mea nolebam impediri.*)

13. The fact that the friend in question is Atticus may even lend this letter a programmatic charge. On the relationship between *ad Fam.* and *ad Atticum*, see my discussion on pp. 20–21.

14. Cicero's hostility to Epicureanism is a consistent theme across his philosophical works and his speeches, and that hostility is also revealed in the light mockery of his Epicurean

its reticence in promoting the interests of its *commendatus*, Patro, and invites us to speculate as to what we gain from reading it first.

One answer lies in the striking image of a house or household of friends that the letter delivers to readers as book 13's opening (and guiding) symbol. · Cicero himself fleshes out this image elsewhere in his oeuvre, where he explicates the significance of the house for Epicurus's view of friendship. In the *de Finibus*, the principal speaker, Torquatus, mentions the house in which Epicurus lived alongside a large number of his followers, who were also his friends, in a kind of commune, as part of his larger discussion of the centrality of friendship to the Epicurean lifestyle (*Fin.* 1.65): *At vero Epicurus una in domo, et ea quidem angusta, quam magnos quantaque amoris conspiratione consentientis tenuit amicorum greges! quod fit etiam nunc ab Epicureis.* ('But Epicurus in a single household, and a cramped one at that, maintained a great host of friends, united by a wonderful bond of affection! And this is still a current feature of Epicureanism.') This concrete image—in the shape of a building—of a *familia* or household of friends will manifest in virtual space in the subsequent book of letters, where Cicero's own *familia* of *familiares* is shown not to inhabit the four walls of a single building but to extend across the furthest reaches of the republican empire. Whoever has placed this letter at the front of *Fam.* 13 has converted the original phenomenon that it describes (Epicurus's house of friends) into a semantic form that represents a social structure, along with its concomitant structure of feeling (*familiaritas*), that plays out in more emergent, intangible ways across the other letters contained within this book.

But there remains a sticking point in this interpretation—more particularly, in the misfit between the Epicurean identity of the community represented by Epicurus's crumbling house and the broad community of *familiares* described across *Fam.* 13 as a whole. For Cicero's circle of friends may include the odd Epicurean, but it is certainly not unified by this philosophical school, which Cicero generally shuns. How to explain the decision to use an Epicurean symbol of friendship to describe the community of friends in *Fam.* 13? In Cicero's response to Torquatus in *de Finibus* 2, he contests the Epicurean view of friendship that Torquatus saw symbolized in Epicurus's

---

friends in the letters (cf., e.g., *Fam.* 7.12, to Trebatius Testa following the latter's conversion to Epicureanism; *Fam.* 9.15–26, to Papirius Paetus; and *Fam.* 15.16–18 to Cassius, whose Epicureanism is the target of Cicero's melancholy humour in this letter sequence). For general discussion of the philosophical grounds for Cicero's rejection of Epicureanism, see Nicgorsky 2002; Stokes 1995; and Striker 1996. For discussion of Cicero's anti-Epicurean polemic in the speeches (esp. *Pis., Sest.* 23 and 138–39, and *Cael.* 39–42), see Maslowski 1974.

household, objecting in particular to the utilitarian value that Epicureans place on friends (*Fin.* 2.84–85):[15]

'Utilitatis causa amicitia est quaesita.' Num igitur utiliorem tibi hunc Triarium putas esse posse quam si tua sint Puteolis granaria? Collige omnia, quae soletis: 'Praesidium amicorum.' Satis est tibi in te, satis in legibus, satis in mediocribus amicitiis praesidii; iam contemni non poteris, odium autem et invidiam facile vitabis, ad eas enim res ab Epicuro praecepta dantur. Et tamen tantis vectigalibus ad liberalitatem utens etiam sine hac Pyladea amicitia multorum te benevolentia praeclare tuebere et munies. 'At quicum ioca seria, ut dicitur, quicum arcana, quicum occulta omnia?' Tecum optime, deinde etiam cum mediocri amico. Sed fac ista esse non importuna; quid ad utilitatem tantae pecuniae? Vides igitur, si amicitiam sua caritate metiare, nihil esse praestantius, sin emolumento, summas familiaritates praediorum fructuosorum mercede superari.

'Friendship is sought on the basis of utility.' So do you really think that Triarius here could provide you with more utility than you would have if you owned the granaries at Puteoli? Gather in all the usual Epicurean maxims: 'Friends give protection.' You can protect yourself well enough, the laws can protect you, and ordinary friendships (*mediocres amicitiae*) can protect you too. You already have too much power to be easily slighted. You will avoid without difficulty incurring resentment and envy, given that Epicurus lays down rules for doing so. In fact, with a handsome income at your disposal with which to demonstrate your largesse, the goodwill of hundreds will ensure you excellent protection and defence, even though you may lack the friendship of a Pylades and Orestes. Who, as the saying goes, will you have to share your thoughts with, be they light-hearted or serious, and your deepest secrets? You will have yourself, best of all, and perhaps some ordinary friend as well. Granted, friendship has its advantages. Still, they are nothing compared to the usefulness of all that money. I hope you see, then, that when friendship is measured by the affection it generates from within, there is nothing to surpass it. If, on the

---

15. Similar objections to a utilitarian estimation of friendship (with particular emphasis on the term *utilitas*) are found in Cic. *Am.* 26–27.

170 SOUVENIRS OF CICERO

other hand, you judge it in terms of profit, then the rent from a valuable estate will outweigh the closest friendship.

Cicero's protestation in this passage that friendship is an object to be completely divorced from money or questions of economic advantage will be news to readers who have read *Fam.* 13 first, since the utility (economic and otherwise) of Cicero's services to his *familiares* is one of the most insistent desiderata sustained across this book of letters. Verboven's conception of 'instrumental friendship', a phrase that captures his view of the role played by *amicitia* in the Roman economy, and of the economic goals that were channelled through informal social networks in late republican Rome, is derived overwhelmingly from this book of letters.[16]

The terminology of utility is embedded in some of the most common formulations of friendship in *Fam.* 13: one way in which Cicero expresses the degree of *familiaritas* connecting him to his *commendatus* is with the phrase '*utor X familiariter/familiarissime*'.[17] If the idea of utility expressed by the verb *utor* in this idiom seems too fossilized to be meaningful or even perceptible, it becomes visible thanks to the recurrence of a complementary closing formula: Cicero's wish that this letter will be of use (*usus*) to the *commendatus*.[18] These opening and closing formulae, which convey the mutual utility of each friend to the other, express a transactional relationship, one that complements the economic function that the vast majority of these recommendation letters serve. Contrary to expectations, it is precisely the utilitarian value that Epicureans place on friendship which makes Epicurus's household of friends an apposite symbol for this book of letters. The editor's decision to place this letter first expresses a wry recognition that the reality of Cicero's friendships

---

16. Verboven 2002. Along with *ad Atticum*, *Fam.* 13 must be the most cited text within this study, not just in the section on 'recommendations and *gratia*' (pp. 287–323), but across the work as a whole. While Verboven's emphasis on the role played by friendships and informal social networks in the Roman economy is to be welcomed, there are certain methodological problems involved in extrapolating generalizations about the Roman economy from this particular book of letters. For further discussion of these problems, see pp. 184–186.

17. The formula appears eighteen times in total in the course of the book.

18. E.g., *Fam.* 13.20, which begins: '**I'm on very familiar terms** with the doctor Asclapo.' (*Asclapone Patrensi medico* **utor valde familiariter**.) And closes: 'So I recommend him to you, and ask you to make an effort to convince him that I have taken special pains in writing on his behalf, and that my recommendation **has been of considerable use to him**.' (*Hunc igitur tibi commendo et a te peto ut des operam ut intellegat diligenter me scripsisse de sese meamque commendationem* **usui magno sibi fuisse**.)

with *familiares*, as shown across *Fam.* 13, is somewhat different from the idealized picture that we receive from his philosophical treatises.[19]

The Domus *as a Principle of Social Structure*

Throughout *Fam.* 13, the function of *familiaritas* is presented as an obligation to protect the property of one's *familiares*. Property takes many forms, ranging from abstract business speculation and other financial interests, vaguely referenced by the catch-all *negotia*,[20] or, even more inscrutable *res*,[21] to the reassuringly concrete. Perhaps the most ostensibly tangible form that the property of a *commendatus* takes is the *domus*; yet the obligation to protect the *domus* of a *familiaris* extends to the people who represent it socially, which range from the slaves, *liberti*, and family members who dwell within it,[22] at one time or another, to the extended network of friends and associates who come into and out of it. In this way, *Fam.* 13 expands on the opening image of Epicurus's house of friends to construct a picture of social obligations in which the house stands as the most significant structuring principle. Roman society at large is presented as a network of intersecting households, the interests of which are facilitated by the ability of its members to move from one to another. This structure, however, gains new meaning within the imperial period, when the *domus* of the emperor, and his *familia* (the *familia Caesaris*), overshadows all others and takes over many of the bureaucratic operations that had been managed by senators and their agents at the time of Cicero's writing.

---

19. The discussion in Hanchey 2013 of Cicero's abhorrence of the Epicurean idea that an important *beneficium* of friendship was the *utilitas* (including commercial/economic *utilitas*) that friends could confer on one another is drawn entirely from Cicero's philosophical treatises and speeches, and notably contains no reference to *Fam.* 13.

20. The term *negotium* (or its variants) appears in thirty-one of the seventy-nine letters.

21. Throughout *Fam.* 13, it is strikingly difficult to distinguish the meaning of *res* as 'matter' or 'case' (as in, 'the matter of the *commendatus* that claims the attention of the addressee'), from its meaning as 'property', since frequently these two things slide into one another (i.e., the case being put to the addressee's attention concerns the property of the *commendatus*).

22. In her discussion of Cicero's habit of casting himself as a quasi-kinsman to the friends of his whose interests he promotes in his letters (e.g., Atticus in *Fam.* 13.1, who is described as *alterum fratrem*), Wilcox 2012, 33 likewise emphasizes the obligations that membership of the same broad household incurs.

172   SOUVENIRS OF CICERO

When the *domus* is mentioned as an object of property to be protected, it frequently arises as part of a list of items that are implicitly either associated or equated with it—most often, *res familiaris*, the broad term for property in general, and the *familia* who live in it or look after it, most commonly its *liberti*.[23] A *domus*, then, is both property and people, house and household.[24] The latter dimension of the *domus*, and the obligations that it incurs, is represented in *Fam.* 13 by the large number of letters that Cicero writes recommending these household members, whether as instruments of their master's *domus* or simply as associates of it.[25]

Immediately after the opening letter to Memmius about the Epicureans, Cicero writes to the same addressee to promote the interests of C. Avianius Evander, the freedman of a friend of Cicero's (M. Aemilius Avianius), and a talented sculptor, whose statues Cicero would later unwittingly purchase through an intermediary.[26] The letter picks up the theme of *Fam.* 13.1 by concerning itself with the question of Evander's lodgings: currently residing in Memmius's *sacrarium*,[27] while he works on a sculptural commission for this building, Cicero writes to Memmius to ask him to sort out the matter of Evander's dwelling while he is currently occupied with a number of pressing commissions. Cicero's concern for a member of Avianius's household is expressed as a concern to reconstitute a physical *domus* for Evander now removed from the *domus* of his patron.

We hear again about Marcus Aemilius Avianius, the patron of Evander, vicariously in some of the letters that Cicero sends to Servius Sulpicius Rufus, governor of Achaea in 46 BCE, recommending another of Avianius's freedman, Hammonius, in his capacity as procurator of (or at) his master's

---

23. Cf., e.g., *Fam.* 13.21: 'I recommend to you, in a greater degree than usual, **his home, which is at Sicyon, his private property, and Gaius Avianius Hammonius, his freedman**, most especially, whom I also recommend to you on his own terms.' (*Commendo tibi in maiorem modum **domum eius quae est Sicyone remque familiarem, maxime C. Avianium Hammonium, libertum eius**, quem quidem tibi etiam suo nomine commendo.*) And *Fam.* 13.38: 'But I recommend his home, his property and his land agents to you.' (*Sed tamen domum eius et rem familiarem et procuratores tibi sic commendo.*)

24. Saller 1994, 80–101.

25. Mouritsen 2011, 62 notes the large number of recommendation letters that Cicero writes on behalf of freedmen. The majority of those that he mentions come from *Fam.* 13.

26. Cf. *Fam.* 7.23. See Deniaux 1993, 466–7 for the full prosopographical portrait.

27. Scholars differ in their interpretation of the location of this building. Treggiari 1969, 137 believes it to be in Rome; while Deniaux 1993, 466 thinks it more likely to be in Athens.

property at Sicyon.[28] In *Fam.* 13.21, Cicero writes to commend Avianius's house, property, and above all, the freedman Hammonius, who, he tells us, has proven his loyalty not only to his master but also to Cicero himself in the days of his exile. When later in the book, in *Fam.* 13.27, Cicero writes to Sulpicius to thank him for acting on the previous recommendation, he draws his addressee into the set of relationships that is structured around Avianius's household by suggesting that even if he (Cicero) had been at Sicyon in person he could not have done more in his friends' interests than Sulpicius has done for them. The letter closes with an account of the close terms on which Cicero is currently living alongside Sulpicius's son at Rome, as if to demonstrate the reciprocity of this relationship.[29] As Sulpicius has protected the household of one of Cicero's friends in his province, so Cicero reciprocates that behaviour by bringing a member of Servius's family into his own company and, implicitly, household at Rome. The structure of social relationships that these two letters describe is conveyed by the capacity of the various individuals mentioned to slide into and out of one other's households, at Rome and abroad. They build on *Fam.* 13.2 by showing how the *domus* of a single patron (here, M. Aemilius Avianius) provides the basis of a network that becomes infinitely extendable, as its members form friendships independent of their patron (or father).

The network of intersecting *domus* may be expressed, as here, across letters, or it may be depicted within the space of a single letter. We see this with peculiar clarity in one of the two letters addressed in this book to Julius Caesar. In *Fam.* 13.16, Cicero writes to Caesar to recommend Apollonius, a freedman of the now dead P. Crassus (son of the triumvir), as a suitable candidate for writing a literary account of Caesar's *acta* in Greek. The letter tracks Apollonius's movement between the entourages of a variety of notable Romans in the course of his peripatetic career. Beginning that career in the household of P. Crassus, he subsequently joined Cicero in Cilicia after Crassus's death, before then joining forces with Caesar in Alexandria, and thereafter in Spain. But what recommends Apollonius in Cicero's eyes is the time he spent studying with Diodotus in Cicero's own house in his youth

---

28. Treggiari 1969, 104 notes how this letter recognizes Hammonius's status as both his patron's procurator and a businessman in his own right (*suo nomine*).

29. *Fam.* 13.27.4: 'I'm living on the most delightful and friendly terms with your son Servius and draw great pleasure from his talent and dedication as well as his virtue and integrity.' (*Ego cum tuo Servio iucundissimo coniunctissime vivo magnamque cum ex ingenio eius singularique studio tum ex virtute et probitate voluptatem capio.*)

(*Fam.* 13.16.4): *Nam domi meae cum Diodoto Stoico, homine meo iudicio eruditissimo, multum a puero fuit.* ('For he was often at my house since his childhood, studying with Diodotus the stoic, a man of great erudition in my opinion.') The structure of relationships connecting P. Crassus, Cicero and Caesar is depicted through the movement of this *libertus* across their households, not just in his professional life, but in the earlier years of his education too.

Cicero's support for Apollonius devolves from his affection for his former master, P. Crassus. But this is not typical of his letters in support of freedmen in *Fam.* 13, for as the letters recommending Evander and Hammonius demonstrate, in many cases the patron who may have provided Cicero with his initial point of access to them is incidental to his affection for them. This dynamic is sustained throughout *Fam.* 13, which emphasizes the extent to which the members of a *domus* are not simply valued as extensions of their master but as social agents in their own right. As *Fam.* 13 progresses, we see that the autonomy of Cicero's affection for the various freedmen he promotes is a mark of their own autonomy as social agents and testifies to their capacity to extend the social structure represented by the *domus* of their patrons in their own right and on their own terms. Even to set up *domus* of their own.

In *Fam.* 13.60, for example, Cicero writes to a C. Munatius to recommend L. Livineius Trypho, the freedman of a friend, Regulus, who has been recently exiled. Cicero claims to have the utmost sympathy for Regulus, but reserves his strongest claims of affection for Trypho, who is identified as having been a source of great practical assistance during the period of Cicero's own exile (*Fam.* 13.60.1): *Sed ego libertum eius per se ipsum diligo; summa enim eius erga me officia exstiterunt his nostris temporibus, quibus facillime benevolentiam hominum et fidem perspicere potui.* ('But I love his freedman for his own qualities, for he extended to me the greatest possible services at that time in my life when I was in the strongest position to discern people's goodwill and loyalty.') Regulus's exile provides the occasion for reflecting on the services that his freedman performed for Cicero at the time of *his* exile, and highlights the preference shown here for the freedman over his patron. The verb *diligere* used here of Trypho recurs repeatedly throughout *Fam.* 13 to describe Cicero's affection for various freedmen, as well as their affection for him. Cossinius's entire household loves Cicero, we are told in *Fam.* 13.23.1, and above all his freedman Anchialus (*tota Cossinii domus me diligit in primisque libertus eius, L. Cossinius Anchialus*), whom Cicero could not commend more highly if he were patron to Anchialus himself, as he urges Sulpicius, his addressee, to admit this freedman into his *amicitia*.[30] And in a later letter, *Fam.* 13.69, Cicero expresses his affection for the freedman of his friend Postumus, C. Curtius Mithres, with whom he often stays when at Ephesus.[31] The autonomy of the freedman as an object of affection and as a social agent in his own right reaches its apex here, where it is represented by the *domus* over which this *libertus* now presides. Cicero who was shown trying to secure temporary housing for Evander in *Fam.* 13.2 is explicitly shown to be the regular recipient of such hospitality from a freedman in *Fam.*13.69.[32]

The freedman's experience offers a particularly useful lens through which to consider the role played by the *domus* as a structuring principle of Roman society because his social mobility bespeaks a quite literal ability to move across households, of various social classes, whether as an intermediary for his social superiors or as an agent in his own right. Tracing the movements of these *liberti* through the *domus* in which they find patronage or refuge in *Fam.* 13 allows us to form a picture of the vertical axis that structures Roman society at this time: from the top strata represented by the households of big men, on whom a *libertus* like Apollonius depends, down to somewhere nearer the bottom, in the household of C. Curtius Mithres at Ephesus. Yet when a freedman is shown hosting Cicero within his own home, it becomes very difficult to locate him on a social spectrum at all, and it highlights rather the extraordinary degree of social mobility that *Fam.* 13 charts. Many of the freedmen singled out for a recommendation in *Fam.* 13 are identified as having helped Cicero during the time of his exile, when his own social status was at its lowest, and when this social injury was marked above all by the loss

---

30. *Fam.* 13.23.2: 'I recommend him to you so warmly that if he were my own freedman and were in the same standing with me as he is with his patron, I couldn't commend him with more enthusiasm. You'll therefore do me a great favour if you take him into your friendship. . . .' (*Hunc tibi ita commendo, ut, si meus libertus esset eodemque apud me loco esset quo est apud suum patronum, maiore studio commendare non possem. Quare pergratum mihi feceris si eum in amicitiam tuam receperis. . . .*)

31. *Fam.* 13.69.1: 'C. Curtius Mithres is of course, as you know, the freedman of my very close friend Postumus, but he respects and pays his dues to me as much as to his patron. At Ephesus, whenever I happened to be there, I stayed at his house and treated it as if it were my own.' (*C. Curtius Mithres est ille quidem, ut scis, libertus Postumi, familiarissimi mei, sed me colit et observat aeque atque illum ipsum patronum suum. Apud eum ego sic Ephesi fui, quotienscumque fui, tamquam domi meae.*)

32. It may be no accident that these two letters come at opposite ends of this book of letters, inviting us to track how far the *libertus* has come in the period that *Fam.* 13 covers (*Fam.* 13.2 and *Fam.* 13.69 are, respectively, the first and last letters in *Fam.* 13 to recommend the interests of a freedman).

176 SOUVENIRS OF CICERO

of his own *domus*. With his own social position now restored, he returns the favour to these low-status *liberti*, aiding them on their own social and physical trajectories in ways that appear to bring senator and freedman onto the same sliding social scale.

The letters in *Fam.* 13 are often taken to testify collectively to the influence that Cicero still commanded after the civil war (when the majority of them were written) among those whom Caesar placed in positions of power. Yet the relatively low status of the people whom he recommends to these Caesareans tells a different story. Not simply that Cicero was reduced to promoting those on the lowest social rung of society. But rather that the social structure configured by the *domus* was currently turning social categories inside out.

Hospitium *and the Empire-wide* Familia*: Cicero's Virtual Household*

Many of the *liberti* who appear as *commendati* in *Fam.* 13 form part of a wider network of friendships that Cicero built up with non-Romans abroad during his years of public service in the provinces, the contours of which are outlined in the course of *Fam.* 13. Letters to M. Acilius Glabrio (*Fam.* 13.30–39), who was proconsul of Sicily in 46–45 BCE, and to other state officials in Sicily at this time,[33] show Cicero recommending a number of Sicilians whose friendship he had cultivated as quaestor in 75 BCE; while letters to Servius Sulpicius Rufus (*Fam.* 13.17–28), who was posted to Achaea in 46 BCE, and a variety of other individuals posted to Asia and other provinces in the Greek-speaking East,[34] show Cicero recommending the various Greeks and Greek-speaking locals whom he had befriended during the educational travels of his youth or his time in exile in 58 BCE or while on tour in Cilicia in 51 BCE or even, more recently, during the civil war. The profusion of Greek names in this book of letters offers striking testament to the actual relationships that Cicero maintained with the people whose culture he admired so greatly in the

---

33. *Fam.* 13.52: to Q. Marcius Rex, propraetor of Sicily in 46; *Fam.* 13.75: to T. Titius, Pompey's legate when the latter was *praefectus annonae*; *Fam.* 13.78–79: to Aulus Allienus, proconsul of Sicily in 46.

34. E.g., Q. Minucius Thermus, propraetor of Asia in 51–50 (*Fam.* 13.53–57); Q. Anchiarius, proconsul of Macedonia in 55 (*Fam.* 13.60); P. Silius, propraetor of Bithynia and Pontus in 51 (*Fam.* 13.61–65); P. Servilius Isauricus, propraetor of Asia in 46 (*Fam.* 13.66–72); Q. Marcius Philippus, pronsul of Asia for a year that remains unknown (*Fam.* 13.73–74), along with his legate, Quintius Gallus (*Fam.* 13.63–64), and proquaestor, Apuleius (*Fam.* 13.65–66).

Structures of Feeling 177

course of his many sojourns into their territory, and make the book participate in the idealized vision of beneficent imperialism that we have seen this letter collection promotes.[35] The *liberti* form part of this picture; but not the whole picture. Cicero's relationships with non-Romans of more equal social status allow us to construct a picture of social exchange across the republican empire in which the *domus* extends not just vertically, in hierarchical terms (as is emphasized in the case of the *liberti*), but spatially as well.

The relationship with foreigners of equal social rank that these letters stress is one of *hospitium*,[36] friendship based on mutual hospitality, which is, as Hellegouarc'h notes, normally reserved for non-Romans, or, at the very least, for Roman friends residing outside Rome.[37] In a number of instances, we hear explicitly that hospitality means opening one's house to the other. This ideal of friendship participates squarely in an idea of the house or household that I want to suggest is integral to the meaning of *familiaritas* that *Fam.* 13 generates and expresses the reciprocity that is assumed to form part of this idea. In *Fam.* 13.19, for example, Cicero writes to Servius Sulpicius Rufus, now stationed in Greece, to recommend admitting a friend of his, Lyso of Patras, into his own inner circle of friends. The grounds for Cicero's friendship with Lyso is, as Cicero notes, *hospitium*: he (Cicero) virtually took Lyso into his own home in Rome following the civil war (in which Lyso had sided with Pompey), when he helped Lyso obtain his pardon from Caesar.[38] While *Fam.* 13 documents only this side of the *hospitium* shared between the two men, the collection as a whole reveals the bond to be reciprocal. Early on in *Fam.* 16, we hear how Lyso had, for his part, taken Tiro into his home in Patras when the

---

35. Rowland 1972, 459–60 colludes with Cicero's (or his editors') vision, concluding: 'The large number of friendships with powerful and influential Greeks acquired by a new man in relatively brief tours of duty abroad is an important testimony to the workings of the Roman system of provincial government—in fact, to the working of the Roman system.'

36. Hellegouarc'h 1963, 50 follows Mommsen 1864 (vol. 1), 324 in viewing *hospitium*, along with *amicitia*, as a relationship reserved for social equals. In *Fam.* 13.69, where he explicitly describes staying with the freedman C. Curtius Mithres, Cicero does not use the term *hospitium* to describe their relationship, nor does he use it to describe his relationship with any other *libertus* in this book of letters.

37. Hellegouarc'h 1963, 51–3. In *Fam.* 13, Cicero notably sticks to the principle of reserving the term *hospitium* to describe relationships with non-Romans or newly enfranchised Romans. Cf. Sherwin White 1973, 301 on the relationship of *hospitium* between Balbus and his provincial friends once he becomes a citizen of Rome.

38. *Fam.* 13.19.1: 'When he spent nearly a year in Rome, with the result that he was living with me....' (*Is cum Romae annum prope ita fuisset ut mecum viveret....*) Lyso's proximity to Cicero during his year at Rome is similarly stressed in *Fam.* 13.24.2: 'When Lyso was in my company

latter fell sick when accompanying Cicero back to Rome from Cilicia.[39] The expectation of reciprocal *hospitium* incumbent on a *hospes* is shown here to extend not just to individual guests but to the other members of their *domus*, as if this bond enabled the entire household of a Roman to rematerialize in the house of his *hospes* many miles away in a distant province.

On top of this, *Fam.* 13.19 speaks to the ways in which friendship with a *hospes* might be expected to extend to others and create further networks— and households—of *familiares* abroad. Servius Sulpicius Rufus, for example, is advised to receive Lyso into his *necessitudo* while stationed in Achaea. More striking, perhaps, is the account this letter gives of another Roman who has already done precisely this. In the course of recommending the protection of Lyso and his family to Servius, Cicero mentions that Lyso has a young son, who has already been adopted by a former client of Cicero's, C. Maenius Gemellus,[40] when the latter was stationed in Patras while in exile from Rome. Gemellus was made a citizen of Patras while he was there, and his adoption of Lyso's son appears to be a condition of the city's 'adoption' of him.[41] But whether his adoption of Lyso's son was voluntary or imposed by his new civic status, the procedure speaks to the formation of new *familiae* that this book of letters thematizes. When Cicero asks Servius to protect the inheritance that is due to Lyso's son as Gemellus's adoptive heir, we see the remarkable situation of a Roman (Servius Sulpicius Rufus) using the authority that the Roman state has given him to protect the rightful property that a Greek (Lyso's son) has inherited from a Roman (C. Maenius Gemellus), according to the civic laws of a Greek city. The various individuals involved in this sprawling *familia* of *familiares* are shown here to be crossing a number of cultural and civic boundaries in order to forge their emergent network far away from Rome.

Within book 13, the bonds of *hospitium* are frequently expressed in terms that convey the timeless antiquity of the mode of indebtedness that this

---

almost every day, and was living with me. . . .' (*Lyso vero cum mecum prope cottidie esset unaque viveret.* . . .) Shackleton-Bailey 1977, 445 stresses that this need not mean living under the same roof.

39. Cf. *Fam.* 16.4, 16.5, and 16.9.

40. We know nothing about C. Maenius Gemellus, nor about the trial in which Cicero defended him.

41. Greenidge 1901, 510 explains the procedure that allowed certain free and federate cities in Italy and the provinces, including Patras, to make an exiled Roman citizen a citizen of their community. It is not clear whether the law that Cicero mentions in this letter, which insisted that a new citizen of Patras had to adopt a native child of the city and make that child his heir,

Structures of Feeling 179

relationship incurs.[42] The inheritance of the bond of *hospitium* across generations is an explicit theme in some of the letters, where, sustained as it is between people of different cultures and languages, it carries an almost Homeric resonance at times.[43] Yet the antiquity of the bond cannot disguise the novelty of the situation in which some of the cultural crossing that takes place in the name of *hospitium* occurs. A number of letters in *Fam.* 13 refer to the *hospitium* that Cicero shares with non-Romans who have recently been made citizens of Rome, and thus provide evidence for the new wave of provincial enfranchisement that Caesar instantiated at this time.[44] Elsewhere in the collection, we hear Cicero lamenting this development.[45] But in this book, he is shown to collude with it, and the *hospitium* that he shares with these newly enfranchised foreigners stands as a microcosm of the *hospitium* displayed by the Roman state as it welcomes them into its rights and laws.

In *Fam.* 13.35, Cicero writes to M. Acilius Glabrio, proconsul of Sicily in 45 BCE, to promote the interests of Avianius Philoxenus, a Sicilian Greek and *hospes* of Cicero, who was one of the five hundred distinguished Greeks enrolled as colonists of Novum Comum under the *Lex Vatinia* in 59 BCE,

---

held for other federate cities too. Cf. also Costa 1927, 63 n. 9 and 85 n. 1 on this letter; and Bernhardt 1971, 119 on the status of Patras as a *civitas foederata*.

42. Mommsen 1864 vol. 1,·329 views *hospitium* as an older relational model than *amicitia*. Hellegouarc'h 1963, 50 shares with Mommsen the view that *hospitium* is hereditary.

43. Cf. esp. *Fam.* 13.34: 'I am bound by ties of hospitality to Lyso of Lilybaeum, dating from his grandfather's day; he is very attentive to me, and I know him to be worthy of his father and grandfather; for he comes from a very noble family.' (*Avitum mihi hospitium est cum Lysone, Lysonis filio, Lilybitano, valdeque ab eo observor cognovique dignum et patre et avo; est enim nobilissima familia.*)

44. Cf. Brunt 1971, 239; Yavetz 1983, 69; and Deniaux 1993, 316 for clear agreement that Caesar's policy of extending citizenship to provincials was more expansive than that of other late republican generals. Caesar's expansion of the franchise takes place in three stages: first, in 59 BCE with the new colony at Comum under the *Lex Vatinia*; second, in 49 BCE with the grant of citizenship to the inhabitants of Cisalpine Gaul under the *Lex Roscia* (on which, see Yavetz 1983, 66–70), and to the inhabitants of Gades under the *Lex Iulia de civitate Gaditanorum* (on which see Yavetz 1983, 70–73); and third, in 47 BCE with the enfranchisement of all doctors practising at Rome, as well as those teaching literature (Suet. *Iul.* 42.1). Millar 1977, 478 notes Caesar's preferential treatment of Greeks in this latter measure, as well as in the various attested cases of his granting citizenship to individual Greeks.

45. *Fam.* 9.15.2 (to Paetus): 'But (whatever you make of it) I'm amazingly fond of jokes, especially those of our country, and most particularly because I see that they're now forgotten, since foreigners are now all over our city, with the influx of trousered tribes from across the Alps, so that not a trace of our old native wit can be found any more.' (*Ego autem (existimes licet quidlibet) mirifice capior facetiis, maxime nostratibus, praesertim cum eas videam primum*

and who obtained Roman citizenship as part of this measure.[46] This letter, which shows Philoxenus pursuing his affairs in Sicily, substantiates the claim that we find in a later source that the Greek colonists never settled in Comum, and further demonstrates the ways in which the *hospitium* of the Roman franchise disregards geographical space and extends the household of Roman citizenship across the provinces:[47] enrolled as a Roman citizen in one provincial city, far from where he comes from, simply by virtue of being a (distinguished) Greek, Philoxenus is shown here taking advantage of that status with a Roman proconsul back in his native Sicily.

The core of this letter is taken up with affirming Cicero's claim to have been the party responsible for recommending Philoxenus to Caesar as a worthy candidate for Roman citizenship, despite the fact that Philoxenus's Roman nomenclature seems to tell a different story. Newly enfranchised citizens commonly took the name of the person who had promoted their candidacy for citizenship,[48] and Philoxenus chose to name himself not after Cicero but after someone with whom he was more *familiaris*—namely, C. Avianius Flaccus, a corn merchant (with apparent interests in Sicily) and *commendatus* of Cicero, about whom we hear more in the course of *Fam.* 13.[49] In taking on the *nomen* (and *praenomen*) of C. Avianius Flaccus upon his enfranchisement, C. Avianius Philoxenus demonstrates the ties of adoptive kinship that Roman citizenship brings with it, as entry into the broader Roman *familia* is

---

oblitas †latio† tum cum in urbem nostram est infusa peregrinitas, nunc vero etiam bracatis et Transalpinis nationibus, ut nullum veteris leporis vestigium appareat.)

46. Suet. *Iul.* 28.3 and Strabo 5.1.6. For discussion of the constitutional peculiarity provided for by the clause in the *Lex Vatinia* that authorized extending the franchise to these Greeks at Comum, see Luraschi 1974, 363–400; Wolff 1979, 169–87; Sherwin White 1973, 231–32.

47. It is not clear how Philoxenus gets round the objections raised by the concept of *postliminium* (on which see Sherwin White 1973, 292 ff.). Sherwin White 1973, 169 traces this idea through the inexorable process of municipalization that took place in Italy over the course of the first century BCE: 'In the Social War the city-state, though overgrown, existed in a very real sense, politically and geographically, and fought a war with its neighbours. By the close of the Republic there is a complete change. *Municipia et coloniae* means Italy apart from Rome; and *Urbs Roma* stands either literally for so much brick and mortar and stone, or else for an idea.'

48. See Deniaux 1993, 368 for the significance of this practice at this time.

49. One of Flaccus's sons, another C. Avianius, is the *commendatus* of *Fam.* 13.79, where Cicero recommends his business in Sicily to A. Allienus, the proconsul there in 46 BCE; Flaccus himself is the *commendatus* of *Fam.* 13.75, which seeks to secure the distribution privileges he enjoyed as a corn merchant under Pompey's tenure of the *cura annonae*. Cf. Deniaux 1993, 463 for the likelihood that he oversaw the transportation of grain from Sicily to Rome at this time.

marked by entry into the *familia* of a particular Roman *gens*. Cicero's way of getting around the fact that Philoxenus did not choose him as his namesake is to suggest that they nevertheless share the bond of *hospitium*: the ties of reciprocal hospitality (or the expectation of such, at any rate) are presented as a form of compensation for Philoxenus's decision to mark his ties of adoptive kinship with another Roman family, and an alternative relational model for Philoxenus's movement into the broader Roman community of citizens.

Other letters similarly play on the tension between *hospitium* and adoptive kinship as alternative models for the procedure of Roman citizenship, even if they organize that tension differently. In *Fam.* 13.36 Cicero claims ties of longstanding *hospitium* with another Sicilian, Demetrius of Megas, who had likewise received Roman citizenship from Caesar under a different authorizing measure.[50] Again, Cicero claims to have played a role in the procedure;[51] yet again, the newly enfranchised individual honours the benefaction of another, in this instance Cicero's son-in-law Dolabella, by taking his *nomen*, Cornelius. But linked as they are by ties of marriage (even if that marriage was now over, the ties that bound father and son-in-law seem to have stuck), Cicero and Dolabella belong to the same extended *familia*, such that Demetrius's new name underscores his ties with Cicero himself. Within the letter, Cicero offers a concrete glimpse of what participating in an extended family like this one looks like in practice, when he describes the assurances that Caesar has given Dolabella that Demetrius's new status was immune from the reparative measures that he was currently taking to remove citizenship from those who had secured it improperly. In describing these assurances, Cicero takes pains to stress that they were delivered within his own hearing, as if destined for his ears as well as Dolabella's.[52] Just as Cicero reaches the

---

50. Deniaux 1993, 314 notes that while no ancient source tells us under what authority Caesar was granting citizenship at this time, it is likely that he was following the precedent of other late republican *imperatores* by enfranchising individuals and communities *virtutis causa*.

51. Cicero claims that Dolabella obtained citizenship for Demetrius at Cicero's request. *Fam.* 13.36.1: 'Dolabella obtained citizenship for him from Caesar at my request, a decision in which I was involved.' (*Ei Dolabella rogatu meo civitatem a Caesare impetravit, qua in re ego interfui.*) Deniaux 1993, 314 notes the peculiarity of a tribune trumping a consular in making this request, but this kind of inversion was presumably characteristic of the strange times of Caesar's dictatorship.

52. *Fam.* 13.36.1: 'And when on account of certain disreputable men, who used to sell Caesar's favours, the latter ordered that the tablet on which the names of those presented with citizenship should be torn down, Caesar told that same Dolabella in my hearing that there was nothing for Megas to fear, that the favour he had shown him remained in place.' (*Cumque*

dictator through his son-in-law, so Caesar reaches Cicero through the same intermediary, delivering his confidences about Demetrius's status in the mutual hearing of father and son-in-law.[53] The relationship between Cicero and Dolabella, which models the relationship of extended kinship that Demetrius has entered into by taking Dolabella's name as a new citizen of Rome, is explicitly conveyed through the situation of their sharing the same social and physical space, such that Demetrius's adoption by name into this family appears as an extension of the *hospitium* that he already shares with Cicero, rather than as alternative to it. *Hospitium* is presented as the foundation for the closer relationship of familial kinship (and, by extension, Roman citizenship).

Fam. 13.36 conveys a striking picture of Julius Caesar at work: bestowing citizenship, and even removing it when it had been granted by his agents through corrupt practices. Either way, his oversight of the procedures of enfranchisement is presented in this letter as absolute.[54] Scholars have emphasized the extent to which Caesar's expansion of Roman citizenship in the course of his consulship and dictatorship stands apart from the measures taken by his predecessors in this regard and anticipates the actions of the emperors. This book of letters provides a crucial contemporary witness to his policies of enfranchisement. In all of the letters in *Fam.* 13 that deal with individuals whom Caesar has made citizens of Rome, Cicero couches his relationship with them in terms of *hospitium*, an age-old bond of friendship based on mutual hospitality that applies particularly to relationships between Romans and foreigners. Yet far from being timeless, this bond expresses a relationship with Cicero that mirrors Caesar's work of Roman enfranchisement, which was currently welcoming foreigners into the *hospitium* of Roman citizenship at unprecedented rates. The nuances of *hospitium* in *Fam.* 13 witness the emergent changes taking place within the wider *domus* of Roman society, which was expanding spatially even as it was transforming vertically at the same time.

---

propter quosdam sordidos homines, qui Caesaris beneficia vendebant, tabulam in qua nomina civitate donatorum incisa essent revelli iussisset, eidem Dolabellae me audiente Caesar dixit nihil esse quod de Mega vereretur; beneficium suum in eo manere.)

53. See Gowers 2019 for discussion of the dynamics of father and son-in-law relationships in ancient Rome that this letter may be seen to exemplify.

54. Millar 1977, 479 comments on this letter: 'Nothing could show more clearly the introduction of typically monarchic social patterns, the acquisition of benefits for their protégés by well-placed intermediaries, the activities of hangers-on of the monarch, and the ultimate dependence of the distribution of favours on the will of the monarch himself.'

Structures of Feeling

The Commerce of Friendship

In a letter in *Fam.* 7, a businessman friend of Cicero's, Manius Curius, who has left Rome to go and live in Greece, writes to ask for Cicero's representation to the new governor of Achaea, Acilius Glabrio. The letter makes a joke of the financial interests that Curius asks Cicero to protect in making the introduction, by couching his relationship with Cicero (and with Atticus) in starkly transactional terms (*Fam.* 7.29):

> 'Suo'; sum enim χρήσει μὲν tuus, κτήσει δὲ Attici nostri. Ergo fructus est tuus, mancipium illius; quod quidem si inter senes comptionalis venale proscripserit, egerit non multum.

> I write 'his own', for I am yours to use, though I am the inalienable possession of our friend Atticus. For I'm a source of profit for you, but I belong to him; though if he were to advertise me for sale in a job lot (as is done for aging slaves), he wouldn't make much.

Amanda Wilcox singles this letter out from the rest of Cicero's correspondence for its refusal to resort to the kinds of euphemism that Cicero and his friends elsewhere rely on to obfuscate the transactional nature of their relationships with one another. The letter only stands out, however, because of its location in the collection; within *Fam.* 13, a book in which this letter could easily stake a claim to belong, the language is hardly exceptional. For throughout this book of letters the terminology of profit, calculation, contracts, debt, and loan is liberally used as part of the language of recommendation and slides seamlessly from the economic interests being promoted in the name of *familiaritas* into an evaluation of the friendship itself.

In *Fam.* 13.50, for example, which is the letter that Cicero writes to Acilius Glabrio in response to Manius Curius's request for a recommendation in *Fam.* 7.29, Cicero mentions the vague *officia* that the businessman Curius has performed for him, and then describes their *amor* for one another as *mutuus*. This seemingly innocent adjective is also, when used as a substantive, the term for an interest-free loan, a financial phenomenon that economic historians identify as one of the most basic expectations of friendship in ancient Rome. In a letter promoting a businessman, mutual affection may also describe 'interest-free affection', or the kind of relationship that is guaranteed by this advantageous mode of financial service. Cicero's central plea that his addressee keep Curius 'in good repair and well-roofed' and free from disaster, damage, and distress (*sartum et tectum, ut aiunt, ab omnique incommodo detrimento, molestia sincerum integrumque conserves*) uses the metaphor of building conservation to refer euphemistically to the business interests of Curius that he wants Acilius Glabrio to protect. But when Cicero closes by promising Glabrio the benefits that he himself will reap from the friendship that will attend such protection, he resorts again to financial terminology to express this reward (*Fam.* 13.50.2): *Et ipse spondeo, et omnes hoc tibi tui pro me recipient, ex mea amicitia et ex tuo in me officio maximum te fructum summamque voluptatem esse capturum.* Cicero pledges (*spondeo*, a verb used in legal contracts) that Glabrio will derive the utmost profit (*fructum*), along with pleasure, from Cicero's friendship if he complies with the latter's request. In this letter, the only thing that is not expressed in explicit financial terminology, it seems, is the financial business of Curius that is the letter's chief object of recommendation.

The use of financial terminology to describe social debts and benefits arises with some frequency in those letters in *Fam.* 13 addressed to bankers, traders, and businessmen.[55] But it is not confined to them: the language spills into letters addressed to other social types, where it arises (euphemistically) in contexts of finance, as well as in other social contexts too.[56] It is easy to look at the sum total of these expressions and infer that they speak in a timeless way about the transactional nature of Roman social relationships. Roman society, and the Roman economy, is premised on relationships of dependence and

---

55. Cf. esp. *Fam.* 13.56, which recommends the interests of Cluvius of Puteoli, and where the language of technical finance that is used metaphorically elsewhere in *Fam.* 13 finds its most literal register. For examples of that metaphorical usage, see *Fam.* 13.22 (of another businessman, T. Manlius, based at Thespiae in Greece), which closes with Cicero's promise that his addressee will derive *fructus* ('profit') from assisting such a deserving beneficiary; and *Fam.* 13.45, in which Cicero uses the adjective *mutuus* (with its' interest-free' connotations) of L. Egnatius, an equestrian businessman friend of Cicero's, with business interests in Asia: 'For I would wish you to see not only that my daily dealings with him are of the closest kind, but that there are considerable mutual services between the two of us.' (*Sic enim existimes velim, mihi cum eo non modo cottidianam consuetudinem summam intercedere sed etiam officia magna et mutua nostra inter nos esse.*)

56. Cf. *Fam.* 13.64, which recommends the interests of one of the most aristocratic individuals promoted in this book, Tiberius Nero. Again, the letter's addressee (P. Silius) is told near the start of the letter that he will derive *fructus* ('profit') from having assisted such a promising young man in his business dealings. Near the end of the letter, Silius is told that he will have made a brilliant investment in Tib. Nero (*apud ipsum praeclarissime* **posueris**) if he gives him the assistance that he needs. A similar phrase is used in *Fam.* 13.55.2 of the investment that Q. Minucius Thermus will derive from assisting Cicero's legate M. Anneius: 'How well **you will be investing** your energy and duty. . . .' (*Quam bene* **positurus sis** *studium tuum atque officium.*) This letter also uses another economic term, *cumulus* ('surplus'), to describe the extra

Structures of Feeling

patronage. The recurrence of expressions that entwine social and economic interests in *Fam.* 13 is taken by scholars as emblematic of the way in which the broader socio-economic system operates over an unspecified (but implicitly extensive) period of time. Parallels with language used in later recommendation letters are taken to bear this out. But *Fam.* 13, as the unique example of this phenomenon that we have from the late Republic, is singled out and made to set the barometer for our expectations of how Roman society worked in general, and of how an elite Roman might encode these workings in the language of social politesse.[57]

This picture may well be broadly correct. But the generalities about Roman society, and about the Roman economy, that *Fam.* 13 is normally used to substantiate may lead us to miss some of the nuances that it presents about Roman social feeling at a particular moment in historical time. These nuances derive from the fact that as letters, written in the present for the present, they provide a unique witness to the kinds of emergent changes taking place within their moment of writing. If we miss these nuances, it may well be because of the work of consolidation that the collection performs on the letters, transforming their emergent witness into a structure that withstands time. Yet *Fam.* 13 has been organized in a way that draws attention to some of the disruptive events that underpin the preoccupation with property that we see throughout this book of letters. Near the outset of the book, we find a series of letters that bear important witness to some of the measures of social and economic redistribution that Caesar was taking in 46–45 BCE, the year when most of the letters within this book were written. This sequence also contains references to measures of redistribution that had been taken by both Caesar and Sulla in the preceding decades. The book has been organized in a way that reminds readers from the very start of the waves of socio-economic restructuring that lie behind its sustained focus on property, and which help explain the feelings that the propertied classes harboured under threat of losing what they believed to be theirs at this time. In foregrounding these measures, *Fam.* 13 invites us to consider how they inflect the propertied sense of *familiaritas*

---

spur that Cicero's recommendation is imagined offering to his addressee's goodwill towards the *commendatus* (*Fam.* 13.55.1): 'So that I do not doubt but that the great **surplus** of my recommendation will add to your goodwill.' (*Ut non dubitem quin ad tuam voluntatem magnus* **cumulus** *accedat commendationis meae.*) For a similar use of the term *cumulus*, cf. *Fam.* 13.66.1 (of A. Caecina, son of Cicero's erstwhile defendant in the *Pro Caecina*, whose business interests in Asia Cicero seeks to protect in this letter): 'So that my letters may bring some profit to these measures' (*Ut ad ea... aliquem afferant* **cumulum** *meae litterae*).

57. On which, see Roesch 2004, 146–49; and Hall 2009a, esp. 29–77.

186 SOUVENIRS OF CICERO

throughout this book of letters, and it enables us to trace the way in which they structure and are in turn structured by this feeling.

In 47 BCE, Appian writes that Caesar declared his intention to settle the veterans either using any remaining public land, or his own, or, if that was not enough, by buying up the rest of what he needed.[58] Five letters near the start of book 13, *Fam.* 13.4–8, provide an important contemporary witness to the efforts undertaken to make good on this promise in the years that followed, and to the feelings of solidarity that they generated among those who found their property threatened as a result of this measure. Because all of them deal with the redistribution of public land, these letters are inevitably a means of rehearsing Cicero's career-long resistance to agrarian reform in the interest of protecting private interests, a resistance that finds its culminating expression in the defence of private property in the *de Officiis*.[59]

The first we hear of it is in *Fam.* 13.4, in which Cicero writes to Q. Valerius Orca, one of the commissioners placed in charge of Caesar's land assignments, and he pleads with him to allow the town of Volterra in Etruria to keep its lands. These lands, we hear, had been confiscated by Sulla and declared public by him,[60] only to be officially freed from that status by Caesar during his consulship in 59 BCE as part of his notorious agrarian reform.[61] Yet now it seems

---

58. App. *B. Civ.* 2.94.

59. Cic. *Off.* 2.78 with Walcot 1975.

60. The punitive measures that Sulla took against Volterra, one of the last strongholds of anti-Sullan resistance until it finally fell to Sulla's siege in 79 BCE, included removing the town's citizen rights (a measure discussed—and contested—in Cicero's defence of the Volterran aristocrat, Aulus Caecina, in Cic. *Caec.* 95–102, on the background to which see Frier 1985, 20–27; and Santangelo 2007, 173–8), and declaring Volterra's surrounding lands *ager publicus*. That Sulla intended Volterra's now public land to be parcelled up and allotted to his veterans, but never followed through on this land assignment, is suggested by the comments that Cicero makes in a letter to Atticus (*Att.* 1.19.4) concerning the agrarian bill proposed by the tribune Flavius in 60 BCE, which sought to implement Sulla's plans for the assignment of Volterran and other Etrurian lands. Cicero's intervention, as he describes it to Atticus, is to remove all the provisions that harmed private interest, including the property of the Volterrans, whose land had been made public but never apportioned: 'By the will of the people's assembly, I removed all those things from that second law which pertained to the inconvenience of private property.' (*Ex hac ego lege secunda contionis voluntate omnia illa tollebam quae ad privatorum incommodum pertinebant.*) Santangelo 2007, 179 n. 29 notes that we have no evidence explaining why Sulla's intended assignment of Volterran land was never implemented. But cf. Brunt 1971, 306 for the suggestion that, as the last city to fall, Volterra's lands were perhaps no longer needed, following the confiscations of so many others'. Unlike Arretium, which did become a colony, there is no archaeological or other evidence to suggest that Volterra ever became a colony.

61. *Fam.* 13.4.2: 'Caesar approved this policy of mine in the agrarian law of his first consulship, and he freed the district and the town of Volterra from all danger for all time.' (*Hanc actionem*

Structures of Feeling

that Caesar is seeking to reappropriate this land, in a reversal of his earlier policy.[62] Cicero's description of the Volterran properties that he wants Orca to preserve resonates strongly with the description of the list of items that Patro seeks to safeguard in the house of Epicurus (*Fam.* 13.4.3): *Eorum ego* **domicilia sedes rem fortunas,** *quae et a dis immortalibus et a praestantissimis in nostra re publica civibus summo senatus populique Romani studio conservatae sunt, tuae fidei iustitiae bonitatique commendo* ('**Their domiciles, abodes, property, and estates**, preserved by the immortal gods and the most outstanding men in our state through the utmost desire of the senate and the Roman people, all these I commend to your honesty, sense of justice, and goodness of heart.')

But the difference between this letter and that written on behalf of the Epicureans is at least as marked as any similarity, for Cicero's interest in protecting the property of the Volterrans is premised on a long history of protection and patronage.[63] The relationship between himself and the community is described as one of *necessitudo*, a form of mutual dependence that expresses itself in this letter as a kind of ownership.[64] Social relationships

---

meam C. Caesar primo suo consulatu in lege agraria comprobavit agrumve Volaterranum et oppidum omni periculo in perpetuum liberavit.) This letter is our only witness to the provisions that Caesar made for Volterra as part of his agrarian legislation of 59 BCE (cf. Deniaux 1991, 216 for discussion). Dio 38.1 is our best source for its other provisions. Gelzer 72–73 stresses the care that Caesar took in drafting this legislation; the provisions for Volterra may be seen as evidence of that care.

62. Brunt 1971, 323 notes that Caesar's appropriation of Volterran land in 47 BCE implies that the protections he had offered in 59 BCE can only have been informal: 'We may suppose that Caesar had then [in 59 BCE] exempted the *ager Volaterranus* from redistribution, without giving the *possessores* better title than they had before.'

63. *Fam.* 13.4.1: 'I have a very close bond with the people of Volterra. Since they have received **an important favour from me**, they paid it back most abundantly, having never failed to support me either in my successes or in my failures.' (*Cum municipibus Volaterranis mihi summa necessitudo est;* **magno enim meo beneficio** *adfecti cumulatissime mihi gratiam rettulerunt; nam nec in honoribus meis nec in laboribus umquam defuerunt.*) Cicero never says explicitly what the *beneficium* that he granted the Volterrans was, nor how they repaid that favour. Deniaux 1991, 220–23 suggests that it must relate to earlier interventions that he had made on their behalf to protect them from Sulla's punitive measures, as seen in his contestation of Flavius's agrarian reform and in defence of their right to citizenship in, e.g., *Dom.* 79 and *Caec.* 18. She suggests that their gratitude, like that of Atella (which is described as bound to Cicero by similar ties of gratitude in *Fam.* 13.7) must have expressed itself in the contributions they made to his electoral campaigns, as well as to his recall from exile.

64. Hellegouarc'h 1963, 71–6 begins his discussion of *necessitudo* by noting its etymology (made up of the negation *ne-* + a substantive derived from *cedo*), which stresses the impossibility of

188   SOUVENIRS OF CICERO

are thus caught up in the logic of possession and alienation that Caesar's literal confiscation of property has made so fraught (*Fam.* 13.4.4): *Si pro meis
pristinis opibus facultatem mihi res hoc tempore daret ut ita defendere possem
Volaterranos* **quem ad modum consuevi tueri meos**, *nullum officium, nullum
denique certamen in quo illis prodesse possem praetermitterem.* ('If I had the
influence of my former days to defend them, **as I have always been accustomed to protect [*tueri*] my own people**, then there is no service or effort
that I would overlook for their benefit.') The object of *tueri* here is not the
property of the Volterrans, but the Volterrans themselves, who are, however,
cast as a form of property for Cicero through the possessive pronoun *meos*,
which stands out in this sentence, with its emphasis on ownership and confiscation, with particular force.[65] Alienated from what's *theirs* by the Roman
state, Cicero would like to be in a position to claim the Volterrans as *his* to
protect. The ties of *necessitudo*, which attach the Volterrans to Cicero (and
vice versa), here attempt to compensate for the broken ties that should attach
them to their own property.

The letter to the community of Volterrans serves as a prelude to the one that
immediately follows it, which is addressed to an individual Volterran, Gaius
Curtius, whose situation allows us to trace the way in which the obligations
and feelings generated by *familiaritas* forge their structure in the gaps that
open up between Caesar's economic and social policies. Curtius held until
recently a *possessio* on Volterran land into which, it seems, he invested all his
money. That *possessio* appears from this letter to have now been confiscated
as a result of Caesar's land assignments, and scholars tend to read the letter
as proof that the preceding plea to Orca to spare Volterra was ineffectual.[66]
Cicero describes Curtius's situation as a *naufragium*, an image that resonates,
again, with the opening image of Epicurus's dilapidated house.[67]

Curtius is described in no uncertain terms as a *familiaris*: Cicero claims
to have treated this man *familiarissime* since his earliest youth (*Fam.* 13.5.1: *C.
Curtio ab ineunte aetate familiarissime sum usus*), and the specifically possessive

---

removing oneself from a relationship defined by this term. Throughout *Fam.* 13, this is the term
used to describe the relational obligations that tie Cicero to towns and communities.

65. *TLL* v. 1 for *meus* meaning *mihi proprius*; *TLL* v. 2 meaning *mihi carus.*

66. Brunt 1971, 323.

67. *Fam.* 13.5.2: 'Curtius has a holding in the territory of Volterra, into which (**like a shipwreck**) he'd invested all that was left to him.' (*Is habet in Volaterrano possessionem, cum in eam
tamquam e naufragio reliquias contulisset.*)

aspect of *familiaritas* emerges towards the end of the letter, when Cicero pleads with Orca to protect Curtius's property as if it were his (Cicero's) own.[68] This plea, to treat the property of X as if it were my own, will become a common one as this book of letters progresses, as will the claim that in favouring the *commendatus* the addressee confers favours on Cicero himself. What is striking about its appearance in this letter is the backdrop of social as well as economic upheaval against which it arises. An important grounds for Cicero's argument that Curtius should be allowed to keep his land is that Caesar has recently made him a senator, and that it is therefore perverse for him to be taking away with one hand the property that befits the new status that he has granted with the other. Underlying the request to treat Curtius's property, and case, as if it were Cicero's own, is the resemblance between their situations. For Cicero, likewise a senator, had also once lost his property, and he understood precisely what this meant for the loss of senatorial prestige.[69]

Technically there may be no contradiction in Caesar's decision to make a senator out of someone he was dispossessing, since under the Republic there was no property qualification for senators.[70] But for Cicero these shifts in wealth and status should move in step, and his letter conveys the perceived absurdity of their working against one another. Curtius, he says, can hardly protect (*tueri*) his new rank of senator if he loses his property (*Fam.* 13.5.2): *Hoc autem tempore eum Caesar in senatum legit; quem ordinem ille ista possessione amissa* **tueri** *vix potest.* ('But at this very moment, Caesar's chosen him to be a member of the senate, a rank that he can hardly **protect** if he loses his holding.') We are reminded again of the opening letter and the list of abstract properties that was safeguarded (*tueri*) with the safeguarding of Epicurus's physical house. Cicero goes on to add that it is unseemly for Curtius to be moved out of land that Caesar is dividing up when he has been allowed to move *ordines* as a result of Caesar's favour (*Fam.* 13.5.2): *Minimeque convenit, ex eo agro qui Caesaris iussu*

---

68. *Fam.* 13.5.3: 'So I beg you all the more especially to treat Curtius's property/case as if it were my own; and whatever you do for my sake, although you may have done it for Curtius, to believe that any favour he obtains through me is one conferred upon me by yourself.' (*Quamobrem te in maiorem modum rogo ut C. Curti rem meam putes esse; quicquid mea causa faceres, ut, id C. Curti causa cum feceris, existimes, quod ille per me habuerit, id me habere abs te.*)

69. For the clearest articulation of what the eradication of his own house on the Palatine meant for Cicero's loss of prestige, see Cic. *Dom.* 100. See also McIntosh 2013 for discussion.

70. Shatzman 1975, 143.

dividatur eum moveri qui Caesaris beneficio senator sit. ('It's hardly fitting that he should be removed from the land which is being divided up under Caesar's orders, when he's been made a senator thanks to Caesar's favour.') The image of centuriated land suggested by the reference to the *ager* being divided up resonates with the grid of socio-political *ordines* that Caesar is also redrawing to Curtius's benefit, and Cicero's hypotactic sentence structure enacts (in faintly parodic terms?) this grid-like structure at the level of the word. For Caesar (the 'cutter'), who re-divides everything—land as well socio-political categories—the grid is the perfect emblem of his will to impose order on Roman society. For Cicero, though, the division that matters is that which separates property from socio-political status, a form of alienation that arises as an unintended consequence of Caesar's hyperactive reforms, and one to which Cicero (the 'new man', who had bought most of his properties) would be especially alert. *Familiaritas*—in the sense of a concern for the property (*res familiaris*) of one's friends (*familiares*)—emerges here in the gap created by the misalignment of Caesar's new grids, as the social glue that would seek to stick property and status back together.

The last letter in this sequence demonstrates how the technical language associated with Caesar's reforms bleeds into the expressions of social affinity and/or esteem with which they are enmeshed. *Fam*. 13.8 is caught up in a conflict between Caesar's land-assignment program and his solution for settling debt in the aftermath of the civil war. Responding to a combination of widespread indebtedness and a shortage of coin at this time, Caesar ordained that real estate should be put up to settle debts in lieu of cash;[71] and that because real estate was substantially deflated at this time, it should be valued by assessors at pre-war prices.[72] The technical term for the evaluation performed by the assessors is *aestimatio*. *Fam*. 13.8 tells the story of C. Albinius, who has received some land, assessed at an *aestimatio*, as payment for a debt owed by a man named M. Laberius, who purchased this land from Caesar when it was auctioned off following its confiscation from the original owner, Plotius, a

---

71. Frederickson 1966, 133–4 notes the confusion over the date of this order in the sources. His solution is to suggest that while Caesar made the decision to institute *aestimationes* in 49 BCE, it was only enshrined in law (the *Lex Iulia de bonis cedendis*) some time in 46/45 BCE.

72. Cf. Frederickson 1966, 132–4 on the credit crisis of 49 BCE, and the measures that Caesar subsequently took to remedy its causes. Andreau 1999, 102–4 further contextualizes the crisis (and the solutions put forward to remedy it) by relating it to the earlier and later crises of debt and liquidity of 63 BCE and 33 CE.

Pompeian who appears to have died in the civil war.[73] That land has somehow been made available for redistribution, and Cicero writes to the relevant land commissioner to ask if this new property of Albinius might be exempted.[74]

The contested transaction at the heart of this letter is one of the most complicated examples in the entire book, involving four named individuals (C. Albinius, Laberius, Caesar, and the probably dead Plotius). The epistolary transaction is equally complex: Cicero writes to Rutilius, the land commissioner concerned, on behalf not of Albinius but of Publius Sestius, Albinius's son-in-law, to whom Cicero owed long-standing political debts.[75] Cicero phrases the constellation of obligations between himself, Sestius, and Albinius in terms that slide readily into the financial debt (and its repayment) that is the object of the letter's plea (*Fam.* 13.8.3): *Magna me adfeceris non modo laetitia sed etiam quodam modo gloria si P. Sestius homini maxime necessario satis fecerit per me, ut ego illi uni plurimum debeo.* ('You will make me not only very happy but even quite proud if Sestius ends up satisfying the claims of a man [Albinius] so closely bound to him because of me, as I owe more to him [i.e., Sestius] than to anyone.' Given the nature of the transaction between Albinius and Laberius,

---

73. The scale of the confiscations at this time is unclear. Brunt 1971, 321 notes the number of sources which suggest how sparing Caesar was in confiscating the property of his enemies, but also draws attention to the contradiction to this view found in Dio 42.51.2, who suggests that land prices in 47 BCE had fallen because of the number of confiscated properties on the market. In the same passage in Dio, we hear that Caesar refrained as far as possible from settling the veterans on confiscated land, which would make the situation presented in this letter something of an anomaly.

74. Cicero argues that in re-appropriating land that he has already sold, Caesar is in fact undermining the *auctoritas* of his sales, as well as the *auctoritas* of the land assignments, which become vulnerable to claims such as this one. Roselaar 2010, 120 n. 122: 'Uncertainty about property could cause problems when trying to sell land. For example, in 45 Caesar tried to have sales made in Sulla's time ratified, so that he would have more authority over those lands that he had bought himself. If his title would remain uncertain, then what possible right of property can his sales carry?' As long as Caesar's title to the land remained uncertain, he could not transfer its ownership by sale. Cf. Brunt 1971, 301–5 on the rapaciousness of Sulla's confiscations. Like Caesar, Sulla preferred to sell the estates he had confiscated rather than re-distribute them for his troops. But in Sulla's case, this was in order to reward his partisans (who bought them at knock-down prices, if at all), whereas in Caesar's case it was because he needed the money (to pay his troops?).

75. *Fam.* 13.8.1: 'My aim in writing you this letter was to explain not only that I am obliged to exert myself on behalf of Sestius, but that Sestius is obliged to go out of his way for Albinius.' (*Hoc idcirco scripsi ut intellegeres non solum me pro P. Sestio laborare debere sed Sestium etiam pro Albinio.*) Sestius, tribune in 57 BCE, when he was a vocal advocate for Cicero's recall, was defended by Cicero in 56 BCE against charges of *vis* for the violence with which he had opposed Clodius the preceding year. Cf. Kaster 2006, 14–18 for an overview of their relationship. Despite Sestius's loyalty towards him, Cicero complains about his actions on his behalf in letters to Atticus from exile and is notably rude about his skills as a writer at *Att.* 7.17.2.

192 SOUVENIRS OF CICERO

the verbs *satisfacio* and *debeo* are particularly interesting here: *satisfacio* can have the more general meaning of making amends to an injured party,[76] or the more specific meaning of giving satisfaction to a creditor by means of a substitute payment (which was precisely what Laberius was doing in giving Albinius the Plotian estate).[77] Financial debts and familial obligations become interchangeable here, as Sestius's concern to see the debt owed to his relative honoured is described in a way that makes him sound like the technical repayer of that debt. And Cicero's own obligations to Sestius become assimilated to the relative's debt problem too, expressed as they are in language that can take on the same financial semantics of loans and debts (*debeo*).

More striking than these observations about how the general terminology of finance slides into these expressions of social obligation is how the technicalities of Caesar's new procedure of *aestimatio* resonate through the language of sociality that Cicero uses as well.

Of all the individuals named in this sequence of letters from *Fam.* 13 (and indeed of many others), P. Sestius is the one whom we might expect to see described as *familiaris*. But this word is not used. Instead, Cicero repeatedly uses the phrase *quanti facio* to convey, through the genitive of value, how highly he values Sestius.[78] And this language spills into the opening compliments that he addresses to Rutilius, the recipient of the letter, as Cicero tactfully balances his high appraisal of Sestius, the person he is representing to Rutilius, against similar compliments of appraisal to Rutilius himself (*Fam.* 13.8.1): *Cum et mihi conscius essem **quanti te facerem** et tuam erga me benevolentiam expertus essem, non dubitavi a te petere quod mihi petendum esset. P. Sestium **quanti faciam**, ipse optime scio; **quanti autem facere debeam**, et tu et omnes homines sciunt.* ('Knowing in my heart **how highly I value you**, and having learned from experience your goodwill towards me, I haven't hesitated to ask you what ought to be asked. **How highly I value** P. Sestius is best known to myself; **how highly I ought to value** him is known both to you and to everyone.') The new financial procedure of *aestimatio* can be seen here resonating through the entire network of relationships affected by its emergent pressures.

---

76. *OLD* v. 1.

77. *OLD* v. 2.

78. While this phrase appears occasionally elsewhere in *Fam.* 13, it is more commonly used to describe the value that Cicero assumes people place on himself (e.g., *Fam.* 13.10.4 and *Fam.* 13.19.3). The iteration of the phrase (three times in the two opening sentences) makes it particularly striking in *Fam.* 13.8.1.

Conclusion

'It is a truth universally acknowledged,' writes Raymond Williams in his study of the English novel, 'that Jane Austen chose to ignore the decisive historical events of her time. Where, it is still asked, are the Napoleonic Wars: the real current of history?'[79] Yet as he points out, history has many currents, and the revolutionary events of the early-nineteenth century, including the Napoleonic Wars, are felt in her fictional portraits of the cultivated rural gentry as social history. In particular, Austen's persistent preoccupation with the sources of income that support the landed households that she describes tells a story of social and economic mobility at this time that belies her novels' veneer of settled tradition. For underpinning the stories of personal relationships is a socio-economic world in flux, wherein fortunes from trade and colonial or military profit are being converted into houses, estates, and social position. Austen's fictional worlds are torn between the competing claims of these emergent economic pressures and the inherited social codes of the past, and the tone of controlled observation with which she narrates their dramas of social conduct and material improvement forms part of a 'structure of feeling' that is forged in response to these conflicting pressures.

Sociolinguistic studies of the language of politesse in *Fam.* 13 frequently treat this language as if it were timeless—as if this book of letters gave us access to eternal truths about the structure of social relationships in Rome and the modes of address proper to those relationships. I have argued instead that the financial nuances of this language make it part of a structure of feeling that emerges in relation to the particular socio-economic upheavals taking place at the time of Cicero's writing. But what feeling does this language denote? As Williams emphasizes, the emergent nature of structures of feeling means that they are frequently spaces of blockage and inarticulation, places where what he calls 'emotional trouble' rubs up against language and resists traditional forms of expression.[80]

Cumulatively these letters say something that individually they may not. Cicero's repeated attempts to protect his *familiares*, the people he calls his own, in defence of the property that is theirs, bespeaks a desperation to cling onto more than property. At stake in these pleas is the idea of the virtual *familia* of *familiares* and the larger social structure of which it forms part, which later

---

79. Williams 1970, 18.

80. Williams 1977, 130–31.

readers could see was crumbling around Cicero and his peers. The opening image of Epicurus's dilapidated house concretizes an emergent feeling that finds expression in the rest of the letters, which can in turn be understood in light of the new hegemony on the horizon. For one prominent social form that monarchy would take in Rome was, after all, the *familia Caesaris* (or 'imperial household'), which saw many of the administrative roles that are filled in *Fam.* 13 by members of the senatorial class handed over to the slaves and freedmen of the emperor's household; and which also saw the state treasury transferred, gradually, to the emperor's private fiscus, and administered not by public officials (as the *aerarium* in the temple of Saturn had been)[81] but by an accounting staff made up of the slaves and freedmen of his own *familia*.[82] The sprawling nature of this gigantic household, concretized for imperial readers in inscriptions found across the empire,[83] symbolized the extent to which the extended network of intersecting households of Cicero's day had been sidelined by the one *familia* that now mattered.

---

81. Millar 1964, 33–4 on the different officials that Caesar and subsequent emperors appointed to this job, before Claudius restored the republican practice of appointing quaestors to the position.

82. But see Brunt 1966, 89 for the notion that in practice it was the accounting staff from the emperor's private household who administered the expenditures from the *aerarium* as well as his private fiscus; and that it is the fact of this singular personnel for both public and private finances that helps produce the amalgamation of the two.

83. For a social analysis of the freedmen and slaves of the *familia Caesaris* recognized for their procuratorial functions in the vast body of inscriptions that mention them, see Weaver 1972.

Conclusion

WHO READ CICERO'S letters in the centuries after his death? Scholars typically answer this question by harvesting citations of the letters by later authors and pointing to these as the best available evidence of readership. The Elder Seneca, and the Younger, Quintilian, Pliny, Plutarch, Gellius, and Fronto (that is, the major prose writers of non-fiction in the two centuries that followed Cicero's death): all accurately cite various letters by Cicero and bear witness to the circulation of his letters, in one collected form or another, throughout this period.[1] Yet to restrict the question of the readership of

---

1. Seneca the Elder provides our first reference to the letters (at *Suas.* 1.5.5 he mentions a letter from Cassius to Cicero, which corresponds to *Fam.* 15.19). Quintilian, however, provides an earlier indirect attestation of *ad Atticum*, with a reference at *Inst.* 6.3.108 to a joke from a letter to Atticus (*Att.* 8.7.2), which he claims to have taken from a treatise on humour by Domitius Marsus, a contemporary of Ovid. Seneca the Younger's direct citations of Cicero's letters are commonly held to form part of a broader project of attempting to marginalize Cicero (on which see Setaioli 2003, 55–77; Gowing 2013, 239–44; and Keeline 2018, 196–222): at *Epist.* 97.4, he alludes to *Att.* 1.16.5 (one of Cicero's letters to Atticus about Clodius and the Bona Dea scandal), only to contrast Cicero with his hero, Cato; while at *Epist.* 118.1–2 Seneca cites *Att.* 1.12.4, where Cicero asks Atticus to write even if he has nothing to say, in order to boast that he (Seneca) will never lack things to write (because his letters are full of more substantive, philosophical content than the political gossip that fills Cicero's letters). Pliny's direct allusions to Cicero's letters are usefully listed in an appendix to Marchesi 2008, 252–56. Keeline 2018, 292–95 discusses Pliny's programmatic allusion to a letter of Cicero's (Cic. *Att.* 1.14.3) in *Epist.* 1.2.4, but elsewhere (pp. 317–34) argues that Pliny alludes less to the actual words of Cicero's letters, than to their general epistolary tone. Any allusions to Cicero's letters in the Plinian corpus must be situated against Pliny's broader view of Cicero, for which see Keeline (pp. 277–317) and Whitton 2019, 151–91. See Gibson and Morello 2012, 83–99 on Pliny's 'Cicero cycle' (the letters in which Pliny mentions Cicero by name). Cugusi 1983, 174 n. 89 notes Suetonius's citations of letters addressed by Cicero to Axius in *Iul.* 9.2 and to Nepos in *Iul.* 55; references to letters contained in *ad Fam.* and *ad Atticum* are found in Suet. *gramm.* 14.2–3 (*Fam.* 9.10.1 and *Att.* 12.26.2). In Fronto we encounter fewer direct citations of Cicero's letters than general appraisals of them (e.g., 3.8): *epistulis Ciceronis nihil est perfectius.* See Cugusi 1983, 174 for discussion. Cugusi (pp. 247–51) also notes what Fronto's two book of letters *ad amicos* may owe

---

Souvenirs of Cicero. Francesca K. A. Martelli, Oxford University Press. © Oxford University Press 2024.
DOI: 10.1093/oso/9780197761960.003.0007

Cicero's letters to the authors who quote them is to assume that authors were the only readers in the ancient world. In this book, I have suggested that we can piece together a broader picture of the readerships of Cicero's letters by looking more closely at the collections in which they were transmitted, and by considering the narrative interests that these collections serve.

For a letter collection like *ad Fam.*, which may have taken some time to come into formation, its seemingly invisible readers may have been authors too, marking their presence—and even their identities—by keeping some letter books in circulation, and perhaps gradually discarding others; such that the very selection of those sixteen books that made it into the final collection demonstrate these readers' collective preferences and prerogatives over time. According to this scenario, *ad Fam.* would offer a good example of distributed authorship, one that challenges assumptions about our ability to isolate the author of the letters (or the editor/s of the collections) from the readerships that played an equally important role in determining the shape of those collections, and which challenges too assumptions about the artistry of literary form belonging either to the individuated author or to restrictive conceptions of the literary. Appropriately enough, the democratizing aspect of this collection's distributed authorship is reflected in its narrative perspectives, for the range of interests served by *ad Fam.* suggests a readership (or readerships) that extended beyond the senatorial class represented by those authors who explicitly cite Cicero. The inclusion of a book of letters addressed to Tiro, for example, significantly expands the purview of this collection beyond the senatorial elite, while the inclusion of *Fam.* 13 expands its horizons far beyond interests located in 'Rome'. If Roman senators were the only figures interested in reading Cicero's letters, it is hard to see the rationale for including these books in *ad Fam.* Their presence suggests rather that Cicero's letters must have developed an appeal for a widening demographic in the centuries in which they circulated, one that the sixteen-book collection had to accommodate when it took the form that it did.

---

to knowledge of the books of Cicero's *ad Fam.* (if not the complete collection), esp. the recommendation letters of *Fam.* 13. For Plutarch's awareness of Cicero's letters (whether directly or through an intermediary source), Cugusi 1983, 174 n. 90 sees specific references to letters found in *ad Fam.* in Plut. *Cic.* 36.6 and *Cic.* 37.3; and to *ad Atticum* in *Cic.* 37.3–4, *Pomp.* 63, and *Brut.* 21.6. However, Pelling 1979, 89 n. 105 is more conservative, arguing that Plutarch restricts his use of the letters as a source to *Cicero* (but does not use them for his other Roman lives). Pelling notes (p. 87 n. 93) that while Plutarch draws on Brutus's letters to Cicero (including recognizable allusions to Cic. *ad Brut.* 1.16 and 1.17) for his *Brutus*, he does not appear to draw on Cicero's letters to Brutus for this life.

Conclusion

To pose the question of who read Cicero's letters is also to ask implicitly why they read them. This question can get lost amid assumptions about the inevitably canonical status of Cicero's works and the celebrity of his person. Yet it is worth considering how these letter collections may have served to create communities of Roman readers as they circulated over space and time, connecting increasingly far-flung readerships to a defining moment (and a key figure) in Roman history with which (and with whom) they would otherwise have had little contact, and transforming this history into a patrimony in which a widening Roman citizenry could share. That connection will have been more immediate than any narrative about the fall of the Republic written in retrospect, because of the intimate nature of the letters concerned: imperial readers read these letters, as we moderns do, over the shoulder of Cicero's immediate addressees, finding themselves readily interpellated by their second-person address. The same quality of intimacy that magnetized readers when the letter collections were rediscovered in the Renaissance may have had a similar effect in antiquity, drawing readers into the narrative of events that the letter sequences construct (and into sympathy with their authors' biases) by virtue of their confiding disclosures. If we are to ask why Cicero's letters kept circulating, quite possibly in a variety of formats, through the imperial period and beyond, this may be at least part of the reason.

A more obvious focus might be to ask *how* Cicero was viewed and read, a question that is also of interest to this study, even if the answers that the letter collections yield differ from the receptions of Cicero that we find in the prose works of other later authors. As a number of scholars have recently shown, the elite prose authors of the early empire inherited a view of Cicero that was heavily shaped by the schoolroom.[2] The complexity of Cicero's life and person was reduced by the rhetoric schools to a number of partially drawn episodes and traits, determined by their popularity as declamation *topoi*: stories of Cicero's consulship, exile, and death dominate the early reception of Cicero as a result of this.[3] At the same time, the early canonization of particular speeches (such as the *Pro Milone* and *Catilinarians*) further enshrined certain episodes

---

2. See esp. Pierini 2003; and Keeline 2018, esp. chapters 1–4.

3. Keeline 2018, 102–46 for the declamatory schools' focus on Cicero's death; and pp. 147–95 for their focus on his consulship, exile, and activities after Caesar's death. Gowing 2013, 235–8 shows how the preoccupation with Cicero's death that takes hold in the early empire comes about, in part, as a result of its potential as a site of exemplarity (the rest of Cicero's life does not lend itself so easily to exemplarization).

from his life as worthy of memory.[4] Many of the prose authors who explicitly cite Cicero's letters are influenced by these schoolroom traditions and situate their piecemeal quotation of the letters within treatments of Cicero that are primarily indebted to these traditions.[5]

While the schoolroom version of Cicero is to some extent reflected in *ad Fam.* simply by virtue of the number of epistolary sequences given over to letters to (and from) younger colleagues for whom Cicero self-consciously played the role of mentor,[6] the narratives that the letter collections yield significantly complicate and circumvent the limited repertoire of reception narratives that derive from the declamation schools and from Cicero's most canonical speeches. The letter collections bypass the high points of his career that were enshrined by the publication of the *Verrines* and *Catilinarians*, two of his best loved and studied speeches,[7] and stop short of recounting Cicero's death, the event from his life that dominates the declamation schools more than any other. At the same time, however, the letter collections draw significant meaning from the fact of Cicero's death, which is a source of narrative irony (and historical regret) for both *ad Fam.* and *ad Atticum*, in particular. In addition, both these collections fill out important details for some of the

---

4. Keeline 2018, 13–72 on the schoolroom reception of the *Pro Milone*; and pp. 78–90 on the canonization of the *Catilinarians*, *Philippics*, and *Verrines* in the early empire, and the role these speeches played in characterizing Cicero as *publica vox*.

5. Keeline 2018, 336 sums up his view (elaborated at length in the preceding chapters) that the younger Seneca, Tacitus, and Pliny were all influenced by the declamatory schools' treatment of Cicero, even if they are not limited to it and attempt to complicate it. All these authors include occasional quotations from Cicero's letters. The fact that they are not influenced by the alternative view of Cicero that we find in *ad Fam.* may in part be due to the possibility that the sixteen-book collection had yet to crystallize.

6. *Fam.* 2, which is largely taken up with letter sequences to Curio (*Fam.* 2.1–7) and Caelius (*Fam.* 2.8–16) may be characterized as the book of letters to errant youth (although see p. xx for discussion as to how young Caelius actually was), while much of *Fam.* 7 is taken up with letters of advice (and encouragement) to Cicero's young protégé, Trebatius Testa (*Fam.* 7.6–22). See Leach 2006 for discussion.

7. The earliest letters in *ad Fam.* (*Fam.* 5.1 and 5.2) post-date the delivery of both the *Verrines* and the *Catilinarians*: *Fam.* 5.1 is commonly dated to January 62 BCE on the grounds that its author Q. Metellus Celer, who identifies himself as PRO COS. in the heading, took up this position in Cisalpine Gaul in 62 BCE, while events to which it alludes took place in early January (e.g., a clash between Cicero and Celer's brother, Q. Metellus Nepos, in the senate on January 1, and Nepos's *contio* on January 3). See Shackleton Bailey 1977, 273–74 for discussion of the date; and Leveghi 2016, 426–7 for discussion of Celer's appointment. *Fam.* 5.2, Cicero's reply to this letter, was evidently written shortly after. The first eleven letters in *ad Atticum* (*Att.* 1.1–11) are dated before Cicero's consulship, between 68 and July 65 BCE. There is then a gap of four years until the correspondence resumes in 61 BCE with *Att.* 1.12, thus leaving a substantial epistolary lacuna in the years immediately before and immediately after Cicero's consulship.

Conclusion 199

months of the final year of Cicero's life and offer important contextual information for another set of canonical speeches, the *Philippics*, that enshrined Cicero's eloquence in the early empire. Yet far from simply affirming that eloquence, both *ad Fam.* and *ad Atticum* supplement the *Philippics* by demonstrating why these speeches failed:[8] simply by virtue of continuing the narrative beyond the battles of Mutina, they track Antony's unexpected recovery following his defeat at the Battle of Forum Gallorum, when the fourteenth and final *Philippic* had declared him a public enemy. Thus the letter collections confront us with Cicero's failures—showing us the very places where history refuses to corroborate the triumphalist rhetoric of his most celebrated speeches.[9] If there is an exemplary value to the letter collections' version of Cicero, it is in showing readers (ancient and modern) how to fail: both how to fail badly and how to fail better.

In refusing the most standard and canonical narratives about Cicero, the letter collections raise complex questions about authorship and influence. We saw in Chapter 4, 'Ordering the Collection: History and Counter-History in *Fam.* 10–12', how Appian's account of the Rhodians' resistance to helping the republicans in their fight with Antony and Dolabella shares striking points of contact with the account of this episode that we find in *Fam.* 12.[10] Yet it remains difficult to say precisely which narrative is influencing the other. The individual letters transmitted as *Fam.* 12. may have influenced Appian, circulating in a format that we cannot know for certain, while Appian's own narrative may subsequently have influenced how this letter book was put together. Or, if this letter book already existed in the format we know of by the time of Appian's writing, Appian's narrative may have determined where this book was placed in the three-book narrative trilogy of Mutina that *Fam.* 10–12 comprise. The anti-republican bias of this narrative may be indebted to Appian's account, which is clearly in sympathy with the Rhodians, even as his account draws critically on the original letters, with their blindly uncomprehending response to the Rhodians' behaviour. Each source acts upon

---

8. See pp. 122–123 above for how the narrative of *Fam.* 10, in particular has been carefully crafted to supplement the *Philippics*; and pp. 125–126 on how *Att.* 14–15 casts problematic light on Cicero's lengthy justification for his sojourn to Greece in *Phil.* 1.

9. See Morello 2017, 153–7 for a similar view.

10. See pp. 158–60.

the other to produce a narrative that ultimately goes expressly against the intentions of the original letter writers.[11]

This particular example also demonstrates the ways in which Cicero's letter collections resist the project of wholly vilifying Antony and his side, a legacy of Cicero's that other later sources capitalize on as part of the post-Actium recuperation of Cicero as a would-be ally of Octavian's cause.[12] What we find in *ad Fam.*, in particular, is a more complex set of attitudes towards the past than the polarizing strategies that both the declamation schools on the one hand and imperial propaganda on the other would have us understand. This complexity derives from the special status of Cicero's letters as artefacts that migrate across historical eras, capable of being put to novel historical use but also refusing at times to shake off the meanings of the past. As we saw from looking in the Introduction at Raymond Williams's discussion of the different rates at which culture moves, Cicero's letters answer to the category of the 'residual', insofar as they are cultural products that continue to circulate (and recirculate) long after their original moment of consumption because they retain a currency that the dominant culture cannot effectively supersede. Like other residual artefacts, they communicate a nostalgia for the past and, with that, an implicit critique of the present, even while they do not shy away from exposing the structural problems and basic disfunction of republican governance at Rome in its final decades. The Republic haunts the imperial period in the very institutions of government (the consulship, for example, and the senate) that persist into the new era, albeit emptied of the power and meaning that they used to hold. In continuing to circulate in this new era, Cicero's letters haunt the imperial present with reminders of a time when these positions held real power and meaning, and, furthermore, offer traces of the alternative paths that history might have taken, had events turned out otherwise. When Cicero asks Plancus at the outset of *Fam.* 10 what hope there can be for a republic in which neither the senate nor the people have any power at all,[13] we have to consider what the force of this question would be for an imperial

---

11. See pp. 159–60 n. 126 above for a further example of Appian's critical stance toward Cicero. Gabba 1957, 327–39 argues that the anti-Ciceronian bias of book 3 of Appian's *B. Civ.* is owed to the influence of Asinius Pollio's *Histories*. See also Gabba 1956, 244–9 for discussion of Pollio's influence on Appian's account.

12. Keeline 2018, 105–10 on how Augustus's post-Actium propaganda made use of Cicero's opposition to Antony (despite the virtual absence of any explicit mention of Cicero by the Augustan poets, which Pierini 2003, 3–15 also discusses); and pp. 110–118 on how this propaganda acted on the declamatory tradition surrounding Cicero's death.

13. Cf. *Fam.* 10.1.1 with discussion on p. 120 n. 19 above.

readership reading this text at a time when neither the senate nor the people had any real power to speak of. The post-republican readerships of this letter book, who read the letters it contains over the shoulder of Cicero's addressees, find themselves addressed by his aspirations for saving the Republic at all costs—at a time when the Republic was long gone, replaced by the system of government that Cicero most dreaded.

The hauntological currency of *ad Fam.* is concretized by the presence within it of letter sequences composed in the aftermath of the civil war in which Cicero describes the lost Republic in explicitly spectral terms. These letter sequences are worth dwelling on because of the tangible images they provide of the broader (if more elusive) effect that the collection as a whole produces when read in its imperial context. The civil war of 49–46 BCE, which is well documented within the collection, presents readers with a template for the historical break that will recur outside it—with the definitive death of the Republic that follows (and draws symbolically on) Cicero's own death. The spectral language that Cicero uses within *ad Fam.* to mark his reaction to losing the Republic in the historical break of civil war offers a suggestive model for readers' reactions to the break that ultimately closes off and delimits the collection, but which stands outside the letters' purview other than as an object of anticipated but unrealized dread.

Spectres of the Republic

Three books in *ad Fam.* track Cicero's reaction to the civil war of 49–46 BCE across sustained letter sequences: book 4, in which his experiences of political loss are entangled with the work of mourning for his dead daughter;[14] book 6, which focuses on the experience of surviving the war; and book 9, which brings together letter sequences with three quite different correspondents— Varro, Dolabella, and Cicero's Epicurean friend and gourmand, Papirius Paetus—from the year 46–45 BCE, and which showcases Cicero's strategies for coping with life under the dictatorship. A motif that runs especially prominently through this book of letters comes from the uncanny way in which the lost Republic keeps returning, haunting the present in the form of doubles and substitutes. We first see this in a letter that Cicero writes to Varro, in which he derives consolation for their mutual political losses from the turn to philosophy that they had both embarked on at this time, and presents the

---

14. See Gibson 2017 for this reading of *Fam.* 4. Martelli 2016 offers further reflections on how these two forms of grief are entangled in *Att.* 12–13.

202

SOUVENIRS OF CICERO

πολιτεῖαι that he describes himself and Varro constructing in their written studies as a virtual substitute for the real thing (*Fam.* 9.2.5):

> *Modo nobis stet illud, una vivere in studiis nostris, a quibus antea delectationem modo petebamus, nunc vero etiam salutem; non deesse si quis adhibere volet, non modo ut architectos verum etiam ut fabros, ad aedificandam rem publicam, et potius libenter accurrere;* **si nemo utetur opera, tamen et scribere et legere** πολιτείας **et, si minus in curia atque in foro, at in litteris et libris, ut doctissimi veteres fecerunt, navare <operam> rei publicae** *et de moribus ac legibus quaerere.*

> Only let us be fixed on this: to live together in those studies of ours in which we formerly simply sought delight, but now seek our salvation too; and if anyone wants to employ us to build up the Republic, not just as master-builders but even as masons, not to hang back but rather to rush forward eagerly. **If nobody wants to avail themselves of our services, at any rate to write and read 'Republics' and if we fail to do so in the senate house and the forum, at all events to support the state with all our energy in literature and books**, as the greatest ancient philosophers have done, and to investigate ethics and laws.

To those readers of the letter collection for whom the 'Republic of letters' was the only Republic that they had ever known, this exhortation will have brought home the extent to which they were living in the shadow of something past.

Later in book 9 (but before *Fam.* 9.2 in the chronology of composition), we see a different kind of republican spectre in the letter that Dolabella writes to Cicero in the midst of the civil war, during the siege of Dyrrhachium, when Cicero was penned in with others in the Pompeian camp by Caesar's blockade. Trying to persuade Cicero to detach himself from the Pompeians, Dolabella writes (*Fam.* 9.9.3): *Reliquum est, ubi nunc est res publica, ibi simus potius quam, dum illam veterem sequamur, simus in nulla.* ('It only remains for us to take our stand there, where there is now a republic, rather than pursue the old one, and find ourselves with none.') Both old and new republics appear as spectral as each other in this formulation: the old Republic has enough agency to act on those who would pursue it, without actually existing; while the new Republic is a patent replica of the old one—a copy of an original that no longer exists. Cicero's letters to Paetus bear out the further spectral consequences of this situation. *Fam.* 9.15 shows Cicero responding to Paetus's

Conclusion 203

protestation that he should not abandon the political scene in Rome altogether by taking up residence near himself in Naples, where Cicero was considering buying a house. Cicero's reply is to say that it no longer matters where he resides since the decisions now made in the name of the senate no longer rely on the physical venues of senate house and forum because they are made by Caesar himself. But Caesar, it seems, was still relying on the semblance of a functioning senate, drafting decrees on the basis of invented senatorial votes, such that Cicero finds himself being thanked by kings for the honours that he has apparently voted them, despite being unaware of their existence.[15] The spectre of the Republic lingers on after its demise, acting on events without existing, as Cicero can personally bear witness.

In *Fam.* 9.17, Cicero replies to an inquiry from Paetus, asking if he knows anything about the land confiscations that were currently underway, which seem to have posed an immediate threat to the property of both correspondents.[16] Cicero replies with the comment that he is past caring about such things, since life itself can be considered a profit, or *lucrum*, given the fallout from the civil war. But he goes on to hedge this, by saying this (*Fam.* 9.17.1): *Si aut hoc lucrum est aut haec vita, superstitem rei publicae vivere.* ('If indeed outliving the Republic can be called life').[17] Again, it is not completely clear where the spectre resides—with the Republic that has died or with those who live on in a life that might as well be death. In many ways, these letters of Cicero's bring out the true paradox of the ghost, which calls into question the distinction between life and death and threatens to overturn its poles. But the term

---

15. *Fam.* 9.15.4: 'Do you really think there will be fewer decrees of the senate, if I'm at Naples? Here am I at Rome and in constant attendance at the Forum, and all the while decrees of the Senate are being drafted at the house of my dear friend who dotes on you. (*Romae cum sum et urgeo forum, senatus consulta scribuntur apud amatorem tuum, familiarem meum.*) Indeed, whenever it occurs to him, my name's put down as a witness to the drafting, and I'm informed that some decree of the senate alleged to have been passed in accordance with my vote has found its way to Armenia and Syria, before the matter's ever been mentioned at all. And please don't think this is simply a joke; you should know that I've received letters from kings in the farthest reaches of the world, in which they thank me for having given them by my vote the title of king—people whom not only did I not know that they were titled kings but even that they'd ever been born.' Shackleton Bailey 1977, 352 follows Tyrrell and Purser 1918 (vol. 4, 2nd ed.), 427 in regarding Paetus's 'friend' (*amator*) here as Balbus, to whom Caesar is likely to have delegated the drafting of new legislation.

16. See pp. 153–60 for discussion of Caesar's land confiscations at this time.

17. *Fam.* 9.17.1: 'But, my dear Paetus, I'm not inquiring into those matters, firstly, because for the last four years or so the very fact of our being alive has been so much clear gain, if indeed it is a gain, or even life at all, **to outlive the Republic**. (*Sed ego ista, mi Paete, non quaero; primum quia de lucro prope iam quadriennium vivimus, si aut hoc lucrum est aut haec vita, **superstitem rei publicae vivere**.*)

204 SOUVENIRS OF CICERO

superstes, which brings out the wraith-like status of the survivors, is particularly striking because of how it makes this letter resonate with a later work of imperial prose that sketches out an analogous vacuum following a period of trauma. In Tacitus's *Agricola*, those who survived Domitian's cruelty are described in an early chapter of the work as survivors (*superstites*) not only of others but even of themselves—haunted by the ghosts of their past selves or, indeed, living ghosts whose very existence seems out of place amid the ubiquitous death of Domitian's aftermath (Tac. *Agr.* 3):

> *Quid, si per quindecim annos, grande mortalis aevi spatium, multi fortuitis casibus, promptissimus quisque saevitia principis interciderunt pauci et, ut ita dixerim, **non modo aliorum sed etiam nostri superstites sumus** exemptis e media vita tot annis, quibus iuvenes ad senectutem, senes prope ad ipsos exactae aetatis terminos per silentium venimus.*

What if for fifteen years, a large expanse of human life, chance and change have cut off many among us; others, and the most energetic have perished by the emperor's ferocity; **while we few who remain have outlived not merely our neighbours but, so to say, ourselves**; for out of our prime have been blotted as many years during which young men reached old age and old men the very bounds of decrepitude, and all without opening their lips.[18]

Authors like Tacitus can be seen here drawing on the spectral terms in which Cicero describes the gaps in the symbolic that open up in the wake of the civil war and using the same terms to reinscribe a comparable vacuum following the trauma of Domitian's reign. As the trauma of civil war is condemned to repeat itself even after the principate takes hold, so the spectre of the lost Republic returns again and again.

An important effect of the residual currency of Cicero's letters is that they not only take us back to the past but also give us access to the past's lost futures as well, allowing us to linger lovingly and regretfully with the hopes and dreams of a future that was anticipated before being cancelled by the path that history actually took. And which might be reactivated again in the right circumstances. We see this effect throughout the narrative of Mutina in *Fam.*

---

18. The programmatic force of the term *superstes* for the political context of the Agricola is confirmed by the way in which it recurs again at the end of this work (Tac. *Agr.* 46): *Agricola posteritati narratus et traditus **superstes** erit.*

Conclusion 205

10–12, where the counter-historical tale of republican hopes is told in the shadow of the post-republican reader's knowledge of the version of history that won out. Elsewhere in the collection these counter-historical aspirations assume a distinctly spectral shape when, at various points, Cicero projects an idealized version of his addressee, only for the reader to recall that the addressee in question would fall short of this ideal for various reasons, note the historical irony and the regret that things were not destined to turn out otherwise. The letter collection is haunted by these idealized (and unrealized) avatars.

Fam. 9 again supplies a notable example of this, when Cicero writes to Dolabella, who as consul in 44 BCE, had made a brief show of resistance to the Caesarean currents of feeling at Rome, by destroying the altar and pillar erected in honour of Caesar following his assassination and punishing his worshippers. Cicero writes to congratulate him for his actions and claims that he can find no better *exemplum* to guide Dolabella's future actions than the model that he has created for himself (*Fam.* 9.14.6): *Proponam tibi claros viros, quod facere solent qui hortantur? Neminem habeo clariorem quam te ipsum; te imitere oportet, tecum ipse certes; ne licet quidem tibi iam tantis rebus gestis non tui similem esse.* ('Shall I remind you of exemplary men, as people often do when exhorting one another? I find no more illustrious example than yourself. It lies with you to imitate yourself and be your own rival. So splendid have been your achievements already that you don't have the right to fall short of your own standard.') This is the last letter in the sequence of letters exchanged between Cicero and Dolabella, as the editor of the book capitalizes on what later readers can supply from their knowledge of how this story would turn out. Which is that Dolabella would shortly side with Antony, against the republican faction, after being offered the province of Syria, plundering the cities of Greece and Asia Minor, and brutally murdering the pro-republican proconsul of Asia, Trebonius, en route to his province. These events are recounted in *Philippic* 11, but do not surface explicitly in *ad Fam.*,[19] which holds open the promise that Cicero invests in Dolabella in this letter from book 9, without referring to how this promise was cancelled by his subsequent actions.[20] Cicero here projects a Dolabella who is shadowed— haunted in advance—by a better version of himself, and the editor leaves this

---

19. See discussion on p. 160 n. 128 above.

20. Another spectacular example of this kind of idealized avatar appears in the sequence of letters from Cicero to Curio that opens *Fam.* 2, which culminates in a letter of congratulations that Cicero sends Curio upon hearing that he has been made tribune (a letter that is, however, hedged with misgivings about the danger of Curio's appointment to this position). Preceding this letter is a sequence written to Curio while he was stationed on official duty in Asia in 53

206 SOUVENIRS OF CICERO

idealized avatar of the wayward ex-son-in-law as the reader's lasting image of him, capitalizing on our knowledge of Dolabella's subsequent behaviour to note the gap between Cicero's hopes and history's refusal.[21]

But Cicero's longing for a better future, pinned on the shoulders of idealized versions of his peers, have wider implications for the residual power structures that carry over from the Republic to a principate. As we have seen, *Fam.* 10 opens with a suite of letters exchanged between Cicero and L. Munatius Plancus, whose capacity to save his neck by changing sides throughout this period would subsequently become famous. Throughout his correspondence with him in 44 to 43 BCE, Cicero reveals his concerns about this tendency, when he tells him repeatedly to ensure that his ending matches his beginning. Plancus had been pre-appointed consul for 42 BCE by Julius Caesar, and in *Fam.* 10.6, after one particular show of potential disloyalty to the republican side, Cicero reminds him that the consulship is a badge of merit, earned by the consular's behaviour towards the Republic, rather than an empty title (*Fam.* 10.6.2 and 10.6.3):[22]

> *Crede igitur mihi, Plance, omnis quos adhuc gradus dignitatis consecutus sis (es autem adeptus amplissimos) eos honorum vocabula habituros, non dignitatis insignia, nisi te cum libertate populi Romani et cum senatus*

BCE, praising him for actions abroad that are now obscure to us, in the course of which Cicero tells Curio that the high reputation he has earned while abroad has established a rival version of himself to emulate (*Fam.* 2.4.2): 'For the extraordinary expectation that you have aroused has established and supplied you with a serious rival here' (*Est enim tibi gravis adversaria constituta et parata incredibilis quaedam exspectatio*). The idealized apparition that these terms of exhortation conjure carries over into the letter that Cicero writes to congratulate Curio upon his being made tribune, where he tells him not to be guided by others but always to listen to himself (*Fam.* 2.7.2): 'But I beg of you, don't let your thoughts and anxieties take a new direction, but do just what I suggested at the start of my letter: have a talk with yourself, invite yourself to a consultation, listen to yourself and pay attention to what you have to say.' (*Sed amabo te, cura et cogita—nihil novi, sed illud idem quod initio scripsi: tecum loquere, te adhibe in consilium, te audi, tibi obtempera.*) As with Dolabella in 44 BCE, Cicero projects a Curio who is shadowed—haunted in advance—by a better version of himself. This idealized avatar is, moreover, the image of Curio that the letter collection leaves us with, since the letter sequence cuts off here, before the point in the narrative when Curio would turn over to the other side and refute the prospect of this version of himself completely.

21. The ironies that arise from the disjunction between the future possibilities and retrospective realities of the self-exemplary script that Cicero projects onto Dolabella in this letter are subsequently picked up by Seneca and channelled to similarly ironic effect when telling Nero that he has no better available *exemplum* to copy as *princeps* than himself at Sen. *Clem.* 1.6. Braund 2009 *ad loc.* notes the allusion to Cic. *Fam.* 9.14.6—but not the irony.

22. See pp. 133–136 for discussion of this letter within the narrative of *Fam.* 10.

Conclusion   207

auctoritate coniunxeris. Seiunge te, quaeso, aliquando ab iis cum quibus
te non tuum iudicium sed temporum vincla coniunxerunt. Complures in
perturbatione rei publicae consules dicti, quorum nemo consularis habitus
nisi qui animo exstitit in rem publicam consulari).

Believe me, Plancus, those steps of promotion you've ascended thus far
(and you've reached the most important of them) will be universally
viewed not as badges of merit, but as mere titles of public office, unless
you align yourself with the liberty of the Roman people and the authority of the senate. Disassociate yourself, I beg you, while there's still
time, from those to whom you're bound by the ties of circumstance
rather than by your own choice. Amid the Republic's turmoil, several
men have been named consul, but not a single one of them has been
truly deemed a consular unless he was a man who stood out for the
consular spirit he displayed toward the Republic.

Plancus would, however, go on to share the consulship of 42 BCE, not with
the republican Decimus Brutus, whom Caesar had appointed as his colleague,
but with Octavian himself, after Plancus moved over from the republican to
the triumviral side. For the later reader, there is an obvious irony to this letter,
as Cicero exhorts Plancus to earn the consulship to which he has been pre-
appointed by remaining true to the Republic, even if, again, it is an irony that
the collection leaves implied, as *Fam.* 10 (and the collection as a whole) tapers
off before Plancus would definitively betray the republic by changing sides.
But this is also an irony that extends beyond Plancus himself to the broader
office of consul that would be held by others long after him. Cicero's reproach
to Plancus addresses all those future consuls of the imperial period who find
themselves occupying the constitutional offices of the old Republic, which
haunt the new monarchical system as empty titles, residual reminders of a
more meaningful past, in perpetuity. Or, alternatively, they may appear as
goads to those like Thrasea Paetus and the stoic resistance under Nero who
would try to stand up to monarchical rule.

Cicero's letter collections haunt later readers, even up to our own day, with
their republican hopes and aspirations (however flawed the system they long
for may have been). In addressing readers in the second person, the letters seem
to want to bridge the historical gap between Cicero and ourselves and draw
us into the (doomed) drama of republican salvation. Yet, as products of a later
era, the collections reopen that gap and reproach us with living in a time of
the aftermath, in which that process of salvation has already failed, reducing

us all to the status of ghosts. Reading Cicero's letter collections now, in an era that has not moved on substantively from that which Derrida describes in *Spectres of Marx*, and which is still punctured by the contradictions and inequalities on which our late-capitalist system is founded to the point of ever worsening crisis,[23] we can map our own twenty-first century vantage point all too easily onto that of the collection's early imperial readers and editors over two millennia ago. For despite the historical disjunction, and the disparate nature and causes of the crises that Cicero and we find ourselves contending with, these moments resonate in the similar effects that they produce for us as historical subjects: in the common experience of political loss; and in the feeling of time standing still—of being stuck, or unable to move on—which characterizes the experience of time in the early Roman Empire and in our own era, and creates the illusion of continuity between them.[24] Cicero's letter collections address us in speaking to this condition.

The question is: What will we reply?

---

23. The ongoing resonance for many fields and discourses of Derrida's diagnosis of the 'perma-crisis' produced by post-communist capitalism (worsened since the publication of *Specters of Marx* by the climate catastrophe and the Covid-19 pandemic), is outlined by Migheli 2022.

24. See pp. xxx–xxxiii on the significance of time being 'out of joint' in the era ushered in by the collapse of Communism, and of the resonance between this moment of untimeliness and that of the early Roman empire.

APPENDIX

The Chronological Order of Letters
in Fam. *10–12*

This appendix is offered to supplement Chapter 4, 'History and Counter-History in *Fam.* 10–12', and to help the reader comprehend the organization of letters in these three letter books in relation to the correspondents involved and to the chronological order in which they were composed.

Chronology is, however, as I noted at the outset of that chapter, a particularly difficult effect to reconstruct in the case of these letter books, which include letters from Cicero along with their replies, and which are written at a time when the time lag between sending and receiving a letter was filled with uncertainty, as communication routes and channels were disrupted by war.

The chronology of events is complicated by this time lag: a letter may communicate news that has been made redundant or superseded by new developments by the time it reaches its correspondent, or it may fail to reach its correspondent altogether. These letters illustrate particularly well how asynchronously the historical events of this period were experienced by the correspondent-protagonists involved. The chronology of the letters' composition is equally difficult to reconstruct: whereas some of the letters are explicitly dated, others are not, and those have to be dated in relation to other letters or events. In some cases, a letter can be approximately dated when it is written in reply to another letter which is either explicitly dated or contains an internal reference to a datable event. In these instances, though, we have to gauge the extent of time that it would have taken for the earlier letter to reach its recipient, which is a highly uncertain estimate, especially in times of war.

For this appendix, I have relied heavily on the chronological sequence painstakingly reconstructed by Shackleton Bailey [SB] 1977 and in various articles by W. Sternkopf. Dates without brackets refer to letters that are explicitly dated. The dates placed in brackets are based on scholars' reconstructions, which I have summarized in the footnotes.

210   *Appendix*

Profectio et Reversio *in* Fam. *10*

Plancus	Other Correspondents	Lepidus	Pollio
1. Cic. to Planc. (Sept, 44 BCE)[1]			
2. Cic. to Planc. (after Sept 19)[2]			
3. Cic. to Planc. (mid-Dec)[3]			
4. Planc. to Cic. (late Dec)[4]			
5. Cic. to Planc. (mid-Jan, 43 BCE)[5]			
	28. Cic. to Trebonius (Feb 2 or 3)[6]		31. Poll. to Cic. (March 16)
6. Cic. to Planc. (March 20)		27. Cic. to Lep. (March 20)[7]	

---

1. Composed after Cicero returned to Rome, following his abortive departure for Greece in August. SB 1977, 479–80 notes the uncertainty as to whether *Fam.* 10.1 should be dated to before or after the senate meeting of September 19, when Antony issued verbal threats against Cicero. But SB 1977, 479 notes that Antony may have delivered similar threats before that occasion, and that this letter may be responding to earlier abuse.

2. Dated to after September 19, on the basis of a reference to the recent occurrence of a senate meeting that took place on that date (from which Cicero was absent).

3. SB, 1977 495 dates this letter to mid-December on the basis of the conjectured date of its reply (*Fam.* 10.4).

4. A reply to *Fam.* 10.3. This letter (*Fam.* 10.4) is dated to late December on the basis of Plancus's eager anticipation (at *Fam.* 10.4.4) of news about what would happen in January.

5. A reply to *Fam.* 10.4.

6. SB 1977, 503 dates this letter to the same moment as *Fam.* 12.4, which is dated to the February 2 or 3 on the basis of details that relate it to the *Eighth Philippic* (which was delivered then).

7. SB 1977, 509: 'On 20 March the Senate had before it letters from Lepidus and apparently from Plancus advocating peace. Cicero dealt with Lepidus' letter with firmness and restraint in the course of his *Thirteenth Philippic*.... This and the next letter [*Fam.* 10.6] were probably written in the evening after the debate.' *Fam.* 10.6 is explicitly dated to March 20.

Plancus	Other Correspondents	Lepidus	Pollio
7. Planc. to Cic. (shortly after mid-March)[8]			
8. Planc. to SPQR (shortly after mid-March)			
10. Cic. to Planc. (March 30)			
12. Cic. to Planc. (April 11)			
	30. Galba to Cic. (April 15)		
9. Planc. to Cic. (after April 26)[9]			
11. Planc. to Cic. (before May 9/10)[10]			
14. Cic. to Planc. (May 5)			
13. Cic. to Planc. (after May 10)[11]			
15. Planc. to Cic. (mid-May)[12]			

---

8. SB 1977, 511 follows T-P in dating this letter, which arrived in Rome with *Fam.* 10.8 around April 7 (as is clear from a detail in *Fam.* 10.12.2), to mid-March, on the grounds that it would have taken about three weeks to travel there from Gaul.

9. SB 1977, 522: 'An answer to *Fam.* 10.10, written on or shortly after 26 April.'

10. SB 1977, 524: 'Since writing *Fam.* 10.9 on *ca* 27 April, Plancus had received *Fam.* 10.12 from Cicero, with the news of the senate's complimentary decree, and a report of Antony's defeat on 21 April. The latter might take about a week to travel the 350 miles or so from Mutina. This letter was certainly sent before 9–10 May.'

11. This letter seems to be an answer to *Fam.* 10.9, which is dated to c. April 27, and which SB 1977, 531 argues cannot have arrived in Rome before May 10.

12. SB 1977, 532 follows Sternkopf 1910, 257 in viewing this letter as most probably the post-script to a lost letter, rather than to *Fam.* 10.11. SB follows Sternkopf 1910, 256 in correcting the internal date at *Fam.* 10.15.3 from *a.d. IIII Id. Mai.* to *a.d. VII Id. Mai.* because 'the despatch of the cavalry was clearly subsequent to the building of the bridge.'

Plancus	Other Correspondents	Lepidus	Pollio
21. Planc. to Cic. (mid-May)[13]			
19. Cic. to Planc. (mid-May)[14]		34a. Lep. to Cic., (after May 18)[16]	
18. Planc. to Cic. (May 18)[15]		34b. Lep. to Cic. (May 22)	
17. Planc. to Cic. (after May 18)[17]	25. Cic. to Furnius, (late May)[18]	35. Lep. to SPQR (May 30)	
16. Cic. to Planc. (after May 25)[19]			
20. Cic. to Planc. (May 29)			
23. Planc. to Cic. (June 6)	26. C to Furnius, (late June)[21]		33. Poll. to Cic., (early June)[20]
22. Cic. to Planc. (late June)[22]	29. C to Appius Claudius (July 6)		32. Poll. to Cic. (June 8)
24. Planc. to Cic. (July 28)			

---

13. Written two days after the despatch of *Fam.* 10.15.

14. SB 1977, 535 follows Walser 1957, 121–23 in regarding this letter as a reply to *Fam.* 10.11—not as (T.-P. take it) to *Fam.* 10.15. He dates *Fam.* 10.19 to mid-May accordingly.

15. SB 1977, 536 dates this letter to May 18: at *Fam.* 10.18.4 Plancus mentions striking camp on this date, presumably after despatching this letter, in the hope of joining Lepidus eight days hence.

16. SB 1977, 537: 'Ventidius was two days' march from Antony on 15 May. . ., and this letter was written after their junction; therefore not earlier than 18 May.'

17. SB 1977, 538 follows Sternkopf 1910, 264 in regarding this letter as being written after May 18 and before May 25, on the march south.

18. SB 1977, 543 assigns this letter to c. May 27, regarding it as contemporaneous with *Fam.* 10.19.

19. SB 1977, 544: 'The official letter mentioned in §1 will have corresponded to [*Fam.* 10.15], and will have arrived in Rome about 25 May.'

20. SB 1977, 550: 'News from Italy took at least forty days to reach Pollio (§5) and the news of the battle of Mutina and events immediately following had been held up en route for nine days (§1).' SB therefore follows Ruete 1883, 112 in dating this letter to the first half of June.

21. SB 1977, 565 suggests that this letter may have been despatched with the two letters that he places immediately before it (*Fam.* 11.15 and 10.22), both of which are dated to late June.

22. SB 1977, 565: 'The identical conclusion indicates that this and the foregoing [*Fam.* 11.15] were composed at a sitting.' SB dates *Fam.* 11.15 to late June on the grounds that news of Plancus and D. Brutus joining forces (mentioned at *Fam.* 11.15.1) would have reached Rome toward the end of June.

Appendix

The Siege of Letters in Fam. *11*

M. Brutus & Cassius	Decimus Brutus	Matius	Oppius
1. D.Brut. to M.Brut. & Cassius (between March 17 and 22, 44 BCE)[23]			
2. M.Brut. & Cassius to M.Ant. (from mid-May)[24]			
3. M.Brut. & Cassius to M.Ant. (Aug. 4)			29. Cic. to Oppius (July)[25]
	4. D.Brut. to Cic. (Sept)[26]	27. Cic. to Matius, (mid-Oct)[27]	
	6. Cic. to D.Brut. (late Sept)[28]	28. Matius to Cic. (late Oct)[29]	

---

23. SB 1977, 463–64 gives a full discussion of the complex question of this letter's date: assigned by many (e.g., Schmidt 1884, 334) to the early morning of March 17 (i.e., before the amnesty and ratification of Caesar's *acta* that were decreed in the Temple of Tellus later on that day), SB follows Ruete 1883, 16–18; Sternkopf 1916, 485–89, and Accame 1934 in assigning the letter to a date shortly after Caesar's funeral.

24. SB 1977, 469: 'After their first flight from Rome following the riots after Caesar's funeral Brutus and Cassius seem to have returned, only to withdraw again to Lanuvium about the middle of April [*Att.* 14.7.1].' At §1, this letter refers to a large number of veterans already gathering at Antony's bidding for the senate meeting on June 1, which was evidently imminent.

25. This letter is dated to July, before Cicero's abortive trip to Greece, but after he had finally resolved to make the trip, on the basis of a reference in §1 to Atticus having relayed to Cicero Oppius's approval of his decision to leave. See SB 1977, 475 on the relative dating of this letter with the last two letters to Atticus [*Att.* 15.26 and 27] that Cicero composed before departing.

26. SB 1977, 480 follows Sternkopf 1901, 302–4; and 1905, 541–42 in dating this letter to September.

27. SB 1977, 486 follows Kytzler 1960, 49–52 in rejecting the generally received date of late August for this letter (shortly after Cicero's abortive trip to Greece and recent return to Rome), and dating it to mid-October, when Cicero would have been in Rome for over a month, on the grounds that the references Cicero makes at §7 and §8 to having repeatedly defended Matius's reputation suggest that he has been in Rome for a sustained period of time.

28. Sternkopf 1901, 299–301 separated this letter from *Fam.* 11.6a, recognizing that this letter was written in response to the senate meeting of September 19, while *Fam.* 11.6a was composed following the senate meeting of December 20.

29. Matius's reply to *Fam.* 11.27.

M. Brutus & Cassius	Decimus Brutus	Matius	Oppius
	5. Cic. to D.Brut. (after Dec 9)[30]		
	7. Cic. to D.Brut. (mid-Dec)[31]		
	6a. Cic. to D.Brut. (on or after Dec 20)[32]		
	8. Cic. to D.Brut. (late Jan, 43 BCE)[33]		
	9. D.Brut. to Cic. (April 29)		
	13b. D.Brut. to Cic. (April 30)[34]		
	10. D.Brut. to Cic. (May 5)		
	11. D.Brut. to Cic. (May 6)		
	13. D.Brut. to Cic. (May 8)[35]		
	12. Cic. to D.Brut. (mid-May)[36]		

30. At *Fam.* 11.5.1, Cicero mentions having arrived back in Rome on December 9.

31. See Sternkopf 1901, 297 for discussion of the date (before the senate meeting of December 20), and the decision to place this letter before *Fam.* 11.6a.

32. This letter, which Sternkopf 1901, 299–301 separates from *Fam.* 11.6, was clearly written shortly after the senate meeting of December 20. It contains references to the support of D. Brutus that Cicero delivered publicly on that day in *Phil.* 3 and 4.

33. S-B 1977, 499 surmises that Cicero wrote this letter in late January, not long before the return of the envoys mentioned in §1.

34. SB 1977, 523: 'The first two words of this letter are preserved in M's Index. If Decimus left Regium on the 29th [April] he might arrive on the same or the following day.'

35. See SB 1977, 529 for discussion of the date of this letter, which he works out relative to the date of the despatch of *Fam.* 11.11 on May 6 and the time it would have taken D. Brutus to reach Pollentia from Statiellenses ahead of Antony, who had set off from Vada.

36. SB 1977, 535: 'Probably written shortly after the arrival of Decimus's three letters (§1) [*Fam.* 11.9–11], the latest of which [*Fam.* 11.11] was despatched from north-west Italy on 6 May. It might take six or seven days to reach Rome.'

Appendix

M. Brutus & Cassius	Decimus Brutus	Matius	Oppius
	18. Cic. to D.Brut. (May 19)		
	19. D.Brut. to Cic. (May 21)		
	20. D.Brut. to Cic. (May 24)		
	23. D.Brut to Cic. (May 25)		
	16. Cic. to D.Brut. (May/June)[37]		
	17. Cic. to M.Brut. (May/June)[38]		
	26. DB to Cic. (June 3)		
	21. Cic. to D.Brut. (June 4)		
	24. Cic. to D.Brut (June 6)		
	14. Cic. to D.Brut. (June 7)[39]		
	13a. Planc. & D.Brut. to SPQR (c. June 9)[40]		

---

37. SB 1977, 571 notes that this seems to have been written in May or June, after the siege of Mutina had been lifted.

38. This letter fulfils the similar function of recommending L. Lamia for the praetorship as *Fam.* 11.16 and must have been written around the same time. In this case, however, although the manuscripts MDVH identify the addressee simply as 'Brutus' (the heading of the letter reads: *Cicero Bruto s.*), the addressee appears to be M. Brutus (not D. Brutus, as in the case of *Fam.* 11.16). SB 1977, 571–72 diverges from Tyrrell and Purser (who try to sustain the case for the addressee being D. Brutus), and follows Schmieder 1799, 60 in viewing this letter as having mistakenly migrated into the wrong collection.

39. SB 1977, 554 argues that the letter Cicero is answering here must have been received after he wrote *Fam.* 11.21 (June 4), and after D. Brutus wrote both *Fam.* 11.20 (May 24) and *Fam.* 11.23 (May 25). But this reply of Cicero's must have been penned before the news of Lepidus's defection reached Rome (on June 8 or 9).

40. SB 1977, 561: '. . . part of an official letter from Plancus and D. Brutus to the Senate, attached in the MSS to [Fam. 11.13]. It was probably written soon after their junction, which had been expected to take place on 9 June.'

M. Brutus & Cassius	Decimus Brutus	Matius	Oppius
	25. Cic. to D.Brut (June 18)		
	15. Cic. to D.Brut. (late June)[41]		
	22. Cic. to D.Brut. (June or July)[42]		

The View from the East in Fam. *12*

Cassius	Other Correspondents	Cicero to Q. Cornificius[43]
		17. (Spring of 46)[44]
		18. (late Sept/early Oct, 46 BCE)[45]
		19. (c. mid-Dec 46 BCE)[46]
1. Cic. to Cassius (May 3, 44 BCE)[47]	16. Trebonius to Cic. (May 25)	

---

41. SB 1977, 565: 'News of Plancus' junction with D. Brutus (§1) will have reached Rome toward the end of June.'

42. This letter, enlisting D. Brutus's support in the senate to restore Appius Claudius's civic rights, appears to have been written around the same time as *Fam.* 10.29 (addressed to Appius Claudius himself, assuring him of Cicero's support, and dated to July 6).

43. For the letters exchanged between Cicero and Cornificius, we only have Cicero's side of the correspondence.

44. SB 1977, 364: 'Q. Cornificius, neoteric poet and orator . . . had taken over Cilicia presumably as *pro quaestore* (not Quaestor, as Broughton; he had been Quaestor in 48) or *legatus pro praetore* (or *pro consule*) in the spring or early summer of 46 (cf. Broughton [1952], 297).'

45. SB 1977, 364–65 notes that an approximate date is indicated by the reference in §2 to *the ludi Victoriae Caesaris*, held in honour of Caesar's victory at Thapsus and dedication on that occasion of the temple of Venus Genetrix. The games took place on September 24/25 according to the current calendar, but between July 20 and 30 once the calendar was reformed.

46. SB 1977, 366 notes that the letter referred to in the opening sentence of seems to be *Fam.* 12.18, and that this letter seems to have been written four to five months later.

47. SB 1977, 465: 'The place and date of writing follow from [*Att.* 14.15.1] *quadriduo ante ad eum scripseram.* Cicero had left Rome for Campania on 7 April. Cassius was with Brutus at Lanuvium.'

Appendix 217

Cassius	Other Correspondents	Cicero to Q. Cornificius[43]
2. Cic. to Cassius (late Sept)[48]		20. (date uncertain, possibly Sept. 2, 44)[49]
3. Cic. to Cassius (early Oct)[50]		22. (late Sept, 44 BCE)[51]
		23. (c. Oct 10, 44, BCE)[53]
4. Cic. to Cassius (Feb 2 or 3, 43 BCE)[52]		22a. (c. Dec 21, BCE)[55]
		24.1-2 (late Jan, 43 BCE)[56]
5. (after Feb 3)[54]		

---

48. SB 1977, 481: 'Written after 19 September (§1) and before 2 October [*Fam.* 12.3.2]. Cassius may still have been in South Italy.'

49. SB 1977, 478: 'The date is uncertain. L. Ganter's highly plausible hypothesis [Ganter 1894, 141] that Cicero wrote the letter at the sitting of the Senate on 2 September 44, after Cornificius had set out for his province of Africa, cannot be proved; cf. Sternkopf 1912, 338. On the other hand, the reference to Cicero's lodge at Sinuessa is against Schmidt's dating to the spring of 46 [Schmidt 1893, 252].' Cicero would appear (from *Fam.* 6.19) to have acquired this lodge in the autumn of 45 BCE.

50. SB 1977, 483: 'Written shortly after 2 October (§2), before Antony's departure from Rome on the 9th.'

51. SB 1977, 484 follows Ganter 1894, 139–40 in separating this letter from *Fam.* 12.22a, and dating it to the latter half of September on the basis of parallels with *Fam.* 10.1, *Fam.* 10.2, and *Fam.* 12.2.

52. SB 1977, 502 dates this letter to February 4 or 5, after the first debate in the senate that took place on February 2 or 3, after the return of the two surviving envoys from Mutina (on February 1 or 2).

53. SB 1977, 485 dates this letter to approximately October 10, apparently on the basis of a reference to Antony's departure for Brundisium on October 9 (§2).

54. SB 1977, 504 notes that this letter must be dated after February 3, since there is a reference in it (§2) to Hirtius's despatch announcing the capture of Claterna, which would have been read out to the senate on that date (as we know from *Phil.* 8.6). How soon this letter was written after February 3 is, however, unclear. SB follows the observation of Nardo 1966, 40–41 that correspondences between the letter and the *Tenth Philippic* do not prove the priority of the speech, the date of which is uncertain.

55. SB 1977, 497 follows Ganter 1894, 139–40 in separating this letter from *Fam.* 12.22. As it stands, *Fam.* 12.22a now opens with a reference to the senate meeting of December 20, which evidently took place shortly before the composition of this letter. At §4, Cicero mentions hurrying to meet the time pressures of Cornificius's messengers.

56. SB 1977, 569 follows Nardo 1966, 60–61 in separating *Fam.* 12.24 into two letters. This first letter is dated by an internal reference to the *occasio* on which the *Third Philippic* was delivered on December 20 (§2).

Cassius	Other Correspondents	Cicero to Q. Cornificius[43]
7. (c. March 7)[57]		21. (44 or 43 BCE)[58]
11. Cassius to Cic. (March 7)		24.3 (44 or 43 BCE)[59]
		26. (43 or 44 BCE)[61]
		27. (43 or 44 BCE)[62]
6. Cic. to Cassius (late March/early April)[60]		25. (after March 19)[64]
		28. (c. March 25)[66]
12. Cassius to Cic. (May 7)	14. Lentulus to Cic. (May 29)	
8. Cic to Cassius (c. June 9)[63]	15. Lentulus to SPQR (June 2)	
9. Cicero to Cassius (mid- or late June)[65]	13. Cassius Parmensis (June 13)	

---

57. SB 1977, 506 places the composition of this letter shortly after the Eleventh Philippic, which is dated by Tyrrell and Purser to March 6 or 7.

58. SB 1977, 569–70: 'This and the following three letters to Cornificius [*Fam.* 12.24.3, *Fam.* 12.26 and *Fam.* 12.27] cannot be dated precisely.' All four of these letters are recommendation letters.

59. See n. 14.

60. SB 1977, 517: 'Seemingly written about the same time as [*ad Brut.* 1.1], which expresses similar anxiety about the course of the war, probably about the end of March or beginning of April.'

61. See n. 14.

62. See n. 14.

63. SB 1977, 560 notes that the news of Lepidus's defection on May 29 (addressed in the opening sentence of this letter) would have reached Rome around June 8 or 9.

64. SB 1977, 513: 'What appears in the earliest editions (not, as T.-P. say, the MSS) as 12.25 was recognized by Corradus as two letters, this and [*Fam.* 12.25a]. The former was evidently written soon after the meeting of the Senate on 19 March.'

65. SB 1977, 564: 'The letter was written, as its contents show, before 30 June, when Lepidus was declared a public enemy, and after [*Fam.* 12.8].'

66. SB 1977, 515: 'Datable after Pansa's departure on 20 March and before 20 April, when the news of Forum Gallorum reached Rome. But §3 will have been written before the end of March, by which time Cicero had become acutely anxious about the situation at Mutina.'

Appendix

Cassius	Other Correspondents	Cicero to Q. Cornificius[43]
10. Cicero to Cassius (c. July 1)[67]		25a. (early May)[68]
		30. (c. June 9)[69]
		29. (first half of 43 BCE)[70]

67. This letter may be dated by the reference in the opening sentence to Lepidus being declared a public enemy on June 30.

68. SB 1977, 525: 'Presumably written soon after the news of the second battle of Mutina reached Rome, i.e. about the beginning of May.'

69. SB 1977, 561 dates this letter to the same date as *Fam.* 12.8 (i.e., June 9), on the basis of similar phrasing used at §2 to describe the war that had been almost snuffed out being resuscitated (as a result of the confirmed news of Lepidus's defection).

70. SB 1977, 570 dates this letter to the first half of 43 BCE, on the grounds that the consuls referred to (*illis consulibus*) at §2 must refer to Antony and Dolabella.

Bibliography

Accame, S. 1934. 'Decimo Bruto dopo i funerali di Cesare'. *Rivista di Filologia* 62: 201–8.

Althusser, L. 2014. *On the Reproduction of Capitalism: Ideology and State Apparatuses*. London and New York: Verso.

Andreau, J. 1999. *Banking and Business in the Roman World*. Cambridge University Press.

Arcellaschi, A. 1997. 'Le *Pro Caelio* et le théâtre'. *RÉL* 75: 78–91.

Austin, R. G. 1933. *M. Tulli Ciceronis 'Pro Caelio Oratio'*. Oxford.

Austin, R. G. 1948. *M. Tulli Ciceronis 'Pro Caelio Oratio'* (revised ed.). Oxford.

Austin, R. G. 1951. *M. Tulli Ciceronis 'Pro Caelio Oratio'* (revised ed.). Oxford.

Austin, R. G. 1960. *M. Tulli Ciceronis 'Pro Caelio Oratio'* (revised ed.). Oxford.

Bachelard, G. 1994. *The Poetics of Space*. Boston: Beacon Press.

Badian, E. 1965. 'M. Porcius Cato and the Annexation and Early Administration of Cyprus'. *Journal of Roman Studies* 55: 110–21.

Balsdon, J. 1952. Review of Carcapino, J. 1951. *Cicero, The Secrets of His Correspondence* (trans. E. O. Lorimer). London: *Classical Review* 2, no. 3/4: 178–81.

Baudrillard, J. 1996. *The System of Objects*. London and New York: Verso.

Beard, M. 2002. 'Ciceronian Correspondences: Making a Book out of Letters'. In T. P. Wiseman (ed.), *Classics in Progress: Essays on Ancient Greece and Rome*. 103–44. Oxford.

Beard, M. 2007. *The Roman Triumph*. Cambridge, MA: Harvard University Press.

Beard, M. 2015. *SPQR: A History of Ancient Rome*. New York and London: Liveright.

Bell, A. J. E. 1997. 'Cicero and the Spectacle of Power'. *JRS* 87: 1–22.

Bell, S., and T. Ramsby, eds. 2012. *Free at Last! The Impact of Freed Slaves on the Roman Empire*. London: Bristol Classical Press.

Bernhardt, R. 1971. *Imperium und Eleutheria. Die Römische Politik gegenüber den freien Städten des Griechischen Ostens*. University of Hamburg.

Biale, D. 1979. *Gershom Scholem: Kabbalah and Counter-History*. Cambridge, MA: Harvard University Press.

Biale, D. 1999. 'Counter-History and Jewish Polemics against Christianity: The *Sefer toldot yeshu* and the *Sefer zerubavel*'. *Jewish Social Studies* 6, no. 1: 130–45.

Bibliography

Bishop, C. 2020. *Cicero, Greek Learning, and the Making of a Roman Classic*. Oxford University Press.

Blake, S. 2012. 'Now You See Them: Slaves and Other Objects as Elements of the Roman Master'. *Helios* 39, no. 2: 193–211.

Boissier, G. 1863. *Recherches sur la manière dont furent recueillies et publiées les lettres de Cicéron*. Paris: Librairie d'Auguste Durand.

Bomgardner, D. 2000. *The Story, of the Roman Amphitheatre*. London and New York: Routledge.

Bonnefond-Coudry, M. 1989. *Le sénat de la republique romaine de la guerre d'Hannibal à Auguste: Pratiques délibératives et prise de decision*. Rome: Ecole Française de Rome.

Boym, S. 2001. *The Future of Nostalgia*. New York: Basic Books.

Braund, S. 2009. *Seneca: De Clementia*. Oxford University Press.

Broughton, T. R. S. 1951–2. *The magistrates of the Roman Republic* (2 vols.). New York: American Philological Association.

Bruns, K. G., ed. 1909. *Fontes Iuris Romani Antiqui*. Tübingen, Germany: P. Siebeck.

Brunt, P. 1966. 'The "Fiscus" and Its Development'. *JRS* 56, nos. 1–2: 75–91.

Brunt, P. 1971. *Italian Manpower 225 B.C. – A.D. 14*. Oxford: Clarendon Press.

Bruwaene, M. Van den. 1953. 'Précisions sur la teneur et l'importance du sénatus-consulte d'octobre 51 avant J.-C'. *Les Etudes Classiques* (*LEC*) 21: 19–27.

Büchner, K. 1939. 'M Tullius Cicero (Tullius 29)'. In Wilhelm Kroll, ed., *Paulys Realencyclopädie* 7A. Stuttgart: J.B. Metzler, 827–1274.

Cammoranesi, S. 2022. *Cicero's Epistulae ad Familiares: Narratives of Civil War*. Manchester University unpublished diss.

Cappello, O. 2016. 'Everything You Wanted to Know about Atticus (but Were Afraid to Ask Cicero): Looking for Atticus in Cicero's ad Atticum'. *Arethusa* 49, no. 3: 463–87.

Carcopino, J. 1947. *Les secrets de la correspondence de Cicéron*, 2 vols. Paris: L'Artisan du Livre.

Celenza, C. 2020. *The Intellectual World of the Italian Renaissance: Language, Philosophy and the Search for Meaning*. Cambridge: Cambridge University Press.

Clay, D. 2009. 'The Athenian Garden'. In J. Warren, ed., *The Cambridge Companion to Epicureanism*. Cambridge University Press, 9–28.

Cliff, M. 1990. 'Object into Subject: Some Thoughts on the Work of Black Female Artists'. In G. Anzaldua, ed., *Making Face, Making Soul/Haciendo Caras: Creative and Critical Perspectives by Women of Color*. San Francisco: Aunt Lute, 271–90.

Coleman, K. 1990. 'Fatal Charades: Roman Executions Staged as Mythological Enactments'. *JRS* 80: 44–73.

Coleman, K. 1993. 'Launching into History: Aquatic Displays in the Early Empire. *JRS* 83: 48–74.

Costa, E. 1927. *Cicerone Giureconsulto I*. Bologna: Nicola Zanichelli.

Crawford, J. 1984. *M. Tullius Cicero: The Lost and Unpublished Orations*. Göttingen, Germany: Vandenhoeck and Ruprecht.

Bibliography

Cugusi, P. 1983. *Evoluzione e Forme Dell'epistolografia Latina Nella Tarda Repubblica e nei primi due secoli Dell'impero*. Rome: Herder.

Deniaux, E. 1991. 'Les recommandations de Ciceron et la colonisation césarienne'. *Cahiers du Centre Gustave Glotz* 2: 215–28.

Deniaux, E. 1993. *Clientèles et Pouvoir à l'époque de Cicéron*. Rome: Ecole Française de Rome.

Derrida, J. 1987. *The Post Card: From Socrates to Freud and Beyond*. Chicago University Press.

Derrida, J. 1993. *Specters of Marx*. New York and Oxford: Routledge.

Derrida, J. 1996. *Archive Fever: A Freudian Impression*. Translated by Eric Prenowitz. Chicago and London:

Dettenhofer, M. 1992. *Perdita iuventus: zwischen den Generationen von Caesar und Augustus*. Munich: C. H. Beck'sche Verlagsbuchhandlung.

Durkheim, E. 1893. *De la Division du Travail Social*. Paris: Félix Alcan.

Durkheim, E. 1897. *Le Suicide: Étude de Sociologie*, Paris: Félix Alcan.

Dyck, A. 2013. *Cicero: Pro Marco Caelio*. Cambridge: Cambridge University Press.

Earlie, P. 2015. 'Derrida's Archive Fever: From Debt to Inheritance'. *Paragraph* 38, no. 3: 312–28.

Eden, K. 2012. *The Rediscovery of Intimacy in the Renaissance*. Chicago: Chicago University Press.

Ernout, A., and A. Meillet. 1967. *Dictionnaire étymologique de la langue latine. Histoire des mots*. Paris: Librairie C. Klincksieck.

Feeney, D. 2007. *Caesar's Calendar: Ancient Time and the Bginnings of History*. Berkeley, Los Angeles and London: University of California Press.

Fineman, J. 1989. 'The History of the Anecdote: Fiction and Fiction'. In H. A. Veeser, ed., *The New Historicism*. London and New York: Routledge, 49–76.

Fisher, M. 2013. 'The Metaphysics of Crackle: Afrofuturism and Hauntology'. *dancecult* 5, no. 2: 42–55.

Fisher, M. 2014. *Ghosts of My Life: Writings on Depression, Hauntology and Lost Futures*. Winchester, UK and Washington, DC: Zero Books.

Fishwick, D. 1993. 'On the Origins of Africa Proconsularis I: The Mmalgamation of Africa Vetus and Africa Nova'. *Antiquités Africaines* 29: 53–62.

Fitzgerald, W. 2000. *Slavery and the Roman Literary Imagination*, Cambridge: Cambridge University Press.

Fitzgerald, W. 2011. 'The Slave as Minimal Addition'. In R. Alston, E. Hall, and L. Profitt, eds., *Reading Ancient Slavery*. London and New York: Bristol Classical Press.

Fletcher, R. 2016. 'Philosophy in the Expanded Field: Ciceronian Dialogue in Pollio's Letters from Spain (*Fam*. 10. 31-3)'. *Arethusa* 49, no. 3: 549–73.

Foucault, M. 2003. *Society Must Be Defended: Lectures at the Collège de France, 1975–76*. New York: Picador.

Fowler, D. 1995. 'Martial and the Book'. *Ramus* 24, no. 1: 31–58.

Bibliography

Frampton, S. 2019. *Empire of Letters: Writing in Roman Literature and Thought from Lucretius to Ovid*. Oxford: Oxford University Press.

Frederickson, M. 1966. 'Caesar, Cicero, and the Problem of Debt'. *JRS* 56: 128–41.

Frier, B. 1985. *The rise of the Roman Jurists: Studies in Cicero's Pro Caecina*. Princeton, NJ: Princeton University Press.

Frow, J. 1982. 'The Literary Frame'. *Journal of Aesthetic Education*, 16, no. 2: 25–30.

Funkenstein, A. 1986. *Theology and the Scientific Imagination from the Middle Ages to the Seventeenth Century*. Princeton, NJ: Princeton University Press.

Funkenstein, A. 1993. *Perceptions of Jewish History*. Berkeley, CA: University of California Press.

Futrell, A. 1997. *Blood in the Arena: The Spectacle of Roman Power*. Austin, TX: University of Texas Press.

Futrell, A. 2006. *The Roman Games: A Sourcebook*: Oxford, UK: Wiley-Blackwell.

Gabba, E. 1956. *Appiano e la storia delle guerre civili*. Florence: La Nuova Italia.

Gabba, E. 1957. 'Note sulla polemica anticiceroniana di Asinio Pollione'. *Rivista Storica Italiana* 69: 317–39.

Galinsky, K. 1996. *Augustan Culture: An Interpretive Introduction*. Princeton, NJ: Princeton University Press.

Gallagher, C., and S. Greenblatt. 2000. 'Counterhistory and the Anecdote'. In *Practicing New Historicism*. Chicago: Chicago University Press, 49–74.

Ganter, L. 1894. 'Q. Cornificius: Ein Beitrag zur Geschichte der Senatspartei in den letzten Jahren der Republik'. *Philologus* 53: 132–46.

Garland, A. 1992. 'Cicero's *Familia Urbana*'. *Greece and Rome* 39, no. 2: 163–72.

Geffcken, K. A. 1973. '*Comedy in the Pro Caelio*'. *Mnemosyne* Suppl. 30, Leiden.

Gelzer, M. 1968. *Caesar: Politician and Statesman*, Cambridge, MA: Harvard University Press.

Gibson, R. 2012. 'On the Nature of Ancient Letter Collections'. *JRS* 102: 56–78.

Gibson, R. 2017. '*Pro Marcello* without Caesar: Grief, Exile and Death in Cicero *ad Familiares* 4'. *Hermathena* 202, no. 3: 105–46.

Gibson, R., and R. Morello. 2012. *Reading the Letters of Pliny the Younger: An Introduction*. Oxford: Oxford University Press.

Golvin, J. C. 2012. *L'amphithéâtre romain et les jeux du cirque dans le monde antique*. Paris: Presses Universitaires de France.

Gowers, E. 2019. 'Knight's Moves: The Son-in-law in Cicero and Tacitus'. *Classical Antiquity* 38: 2–35.

Gowing, A. 1992. *The Triumviral Narratives of Appian and Cassius Dio*. Ann Arbor, MI: University of Michigan Press.

Gowing, A. 2005. *Empire and Memory: The Representation of the Roman Republic in Imperial Culture*. Cambridge, UK: Cambridge University Press, 233–50.

Gowing, A. 2013. 'Tully's Boat: Responses to Cicero in the Imperial Period'. In C. Steel, ed., *The Cambridge Companion to Cicero*. Cambridge, UK: Cambridge University Press.

Greenidge, A. H. J. 1901. *The Legal Procedure of Cicero's Time*. Oxford: Clarendon Press.

Griffin, M. 1989. 'Philosophy, Politics, and Politicians at Rome' In M. T. Griffin and J. Barnes, eds., *Philosophia Togata: Essays on Philosophy and Roman Society*. Oxford: Clarendon Press, 1–37.

Griffin, M. 1995. 'Philosophical Badinage in Cicero's Letters to his Friends'. In J. G. F. Powell, ed., *Cicero the Philosopher*. Oxford: Clarendon Press, 325–46.

Grillo, L. 2015a. 'Reading Cicero's *ad Familiares* 1 as a Collection'. *CQ* 65, no. 2: 655–68.

Grillo, L. 2015b. *Cicero's De Provinciis Consularibus Oratio*. Oxford: Oxford University Press.

Grillo, L. 2016. 'The Artistic Architecture and Closural Devices of Cicero's *ad Familiares* 1 and 6'. *Arethusa* 49, no. 3: 399–413.

Gruen, E. 1969. 'Pompey, the Roman Aristocracy, and the Conference of Luca'. *Historia* 18, no. 1: 71–108.

Gruen, E. 1974. *The Last Generation of the Roman Republic*. Berkeley and Los Angeles: University of California Press.

Gunderson, E. 1997. 'The Ideology of the Arena'. *ClAnt* 15, no. 1: 113–151.

Gunderson, E. 2007. 'S.V.B.; E.V.'. *Cl Ant*. 26: 1–48.

Gunderson, E. 2016. 'Cicero's Studied Passions: The Letters of 46 BCE'. *Arethusa* 49, no. 3: 525–47.

Güthenke, C. 2020. 'For Time Is / Nothing If Not Amenable' — Exemplarity, Time, Reception'. *Classical Receptions Journal* 12, no. 1: 46–61.

Habinek, T. 2005. 'Slavery and Class'. In S. Harrison, ed., *A Companion to Latin Literature*. Oxford: Oxford University Press, 385–93.

Hall, J. 2009a. *Politeness and Politics in Cicero's Letters*. Oxford: Oxford University Press.

Hall, J. 2009b. 'Serving the Times: Cicero and Caesar the Dictator'. In W. J. Dominik, J. Garthwaite, and P. A. Roche, eds., *Writing Politics in Imperial Rome*. Leiden, The Netherlands: Brill, 89–110.

Hanchey, D. 2013. 'Cicero, Exchange and the Epicureans'. *Phoenix* 67, no. 1: 119–34.

Harnett, B. 2017. 'The Diffusion of the Codex'. *Cl. Ant.* 36, no. 2: 183–235.

Hellegouarc'h, J. 1963. *Le Vocabulaire Latin des Relations et des Partis Politiques sous la Republique*. Paris: Les Belles Lettres.

Henderson, J. 2002. *'Oxford Reds': Classic Commentaries on Latin Classics*. London: Duckworth.

Henderson, J. 2016. 'Cicero's Letters to Cicero, *ad QFr*: Big Brothers Keepers'. *Arethusa* 49, no. 3: 439–61.

Hendrickson, T. 2018. 'Spurious Manuscripts of Genuine Works: The Cases of Cicero and Virgil'. In A. Guzman and J. Martínez, eds., *Animo Decipiendi? Rethinking Fakes and Authorship in Classical, Late Antique, and Early Christian Works*. Groningen, The Netherlands: Barkhuis, 125–38.

Hickson-Hahn. 2000. 'Pompey's "Supplicatio Duplicata": A Novel Form of Thanksgiving'. *Phoenix* 54, nos. 3/4: 244–54.

Hinds, S. 1985. 'Booking the Return Trip: Ovid and *Tristia* 1'. *CCJ* 31: 13–32.

Bibliography

Hinds, S. 2004. 'Petrarch, Cicero, Virgil: Virtual Community in *Familiares* 24.4'. *MD* 52: 157–75.

Hinds, S. 2005. 'Defamiliarizing Latin Literature, from Petrarch to Pulp Fiction'. *TAPA* 135: 49–81.

Hölkeskamp, K.-J. 1995. '*Oratoris maxima scaena*: Reden vor dem Volk in der politischen Kultur der Republik'. In M. Jehne, ed., *Demokratie in Rom? Die Rolle des Volkes in der Politik der römischen Republik*. Stuttgart: Steiner.

Houston, G. W. 2014. *Inside Roman Libraries: Book Collections and their Management in Antiquity*. Chapel Hill: University of North Carolina Press.

Howley, J. 2018. *Aulus Gellius and Roman Reading Culture: Text, Presence and Imperial Knowledge in the Noctes Atticae*. Cambridge, UK: Cambridge University Press.

Hunt, J. M., R. A. Smith, and F. Stok. 2017. *Classics from Papyrus to the Internet: An Introduction to Transmission and Reception*. Austin, TX: University of Texas Press.

Hutchinson, G. O. 2001. 'The Date of *De Rerum Natura*'. *Classical Quarterly* 51, no. 1: 150–62.

Jenkins, H., S. Ford, and J. Green. 2013. *Spreadable Media: Creating Value and Meaning in a Networked Culture*. New York: New York University Press.

Johnson, B. 1988. 'The Frame of Reference: Poe, Lacan, Derrida'. In J. P. Miller and W. J. Richardson, eds., *The Purloined Poe: Lacan, Derrida and Psychoanalytic Reading*. Baltimore: Johns Hopkins University Press, 213–51.

Johnson, W. 2004. *Bookrolls and Scribes in Oxyrhynchus*. Toronto: University of Toronto Press.

Johnson, W. 2010. *Readers and Reading Culture in the High Empire: A Study of Elite Reading Communities*. Oxford: Oxford University Press.

Jones, C. P. 2015. 'The Greek Letters Ascribed to Brutus'. *Harvard Studies in Classical Philology* 108: 195–244.

Kaster, R. 1998. 'Becoming 'CICERO'. In P.E. Knox and C. Foss, eds., *Style and Tradition: Studies in Honor of Wendell Clausen*. Stuttgart: B. G. Teubner, 248–63.

Kaster, R. 2006. *Cicero: Speech on behalf of Publius Sestius*. Oxford: Oxford University Press.

Keeline, T. 2018. *The Reception of Cicero in the Early Roman Empire: The Rhetorical Schoolroom and the Creation of a Cultural Legend*. Cambridge: Cambridge University Press.

Kennedy, D. 1999. 'A Sense of Place: Rome, History and Empire Revisited'. In C. Edwards, ed., *Roman Presences: Receptions of Rome in European Culture, 1789–1945*. Cambridge: Cambridge University Press, 19–34.

Kenyon, F. 1932. *Books and Readers in Ancient Greece and Rome*. Oxford: Clarendon Press.

King, W. D. 2008. *Collections of Nothing*. Chicago: Chicago University Press.

Kytzler, B. 1960. 'Beobachtungen zu den Matius-Briefen (Ad Fam. 11.27/28)'. *Philologus* 104: 48–62.

Lacan, J. 1997. *The Seminar of Jacques Lacan: The Psychoses (Book 3)*. Translated by Jacques-Alain Miller. New York and London: Norton.

Bibliography

Lacan, J. 2006. *Écrits*. Translated by Bruce Fink. New York and London: Norton.

Lacan, J. 2015. *On the Names-of-the-Father*. Translated by Bruce Fink. Cambridge, UK: Polity.

Lavan, M. 2011. 'Slavishness in Britain and Rome in Tacitus' *Agricola*'. *CQ* 61, no. 1: 294–305.

Leach, E. W. 1999. 'Ciceronian "Bi-Marcus". Correspondence with M. T. Varro and L. P. Paetius in 46'. *TAPA* 129: 139–79.

Leach, E. W. 2006. '"*An gravius aliquid scribam*": Roman *seniores* write to *iuvenes*'. *TAPA* 136: 247–67.

Leach, E. W. 2016. 'Cicero's Cilician Correspondence: Space and *Auctoritas*'. *Arethusa* 49, no. 3: 503–23.

Lebek, W. D. 1970. *Verba Prisca: die Anfänge des Archaisierens in der lateinischen Beredsemkeit und Geschichtsschreibung*. Göttingen, Germany: Vandenhoeck & Ruprecht.

Leigh, M. 2004. 'The *Pro Caelio* and Comedy'. *Classical Philology* 99, no. 4: 300–335.

Leveghi, C. 2016. 'Libro Quinto'. In A. Cavarzere, ed., *Cicerone: Lettere ai familiari* (2 vols.). Milan: RCS Libri, 415–529.

Lintott, A. 1993. *Imperium Romanum: Politics and Administration*. New York and London: Routledge.

Lintott, A. 2003. *The Constitution of the Roman Republic*. Oxford: Oxford University Press.

Lintott, A. 2008. *Cicero as Evidence: A Historian's Companion*. Oxford: Oxford University Press.

Luraschi, G. 1974. 'La "lex Vatinia de colonia Comum deducenda" ed i connessi problemi di storia costituzionale romana'. In *Proceedings of the Conference to Mark the Centenary of the Rivista archeologica Comense*, Noseda, Como, 363–400.

Luraschi, G. 1979. *Foedus ius Latii civitas: aspetti costituzionali della Romanizzazione in Transpadana*. Padua, Italy: Casa Editrice Dott.

Magie, D. 1950. *Roman Rule in Asia Minor* (2 vols.). Princeton, NJ: Princeton University Press.

Magnino, D. 1984. *Appiani Bellorum civilium liber tertius*. Florence: La Nuova Italia.

McCutcheon, R. 2016. 'A Revisionist History of Cicero's *Letters*'. *Echos du monde classique* 13, no. 1: 35–63.

McDermott, W. C. 1972. 'M. Cicero and M. Tiro'. *Historia* 21: 259–86.

McKenzie, D. 1999. *Bibliography and the Sociology of Texts*. Cambridge, UK: Cambridge University Press.

McIntosh, G. 2013. 'Cicero and Exile: Building a House of Letters'. *Syllecta Classica* 24: 47–76.

McLaughlin, M. 2015. 'Petrarch and Cicero: Adulation and Critical Distance'. In W. H. F. Altman, ed., *Brill's Companion to the Reception of Cicero*. Leiden-Boston: Brill, 19–38.

Bibliography

McLean, R. 2018. *Freed Slaves and Roman Imperial Culture*. Cambridge, UK: Cambridge University Press.

McLuhan, M. 1964. *Understanding Media: The Extensions of Man*. New York: Mentor.

Manuwald, G., ed. 2007. *Cicero, Philippics 3–9, Vol. I: Introduction, Text and Translation, References and Indexes; Vol. II: Commentary (Texte und Kommentare 30)*. Berlin: de Gruyter.

Marchesi, I. 2008. *The Art of Pliny's Letters: A Poetics of Allusion in the Private Correspondence*. Cambridge, UK: Cambridge University Press.

Martelli, F. 2016. 'Mourning Tulli-a: The Shrine of Letters in *ad Atticum* 12'. *Arethusa* 49, no. 3: 415–37.

Martelli, F. 2020. *Ovid* (Research Perspectives on Ancient Poetry). Leiden: Brill.

Martelli, F. 2017. 'The Triumph of Letters: Rewriting Cicero in *Fam.* 15'. *JRS* 107: 90–115.

Martelli, F. Forthcoming. 'The Spectral Life of Friends: Derrida, Cicero, Atticus'. In S. Gurd and M.Telò, eds., *The Before and the After*. Tangent.

Maslowski, T. 1974. 'The Chronology of Cicero's Anti-Epicureanism'. *Eos* 62: 55–78.

Migheli, G. 2022. 'Specters of Specters of Marx: A Ghost That Was Named Derrida'. *Ephemera* 22, no. 3: 275–85.

Millar, F. 1964. 'The Aerarium and Its Officials Under the Empire'. *JRS* 54, nos. 1–2: 33–40.

Millar, F. 1977. *The Emperor in the Roman World*. London: Duckworth.

Mitchell, H. 2019. 'The Reputation of L. Munatius Plancus and the Idea of "Serving the Times"'. In K. Morrell, J. Osgood, and K. Welch, eds., *The Alternative Augustan Age*. Oxford: Oxford University Press, 163–81.

Mitchell, T. 1969. 'Cicero before Luca (September 57–April 56 B.C.)'. *TAPA* 100: 295–320.

Mitchell, T. 1991. *Cicero: The Senior Statesman*. New Haven, CT: Yale University Press.

Mommsen, T. 1864. *Römische Forschungen* (2 vols.). Berlin: Weidmann.

Morello, R. 2017. 'Further Voices and Familiar Perspectives in Cicero's Letters'. *Hermathena* 202, no. 3: 147–84.

Morgan, L. 2000. 'The Autopsy of Asinius Pollio'. *JRS* 90: 51–69.

Morgan, L., and B. Taylor. 2017. 'Memmius the Epicurean'. *CQ* 67, no. 2: 528–41.

Morstein-Marx, R. 2021. *Julius Caesar and the Roman People*. Cambridge: Cambridge University Press.

Moss, C. 2023. 'The Secretary: Enslaved Workers, Stenography, and the Production of Early Christian Literature'. *The Journal of Theological Studies* 74, no. 1: 20–57.

Mouritsen, H. 2011. *The Freedman in the Roman World*. Cambridge: Cambridge University Press.

Nake, B. 1866. *De Planci et Ciceronis Epistulis*. Berlin: Franzkrüger.

Nardo, D. 1966. *M Tulli Ciceronis epistularum ad familiares: liber 12*. Milan: Mondadori.

Nicgorski, W. 2002. 'Cicero, Citizenship, and the Epicurean Temptation'. In D. Allman and M. Beaty, eds., *Cultivating Citizens: Soulcraft and Citizenship in Contemporary America*. Lanham, MD: Lexington Books, 3–28.

Bibliography

Nicholson, J. 1998. 'The Survival of Cicero's Letters'. In C. Deroux, ed., *Studies in Latin Literature and Roman History IX*. Brussels: 63–105.

Novati, F. 1888. *La giovinezza di Coluccio Salutati*. Turin, Italy: Ermanno Loescher.

O'Brien Moore, A. 1935. 'Senatus Consultum'. *RE Suppl.* 6: 800–812.

Oost, S. I. 1955. 'Cato Uticensis and the Annexation of Cyprus'. *CP* 50, no. 2: 98–112.

Osgood, J. 2006. *Caesar's Legacy: Civil War and the Emergence of the Roman Empire*. Cambridge: Cambridge University Press.

Owens, W. 2020. *The Representation of Slavery in the Greek Novel*. London and New York: Routledge.

Pêcheux, M. 1982. *Language, Semantics and Ideology*. London: Macmillan.

Pelling, C. 1979. 'Plutarch's Method of Work in the Roman Lives'. *JHS* 99: 74–96.

Pelling, C. 2011. *Plutarch: Caesar* (translated with in introduction and commentary). Oxford: Oxford University Press.

Pettit, T. 2009. 'Containment and Articulation: Media, Cultural Production, and the Perception of the Material World'. 2009. Accessed 18 March 2024. (http://web.mit.edu/comm- forum/mit6/papers/Pettitt.pdf)

Pierini, R. Degl'Innocenti. 2003. 'Cicerone nella prima età imperiale. Luci ed ombre su un martire della repubblica'. In E. Narducci, ed., *Aspetti della fortuna di Cicerone nella cultura Latina*. Florence: Le Monnier, 3–54.

Pinkster, H. 2010. 'Notes on the Language of Marcus Caelius Rufus'. In E. Dickey and A. Chahoud, eds., *Colloquial and Literary Latin*. Cambridge: Cambridge University Press, 186–202.

Ramsay, W. M. 1922. 'Studies in the Roman Province of Galatia III: Imperial Government of the Province Galatia'. *JRS* 12: 147–86.

Rawson, E. 1975. *Cicero: A Portrait*. London: Bristol Classical Press.

Rawson, E. 1986. 'Cassius and Brutus: The Memory of the Liberators'. In I. S. Moxon, J. D. Smart, and A. J. Woodman, eds., *Past Perspectives: Studies in Greek and Roman Historical Writing*, Cambridge: Cambridge University Press, 101–19.

Rawson, E. 1987. '*Discrimina Ordinum*: The *Lex Julia Theatralis*'. Papers of the British School at Rome 55: 83–114.

Reeve, M. 1991. 'The Rediscovery of Classical Rexts in the Renaissance'. In O. Pecere, ed., *Itinerari di testi antichi*. Rome: L'Erma di Bretschneider, 115–17.

Reeve, M. 1996. 'Classical Scholarship'. In J. Kraye, ed., *The Cambridge Companion to Renaissance Humanism*. Cambridge, UK: Cambridge University Press, 20–46.

Reynolds, L. D. 1983. *Texts and Transmission: A Survey of the Latin Classics*. Oxford: Clarendon Press.

Reynolds, S. 2011. *Retromania: Pop Culture's Addiction to Its Own Past*. New York: Farrar, Strauss and Giroux.

Richlin, A. 1999. 'Cicero's Head'. In J. Porter, ed., *Constructions of the Classical Body*, Ann Arbor, MI: University of Michigan Press, 190–211.

Roberts, C. H., and T. C. Skeat. 1983. *The Birth of the Codex*. Oxford: Oxford University Press.

230 Bibliography

Roesch, S. 2004. 'La politesse dans la correspondance de Cicéron'. In L. Nadjo and E. Gavoille, eds., *Epistulae antiquae III: Actes du IIIe colloque international 'L'Épistolaire antique et ses prolongements européens*. Leuven, Belgium: Peeters, 139–52.

Rohrbacher, D. 2016. *The Play of Allusion in the Historia Augusta*. Wisconsin: University of Wisconsin Press.

Roselaar, S. 2010. *Public Land in the Roman Republic. A Social and Economic History of Ager Publicus in Italy, 396–89 BC*. Oxford: Oxford University Press.

Rowland, R. J. 1972. 'Cicero and the Greek World'. *TAPA* 103: 451–61.

Ruete, E. 1883. *Die Correspondenz Ciceros in den Jahren 44 und 43*. Marburg, Germany: N.G. Eltwert'sche Verlags Buchhandlung.

Saller, R. 1994. *Patriarchy, Property and Death in the Roman Family*. Cambridge, UK: Cambridge University Press.

Salutati, C. 1891. *Epistolario* (Vol. 1). Edited by F. Novati. Rome: Forzani.

Santangelo, F. 2007. *Sulla, the Elites, and the Empire: A Study of Roman Policies in Italy and the Greek East*. Leiden, The Netherlands: Brill.

Schiller, A. 1978. *Roman Law: Mechanisms of Development*. The Hague, Paris, and New York: Mouton.

Schmidt, O. E. 1884. 'Zur Chronologie der Correspondenz Ciceros seit Caesars Tode'. *Neue Jahrbücher für Philologie und Pädagogik* 129: 331–50.

Schmidt, P. 1983. 'Die Rezeption des römischen Freundschaftesbriefes (Cicero-Plinius) im frühen Humanismus (Petrarc-Coluccio Salutati)'. In F. J. Worstbrock, ed., *Der Brief im Zeitalter der Renaissance*. Weinheim, Germany: Acta Humaniora, 25–59.

Schmidt, O. E. 1893. *Der Briefwechsel des M. Tullius Cicero von seinem Prokonsulat in Cilicien bis zu Caesars Ermordung*. Hildesheim: Olms.

Schmieder, B. F. 1799. *Historisch-philologische Bemerkungen zur Erläuterung der Briefe Cicero's ad diversos*. Halle, Germany: Hemmerde und Schwetschke.

Setaioli, A. 2003. 'Seneca e Cicerone'. In E. Narducci, ed., *Aspetti della fortuna di Cicerone nella cultura Latina*. Florence: Le Monnier, 55–77.

Shackleton Bailey, D. R. 1965–70. *Cicero: Epistulae ad Atticum* (7 vols.). Cambridge, UK: Cambridge University Press.

Shackleton Bailey, D. R. 1977. *Cicero: Epistulae ad Familiares* (2 vols.). Cambridge, UK: Cambridge University Press.

Shackleton Bailey, D. R. 1980. *Cicero: Epistulae ad Quintum Fratrem et M. Brutum*. Cambridge, UK: Cambridge University Press.

Shatzman, I. 1975. *Senatorial Wealth and Roman Politics*. Brussels: Latomus.

Sherwin-White, A. N. 1973. *The Roman Citizenship*. Oxford: Clarendon Press.

Sherwin-White, A. N. 1984. *Roman Foreign Policy in the East, 168 B.C. to A.D. 1*. London: Duckworth.

Sommer, R. 1926. 'T. Pomponius Atticus und die Verbreitung von Ciceros Werken'. *Hermes* 61: 389–422.

Stacey, P. 2007. *Roman Monarchy and the Renaissance Prince*, Cambridge, UK:

Bibliography

Standage, T. 2013. *The Writing on the Wall: Social Media — The First 2000 Years*, London: Bloomsbury.

Stearns, J. B. 1931. 'A note on Gaius Memmius'. *The Classical Weekly* 24: 161–62.

Stem, R. 2006. 'Cicero as Orator and Philosopher: The Value of the "Pro Murena" for Ciceronian Political Thought'. *The Review of Politics* 68, no. 2: 206–31.

Sternkopf, W. 1901. 'Ciceros Briefwechsel mit D. Brutus und die Senatssitzung vom 20. Dezember 44'. *Philologus* 60: 282–306.

Sternkopf, W. 1905. 'Zu Cicero *ad Familiares* XI 6'. *Hermes* 40, no. 4: 529–43.

Sternkopf, W. 1910. 'Plancus, Lepidus und Laterensis im Mai 43'. *Hermes* 45: 250–300.

Sternkopf, W. 1912. 'Die Verteilung der Römischen Provinzen vor dem Mutinensischen Kriege'. *Hermes* 47, no. 3: 321–401.

Sternkopf, W. 1916. 'E. T. Merrill. 1. On the date of Cic. fam. XI.1; 2. Cicero and Bithynicus.Sonderabdruck aus Classical Philology, Bd X, Nr. 3 (S. 241-259) and Nr. 4 (S. 432-437). Chicago 1915'. *Wochenschrift für klassische Philologie* 33, no. 21: 485–91.

Stewart, S. 1993. *On Longing*. Durham, NC: Duke University Press.

Stokes, M. 1995. 'Cicero on Epicurean Pleasures'. In J. G. F. Powell, ed., *Cicero the Philosopher*. Oxford: Clarendon Press, 145–70.

Strasburger, H. 1968. *Caesar im Urteil seiner Zeitgenossen*. Darmstadt, Germany: Wissenchaftliche Buchgesellschaft.

Straw, W. 2007. 'Embedded Memories'. In C. Acland, ed., *Residual Media*. Minneapolis: University of Minnesota Press, 3–15.

Striker, G. 1996. 'Epicurean Hedonism'. In G. Striker, ed., *Essays on Epicurean Epistemology and Ethics*. Cambridge: Cambridge University Press, 196–208.

Sumner, G. 1971. *The Orators in Cicero's Brutus: Prosopography and Chronology*. Toronto: University of Toronto Press.

Syme, R. 1939. *The Roman Revolution*. Oxford: Clarendon Press.

Syme, R. 1939b. 'Observations on the Province of Cilicia'. In W. M. Calder and J. Keil. eds., *Anatolian Studies Presented to William Hepburn Buckler*. Manchester, UK: Manchester University Press, 299–332.

Telò, M. 2020. *Archive Feelings: A Theory of Greek Tragedy*. Columbus, OH: Ohio State University Press.

Treggiari, S. 1969. *Roman Freedmen during the Late Republic*. Oxford: Clarendon Press.

Treggiari, S. 1969b. 'The Freedmen of Cicero'. *Greece and Rome* 16, no. 2: 195–204.

Tyrrell, R., and L. C. Purser. 1879–1901. *The Correspondence of M. Tullius Cicero, Arranged According to Its Chronological Order, with a Revision of the Text, a Commentary and Introductory Essays on The Life of Cicero, and The Style of His Letters* (7 vols.). Dublin: Hodges & Figgis.

Tyrrell, R., and L. C. Purser. 1885–1933. *The Correspondence of M. Tullius Cicero, Arranged According to Its Chronological Order, with a Revision of the Text, a Commentary and Introductory Essays on The Life of Cicero, and The Style of His Letters* (6 vols.) (2nd ed.). Dublin: Hodges and Figgis.

Tyrrell, R., and L. C. Purser. 1904. *The Correspondence of M. Tullius Cicero, Arranged According to Its Chronological Order, with a Revision of the Text, a Commentary and Introductory Essays on The Life of Cicero, and The Style of His Letters* (vol. 1) (3rd ed.). Dublin: Hodges and Figgis.

Ullman, B. 1963. *The Humanism of Coluccio Salutati*. Padua, Italy: Editrice Antenore.

Vasaly, A. 1985. 'The Masks of Rhetoric: Cicero's *Pro Roscio Amerino*'. *Rhetorica* 3, no. 1: 1–20.

Verboven, K. 2002. *The Economy of Friends. Economic Aspects of Amicitia and Patronage in the Late Republic*. Brussels: Latomus.

Veyne, P. 1976. *Bread and Circuses: Historical Sociology and Political Pluralism*. London: Penguin.

Von Streng, A. 1885. *De Ciceronis ad Brutum epp. lib. II* (dissertation). Helsinki.

Walcot, P. 1975. 'Cicero on Private Property: Theory and Practice'. *Greece and Rome* 22, no. 2: 120–28.

Walser, G. 1957. *Der Briefwechsel des L. Manutius Plancus mit Cicero*. Basel, Switzerland: Helbing & Lichtenhahn.

Watkins, T. H. 1997. *L. Munatius Plancus: Serving and Surviving in the Roman Revolution*. London and New York: Routledge.

Watt, W. S. 1982. *M. Tulli Ciceronis Epistulae (Tomus I): Epistulae ad Familiares*. Oxford: Clarendon Press.

Watt, W. S. 1982. *M. Tulli Ciceronis Epistulae (Tomus II): Epistulae ad Atticum*. Oxford: Clarendon Press.

Weaver, P. R. C. 1972. *Familia Caesaris. A Social Study of the Emperor's Freedmen and Slaves*. Cambridge, UK: Cambridge University Press.

Wegehaupt, W. 1878. *Das Leben des M. Caelius Rufus*. Breslau, Poland: Fiedler & Hentschel.

Welch, K. 2007. *The Roman Amphitheatre: From Its Origins to the Colosseum*. Cambridge, UK:

Weyssenhoff, C. 1966. *De Ciceronis epistulis deperditis*, Wroclaw, Poland: Wydawnictwo polskiej Akademii Nauk.

White, H. 1987. *The Content of the Form*, Baltimore: Johns Hopkins University Press.

White, P. 2010. *Cicero in Letters*: Oxford and New York: Oxford University Press.

Whitton, C. 2017. 'Last but not Least: ad M. Brutum'. *Hermathena* 202, no. 3, 185–224.

Whitton, C. 2019. *The Arts of Imitation in Latin Prose: Pliny's Epistles/Quintilian in Brief*. Cambridge, UK: Cambridge University Press.

Wilcox, A. 2012. *The Gift of Correspondence in Classical Rome: Friendship in Cicero's Ad Familiares and Seneca's Moral Epistles*. Madison, WI: University of Wisconsin Press.

Williams, R. 1970. *The English Novel from Dickens to Lawrence*, Oxford: Oxford University Press.

Williams, R. 1977. *Marxism and Literature*. Oxford and New York: Oxford University Press.

Bibliography

Willis, I. 2017. 'Lucan, Reception, Counterhistory'. In R. Alston, ed., *Foucault and Roman Antiquity: Foucault's Rome* (*Foucault Studies* Special Issue 22), 31–48.

Winterbottom, M. 1981. 'Cicero and the Silver Age'. In W. Ludwig, ed., *Éloquence et Rhétorique chez Cicéron*. Vandoeuvres-Geneva: Fondation Hardt.

Wiseman, P. 1985. *Catullus and His World: A Reappraisal*. Cambridge, UK: Cambridge University Press.

Witt, R. G. 1983. *Hercules at the Crossroads: The Life, Works and Thought of Coluccio Salutati*. Durham, NC: Duke University Press.

Wolff, H. 1979. 'Caesars Neugründung von Comum und das sogenannte ius Latii maius'. *Chiron* 9: 169–87.

Woolf, G. 2006. 'Pliny's Province'. In T. Bekker-Nielson, ed., *Rome and the Black Sea Region*. Aarhus, Denmark: Aarhus University Press, 93–108.

Wright, A. 2001. 'The Death of Cicero. Forming a Tradition: The Contamination of History'. *Historia* 50, no. 4: 436–52.

Yavetz, Z. 1983. *Julius Caesar and His Public Image*. Ithaca, New York: Cornell University Press.

Zetzel, J. 1973 'Emendavi ad Tironem: Some Notes on Scholarship in the Second Century A.D.'. *HSCP* 77: 225–43.

Žižek, S. 1992. *The Sublime Object of Ideology*. London and New York: Verso.

Index Locorum

For the benefit of digital users, indexed terms that span two pages (e.g., 52–53) may, on occasion, appear on only one of those pages.

Appian

B. Civ. 2.17.62: 70–71n.32
B. Civ. 2.94: 186n.58
B. Civ. 3.90-93: 151n.104
B. Civ. 3.97-98: 120n.16
B. Civ. 3.97: 120n.17
B. Civ. 4.2-4: 120n.18
B. Civ. 4.61: 155n.118
B. Civ. 4.64: 155n.116
B. Civ. 4.65-73: 154n.115
B. Civ. 4.76-80: 157n.121

Cicero

Am. 26-27: 169n.15
Am. 97: 96n.30

Att. 1.1-11: 198n.7
Att. 1.12: 198n.7
Att. 1.12.4: 195–96n.1
Att. 1.14.3: 195–96n.1
Att. 1.16.5: 195–96n.1
Att. 1.18.7: 80–81
Att. 1.19.4: 165–66n.7, 186n.60
Att. 4.4: 86n.5
Att. 4.15-18: 166n.9
Att. 5.1-11: 67n.29

Att. 7.1.1: 109n.62
Att. 7.7: 109n.62
Att. 7.17.2: 191n.75
Att. 8.7.2: 34–35n.2, 195–96n.1
Att. 12.4.2: 80–81
Att. 12.26.2: 195–96n.1
Att. 13.44: 86n.5
Att. 14.1.1: 142n.79
Att. 14.6.2: 122n.25
Att. 14.9.2: 122n.25
Att. 14.13.3: 125n.35
Att. 14.16.3: 125n.35
Att. 14.19: 125n.35
Att. 15.15.4: 45n.33
Att. 15.23: 125n.35
Att. 15.25: 125n.35
Att. 16.1.1: 23n.53
Att. 16.3: 35n.3
Att. 16.5.5: 15n.35, 37–38n.12
Att. 16.7.3: 125
Att. 16.7.5: 125n.36
Att. 16. 75-76: 124n.32

ad Brut. 1.4.2-3: 130n.46
ad Brut. 1.4a.2-3: 139n.72
ad Brut. 1.5: 136n.63

236 *Index Locorum*

ad Brut. 1.12.1: 140n.75
ad Brut. 1.12.2: 134n.60
ad Brut. 1.15.9: 134n.60
ad Brut. 1.16-17: 139n.69
ad Brut. 1.16: 139n.71, 195–96n.1
ad Brut. 1.17: 139n.71, 195–96n.1
ad Brut. 2.1.1: 140n.75
ad Brut. 2.2.2: 140n.75

Brut. 190: 96n.30

Cael. 95-102: 186n.60
Cael. 9: 100n.36
Cael. 39-42: 167–68n.14

de Or. 2.338: 96n.30

Dom. 100: 189n.69

Fam. 1: 6n.14, 15–16, 26–27, 28, 62–63,
        65–67, 73, 74–77, 79–80, 81–83, 84
Fam. 1.6.2: 67–68
Fam. 1.7.2: 68
Fam. 1.7.8: 69
Fam. 1.9: 70–71, 79–80
Fam. 1.9.2: 74
Fam. 1.9.17: 69–72

Fam. 2: 12, 13–14n.34, 23n.52, 87–88, 89–
        90, 109n.61, 198n.6, 205–6n.20
Fam. 2.3: 111n.64
Fam. 2.4: 205–6n.20
Fam. 2.6.2: 205–6n.20
Fam. 2.8: 23n.52, 23n.53
Fam. 2.8.1: 89n.11, 90–91, 96
Fam. 2.9.1: 90n.14
Fam. 2.10: 90n.14
Fam. 2.11: 93n.21
Fam. 2.11.1: 67n.29, 107–8n.57
Fam. 2.12.1: 90n.14
Fam. 2.12.2: 67n.29
Fam. 2.12.3: 107–8n.57

Fam. 2.13.3: 90n.14
Fam. 2.13.4: 67n.29
Fam. 2.16: 108–9n.60
Fam. 2.19: 23n.53

Fam. 3: 6n.14, 22n.47, 23, 35n.4, 66n.26
Fam. 3.7.5: 65nn.22–24

Fam. 4: 6n.14
Fam. 4. 2-6: 163n.1

Fam. 5.1: 198n.7
Fam. 5.2: 198n.7
Fam. 5.12: 163n.1
Fam. 5.12.4: 43n.31
Fam. 5.12.7: 82n.52

Fam. 6: 6n.14, 13n.32
Fam. 6.12.2: 48n.38
Fam. 6.9.1: 13n.32
Fam. 6.10.6: 13n.32

Fam. 7: 198n.6
Fam. 7.29: 183

Fam. 8: 10–12, 26–27, 28–29, 86–92, 93,
        100–1, 107–8
Fam. 8.1: 89n.11, 100–1
Fam. 8.1.1: 98–99
Fam. 8.1.2: 100n.36, 101n.38
Fam. 8.1.3: 90n.13, 105n.51, 106n.53
Fam. 8.1.4: 90n.13
Fam. 8.2.2: 90n.13, 92n.16, 101n.38
Fam. 8.3: 107–9
Fam. 8.3.1: 90n.14, 107
Fam. 8.3.2: 108n.58
Fam. 8.4: 100–1
Fam. 8.4.4: 100–1, 105n.51
Fam. 8.4.5: 92n.17
Fam. 8.5.2: 90n.12
Fam. 8.5.2-3: 100–1
Fam. 8.5: 101n.38

Fam. 8.6: 91–92, 92n.18

Fam. 8.8: 91–92, 102n.39, 105n.51

Fam. 8.8.10: 92n.19

Fam. 8.8.4: 102–4

Fam. 8.8.8: 105n.47

Fam. 8.8.9: 106n.53

Fam. 8.9: 91–92

Fam. 8.9.2: 92n.20, 102nn.39–42

Fam. 8.9.3: 91–92, 111n.64

Fam. 8.9.5: 106n.53

Fam. 8.8.10: 111n.64

Fam. 8.10.3: 101n.38

Fam. 8.11.3: 106n.54

Fam. 8.13: 106n.54

Fam. 8.14.2: 106n.54

Fam. 8.14.3: 109n.61

Fam. 8.14.4: 95

Fam. 8.16: 108–9

Fam. 8.16.1: 108–9n.60

Fam. 8.16.5: 108–9n.60

Fam. 8.17.1: 108–10

Fam. 9: 6n.14, 22n.47, 64n.20, 160–61, 205–6

Fam. 9.2: 202–3

Fam. 9.2.5: 201–2

Fam. 9.9.3: 142n.77, 202–3

Fam. 9.10.1: 195–96n.1

Fam. 9.14.6: 205–6

Fam. 9. 15-26: 167–68n.14

Fam. 9.15: 202–3

Fam. 9.15.2: 179–80n.45

Fam. 9.15.4: 203n.15

Fam. 9.17.1: 203–4

Fam. 10: 23, 29–30, 121, 122–23, 126–27, 132, 199n.8

Fam. 10.1-24: 119n.13

Fam. 10.1: 122–23

Fam. 10.1.1: 120n.15, 120n.19, 124, 160–61, 200n.13

Fam. 10.2: 120n.20, 136n.64

Fam. 10.3.3: 132n.53

Fam. 10.6: 126n.37, 136n.64, 206

Fam. 10.6.2: 133

Fam. 10.6.2-3: 206–7

Fam. 10.7: 134–35

Fam. 10.7.2: 134n.58

Fam. 10.8: 134–35

Fam. 10.8.4-7: 126n.37

Fam. 10.9: 126–27n.38

Fam. 10.9.3: 132n.54

Fam. 10.10-13: 160n.129

Fam. 10.10: 135–36

Fam. 10.10.1: 134–35

Fam. 10.11: 134n.61

Fam. 10.11.2: 121n.23

Fam. 10.12: 134–36

*Fam.*10.13: 134n.61

Fam. 10.13.2: 120n.20

Fam. 10.15: 126–27n.38

Fam. 10.15.3: 121n.23

Fam. 10.16.2: 145n.91

Fam. 10.17: 126–27n.38

Fam. 10.18: 126–27n.38

Fam. 10.21.1: 126–27n.38, 137–38

Fam. 10.23: 126–27n.38

Fam. 10.23.1: 138

Fam. 10.24: 52n.53, 123n.28

Fam. 10.24.1: 138–39

Fam. 10.24.6: 139n.69

Fam. 10.27: 121n.21, 134n.59, 136–37

Fam. 10.30: 48n.39, 151n.105

Fam. 10.31-33: 121n.22

Fam. 10.31: 136–38

Fam. 10.31.2: 137n.66

Fam. 10.31.5: 137n.65

Fam. 10.32.1: 137n.66

Fam. 10.32.5: 137n.65

Fam. 10.33: 11n.27, 130–32, 130n.45, 132n.54

Fam. 10.33.1: 129–30

Fam. 10. 33.2-3: 130n.45

Fam. 10.33.4: 48n.40, 127–29

Index Locorum

Fam. 10.33.5: 129–30n.44
Fam. 10.34a: 121n.21, 136–37
Fam. 10.34b: 121n.21
Fam. 10.35: 121n.23, 126–27n.38, 136–37

Fam. 11: 120n.20, 140–41, 152
Fam. 11.1-3: 140n.74
Fam. 11.1-2: 163n.1
Fam. 11.1: 11–12n.28, 142n.78, 143–45
Fam. 11.1.1: 143–45, 143n.82
Fam. 11.1.4: 141
Fam. 11.2-3: 142n.78
Fam. 11.2: 11–12n.28, 151–52
Fam. 11.2.1: 143n.83
Fam. 11.3.1: 143n.84
Fam. 11.4-26: 119n.14, 140n.74
Fam. 11.4: 120n.20
Fam. 11.5: 143–45
Fam. 11.5.2: 144n.85
Fam. 11.5.3: 120n.20
Fam. 11.6: 144n.88
Fam. 11.6a: 143–45
Fam. 11.7: 143–45, 148n.98, 151–52
Fam. 11.7.2: 145n.91
Fam. 11.9: 146n.93
Fam. 11.9.2: 127n.39
Fam. 11.10.4: 151n.106
Fam. 11.10.5: 160n.127
Fam. 11.11.1: 127n.39, 131n.49, 131nn.51–52
Fam. 11.1.4: 141
Fam. 11.12-14: 128n.41
Fam. 11.12: 145–46n.92
Fam. 11.13a.1-2: 128n.41
Fam. 11.13a.3: 151n.106
Fam. 11.13b: 141n.76
Fam. 11.14-15: 123n.28
Fam. 11.14: 123n.29
Fam. 11.14.1: 134n.58, 146
Fam. 11.14.2: 153n.111
Fam. 11.14.3: 146n.94
Fam. 11.18.1: 131n.52
Fam. 11.20: 148–49

Fam. 11.20.1: 148–49, 149–50n.102
Fam. 11.21: 123n.28, 148
Fam. 11.24-–26: 123n.28
Fam. 11.25.2: 153n.111
Fam. 11.26: 120n.20, 153n.111
Fam. 11.27-29: 140n.74, 142n.78
Fam. 11.27: 142n.81
Fam. 11.27.2-5: 142n.80
Fam. 11.29: 142n.81

Fam. 12: 153–54, 158n.123, 159–60,
   199–200
Fam. 12.1-12: 152n.107
Fam. 12.5: 140n.75
Fam. 12.5.2: 131n.52
Fam. 12.6: 140n.75
Fam. 12.6.2: 153n.112
Fam. 12.8-10: 123n.28
Fam. 12.10.4: 153n.112
Fam. 12.11-12: 159–60n.126
Fam. 12.12.1: 160n.128
Fam. 12.13-15: 154, 159–60
Fam. 12.13: 123n.28, 152n.108
Fam. 12.13.4: 154–55
Fam. 12.14-15: 152n.108
Fam. 12.14.3: 155–56
Fam. 12.14.5: 160n.128
Fam. 12.15: 123n.28
Fam. 12.15.2: 156n.119
Fam. 12.15.3: 156–57
Fam. 12.15.4: 160n.128
Fam. 12.16: 153–54n.113
Fam. 12.17-30: 152n.109, 154n.114
Fam. 12.17.2: 154n.114
Fam. 12.18.2: 154n.114
Fam. 12.20: 154n.114
Fam. 12.30: 123n.28

Fam. 13: 13–14n.34, 25–27, 30–31, 37–
   38n.12, 40n.21, 83n.53, 163–64,
   165–66, 168–69, 170–71, 175–76,
   183, 184–86

Index Locorum

Fam. 13.1: 166, 171n.22, 172
Fam. 13.1.3: 167n.12
Fam. 13.1.4: 167
Fam. 13.2: 172–73, 174–75
Fam. 13.4-8: 186
Fam. 13.4: 186–87
Fam. 13.4.1: 187n.63
Fam. 13.4.2: 186–87n.61
Fam. 13.4.3: 186–87
Fam. 13.4.4: 187–88
Fam. 13.5.1: 188–89
Fam. 13.5.2: 188n.67, 189–90
Fam. 13.5.3: 189n.68
Fam. 13.7: 187n.63
Fam. 13.8: 190–91
Fam. 13.8.1: 191n.75, 192
Fam. 13.8.3: 191–92
Fam. 13.10.4: 192n.78
Fam. 13.16.4: 173–74
Fam. 13.17-28: 176–77
Fam. 13.19: 177–78
Fam. 13.19.1: 177–78n.38
Fam. 13.19.3: 192n.78
Fam. 13.20: 170n.18
Fam. 13.21: 172–73, 172n.23
Fam. 13.22: 184n.55
Fam. 13.23.1: 174–75
Fam. 13.23.2: 175n.30
Fam. 13.24.2: 177–78n.38
Fam. 13.27: 172–73
Fam. 13.27.1: 173n.29
Fam. 13.30-39: 176–77
Fam 13.34: 179n.43
Fam. 13.35: 179–80
Fam. 13.36: 181–82
Fam. 13.36.1: 181–82nn.51–52
Fam. 13.38: 172n.23
Fam. 13.45: 184n.55
Fam. 13.50: 183–84
Fam. 13.50.2: 183–84
Fam. 13.52: 176n.33
Fam. 13.53-57: 176n.34

Fam. 13.55.1: 184–85n.56
Fam. 13.55.2: 184–85n.56
Fam. 13.56: 184n.55
Fam. 13.60: 174–75
Fam. 13.60.1: 174–75
Fam. 13.61-65: 176n.34
Fam. 13.63-64: 176n.34
Fam. 13.64: 184–85n.56
Fam. 13.65-66: 176n.34
Fam. 13.66.1: 184–85n.56
Fam. 13.66-72: 176n.34
Fam. 13.69: 174–75, 177n.36
Fam. 13.69.1: 175n.31
Fam. 13.73-74: 176n.34
Fam. 13.75: 176n.33, 180n.49
Fam. 13.78-79: 176n.33
Fam. 13.79: 180n.49

Fam. 14: 6n.14, 10–12, 30–31,
    83n.53, 164n.3
Fam. 14.20: 53–54

Fam. 15: 6n.14, 10–12, 13–14n.34, 16n.37,
    28, 31n.57, 35n.4, 62–63, 73, 74–77,
    84, 164–65
Fam. 15.1-13: 63n.15
Fam. 15.1.1: 63n.16
Fam. 15.2-4: 76n.44, 77n.46
Fam. 15.2.6: 76n.43
Fam. 15.4: 74–76
Fam. 15.4.1: 75n.39
Fam. 15.4.6: 76nn.43–44
Fam. 15.5.1-3: 78–79
Fam. 15.5.3: 79–80
Fam. 15.4.16: 79n.48
Fam. 15.5: 81–82
Fam. 15.6: 82n.52
Fam. 15.7-11: 75n.40
Fam. 15.14-21: CP32 n.41
Fam. 15.16-18: 167–68n.14
Fam. 15.17.3: 48n.38
Fam. 15.18: 195–96n.1

240   *Index Locorum*

Fam. 15.19: 34–35
Fam. 15.19.2: 48n.38

Fam. 16: 6n.14, 26–28, 37–38, 39, 42, 51–52, 54–55, 56–57, 61–62
Fam. 16.1: 38–39, 43n.30, 49
Fam. 16.2: 39n.18
Fam. 16.3: 39n.18
Fam. 16.4: 163n.1, 178n.39
Fam. 16.4.4: 43–44
Fam. 16.5: 38–39, 163n.1, 178n.39
Fam. 16.5.1: 39n.18
Fam. 16.6.2: 39n.18
Fam. 16.7: 39n.18
Fam. 16.9: 163n.1, 178n.39
Fam. 16.10: 43n.30, 45–46
Fam. 16.11-14: 39n.18
Fam. 16.11: 38n.14, 163n.1
Fam. 16.11.1: 49
Fam. 16.12.6: 50n.42
Fam. 16.16.1: 39n.18
Fam. 16.18.1: 38–39n.15
Fam. 16.18.4: 44n.32
Fam. 16.1: 39n.18
Fam. 16.20: 44
Fam. 16.21.1-2: 44–45
Fam. 16.22: 86n.5
Fam. 16.26: 46

*Fin.*1.65: 166n.11, 168
*Fin.*2.84-85: 168–70

ND 1.93: 166n.11

Off. 2.78: 165–66n.7

Orat. 70-74: 96n.30

Phil. 1: 199n.8
Phil. 1.1: 123
Phil. 1.16-17: 122n.25
Phil. 2: 114n.1

Phil. 3.1-2: 130n.46
Phil. 3.12: 144n.87
Phil. 3.29: 140n.75
Phil. 3.38: 122n.25
Phil. 5.30: 130n.46
Phil. 5.35-37: 134n.58
Phil. 5.38-41: 134n.58
Phil. 5.39: 140n.75
Phil. 5.42-52: 134n.58
Phil. 6.19: 140n.75
Phil. 7.1: 140n.75
Phil. 7.12: 140n.75
Phil. 8: 132n.54
Phil. 8. 29: 140n.75
Phil. 9.6: 140n.75
Phil. 10.1: 130n.46
Phil. 10.14: 140n.75
Phil. 10.19: 151n.104
Phil. 11: 160n.128
Phil. 12.5-6: 122n.26
Phil. 12.17: 122n.26
Phil 13: 126n.37
Phil. 13.43: 134n.60
Phil. 13.47-48: 122n.26
Phil. 14.1-5: 146n.94
Phil. 14.3: 140n.75

Qfr. 3.2.1: 166n.8
Qfr. 2.12.4: 43n.31

Sest. 23: 167–68n.14
Sest. 138-139: 167–68n.14

Caesar
BC 3.1: 109n.62
BC 3.20.1: 109n.62
BC 3.20-22: 109n.63
BGall. (Hirt.) 8.53.1: 100n.35

Dio
38.1: 186–87n.61
42.22.2: 109n.62

42.22-25.: 109n.63
42.51.2: 191n.73
46.29.6: 132n.54
47.31.1: 155n.116
47.34: 157n.121
77.33.1: 155n.118

Diogenes Laertius
10.16.21: 166n.11

Fronto
Ep. ad M. Caes. 1.7.4: 36n.9
Ep. ad Anton. Imp. 3.8: 195–96n.1

Gellius
NA 1.7.1: 36n.9
NA 1.22.19: 11n.27
NA 4.9.6: 11n.27
NA 13.9.1-3: 53n.54
NA 13.21.6: 36n.9

Nepos
Att. 16.3: 35n.3

Pliny (Elder)
HN 7.165: 87n.6
HN 36.15.117-20: 112n.65
HN 35.201: 56n.60

Pliny (Younger)
Epist. 1.2.4: 195–96n.1
Epist. 7.4.3-6: 50n.43

Plutarch
Brut. 21.6: 195–96n.1
Caes. 21.5: 70–71n.32
Cat. Min. 35-38: 80n.50

Cic. 36.6: 195–96n.1
Cic. 37.3: 195–96n.1
Cic. 49.4: 153–54n.113
Pomp. 51.4: 70–71n.32
Pomp. 63: 195–96n.1

Quintilian
Inst. 6.3.5: 36n.9
Inst. 6.3.108: 195–96n.1
Inst. 10.7.30-31: 36n.9
Inst. 12: 88n.8

Seneca (Elder)
Cont. 7.2: 48n.41
Suas. 1.5.5: 34–35n.2, 195–96n.1
Suas. 6: 48n.41, 114n.1
Suas. 6.17: 7n.15
Suas. 7: 48n.41

Seneca (Younger)
Clem. 1.6: 206n.21
Epist. 1.2.4: 195–96n.1
Epist. 97.4: 195–96n.1
Epist. 118.1-2: 195–96n.1

Suetonius
Iul. 9.2: 195–96n.1
Iul. 28.2: 100n.35
Iul. 28.3: 180n.46
Iul. 42.1: 179n.44
Iul. 55: 195–96n.1
Aug. 44: 97n.32
gramm. 14.2-3: 195–96n.1

Tacitus
Agr. 3: 203–4
Agr. 46: 204n.18

Index

For the benefit of digital users, indexed terms that span two pages (e.g., 52–53) may, on occasion, appear on only one of those pages.

Actium, Battle of, 153–54, 200–1

Aemilius, M. Lepidus, 52n.53, 119–22, 126–27, 128–30, 132, 133–35, 136–38, 152, 159–60

aestimatio. See property: valuation of (*aestimatio*)

ager publicus (public land) 165–66n.7, 186, 186n.60

Althusser, L., 85–86

amphitheatre, 28–29, 94–99

    Augustan seating arrangements, 94–95

    Curio's, 110–11

    Flavian (Colosseum) 93–94

    ideology of, 97–98

    in Pompeii, 94n.23

    as symbol of Romanization under empire, 93–94

anachronism, 28–29, 57

anecdote. *See* counter-history: anecdote

Antonius (Antony), M., 23, 48, 56n.59, 118–19n.12, 120n.20, 121, 122–23, 124–25, 126–27, 128–29, 132–34, 136–37, 138, 139–41, 143–45, 146, 149, 151–54, 156, 160–61, 198–201, 205–6

Appian, 155n.116, 157–59, 186, 199–200

archive, 2–3, 4–7, 8–10, 12–15, 35–36

    media of, 9–10

    vulnerability of physical, 12–13

    See also Derrida: *Archive Fever*

arena. *See* amphitheatre

Asinius, G. Pollio, 48n.40, 121–22, 126–27n.38, 127–30, 136–38, 200n.11

Augustus, 22–23, 35–36, 56n.59, 94n.23, 97, 200n.12, *See also* Octavian

Austen, Jane, 193

authorship, distributed, 17–18, 196

Bachelard, Gaston, 59–60

Beard, Mary, 6nn.13–14, 7n.17, 12n.30, 48

Benjamin, Walter, 115–16, 119

Boccaccio, Giovanni, 3n.4

book roll, 9–12, 16n.38, 19–21, 58–59, 60, 83n.54, 84, 95–96

Boym, Svetlana, 51–52, 52n.52

Brundisium, Pact of, 152–54

Caelius, M. Rufus, 10–12, 86–94, 98–99, 106–10

    as aedile, 23n.52, 28–29, 91–92, 93–94

    age of, 88–90

244   *Index*

Caelius, M. Rufus (*cont.*)
    on events in the senate in 51–50 BCE,
      12, 89–92
    on panthers for his games, 91–
      94, 110–11
    as praetor, 108–9
    in *Pro Caelio*, 88–91, 107–8
    vocabulary of, 89–90
Capelli, Pasquino, 3–6, 13–15
Cassius, G. Longinus, 11–12n.28, 74–76,
      113–14, 116–17, 139n.71, 140nn.74–
      75, 141, 142–43, 152–55, 157–60,
      167–68n.14
Cassius Parmensis, 152n.108, 154–55, 157,
      158n.123
Cicero. *See* Tullius, M. Cicero
Claudius, A. Pulcher, 62n.10, 65–67,
      74, 109–10
codex, 9–12, 15–16, 19–20, 23–25, 28–29,
      57, 58–59, 60–62, 82–84, 93–96
copyists. *See librarii*
Cornelius, L. Sulla, 165–66, 185–87,
      191n.74
Cornelius, P. Dolabella, 142n.77, 154–58,
      160n.128, 181–82, 199–200, 201–
      3, 205–6
Cornificius, Q., 152, 154n.114, 159–60
counter-history, 29–30, 114–16, 130–32,
      147, 150–51, 154, 157, 204–5
    the anecdote as a form of, 147–
      48, 151–52
    and sovereign history, 116–17, 157–
      59, 161

Derrida, Jacques, 131n.48
    Archive Fever, 5n.10, 6n.12, 8–10, 12–13
    Spectres of Marx, 21, 22–25, 207–8
    See also hauntology
digital media, 18, 59
domus, 171–76

editorship, distributed, 16–18, 26–27

elections
    of aediles, 90n.13, 90n.14, 97
    consular, 22–x, 166n.9
Epicureans, community of, 31,
      168, 170–71
Epicurus
    his garden, 166n.11
    his house, 31, 166–67, 168, 186–87, 188,
      189–90, 193–94
Epistulae ad Atticum (Cicero) 3–6,
      8–12, 13–14n.34, 20–21, 33–34n.1,
      34–35n.2, 35–36, 64–65, 195–
      96n.1, 198–99
Epistulae ad Familiares (Cicero)
    editors of, 1, 2–3, 17–18, 26–28, 29–30,
      82–83, 85–87, 118, 129–30, 159–60,
      170–71, 196, 205–6
    imperial readerships of, 1–2, 8–10,
      15–17, 18, 21–23, 25–29, 30–31, 55–57,
      84, 94–95, 129–30, 136–37, 139–40,
      161, 162–63, 164, 193–94, 195–97,
      200–1, 202, 205–6, 207–8
    organization of collection, 1–3, 9–10,
      17–18, 20–21, 23–25, 36–38, 56–57,
      60–61, 84, 114, 162
    process of formation, 1–3, 10–12, 16–
      17, 20–21, 25–27, 58–59, 62–x, 196
exile, 178–79n.41
    proconsular command as a form of, 28,
      65–67, 68
    See also Tullius, M. Cicero: exile

familia Caesaris, 31, 171, 193–94
familiaritas, 7–8, 30–31, 163–64, 165–66,
      168, 170–71, 177–78, 183, 184–
      85, 188–65
Fisher, Mark, 23–25
Fitzgerald, William, 41, 42–43, 55
Forum Gallorum, Battle of, 121n.23, 127–
      28, 151–52, 198–99
Foucault, Michel, 97–98n.33, 115–17,
      117n.10

Index

freedmen, 25–26, 27–28, 30–31, 42, 54–55, 56nn.60–61, 172–76, 177n.36

Freud, Sigmund, 5n.10, 8n.20
death drive, 6n.12

friendship, 142–43, 166n.11, 168–71, 176–78, 182. *See also familiaritas*

Funkenstein, Amos, 115–16, 117n.8

Gellius, A., 10–12, 34–35n.2, 39–40n.19, 51n.48, 53n.54, 195–96

gladiatorial games, 112. *See also* spectacle entertainment

Gunderson, Erik, 97–88

Gutenberg revolution, 28, 58–59, 60

hauntology, 21–22
and lost futures, 118–19, 127–28, 129–30, 135–36, 145, 204–6

Hegel, Georg Willhelm
on master and slave, 55–56

hospitium, 176–82

humanism, Renaissance, 3n.4, 4–6

irony
historical, 29–30, 77, 118, 120n.15, 136–37, 198–99, 204–5, 206n.21, 207

Josephus, 158–59

Julius, G. Caesar
assassination of, 118–19n.12, 125, 130n.46, 141, 142n.78, 143–45, 153–54, 205–6
calendar reform, 22–23
and civil war, 23, 74–76, 91, 108–9, 143–45, 160–61, 176, 177–78, 190–91, 202–3
dictatorship of, 22–23, 31, 132n.53, 142–43, 160–61, 181–82, 201–2
expansion of franchise, 178–82
land confiscations, 187–88, 190–91, 203–4 (*see also* property: redistribution of)

pre-appointment of consuls, 22–23, 119–20, 121–22, 133, 206
recall from Gaul, 100–1
veterans, 143, 149, 151–52, 186, 191n.73

Junius, D. Brutus, 23, 119–20, 122n.25, 126–27nn.37–39, 128n.41, 130n.46, 133n.56, 134n.58, 139, 140–46, 147, 148–52, 153–54, 159–60, 207

Junius, M. Brutus, 11–12n.28, 113–14, 116–17, 124n.32, 125n.36, 134n.60, 136n.63, 139–40, 140nn.74–75, 141, 142–43, 153–54, 157–59, 163n.1

Kennedy, Duncan, 117

King, William Davies, 53–54

Lacan, Jacques, 28, 85–86
on *nom-du-père*, 42–43, 45

Laodicea, 62n.10, 154–55

Lentulus, P. Spinther, 61–73, 74–77
his homonymous son, 154, 155–57, 158n.123

letters (Cicero's)
imperial readers of, 1–2, 13–15, 16–17, 19–20, 22–23, 25–27, 30–31, 55–56, 57, 160–61, 162, 163, 164, 197, 200–1, 207–8
intimacy of, 7–9, 33, 163–64, 197
of recommendation, 162–63, 170–71, 172n.25, 175–76, 183
as source of historical information, 7–8, 10, 16–18, 86–87, 98–101, 114, 130–32
See also Epistulae ad Atticum (Cicero); *Epistulae ad Familiares* (Cicero)

librarii, 86n.5

literary frame, 61–62. *See also* paratext

Luca, conference at, 70–71

Lycia, free states of, 157–59

Marx, Karl, 21–22, 115n.3

Marxism, 18–19, 21–22, 115–16n.5

mass media, 18

Memmius, G., 74, 166–67, 172

memory
collective, 10–12, 16–17, 25–26
historical, 148, 162, 163, 164, 165–66, 197–98

monarchy. *See* Roman empire as system of government

Munatius, L. Plancus, 119–23, 126–28, 132–40, 163n.1, 200–1
consulship of, 121–22, 133–34, 206–7
as 'time-server', 132

Mutina
Battle of, 10–12, 25–26, 48, 113–14, 128–30, 140–41, 143, 146, 152, 198–200, 204–5
Siege of, 145

nostalgia, 18–20, 21–22, 31–32, 51–53, 84, 200–1

Octavian, 21–22, 35–36, 52n.53, 118–19n.12, 121, 126–27, 128–29, 133–34, 135–36, 139–40, 148–52, 200–1, 207

optimates, 25–26, 70–73, 74–76

paratext, 27–28
enclosing effect of, 28, 51–52, 61–62
as location for editorial commentary, 27–28, 36–38, 61–62

Petrarch, 3–7, 8–10, 163–64
epistulae ad Familiares, 3–4, 7–10, 40n.22
letters to ancient authors, 3–4, 8–9

Pettit, Thomas, 59–60, 83–84

Philippi, Battle of, 48n.41, 113–14, 152–54

Pliny the Younger, 23–25, 50n.43, 62–63, 195–96, 198n.5

Pompey, 21–22, 28–29, 65–67, 70–71, 73, 95, 100–1, 103, 104–6, 110, 142–43

populares, 25–26

Porcius, M. Cato, 73, 74–77, 78–82

principate. *See* Roman empire

printed book, 28, 59–60
effect of containment, 28, 59–61, 83–84

property (*res familiaris*) 31, 165–66, 172, 189–90
redistribution of, 31, 165–66, 185–86, 190–91
valuation of (*aestimatio*) 190–91, 192

Ptolemy Auletes, 62–63, 67, 76–77

public land. *See ager publicus* (public land)

Quintilian, 36n.9, 88–89, 195–96

remediation, 23–25, 87–88, 89–90, 95–96, 97, 99–100
and obsolescence, 23–25, 84

res familiaris. *See* property

residual media, 18–19

Rhodes, 155, 156, 157–59

Roman calendar
Caesar's reforms of, 22–23
Republican, 23–25

Roman empire (principate)
as historical period, 6–7, 15–16, 56–57, 116–17, 118–19, 171, 197, 200–1, 204, 207
as monarchical system of government, 21–22, 26–27, 29–30, 31, 62–63, 116–17, 165, 193–94, 206

Roman provinces
Cilicia, 12–13, 28, 61–67, 68, 73, 74–77, 84, 86, 88–89, 90–91, 176–78
consular, 104–6
Galatia, 62–63, 77
Gaul (Transalpine) 47, 70–71, 90n.13, 91, 100–2, 104–6, 129, 151–52
Imperial, 62–63, 77
praetorian, 105n.47
Syria, 62–63, 152, 154–55, 160n.128, 205–6

Index

247

Roman republic
  fall of, 1–3, 6–7, 21, 29–30, 35n.5,
    48n.41, 113–14, 116–17, 154, 197
  society of, 25–26, 30–31, 162–63, 164,
    165, 171, 175–76, 182
  as system of government, 29–30, 37–
    38, 48, 52–53, 62–63, 72–73, 77, 84,
    86–87, 91, 113–14, 121
Roman revolution, 55–56

Salutati, Coluccio, 3–8, 9–10, 13–15
secretaries. *See librarii*
Segulius, Labeo, 148–49, 150–52
senatus consultum, 102–3
  transcript of, 102, 104–6
Seneca, the Elder, 7n.15, 34–35n.2,
    48n.41, 195–96
Seneca, the Younger, 195–96, 198n.5,
    206n.21
Shackleton Bailey, D. R., 9–10nn.23–24
social media, 17, 28–29, 110–11, 112, 160–61
social network, 17–18, 30–31, 86–87,
    106–7, 170
souvenir, 18–19, 23–25, 26–28, 31–32.
    See also Stewart, Susan: on the
    souvenir
spectacle entertainment, 28–29, 94–96,
    97–99. *See also* amphitheatre;
    gladiatorial games
spreadable media, 18, 57
Stewart, Susan
  on the antiquarian, 53–54
  on collecting, 53–54
  On Longing, 50–54
  on the souvenir, 50–52
Sulla. *See* Cornelius, L. Sulla

Tarsus, 154–55
theatre, 59, 88–89, 96, 97n.32
'Time is out of joint'
  in *Hamlet*, 22–23

and Mark Fisher's 'Metaphysics of
    Crackle', 23–25
Trajan, 62–63
Trebonius, G., 74–76, 109n.61, 153–54,
    159–60, 205–6
triumvirate
  first, 25–26, 70–71, 72–73
  second, 52–53, 119–20, 152, 157–59,
    161, 207
Tullius, M. Cicero
  as author function, 37–39, 40, 54–
    55, 86–87
  death of, 1, 6–7, 10–12, 15–16, 20–
    21, 26–27, 34–35, 36–38, 43, 48,
    62–63, 113–14, 152, 195–96, 197–
    99, 200–1
  as defender of private
    property, 165–66
  exile, 52–53, 65–67, 68–69, 172–73,
    174–77, 187n.63, 197–98
  imperial reception of, 1–2, 13–16, 26–
    27, 82–83, 197–99
  late antique reception of, 1–2, 13–16,
    26–27, 84
  lost letter collections, 11–12n.28,
    15n.35, 40
  manuscript tradition of his works,
    3, 11n.27, 13n.32, 13–15, 34, 38–
    39, 86n.4
  Marcus Junior, 10–12, 35–36, 39n.18,
    40, 44–46, 47–48, 57n.64,
    153–54n.113
  supplicatio, 62–63, 74–76, 78–80,
    106n.54
Terentia, 38n.14, 53–54
Tullia, 38n.14, 45–46, 106n.54
  See also *Epistulae ad Atticum* (Cicero);
    Epistulae ad Familiares (Cicero);
    letters (Cicero's)
Tullius, M. Tiro
  as antiquarian, 53–54

Tullius, M. Tiro (*cont.*)
    Cicero's longing for, 27–28, 46n.35,
        49, 51–52
    as editor of *ad Fam.*, 27–28, 36–38,
        39, 41–42, 43, 47–48, 50, 51–52,
        53–54, 55–57
    as freedman, 27–28, 54–56
    illness of, 27–28, 49, 177–78
    manumission of, 27–28,
        42, 46
    name of, 38–41
    as paternal proxy to Marcus
        Junior, 45–46
    servile status of, 39–44, 47–48,
        50, 54–55
Tullius, Q. Cicero, 38–39, 39n.18, 40,
    46, 47–48, 64n.19

Tyrrell, R. & Purser, L. C., 6n.13, 9n.23,
    12n.30, 36n.7

Volterra, 165–66, 186–88

White, Hayden, 147–48
White, Peter, 15n.35, 34–35nn.2–3
Williams, Raymond
    on the 'residual', 18–19, 200–1
    'structure of feeling' 31, 164–65, 193
    on variable speeds of cultural change,
        18–19, 31, 164–65
Woolf, Greg, 62–63

Xanthus, 157–59

Yerushalmi, Yosef Hayim, 5n.10, 8n.20